THE FILMS OF JOSEPH H. LEWIS

CONTEMPORARY APPROACHES TO FILM AND MEDIA SERIES

A complete listing of the books in this series can be found online at wsupress.wayne.edu

General Editor
Barry Keith Grant
Brock University

Advisory Editors

Robert J. Burgoyne
University of St. Andrews

Caren J. Deming
University of Arizona

Patricia B. Erens
School of the Art Institute
of Chicago

Peter X. Feng
University of Delaware

Lucy Fischer
University of Pittsburgh

Frances Gateward
California State University,
Northridge

Tom Gunning
University of Chicago

Thomas Leitch
University of Delaware

Walter Metz
Southern Illinois University

THE FILMS OF JOSEPH H. LEWIS

Edited by Gary D. Rhodes

Foreword by Francis M. Nevins

Wayne State University Press Detroit

© 2012 by Wayne State University Press, Detroit, Michigan 48201. All rights reserved. No part of this book may be reproduced without formal permission.

16 15 14 13 12   5 4 3 2 1

Library of Congress Cataloging-in-Publication Data
The films of Joseph H. Lewis / edited by Gary D. Rhodes.
p. cm. — (Contemporary approaches to film and media series)
Includes bibliographical references and index.
ISBN 978-0-8143-3462-1 (pbk. : alk. paper) —
ISBN 978-0-8143-3599-4 (ebook)
1. Lewis, Joseph H., 1907–2000—Criticism and interpretation. I. Rhodes, Gary D., 1972–
PN1998.3.L4683F55 2012
791.4302'33092—dc23
2012001064

Typeset by Maya Rhodes
Composed in Warnock Pro and Meta

For Kevin Brownlow

Contents

Foreword by Francis M. Nevins: Joseph H. Lewis, 1907–2000 ix
Acknowledgments xiii

Introduction 1
GARY D. RHODES

Part I: Texts and Contexts

1. Style Development and Product Upgrading: Monogram Pictures, the Ambitious B Movie, and the East Side Kids Films Directed by Joseph H. Lewis 11
YANNIS TZIOUMAKIS

2. Partition and Desire in the Films of Joseph H. Lewis 38
HUGH S. MANON

3. The Joseph H. Lewis Nobody Knows: The Television Films 62
MICHAEL E. GROST

Part II: Individual Works

4. "A House Where Anything Can Happen and Usually Does": Joseph H. Lewis, Bela Lugosi, and (*The*) *Invisible Ghost* 81
GARY D. RHODES

5. B Is for Belief: Joseph Lewis's Experiments with the *Mad Doctor of Market Street* 98
LANCE DUERFAHRD

6. Joseph H. Lewis, Anna May Wong, and *Bombs over Burma* **116**
   BRIAN TAVES

7. "People Can Think Themselves into Anything": The Domestic Nightmare in *My Name Is Julia Ross* **134**
   MARLISA SANTOS

8. "A Matchless Stylist Exercise": Joseph H. Lewis and *So Dark the Night* **146**
   BRIAN HOYLE

9. *The Undercover Man* and the Police Procedural **163**
   DAVID J. HOGAN

10. The "How Big Is It?" Combo: Noir's Dirty Spectacles **178**
    ROBERT SINGER

11. *The Halliday Brand* and *Terror in a Texas Town*: Western Allegories of the Blacklist **199**
    TONY WILLIAMS

Part III: *Gun Crazy*

12. Rejecting Everything: *Gun Crazy* and the Radical Noir of Joseph H. Lewis **223**
    CHRISTOPHER JUSTICE

13. Music, Masculinity, and Masochism in *Gun Crazy* **242**
    MICHAEL LEE

14. Ethos and Ethics: Reconsidering *Gun Crazy* **255**
    PHILLIP SIPIORA

List of Contributors **271**
Index **275**

Foreword
Joseph H. Lewis, 1907–2000

The last time I saw the man who directed *Gun Crazy* (1950), we had lunch on the terrace of the Del Rey Yacht Club. It was the summer of 1999 and he was a small, trim man, ninety-two years old, who walked very tentatively, as if he were afraid at every step of falling. He had actually taken a fall a few months ago, he said, and still needed to go in for therapy two or three times a week. He didn't eat much, just a little fruit salad with cottage cheese. After lunch he felt like strolling over to the slip where his boat was moored. He hadn't seen the *Buena Vista* since his fall, he said. We wove along walkways amid the fleet of small craft glistening in their berths under the bright sun but when we reached his boat he couldn't find the key. He had been losing any number of small objects lately, he told me. We walked back to his car and searched, and I found a key in the glove compartment. "That's not it," he said. Somehow I thought it might be. I left him in the yacht club lounge and went out again to the *Buena Vista*'s slip and tried the key in the door and it fit. On the dining table was the book he'd been reading the last time he was on board: one of Lawrence Block's Burglar novels. I went back to the clubhouse and gave him the good news, which meant that he was spared an expensive appointment with a locksmith, and the two of us returned to the cabin where several years before we had taped the conversations that had become the first book about his life and world. He had owned and loved the *Buena Vista* for more than thirty years but had recently put it up for sale because he knew that at his age he could never take it out again. But he wasn't too old to drive and at the end of my visit he tucked me into his tiny sports car and sped me unerringly back to my hotel. That was the last time I saw Joseph H. Lewis.

Francis M. Nevins is the author of *Joseph H. Lewis: Overview, Interview, and Filmography* (Lanham, MD: Scarecrow Press, 1998).

Joseph H. Lewis on his yacht in Marina del Rey, California. (Courtesy of Francis M. Nevins)

He was born in New York City to Russian Jewish émigré parents on April 30, 1907, and grew up on the Upper East Side, within walking distance of Columbia University. In his teens he may well have crossed paths with another youth of Russian Jewish roots who lived in that neighborhood and would also make huge contributions to the creative genre we call noir: Cornell Woolrich. During the late 1940s when he was directing films at Columbia, Joe told me, he spent several months preparing a feature based on a Woolrich novel but was never able to adapt the book into a viable screenplay. It was well over forty years later when we had this conversation and he had forgotten the novel's title but I suspect it must have been *Rendezvous in Black* (1948), Woolrich's then most recent book and his only suspense novel that hadn't already been filmed. (It still hasn't.) I can't help feeling that a picture based on this novel and directed by Joe might well have become one of the cornerstone works of film noir.

I met him when he was in his early eighties. Before long, whenever I was in Southern California we would hang out on his boat and tape the conversations that eventually became the nucleus of my own book on Lewis. The words he used most often in discussing his life were *pride, dignity, respect.*

As a director a compulsive perfectionist and tough taskmaster, off the set a loving husband and father and grandfather and a generous and thoughtful friend—these impressions that I formed of him during our tapings were confirmed again and again over the rest of his life.

The last time I talked to Joe was about a year after my lunch with him at the yacht club. I had been invited to Canada by a filmmaker who wanted to discuss working with me on a documentary about Woolrich. One thing we needed for the film we had in mind was just the right person to serve as the Woolrich voice, reading from that haunted man's autobiographical writings. I had brought with me a copy of Christian Bauer's 1987 documentary on Lewis, and as we watched Joe and listened to his marvelously expressive voice and remembered how much he and Woolrich had in common—virtually the same age, the same ethnic roots and Upper East Side adolescence, and of course the same enormous significance in the literature and film we have come to call noir—we both knew who our Woolrich should be. We called Joe that day. He seemed interested but of course nothing could happen until our documentary was funded. A few weeks later and back in St. Louis I called Joe again. He was in bed, he said; just the flu, nothing serious. That was on August 20. I never heard his voice again.

Gail Reingold, a psychoanalyst and Joe's close friend for more than forty years, told me about the director's last few weeks.

> There had been an invitation to a *Gun Crazy* screening at UCLA and Joe and Buena [Joe's wife] came to that screening along with my wife and myself. He was pretty enfeebled at that point. I had been taking him to lunch on maybe a two-times-a-month basis but at that time he seemed weaker and a little disoriented, and he got into a very irascible discussion with the moderator and gave her a hard time. And I thought to myself: I wonder if he's ever going to do this again. Looks to me like he's sort of come to the end of the road.
>
> About a week later I called him and asked him if he'd like to go to lunch and he said, "Well, not this particular week, I'm tired, but next week let's do it." So I called about a week later and he said: "No, I have something to do today, but I'll call you."
>
> Maybe it was three or four days later when I got a message to call Georgia Sangster, his granddaughter, and I knew something must have happened. She said: "My grandmother wanted me to call and tell you that my grandfather died yesterday." I said: "My God, what happened?" She said: "Well, he was at the yacht club and evidently he had a heart attack at the yacht club." And she said

they were just marvelous to him there, they rushed right over to him and they got 911 and the ambulance came and I believe they took him to Cedars-Sinai....

She was a little confused, I thought, but she said to me: "They thought my grandfather was okay and they were going to send him home." And I understood her to say that he was about to be put in the wheelchair and they would wheel him downstairs where the car would be brought around to pick him up, and suddenly he collapsed and they were right there on top of him immediately and he went into unconsciousness and they couldn't resuscitate him and he passed away.

It could almost have been a scene out of a Woolrich novel or for that matter a Lewis film noir. Joe's granddaughter is waiting downstairs to take him home and the doctors have to tell her that Joe is dead and she has to go back and tell Joe's wife.

I mourn his passing but can't help considering how lucky he was. To have lived so long, to have enjoyed health and wealth and honors and a loving family, and to die with so little pain—who wouldn't wish to have had his life?

For as long as I remember anything I'll remember him fondly.

Francis M. Nevins

Acknowledgments

These essays and the resulting anthology would have been impossible without the insights and hard work of all of the contributing essayists, each of whom I would like to thank. A number of other persons have also assisted on this volume, ranging from providing intellectual support to offering important illustrations. As a result, I also would like to extend great appreciation to Mark Bould, Kristin Dewey, Jack Dowler, Phillip Fortune, Jim Kitses, Michael Lee, Gregory William Mank, Marina McDonnell, Desmond O'Rawe, Don and Phyllis Rhodes, Annie Ross, Robert Singer, Tom Weaver, Glenn P. White, Devin Williams, and—of course—the late Joseph H. Lewis, who was so very kind in meeting with me years ago and sharing his memories.

Gary D. Rhodes, PhD
The Queen's University of Belfast

Gary D. Rhodes

Introduction

It was a beautiful day in Southern California in the spring of 1996. Working with a camera crew, I had just spent over one week in the Los Angeles area shooting interviews for a documentary film, but in many ways our work in Marina del Ray that afternoon promised to be the most interesting, and not just because it was our only shoot scheduled aboard a ship. It was because I was to meet Joseph H. Lewis for the first time.

In person, Lewis was much the same as he had been on the phone: friendly, gracious, and unassuming. But his personality seemed to loom larger on his boat. At the age of eighty-nine, he was a man of enthusiasm and vigor, whether it was his initial hearty wave or his insistent effort to help carry some of our film equipment. Time had not at all diminished the image so many of us had always held of him: a man's man who had fought to make his films his way. Nor had the endless accolades inflated his ego or clouded his honesty.

Lewis possessed a remarkable ability to speak of his films affectionately in one breath, smiling as if he was describing his own children, while stepping outside of himself in the next breath in order to judge his work with an amazing level of objectivity. Of course he had worked in the B movies, and of course they were not perfect, but he had achieved a high level of quality through grim determination. And of course he had worked in television, but his work in the medium had not been a comedown. His television episodes were themselves finished to a high quality; it was simply that they had been broadcast rather than projected. Those were just a few of his thoughts that day, which ranged from fleeting memories of Bela Lugosi to the rigors of film directing on low budgets.

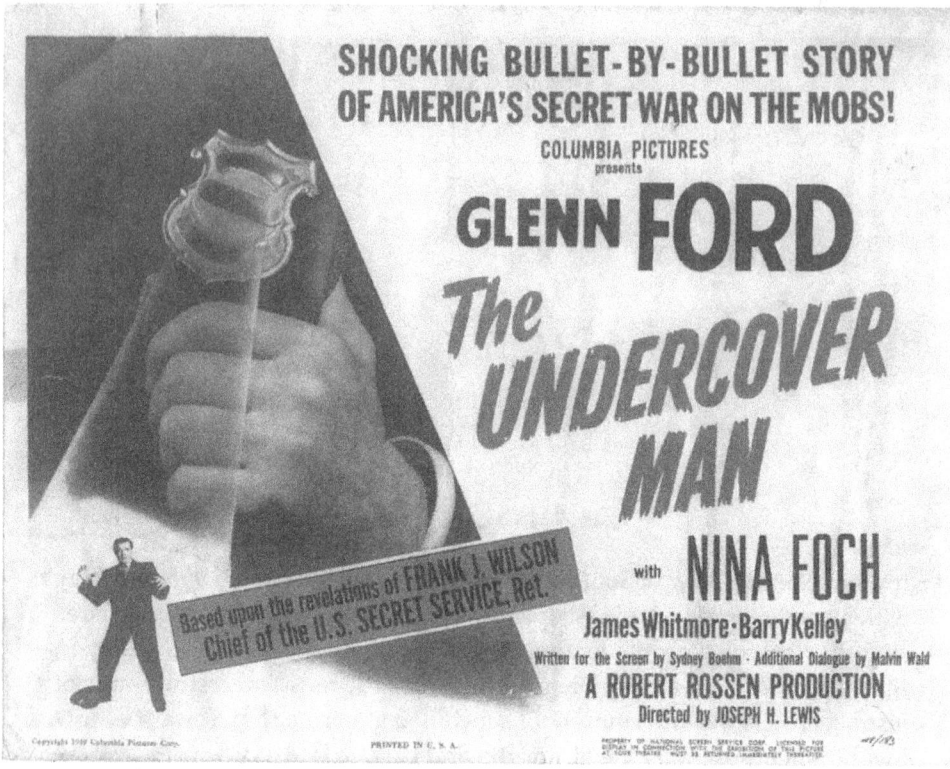

Title card for *The Undercover Man* (1949).

However, interviewing Lewis was simultaneously fascinating and frustrating, exhilarating and exasperating. We talked and we laughed, but when it came to him addressing specific, prepared questions on particular films, he was often brief in his answers. Lewis seemed willing to spend his entire day with us but seemed unwilling to spend more than a few minutes discussing the finer points of individual films. It was as if what he had to say about his films was voiced through their very production.

Joseph H. Lewis's films—created over some three decades—represent what in many ways was a sustained visual style. He emphasized depth in his cinematography, joking to me in our interview about his nickname "Wagon Wheel Joe," which he earned for repeatedly shooting western scenes through wagon wheels. But he also remained ever mindful of the z-axis, employing moving camera from his earliest films to his final television programs. Lewis referred to his instinctual emphasis on moving camera as his "third eye," which so regularly explored his indoor sets and outdoor locations. His camera synthesizes space, familiarizing the audience with unfamiliar terrain. During the first scene of *Gun Crazy* (1950), for example, the camera moves backward from a rainy street to reveal the interior of a hardware store that sells guns, guns that obsess the lead character Bart Tare.

And yet, even with all his emphasis on depth and roving camera, Lewis was always cautious about what visual information he revealed to the audience and—importantly—what visual information he concealed from it. Lewis allows for extreme close-ups of Bela Lugosi in *Invisible Ghost* (1941) as he strangles a victim; by contrast, he intentionally does not allow us to see Daniel Halliday's (Joseph Cotten's) face at the beginning of *The Halliday Brand* (1957) or Johnny Crale's (Nedrick Young's) face at the opening of *Terror in a Texas Town* (1958). At times we are forced to witness violence at great length, as in the bar fight in *A Lawless Street* (1955) that leaves Marshal Calem Ware's (Randolph Scott's) shirt in tatters. In other cases, Lewis intentionally prevents us from seeing violence: when Cassin finds Mama Michaud's (Ann Codee's) body in *So Dark the Night* (1946), Lewis only shows us her dead hand, keeping her body obscured by a kitchen countertop. Similarly, Nils Dreyer (John Hoyt) is shot down offscreen in *The Big Combo* (1955), and the camera in *Terror in a Texas Town* keeps us at a distance from the murder of Sven Hanson (Ted Stanhope).

By lingering on some visuals, Lewis can actually keep important information at bay, as in Captain Tom Benson's (Randolph Scott's) lengthy point of view pan shot of the deserted fort at the beginning of *7th Cavalry* (1956); the more we see, looking through Benson's eyes, the more we have to ponder the mystery of what has occurred. That we see the mysterious initials "MH" in so many places in Julia's (Nina Foch's) bedroom in *My Name Is Julia Ross* (1945) hardly explains their meaning. Nowhere is this approach treated more expertly than in the famous *Gun Crazy* bank robbery; we must wait in the car with Annie Laurie Starr (Peggy Cummins) while Bart Tare (John Dall) pulls the job. The more Lewis's camera shows us, the more we sometimes have to wonder about what we don't know.

What we know and what we don't know. Certainly Francis M. Nevins's book *Joseph H. Lewis: Overview, Interview, and Filmography* sheds important light on Lewis's biography and career; similarly, Jim Kitses's *Gun Crazy* offers an important and in-depth examination of Lewis's most famous film. Many essays in various journals and anthologies over the years have also attempted to bring Lewis's work into sharper focus. At the same time, however, a great number of his films have languished in obscurity, underappreciated by film buffs and scholars. Some have hardly been discussed; others—such as *Gun Crazy* and *The Big Combo*—cry out to be revisited. The present collection of essays proposes to remedy this situation, at least

Title card for *Gun Crazy* (1950).

in part, by exploring not the man Joseph H. Lewis but the cinematic world that he created; in other words, to reveal—at least in some small measure—what has hitherto been concealed.

Part 1 of this anthology investigates various texts and contexts important to Lewis's film and television career. Yannis Tzioumakis initiates the discussion by examining Lewis's trio of East Side Kids films at Monogram Studios, thus illustrating the emergence of his coherent visual style; his essay sheds much light on the connections between the budgetary constraints and aesthetic design of Lewis's early career. Hugh Manon follows with a perceptive discussion that examines spatial and temporal partition and desire across a range of Lewis's most important films, resulting in a simultaneously rigorous and subtle exploration of what he terms "a cinema of the *drive*, a cinema at odds with the mainstream because it satisfies the circulatory imperative of the drive in unexpected ways." Then, in his essay "The Joseph H. Lewis Nobody Knows," Michael E. Grost concludes part 1 by exploring what has been perhaps the most ignored area of Lewis's career: his work in television. Grost investigates major themes and issues that emerge in Lewis's "television films," as he calls them, which he views as an unbroken extension of the visual, narrative, and thematic world of Lewis's theatrical films.

Part 2, "Individual Works," provides ever more specific analyses by presenting an array of essays on specific films, such as my own examination of Lewis's remarkable and prescient *Invisible Ghost*; I argue that—in an effort to grapple with and overcome Bela Lugosi's image and the expectations of a typical Lugosi B movie—Lewis created a horror film that was ahead of its time in its use of dark comedy and in its presentation of film characters under siege in a single location. Lance Duerfahrd then engages with Lewis's other key work in the horror genre, the underappreciated *The Mad Doctor of Market Street* (1942); his essay provides a distinctive examination of a film that he does not claim to be "great" in which he importantly invokes the broader context of the B movie rather than confining himself strictly to Lewis's filmography. Then, Brian Taves investigates *Bombs over Burma* (1942), scrutinizing Lewis's only screenplay credit and the ways in which his writing and direction dealt with issues of World War II, China, and the star persona of Anna May Wong; as Taves suggests, both Lewis and Wong created important work at the "margins of Hollywood."

The section continues with an examination of the noir and crime films for which Lewis is perhaps best known. Marlisa Santos addresses psychology and identity in *My Name Is Julia Ross*, which leads her to suggest that the film should be read as a dream. Brian Hoyle focuses on issues of style

Title card for *Cry of the Hunted* (1953).

in *So Dark the Night*, a film in which he claims "style becomes substance" due to the fact that its "formal qualities and increasingly dark lighting scheme reflect the changing personality of the protagonist." David J. Hogan brings much-needed attention to *The Undercover Man* (1949) by viewing it against the context of the police procedural film of the late 1940s, concluding with the belief that Lewis was himself "one of Hollywood's great procedurists." Robert Singer then leads us into a monumental rethinking of *The Big Combo* by offering a suitably witty *and* serious essay on what he calls a "historically unique narrative of gender-specific sexual craving and humiliation." To complete the section, Tony Williams interrogates two of the director's most notable westerns—*The Halliday Brand* and *Terror in a Texas Town*—by viewing them as important allegories of the Hollywood blacklist.

Part 3 presents a case study of a single Lewis film, offering a trio of quite different approaches to his most famous and—arguably—most important

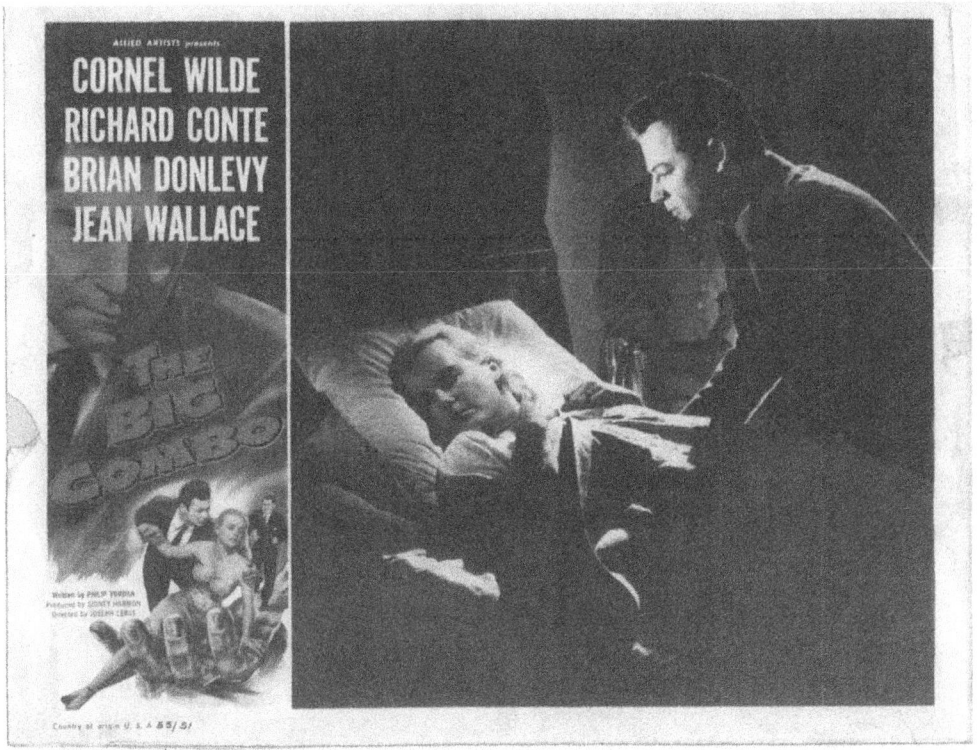

Poster artwork for *Gun Crazy* (1950).

work, *Gun Crazy*. Christopher Justice initiates the case study by situating *Gun Crazy* within the ever-problematic and rich category of film noir as well as providing insight into the ways in which Lewis created a work that is both modernist and postmodernist. Michael Lee's compelling essay scrutinizes *Gun Crazy* and its relationship to masculinity and masochism, arguing that the film's music speaks for the male lead's particular desires in a reversal of Hollywood conventions. Philip Sipiora then concludes the case study and the anthology by reconsidering *Gun Crazy* in terms of ethos and ethics, a particularly fitting way to end a book-length examination of the films of Joseph H. Lewis. "Character is destiny," Sipiora writes, words that could also provide an appropriate and fitting epitaph for Lewis the man.

These essays offer fresh perspectives on a range of Lewis's important theatrical and television films. Taken as a whole, they can be read as an extended and hopefully fertile conversation about Lewis the auteur, a director responsible for individually unique works as well as a sustained and coherent style fostered against the travails of budgetary constraints. Certainly the sheer number of Lewis films—as well as the complexities of his greatest achievements—suggests to all of us involved in this anthology that future studies of Lewis will be necessary. It is our hope to present an important voice in what will be an ongoing conversation.

1
Texts and Contexts

1

Yannis Tzioumakis

Style Development and Product Upgrading

Monogram Pictures, the Ambitious B Movie, and the East Side Kids Films Directed by Joseph H. Lewis

In his reference book *Joseph H. Lewis: Overview, Interview, and Filmography* (1998), Francis M. Nevins observes that "for the vast majority of film scholars Lewis's career begins in 1945 with *My Name Is Julia Ross* and ends in 1954 with *The Big Combo* or at latest in 1958 with *Terror in a Texas Town*."[1] The last of these bookmarks (1958) leaves out Lewis's significant television credits. He directed episodes of twelve different series, including *Daniel Boone* (NBC, 1964–70), *Gunsmoke* (CBS, 1955–75), *The Rifleman* (ABC, 1958–63), and *The Big Valley* (ABC, 1965–69).[2] The first bookmark, however, excludes important work in the medium of cinema: twenty-four feature films directed by Lewis in an eight-year period from 1937 to 1944, as well as an additional thirty-four films in which he worked as an editor between 1935 and 1937. Given that from *My Name Is Julia Ross* to *Terror in a Texas Town* Lewis made only sixteen films, it is not unfair to argue that many film critics have viewed his work with unnecessary, even problematic, limitations.

According to Nevins, one of the main reasons behind this very partial examination of Lewis's film work was the adoption of Andrew Sarris's auteurist approach to filmmakers, which sought to find common stylistic and thematic elements throughout a filmmaker's output. Sarris determined that any efforts to construct Lewis as an auteur filmmaker were bound to prove futile, as the filmmaker's earlier films—especially the seven he directed in 1940—seemed too heterogeneous to even merit any examination in search of markers of authorial signature.

However, Lewis's post-1945 work on a number of crime films that were characterized by strong noir elements—films such as *My Name Is Julia*

Ross, *So Dark the Night* (1946), *The Undercover Man* (1949), *Gun Crazy* (1949), *A Lady without Passport* (1950), *Cry of the Hunted* (1953), and *The Big Combo* (1955)—ensured his considerable visibility in the large number of critical studies on the subject of film noir.[3] Such studies led to more focused, rigorous examinations of films that were perceived as essential to the Lewis noir canon, particularly *Gun Crazy* and *The Big Combo*, which have been widely perceived to be not only Lewis's masterpieces but also key examples of film noir in general.[4]

Although such an approach certainly threw ample critical light on a lesser-known filmmaker's work, it nevertheless all but branded the rest of Lewis's films as unworthy of similar scholarly attention, with the possible exception of his later westerns.[5] This was particularly the case for Lewis's pre-1945 films, which were B movies and—with the exception of RKO's *The Falcon in San Francisco* (1945)—were made for Poverty Row studios such as Grand National, Monogram, and Producers Releasing Corporation (PRC) or for Columbia and Universal, two of the so-called Little Three Hollywood studios. Lewis's firm association with the B movie and the lower echelons of the American film industry in the pre-1945 period of his career further explains the absence of interest critics hold for his early films.

This imbalance has not been redressed in the years following the publication of Nevins's book, despite a surge in critical work on Lewis's cinema. In particular, the filmmaker's death in 2000 gave interested film scholars a new motivation to revisit his career. Detailed profiles of Lewis thus appeared in several journals, but, despite the new work, the critics' emphasis remained firmly within the 1945–58 period and on his much-studied noir films such as *Gun Crazy* and *The Big Combo*.[6] With this problem in hand, the present chapter aims to "open up" Joseph H. Lewis–centered film criticism through an examination of a trio of films from his pre-1945 work. Specifically, the three films Lewis directed for Monogram's East Side Kids series—*Boys of the City* (1940), *That Gang of Mine* (1940), and *Pride of the Bowery* (1941)—are permeated by an often remarkable consistency of stylistic choices, especially as articulated in terms of mise-en-scène, cinematography, and editing. This consistency not only suggests the emergence of an authorial signature as early as 1940 but also underscores the need for a reexamination of a number of films made at Hollywood's Poverty Row.[7]

In order to explore Lewis's use of visual style in the appropriate context, the chapter will begin with an examination of Monogram Pictures and its practices as a Poverty Row studio. This will be followed by a discussion of the series film as an integral part of B movie production for a company like Monogram. The chapter will then move to offer a detailed analysis of the three Lewis films, paying particular attention to his stylistic choices; it will also compare them to the two East Side Kids films that preceded and followed the Lewis films: *East Side Kids* (Robert F. Hill, 1940, the first film of the series) and *Flying Wild* (William West, 1941, the fifth film of the series). In addition to drawing attention to stylistic consistency across the three Lewis-directed films, the chapter will note that his use of visual style is clearly different than that employed by the other two craftsmen filmmakers, Hill and West, in their own East Side Kids films. In this respect, the chapter will argue that even extremely standardized genre filmmaking at the low end of the American film industry did indeed allow space for stylistic experimentation and personal expression, which filmmakers like Lewis could exploit, even if only for reputation-building exercises. Contrary then to what Andrew Sarris professed, there is certainly at least some logic in Lewis's 1940 record.

Poverty Row, Monogram Pictures, and the Film Series

Poverty Row

Monogram remains one of the best-known Poverty Row studios of the 1930s and 1940s. Alongside Republic Pictures, Mascot, and Grand National in the 1930s, as well as PRC in the 1940s, Monogram represents the tip of the iceberg of a large number of very small and thinly capitalized film production and/or film production and distribution companies that had existed under the heavy shadow of the Big Five (Paramount, MGM, Warner Bros., RKO, and Fox [Twentieth Century Fox since 1936]) and the Little Three (Columbia, Universal, and United Artists) studios. Although the designation "Poverty Row" for companies like Monogram and Republic originates from the geographical location in Hollywood where they were in business, it nonetheless came to signify those film companies that operated with extremely slim profit margins and also practiced a very particular type of filmmaking that differed substantially from the mode of film practice associated with the eight majors.[8] This means that Poverty Row films could not generally have been confused with their differently made and certainly glossier studio counterparts.

In terms of financial operations, comparisons between Monogram and various studios underscore the difference. According to Thomas Schatz, Monogram's annual profit for 1941, the year in which *Pride of the Bowery* was released, was a paltry $11,000 on rentals of just over $2.0 million.[9] This figure pales in comparison to the net profits of leading major studios such as Paramount ($9.2 million) or MGM ($11.0 million) or even with the considerably lower profits of the Little Three studios, such as Universal ($2.7

million) and Columbia ($0.6 million), for the same year. It is obvious then that even one of the leading Poverty Row companies could not be taken seriously as competition by the established powers of the Hollywood film industry.[10]

The limited financial capital indicates that there was no margin for mistakes. As Charles Flynn and Todd McCarthy remarked, "A day or two over schedule, a thousand or two over budget could spell the difference between profit and loss."[11] For this reason, companies like Monogram and Republic depended on an extreme standardization of product that, on certain occasions, was almost mathematically guaranteed to return a projected profit. This was mainly because films from Poverty Row studios were licensed to theaters for a flat fee (as opposed to a percentage of box office takings, which studio films normally enjoyed). For instance, a company like Mascot Pictures, which traded primarily in twelve or fifteen chapter serials such as *The Phantom Empire* (Brower and Eason, 1935) and *Undersea Kingdom* (Eason and Kane, 1936) for matinee shows, could make precise profit projections. With each chapter selling for $5 per theater for a period of twelve or fifteen weeks and with the company servicing approximately ten thousand theaters during the Depression era, Mascot stood to receive $600,000 on a twelve-chapter serial and $750,000 for fifteen chapters. It then needed only to keep the production costs in check to secure projected profits.[12]

The operation of Poverty Row companies on these principles meant that production values and aesthetic beauty were all but absent from their managerial agendas. Writing about Republic Pictures, the preeminent Poverty Row company, Richard Maurice Hurst noted that "the studio was not interested in art but in economics," and that it "utilized efficient and often clever means to save money."[13] Hurst continues: "Republic relied heavily and very professionally on such devices as expert use of stock footage (action sequences of merit good enough for multiple reuse), inexpensive character actors and actors on the way up or down, re-releases, strict budgets and shooting schedules, and no-nonsense writing and directing."[14] This philosophy clearly suggests that Poverty Row studios certainly did not encourage aesthetic experimentation and artistic pretension, unless the experimentation was concretely geared toward responding to the logistics of an often impossibly tight production schedule or was indeed deemed a money-saving strategy. This was certainly the case with Lewis's contemporary Edgar G. Ulmer, whose use of a puppet (instead of an actor) for the extensive underwater sequences in the film *Monsoon* (1945) both kept the film firmly on budget and provided it with a number of scenes that conveyed a distinct, almost "otherworldly" feel that makes them stand out from the rest of the narrative.[15] However, as I will argue in the following sections, Lewis's experimentation in the East Side Kids films was not a response to concerns over budget or logistics but a concerted effort to develop a fluid visual style.

The B Movie

The B movie is a label that characterized a significant number of major studio films, as well as all productions made by Poverty Row companies, at least until the mid-1940s. The label owes its existence to the introduction of the double feature presentation in 1930 as a measure to bolster cinemagoing after the economic crash of 1929 and the first signs of the Great Depression. Given the increased value of the price of theater admission that it offered (two films for the price of one), the success of the double bill was so overwhelming that a year later more than eight thousand cities in the country had adopted the practice.[16] This development had a far-reaching effect in the film industry, as it allowed for the emergence of the B movie, a relatively low-budget picture that was specifically created to accompany a more expensive, glossier, and with more evident production values A movie on the double bill. This meant that the B film was first and foremost "a creation of the law of economics" that served a very particular industry objective.[17]

With the double bill increasing the need for more films and with the major studios operating at full capacity producing and distributing both A and B pictures, smaller companies such as Victory Pictures, Supreme Pictures, Invincible Pictures, Empire Films, and others had the opportunity to carve a niche in the film market by solely supplying B movies. However, despite the existence of such a significant number of independent B film production outfits, only Republic and Monogram managed to survive for an extended period of time.[18]

Monogram Pictures

W. Ray Johnston and Trem Carr began various production/distribution companies, starting with Rayart in 1924 and continuing with Continental Talking Pictures and Syndicate Film Exchange before establishing Monogram in 1931.[19] The company was formed as a cooperative with the participation of several independent film exchange owners from various US territories. Under this arrangement, each exchange owner would contribute to the production costs of a set number of films per year and would then obtain the rights to all Monogram films for the territory they represented. This meant that a Monogram stakeholder was guaranteed a steady flow of product, which amounted to approximately thirty films per year during the first years of the company's operation.[20]

Monogram's business plan and, perhaps most important, its creation of a distribution network that expanded throughout America, as well as to a small number of overseas markets, quickly established it as the leading B studio in the first half of the 1930s. However, a number of factors—including the effects of the Great Depression in the 1932–33 period (when even big players such as Fox, Warner Bros., and RKO recorded huge net annual losses) and the major studios' efforts to end the double bill—caused Monogram's management to examine the possibility of consolidation within a larger structure. In early 1935, Monogram merged with Republic Pictures, a new Poverty Row studio that had emerged through Consolidated Film Industries' takeover of Chesterfield and Majestic and the subsequent merger of the new outfit with Liberty Pictures. This created a "super Poverty Row studio" that had the potential to become a major player in the B film market and even compete directly with studios like Columbia and Universal. However, despite the auspicious start, intense management and ownership problems led to the gradual disintegration of the super B studio; one by one the ex-owners of the companies that helped formed Republic walked out and re-formed their old companies.

In 1937, Monogram became the first to be revived and was, moreover, conceived in relatively grander terms compared to its status before the Republic merger. This time thirty-one exchange owners agreed to fund and distribute the Monogram product.[21] Even the number of releases per year increased considerably with forty-two films announced for distribution in the 1937–38 season, the largest program in the history of the company.[22] However, despite upping the stakes, the box office performance of the company's films was not correspondingly higher than its pre-1935 years, to the extent that Monogram recorded a significant net loss of almost $250,000 for the year, posing serious questions about its sustainability.[23] Its problems included competition not only from the reconfigured Republic Pictures but also from Grand National, a newly formed Poverty Row studio that had managed to contract James Cagney for a series of pictures.

With signs of an easing of the Depression becoming visible toward the end of the decade, Monogram decided to risk further its precarious financial situation by opting to stick with the same number of releases for the 1938–39 season.[24] A significant factor in making this decision was Monogram's increasing presence in the independent theater circuit, where it had managed to secure more than six thousand cinemas to screen its films.[25] More important, however, Monogram had begun establishing a number of commercial or exploitable properties that it believed could help strengthen its position in the market. These properties included child star Jackie Cooper, whose film *Boy of the Streets* (Nigh, 1937) proved a major hit for Monogram and which, according to *Variety*, could even "open houses to Mono product heretofore closed to any but major features."[26] Additionally, there was Monogram's contract with Boris Karloff, who was immediately assigned the role of *Collier's* magazine detective character James Lee Wong in a series of four films, all scheduled for the 1938–39 season.[27] The latter meant that Monogram was dynamically entering the film series market with a franchise that could pose competition to the extremely successful Charlie Chan and Mr. Moto series that were produced by Twentieth Century Fox's B units.

The Film Series

The film series is yet another phenomenon that was intricately linked with the Depression, the double bill, and the B picture. With most of the major studios hit by net losses inflicted by the Great Depression during the early 1930s, studio executives were increasingly searching for film product that could offer guaranteed profits. In this respect, the film series was seen as a particularly attractive option given the economic climate and a Hollywood film industry in transition due to the introduction of the double bill. The majority of film series were conceived as B productions (and therefore produced on low budgets), adhered to tested generic formulas, and featured inexpensive unknown actors or minor stars, making it clear that an established and successful film series could prove a lucrative property for any company and not just for the Poverty Row firms.

With the exception of Warner Bros. and United Artists, all the major studios tried to cultivate film series during the 1930s. Arguably the most commercially successful were MGM's Andy Hardy films starring Mickey Rooney. Between 1937 and 1946, MGM produced eighteen Andy Hardy films, some of which were so commercially successful they turned the films' young star into MGM's most valuable property in 1939.[28] Other successful series included Paramount's Hopalong Cassidy western series (1935–41, with the series moving to United Artists in the 1940s when the latter was desperate for product) and RKO's Murder On series (1932–37, starring Edna May Oliver and James Gleason) and the Falcon crime series (1942–46, one of which was directed by Lewis, his first major studio feature as a director). However, the studio that became an industry leader in successful film series in the 1930s was Fox.

Under the leadership of Sol Wurtzel, B movie units at Fox (and later Twentieth Century Fox) demonstrated an exceptional capacity for efficient genre filmmaking that contributed between ten and twenty-five films per year to the studio's output, all of them costing a fraction of the company's

A movie product.[29] At the cornerstone of the unit's success was the film series, which Wurtzel had highlighted as a key strategy to battle the precarious business of filmmaking in Depression Hollywood.[30] The Charlie Chan series, the rights for which Wurtzel had bought after Universal unsuccessfully tried to launch the series in 1929, became the jewel in Fox's B movie crown. The series carried twenty-seven installments over a ten-year period (1932–42), often bringing spectacular profits for the studio, as certain individual films (on budgets of $250,000–$275,000 each) grossed more than $1 million. Indeed, the Charlie Chan films were so successful that Fox managed to arrange distribution deals for these B films on a percentage basis as opposed to the flat fee that was customary for all other B product.[31] Following the success of the Charlie Chan series, Fox proceeded to launch a number of series, some less successful than others, including the Mr. Moto film series (eight films during 1937–39) and the Jones family film series (sixteen films during 1936–40).

With major studios such as Twentieth Century Fox and RKO firmly in the business of producing film series as a form of protection against the economic woes of the Great Depression, it was no surprise that the much more vulnerable Poverty Row studios made the film series and movie serials their preferred type of product. With Republic focusing on serials after its merger with Mascot (a company that specialized in that particular type of filmmaking), the revamped Monogram turned its attention to the film series market, as the Boris Karloff–James Lee Wong films clearly demonstrate.

With this revised business plan in place and with an improved net loss of $180,000 in 1938–39 (compared to $250,000 in 1937–38), Monogram announced a record forty-six films for the 1939–40 season.[32] Table 1 contains the company's release schedule for the 1939–40 season, which was divided into two brackets. The top bracket consisted of three categories of films. The first category included the company's prestige productions, which were "sponsored" by Monogram's chairman and cofounder, W. Ray Johnston. The other two categories, "box office attractions" and "showman's success stories," included the regular releases, the majority of which were films belonging to a given series. Finally, the lower bracket included two western series, a genre that was in critical disrepute for most of the 1930s and therefore relegated to the very low end of production.

As table 1 suggests, Monogram's roster included a number of films with relatively exploitable elements. Besides the four film series, the company also put into production films adapted from literary sources (like Jack London novels and Washington Irving stories), while even the extremely low-budget Jack Randall westerns had additional exploitation elements,

Table 1. Monogram release schedule, 1939–40

	W. Ray Johnston Anniversary Specials	
1	*Rip Van Winkle*, based on a story by Washington Irving	
2	*Queen of the Yukon*, based on *Daughter of the Aurora* by Jack London	
3	*Son of the Navy*	
4	*His Father's Son*	
5	*Under Northern Lights*, based on Jack London's novel	
6	Jackie Cooper Special	
	Box-Office Attractions	
1	*Law and the Man*	
2	*Heroes in Blue*	
3	*The Girl Next Door*	
4	*Midnight Limited*	
5	*Secret Service Sanders*	
6	*Freckles Comes Home*	
7	*Night Edition*	
8	*One Glorious Adventure*	
9	*Mr. Wong Vanishes*	
10	*Mr. Wong in Havana*	James Lee Wong film series
11	*Mr. Wong's Chinatown Squad*	
12	*Mr. Wong in New York*	
	Showman's Success Series	
1	*Arm of the Law*	
2	*East Side Kids*	East Side Kids films series
3	*That Gang of Mine*	
4	*Boys of the City*	
5	*Aces of the Air*	
6	*Transcontinental Plane*	Tailspin Tommy film series starring John Trent
7	*Danger Flight*	
8	*Sky Patrol*	
9	*Tomboy*	
10	*Hoosier Schooldays*	Film series targeting youth audiences
11	*Haunted House*	(starring Marcia May Jones and Jackie Moran)
12	*Kid Reporters*	

Table 1. Continued

Westerns

	Starring Jack Randall	Starring Tex Ritter
1	The Prairie	The Colorado Trail
2	The Pioneers	Riders of Sundown
3	Kit Carson's Pony Express	Under Western Stars
4	Days of Daniel Boone	Oklahoma Land Rush
5	The Covered Wagon Trails	South of Rio Grande
6	The Last Outlaw	The Kid from Panhandle
7	The Cowboy and the Bandit	The Man from Hell's River
8	The Cheyenne Kid	Redskin Trail
Total		
	Forty-six films	

Source: Louis S. Lifton, "Monogram Pictures: With Business at a New Low Mark Ray Johnston Decides to Launch Another Company," in *The Film Daily Cavalcade* (New York: Film Daily, 1939), 1–10; "Monogram Raises Product to 46; Budget and Sales Quota Increase," *Motion Picture Herald*, May 6, 1939, 1.

given that *The Prairie* and *The Pioneers* were based on James Fenimore Cooper stories and thus were advertised as such.[33] However, it is clear that film series were at the cornerstone of the company's expansion plans, as sixteen of its thirty features were installments of series films (with the number rising to thirty-two out of a total of forty-six films, if one counts the western series).

It is at this transitional stage in Monogram's history that Joseph H. Lewis joined the company as a unit director after a brief stint at Columbia where he made five B westerns in six months.[34] As I will argue, Lewis's films could be seen to have epitomized the revamped Monogram's small-scale ambitions for expansion and upgrade of its product. This is particularly impressive given that Lewis's stylistically fluid films were not made under the umbrella of W. Ray Johnston's "anniversary specials," which could at least boast the pretence of artistic production. Instead, Lewis's films materialized in the lower production brackets, which rarely attracted any critical attention. It was in the production milieu of the film series where Lewis found opportunities to develop his skills as a filmmaker, making films with a distinct visual language (at least compared to the other films in the same series), while also offering Monogram a modicum of respectability (at least in the eyes of trade publications reviews, since Monogram films hardly registered with the mainstream press). For all these reasons, it is essential for critics to be aware of the institutional environment that characterized Monogram when Lewis began work on the newly developed East Side Kids film series.

THE EAST SIDE KIDS FILM SERIES AND THE AMBITIOUS B FILM

Sam Katzman and the East Side Kids

At the time of Lewis's arrival at Monogram, the company (like the rest of Hollywood) was organized under a strict producer-unit system of production, with a small number of producers (eight at the time of Lewis's arrival) heading the company's units.[35] Each producer was generally responsible for one film series while also supervising various stand-alone productions. Monogram's roster of unit producers included such persons as William T. Lackey, who was responsible for the Mr. Wong film series, but who also supervised Marcia May Jones and Jackie Moran films; Edward F. Feeney, who produced the Tex Ritter westerns; and Paul Malvern, who supervised the John Trent / Tailspin Tommy film series and other stand-alone productions such as the *Queen of the Yukon* special.

Shortly before Lewis's arrival at Monogram, producer Sam Katzman joined the company. Katzman eventually became one of the most prolific producers in B movie production, racking up more than two hundred credits on Poverty Row and major studio films. Prior to working at Monogram, Katzman had produced more than forty films for small Poverty Row outfits such as Supreme Pictures and especially Victory Pictures for which he produced the majority of its films during 1935–39. When Victory folded in 1939, Katzman went to work for Monogram, where he was allowed to organize his production duties under various corporate production outfits, such as Four Bell Productions and Banner Productions. In effect, he became an in-house independent producer who supplied films for Monogram's expanding distribution pipelines. The property with which the producer launched his Monogram career was a commercially promising new film series: the East Side Kids.

The series was the latest incarnation of a commercially proven formula that involved representations of parentless young adults living in the streets of New York and their ties to urban crime. These representations had their origins in major independent and studio productions such as *Dead End* (Wyler, 1937) and *Angels with Dirty Faces* (Curtiz, 1938), which introduced teen actors Leo Gorcey, Bobby Jordan, and a number of other young performers in supporting roles as "tough kids" involved with gangsters. The success of these crime/gangster films made these young actors and the types of young criminals they portrayed popular to the extent that Warner Bros., which held the contracts with the specific teen actors and owned the rights to the characters they portrayed, started using them in similarly themed films under the collective name the "Dead End Kids." Such films included *They Made Me a Criminal* (Berkeley, 1938); *The Angels Wash Their Faces* (Enright, 1938); and *On Dress Parade* (Clemens, 1939). At the same time, Warner Bros. loaned some of these performers to Universal, which created a successful spin-off film series, originally under the title "Little Tough Guys." The continuing success of these films caused Monogram to decide to launch their own film series built on young criminals.

Katzman's arrival at Monogram proved the linchpin as the Poverty Row studio was developing its own young criminals series for one of its in-house stars, Frankie Darro, who had earlier appeared in such Warner Bros. crime films as *Wild Boys of the Road* (Wellman, 1933).[36] However, Katzman managed to secure a number of young actors with credits in the Little Tough Guys films (such as Hal E. Chester and Harris Berger), as well as Frankie Burke (who, like Harris Berger, had appeared in Warner's acclaimed *Angels with Dirty Faces*), and convinced Monogram to launch its new series with the more easily exploitable former Dead End Kids as stars. In this respect, the first installment of the new series, the titular *East Side Kids*, assumed a considerably different direction than Monogram had originally intended. However, the company felt that there was enough space for more tough kid films and therefore assigned Darro to projects such as *Laughing at Danger* (Bretherton, 1940) and *Up in the Air* (Bretherton, 1940).

East Side Kids was a straightforward crime drama about the manner in which a gangster uses a young kid—whose older brother is in prison awaiting execution—as a pawn in a counterfeit money scheme. The film, which will be discussed briefly later, continued the tradition of the Dead End Kids series with its emphasis on drama and on how parentless teenagers can be easily manipulated unless they are taken off the streets and placed in appropriate spaces where they can be nurtured properly under the appropriate supervision.

However, the particular generic, thematic, and formal direction of this first film of the series was short-lived. As Warner realized in 1939 that the main cycle of the Dead End Kids was reaching its end as a commercial property (at least for a major studio), it terminated the contracts of the young actors, including Leo Gorcey and Bobby Jordan, who had been most identified with the Dead End Kids phenomenon. This was the opportunity that Monogram and Katzman needed to make their series even more exploitable; the signing of Gorcey, Jordan, and certain other actors provided them with an even stronger marketing strategy than the one employed in producing *East Side Kids*. Alongside the new stars, Katzman decided to reshuffle his unit considerably by bringing in a number of new faces, some of which would stay for a number of installments. These included the experienced cinematographer Robert E. Cline, veteran editor Carl Pierson, and newly contracted director Joseph H. Lewis.

This means that Lewis's arrival at Monogram also coincided with the establishment of what in effect was a new unit composed of some very experienced craftsmen under the supervision of an extremely efficient producer working for a Poverty Row studio en route to the expansion and upgrading of its product. Given these conditions, one could argue that Lewis found at Monogram a climate conducive to the needs of an ambitious filmmaker who wanted to build a reputation in order to eventually move on to studio pictures. While Paul Kerr has suggested that conditions openly encouraging ambitious B filmmakers to differentiate their films though distinctiveness of style did not fully materialize until 1942 when the US government "reached a temporary settlement with the major studios in the so-called Paramount case," one could argue that the first signs of such a climate could be seen in 1940 and at a studio like Monogram.[37]

The signing of Bobby Jordan (*left*) and Leo Gorcey (*right*) provided Monogram with a strong marketing hook that would help establish the East Side Kids series.

Style Development and Product Upgrading

The Ambitious B Movie

According to Kerr, the temporary settlement of the Paramount case curtailed the practices of block booking and blind bidding, which meant that each studio had to start negotiating the sale of its films on an individual basis, including B movies, which had generally been sold for a flat fee. Given the low budget, the slim production values, and the relative absence of strong selling points, entities producing B movies started encouraging filmmakers to achieve distinction for the films through alternative means, which often involved "the contravention of current formulas and standard stylistic practices (too often referred to as the Classic Hollywood style), as indulgence in excess, individuality, idiosyncrasy, virtuosity as if for its own sake."[38] In this respect, a number of filmmakers working on B productions managed to produce work that challenged mainstream aesthetic norms while also developing reputations as notable directors.

Although Kerr correctly points to the temporary settlement of the Paramount case as the cornerstone of this phenomenon and 1942 as the year when the effects of this settlement started materializing clearly, his account nonetheless refers to the Consent Decree that was signed much earlier, on October 29, 1940. As I have argued elsewhere, the main effect of that decree was that it signaled the gradual phasing out of B film production by the major studios in order to concentrate on the production of films that would be more competitive in the marketplace.[39] More importantly for the purposes of this chapter, the Consent Decree meant that Poverty Row studios like Monogram and Republic would eventually be left alone to produce films for the bottom half of the double bill. This development immediately marked a period of expansion for these companies, because for the first time they would not have to compete against the B production units at major studios. This can be seen extremely clearly in Republic's decision to start producing and distributing films at capacity levels, after announcing sixty-two films for the 1940–41 season; sixty-six for the 1941–42 season; and sixty-eight films for the 1943–44 and 1944–45 seasons.[40] The effects of the Consent Decree of 1940 also provided the impetus for the formation of a new Poverty Row studio, PRC, which took its final shape in late 1940.

In this respect, Lewis's work at Monogram must also be understood as occurring at the very beginning of particular institutional developments that not only encouraged ambitious B filmmaking (especially for filmmakers such as Jacques Tourneur and Anthony Mann who worked at the studios' B units) but also allowed companies like Monogram that had minimal financial capital to start operating profitably in the marketplace. It is under this more general climate that Lewis found little resistance in building up a personal visual style that was characterized by several "excessive" elements.

The Lewis Style

Boys of the City *(1940)*

Lewis's first contribution to the series, *Boys of the City*, could not have been more different than *East Side Kids*, the series-inaugurating film that preceded it. In addition to the new actors, Lewis brought in a mixture of generic elements that made the film much less a crime film and more a comedy mystery picture. Furthermore, he opted for a slower narrative pace by structuring his film around a smaller number of scenes as compared to *East Side Kids*, a decision that allowed for some narrative development that was largely missing from the first (and much more fast-paced) film of the series. More important, however, Lewis utilized a fluid visual style that made the film (and the rest of his contributions) stand out from the other films in the series, especially those made in the early 1940s, as well as from the majority of the Monogram fare. This fluidity of style, nevertheless, was not noticed by the trade publications of the time, at least not until Lewis's second entry to the series, *That Gang of Mine*, was released later in 1940. For *Boys of the City*, *Variety* acknowledged the entertainment value of the film, which played on "full house[s]" that "seemed to enjoy Leo Gorcey, Bobby Jordan & Co. wrassling a mystery, the reason for which is never clearly explained, to a conclusion." However, the review also pointed out that the film is "crammed full with faults in photography, direction, story and emoting," problems that were certainly not a rare phenomenon with the majority of B film productions by Poverty Row studios.[41]

Yet the *Variety* review was somewhat unjustified and misleading. Although the psychological motivation of certain characters can certainly be questioned and the cause-and-effect logic seems at times problematic when compared to A films, B films were rarely distinguished for their narrative nuance. As Brian Taves has put it, "The familiarity of the most undemanding and rigid formulas were both expected and desired," making for narratives that did not have to rely on clear motivation in order to advance the story, irrespective of their specific generic properties.[42] In this respect, the narrative indeterminacy of *Boys of the City* does not impinge at all on the film's objective to provide entertainment to the youthful audiences that attended it.

On the other hand, and as trade publications' reviewers had not been used to looking for signs of fluidity in terms of visual style at the bottom half of double bills, the *Variety* reviewer should be forgiven for highlighting the number of technical problems that were also anticipated in films of B designation. This means, however, that the reviewer missed the op-

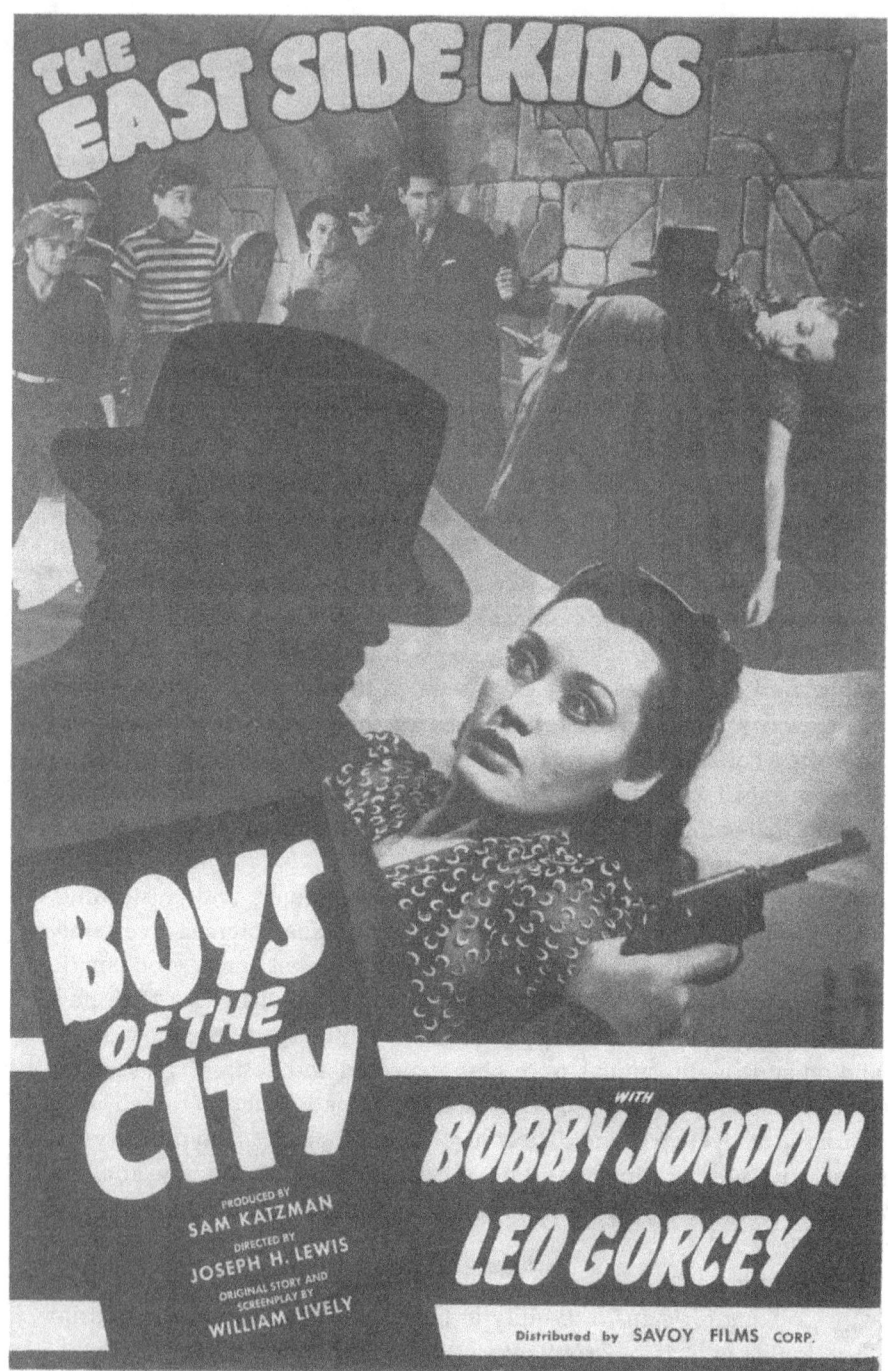

The press book cover for *Boys of the City* (1940), Joseph H. Lewis's first entry in the East Side Kids series.

portunity to name a number of key stylistic features, especially in terms of mise-en-scène, cinematography, and editing that demonstrate both the film's ambition and the emergence of a filmmaker characterized by a distinct use of visual style.

In terms of framing, lighting, and mise-en-scène in general, Lewis relies on certain unusual techniques. In one of the early sequences, as the East Side Kids are lazily trying to find ways to cool off on what seems to be a hot summer day, there is an abrupt entrance to the frame by one of the boys from the top right corner. This is offscreen space that is rarely considered a part of the diegesis, as space from where narrative events can originate, at least in classical filmmaking, and therefore takes the spectator by surprise. Later on, and as the kids are in the "haunted mansion," Lewis chooses to frame a scene from behind the flames of a fireplace, with the camera occupying the inside of the fireplace. This seemingly unmotivated framing of a conversation between the judge and his aide suggests a stylistically excessive choice for the scene, potentially to achieve a more dramatic impact. However, it later becomes clear that the room with the fireplace also includes a secret passage that leads to an elaborate set of tunnels where much of the plot will take place. In this respect, Lewis's unmotivated and unusual shot is later revealed to have been an unattributed point of view shot that suggests the judge was under constant surveillance from the time he arrived at the mansion. This is also confirmed in the scene where the judge is murdered. Lewis's decision to show the murder in shadows (created through low-key backlighting) not only has a narrative function (by withholding the identity of the killer) but also has a clear aesthetic function: the judge is literally killed by a "shadowy presence" that could inhabit any place in the mansion.

Lewis's mise-en-scène choices seem to become particularly excessive in two shots where he employs the technique of the extreme close-up in order to frame the mysterious housekeeper, Agnes. On the first occasion, the extreme close-up of Agnes's face is used to emphasize her exaggerated facial characteristics, especially as she tells the kids that there is a ghost in the mansion. If Agnes's facial features are indeed overstated by this stylistic choice in order to achieve a dramatic effect, Lewis's second use of extreme close-up seems to be far less motivated. In one of the final scenes of the film, the undercover assistant district attorney questions Agnes about her involvement in the judge's murder. Toward the end of the scene, Agnes is framed in an unflattering extreme close-up shot without any explicit narrative justification. The protracted duration of the image (approximately twelve seconds) makes for an unsettling shot that draws attention to technique, signaling that the director has made an aesthetic choice.

Although that final close-up of the housekeeper is the only instance when the film's mise-en-scène moves to excessive levels, Lewis's camerawork draws considerable more attention to technique than his use of mise-en-scène. *Boys of the City* contains a substantial number of elegant tracking shots that exceed narrative requirements. The most protracted of those shots is in a narratively insignificant scene that occurs approximately twenty-five minutes into the film. After being served a formal dinner at the haunted mansion, the kids engage in jokes, pretending to be members of a board sitting around a big table and smoking cigars. By use of a dissolve, the narrative jumps forward in time. The boys are still sitting around the table surrounded by a cloud of smoke created by the cigars and coughing loudly. This scene lasts approximately thirty seconds and consists of a single-take tracking shot with the camera moving around the table and registering the general feel of distress that follows excessive eating, drinking, and cigar smoking. The extended length of the shot makes a narratively insignificant sequence stand out from the rest of the narrative while at the same time also attracting considerable attention to Lewis's technique.

A few scenes later, the unmotivated tracking shot make its appearance again. This time the camera moves around a room where a piano seems to play on its own (suggesting the presence of a ghost) until the camera comes to a halt in the previously mentioned extreme close-up of Agnes. This is followed by yet another tracking shot in the following scene, which this time reveals the illusion of the narrative world. As the judge comes out of his room to silence the noisy boys in the corridor of the mansion, a tracking shot starts moving through the walls of his room and arrives in the corridor at the exact moment as the judge, elegantly revealing the artifice of the setting. Lewis utilizes the same technique a few scenes later when the camera starts moving behind the fireplace and through an impossible space (which should have been occupied by walls) until it is in an optimum position to reframe characters inside the room. These artistically motivated tracking shots are also supplemented by some examples of moving camera that are narratively motivated, particularly in the scenes that take place in the secret tunnels. Taken together, Lewis's extensive use of tracking shots offers a visual fluidity that stands at odds with the narrative rigidity of the haunted mansion "whodunit" that structures *Boys of the City*.

Lewis's achievement in *Boys of the City* can be seen more clearly if one compares the filmmaker's stylistic choices to the ones made by Robert F. Hill in the preceding film of the series, *East Side Kids*. Both in terms of mise-en-scène and cinematography, Hill avoided any choices that were either narratively unmotivated or that could attract attention to technique. This is particularly evident in terms of camera movement, which is minimal and includes only subtle pans that follow the action and corrective pans and tracks that tend to be used for reframing purposes. There are no tracking shots, with the exception of a couple of slow dolly movements that start from a close-up of a character and gradually open up the shot to reveal the surrounding setting.

Initially, the editing of *Boys of the City* seems relatively pedestrian. Scenes adhere clearly to the rules of continuity editing and normally include four to five camera setups that allow the filmmaker and editor considerable choice in terms of frequently cutting among these four to five setups, thus creating a somewhat fast-paced narrative. Lewis also employs a variety of editing techniques to link scenes together, including the cut, the wipe, the dissolve, and the fade. On a few occasions, his use of editing markers achieves standards of virtuosity that are not usually associated with Poverty Row filmmaking. This is particularly clear in an early scene of the film when the use of a wipe from screen right to screen left coincides with the move of a van that follows the same direction, blending beautifully the diegetic world with techniques of narration.

If Lewis's expertise in editing techniques is not surprising given his work as an editor on over thirty films during the mid-1930s, it is his use of parallel editing as the primary stylistic device in advancing the narrative that becomes particularly evident in *Boys of the City*, emerging as an extremely strong marker of an authorial presence. Specifically, in a large number of scenes, Lewis chooses to establish two or more areas of action with the spectator left unaware of how they might be connected, if indeed they are. Hence, on several occasions, it is possible for the spectator to think that a scene might have ended and that the narrative has moved to a different spatiotemporal sequence of events, only to find out that the two separate actions were indeed taking place in the same geographical space or at the same time and in fact were components of the same narrative incident or scene.

This is particularly evident in the fourth scene of the film. The first field of action involves the boys unscrewing a fire hydrant and flooding the street with water. Nearly one minute of screen time later, a cut moves the action to a street vendor and his stall. Although it is possible that this is the same street, no clear stylistic or narrative sign is provided for the benefit of the spectator to understand that this is the case; for example, the kids' loud voices are not audible. Given the absence of such a sign, the spectator is encouraged to think that this is a new scene and that the narrative has moved forward, with the previous scene having achieved its objective: to establish the kids as mischievous characters tampering with public property. A few seconds later, however, the street vendor scene cuts back to the boys further enjoying the water on the street. It is only then—thanks to a camera pan—that the spectator understands that the street vendor had set up his stall close to the first field of action, as the water on the street soon approaches the wood that holds the stall up. Not surprisingly, the water sweeps the wood away, bringing the stall down and causing a fight between the vendor and the East Side Kids. It is clear only then that the two fields of action were indeed running parallel to each other rather than being in a chronological sequence.

Such a connection between narration and editing is employed with impunity throughout the film. It is used to link events together within a particular scene (as the fire hydrant example suggests), and it is employed to bring scenes together that start in different geographies and then converge at the same location. For instance, early in the film, Lewis alternates scenes of the judge's car driving away from the city with scenes of a van transporting the kids. It is only after four scenes when the narration brings the two separate areas of action (this time also separate scenes) together when the judge's car overtakes the van, forcing it off the road.

This use of parallel editing also allows Lewis to exploit the main assets of his film, his young actors. This becomes particularly clear in the main body of the film, which takes place in the haunted mansion. In these scenes, Lewis splits the East Side Kids into smaller groups and various areas of action, which allows him to play up the mystery element of the film as well as to highlight the comedy. Scenes unfold in a parallel fashion in various parts of the mansion and in its secret tunnels without the spectator knowing exactly how they are (or if they will be) connected, not only spatiotemporally, but also in terms of cause-effect logic. In this sense, the use of crosscutting allows Lewis to create an elegant and complex level of narration over a pedestrian and extremely formulaic narrative.

That Gang of Mine *(1940)*

Although Lewis's achievements with *Boys of the City* were unnoticed by the reviewers of the time, his work on his second (and the series' third) installment, *That Gang of Mine*, was received favorably, at least by some of the trade publications. *Film Daily* labeled both direction and cinematography as "good" while reiterating that "Joseph Lewis [turned] in a good job of directing."[43] Although other publications were less impressed, the fluidity in Lewis's use of visual style was once again evident.[44] His choices in terms of cinematography, mise-en-scène, and editing once again offered some complexity to, and in a number of instances exceeded the requirements of, another weak narrative. This time the story focused primarily on Muggs (Gorcey), who wants to race as a jockey in a major horse-racing event. Rather improbably, he manages to secure a horse, but he and the gang then stumble onto a group of crooks who try to manipulate them and the race for their own benefit. After many adventures and setbacks, Muggs has a more suitable jockey ride the horse, which, predictably, wins the race.

The similarities with Lewis's stylistic choices in *Boys of the City* are many. In terms of mise-en-scène, for the most part Lewis makes functional choices that ensure that spectators will focus on the story told and not on the manner of its telling. Lighting, framing, and the staging of actors are overall straightforward. However, once again Lewis includes a small number of choices that are not fully motivated by narrative and therefore attract attention to his craft. In this film, these choices have to do with camera position, which on a few occasions is placed behind objects, making for evocative shots. For instance, on two different occasions he places his camera behind a wagon wheel (a camera setup that Lewis had used a lot in his early westerns), as well as behind a ceiling fan in a nightclub.[45] All these choices distract the spectator from the narrative by breaking with the tradition of a seamless, invisible style.

Similarly, a number of tracking shots make their appearance and certainly add to the film's ambition to stand out stylistically from the rest of Monogram's fare. The most audacious examples of moving camera are once again narratively unmotivated shots that interrupt the overall functionality of the film's visual style. For instance, during a scene in the stables, Ben, the horse's trainer, starts singing a song to his horse and the camera moves, slowly registering the expression on each boy's face as they all listen to the song; the shot is reminiscent of the tracking shot at the dining table in *Boys of the City*. Arguably, Lewis's most audacious tracking shot comes when he combines an elaborate pan and tracking shot during a scene in which one of the kids "blackmails" his father for money to support Muggs's horse-racing dream. While the father and son have fixed places in the frame and could be shot very easily in a medium shot, the camera's elaborate movement removes the emphasis from the comic scene and shifts it to the virtuoso technique.

However, the most memorable stylistic element in *That Gang of Mine* comes through editing. Here Lewis once again uses the full range of editing techniques to link scenes, with his use of fades being particularly pronounced. This time, however, he does not resort to parallel editing, at least not to the extent he utilized it in his previous film. Instead, he opts for a considerably larger number of shots that give the film a much faster pace than *Boys in the City*. The fast pace appropriately supports the subject of the film, especially as the narrative contains two race scenes that are constructed from a large number of shots. Interestingly, however, Lewis also resorts to quick editing in scenes that do not lend themselves to this particular stylistic choice. In this sense, editing becomes excessive on several occasions, demonstrating once again the film's status as an ambitious B production. This becomes particularly evident in an early scene at the stables, when Muggs's horse becomes restless when he rides it for the first time. Within the space of one minute of screen time, Lewis uses no less than thirty shots, which creates a particularly dizzying effect for the spectator at an unsuspected time in the narrative.

Pride of the Bowery *(1941)*

Lewis's editing choices become even more pronounced in the third and final film he contributed to the East Side Kids series, *Pride of the Bowery*. With the narrative of the film containing three boxing matches, including one that is split into different scenes and takes more than five minutes of screen time, Lewis was offered an opportunity to try various editorial strategies, including a substantial use of parallel editing. Indeed, the first and longest boxing match clearly demonstrates Lewis's approach. As in the race sequences in *That Gang of Mine*, he uses a large number of shots, giving the boxing match a rapid pace. These shots include various images of the audience members and a large number of close-up shots of the fight. The camera is often located very close to the action, sometimes assuming the point of view of a boxer.

The swift pace of the film is suddenly interrupted when the camera leaves the boxing match and follows a young boy as he tries to walk away from it without being noticed by the rest of the kids. Following a cut, this same boy is now in the office of the captain of the Civilian Conservation Corps camp that plays host to the East Side Kids' adventures for the film. The boy opens the safe in the office and seems to be ready to steal the contents, but a wipe withholds the outcome of his action and the scene moves a few seconds forward in time as he opens the office door to leave. Another cut and the action moves back to the ring where the boxing game continues with the same relentless pace until the captain declares it a draw.

The fast editing that marks this boxing match is not replicated in the other two matches that take place later in the film, even though parallel editing remains very much their key structural component. The second match occurs almost three-quarters into the film's running time. Here Lewis starts with his trademark tracking shot, the camera approaching the ring from a distance before moving inside it. At this point, however, he avoids the fast edits and the point of view shots, opting instead for a series of dissolves that link a small number of shots together. The technique creates a montage effect that seems to complement the narrative objective of the scene in which Muggs agrees to box in order to raise funds to help the boy who stole the money during the first boxing match.

The third boxing match occurs in the penultimate scene of the film, and it features Lewis utilizing yet another editing style. Now he avoids dissolves, but his straight cuts create a somewhat slow pace. Despite coming at the conclusion, this third boxing match is narratively insignificant (or certainly less significant than the other two), as its function is to lead to the end of the film, which comes only a few seconds later. For that reason, Lewis seems to treat it like a normal scene and not as one of the showpieces of the film as he does with the other boxing matches.

Although it is editing that once again stands out stylistically in *Pride of the Bowery*, mise-en-scène and cinematography prove almost equal contributors to the film's fluid style. Besides the unexpected (and unmotivated) tracking shot at the beginning of the second boxing match, Lewis uses other such shots that attract attention to technique, including a fast tracking shot that halts at a close-up of a boy that adds a particularly (melo)dramatic dimension to the scene. Additionally, in one scene, Lewis includes a protracted tilt movement (to show the great height of a particular tree in a forest), which he juxtaposes with three consecutive extreme close-up shots of boys who are incapable of warning another boy from imminent danger when the tree falls. The combination of cinematography and editing here make for one particularly complex and sophisticated scene that once again interrupts the seamless classical style that marks much of the rest of the film.

By that time, some reviewers of *Pride of the Bowery* had apparently become well aware of Lewis's effort to upgrade the series and potentially launch himself as a filmmaker with a future away from the low depths of Poverty Row. For a Monogram film, *Pride of the Bowery* was reviewed very favorably by the trade press, while also registering with the mainstream press, which, as mentioned earlier, rarely reviewed films from Poverty Row companies. "Blessed with a logical story, good performances and excellent photography of beautiful country, the picture is cinch to garner new audiences for the series on its release," remarked the critic for the *Hollywood Reporter*, while also not forgetting to mention Lewis, whose "direction account[ed] for lots of fan-pleasing fast action and good performances."[46] "For a picture which cost 'peanuts' it's worth much more in entertainment value," said Irene Thirer in the *New York Post*.[47] "It's done in a sound, standardized manner, has some good acting and excellent camera work," observed the reviewer of the *New York World-Telegram*.[48] Even *Variety*, which

Style Development and Product Upgrading 33

had not been impressed by either *Boys of the City* or *That Gang of Mine*, admitted that the "tale [was] straightforwardly told with pleasing simplicity and with more than adequate thespic and directorial skill."[49] With such reviews, it is clear that Lewis had managed to differentiate this particular Monogram product and to demonstrate his proficiency in filmmaking. And Lewis's proficiency in filmmaking was evident both by the fluidity in his use of visual style and the consistency of this fluidity throughout the three East Side Kids installments.

Following the success of *Pride of the Bowery*, Lewis was promoted to directing "special" Monogram productions but remained under Katzman's supervision. Lewis's fourth film for the company was the horror story *Invisible Ghost* (1941) starring Bela Lugosi. To replace Lewis in the East Side Kids series, Katzman brought in an inexperienced contract director, William West. In a brief comparison with *Flying Wild*, West's first contribution to the series (which became the fifth East Side Kids film), one can see beyond any doubt the fundamental ways in which Lewis's East Side Kids films differ from the rest of the series.

Flying Wild has the kids stumbling onto a scheme in which a gang of crooks use an airplane ambulance to smuggle plans for aviation designs and other sensitive documents. Although the film retains the comedy and adventure generic mix that was initiated by Lewis's *Boys of the City*, it has more stylistic similarities with the first installment of the series, *East Side Kids*, than with any of the Lewis-directed films. Mise-en-scène is used in a purely functional manner, with all choices made firmly in the service of the narrative; editing adheres to the rules of continuity and does not use markers that attract attention to technique. Even the use of wipes, which were commonly used in films of the era, is greatly decreased in *Flying Wild*. Similarly, cinematography avoids any unmotivated or excessive camerawork, while camera movement remains minimal and takes the form of a couple of shots where tracking either opens up a shot or makes it tighter and of shots where tracking movement is used to follow characters who are moving. Despite the achieved efficiency, the result made for extremely unimaginative filmmaking, even for Monogram standards, to the extent that West was replaced on the sixth East Side Kids film entry by veteran filmmaker Wallace Fox.

Conclusion

Following his short stint at Monogram—*Invisible Ghost* became his fourth and last film for the company—Joseph H. Lewis continued his career in B movies by alternating between making films for Poverty Row companies, such as PRC, and for Universal, which did not phase out its B production until well into the 1950s. During these four years (late 1941 to 1945), Lewis made nine films, before the commercial success of *My Name Is Julia Ross* led him into A film production, studio projects, and subsequent critical recognition. These nine films (as well as the eleven films he made before his work at Monogram) have generally been ignored. In the rare instances critics have examined these films, such as Wheeler Dixon's collection on PRC,[50] Lewis has usually been heralded as a filmmaker with a rich visual style, whether in war films like *Bombs over Burma* (1942) or in crime films like *Secrets of a Co-Ed* (1943).[51]

Furthermore, it was his films alongside the films of Edgar G. Ulmer that brought a modicum of respectability to PRC, a company that, according to some critics, represented "the nadir of independent film operations."[52] Just as his entries to the East Side Kids film series started changing the perception of trade publications about the quality of filmmaking at Monogram, his contributions to the PRC roster of releases were seen as the part of the company's efforts to transcend the limitations of its mode of operation. As William K. Everson put it, "PRC was at its very best when it had very little—and relied on Edgar Ulmer and Joseph H. Lewis to make it look like far more."[53]

Lewis's films at PRC and certainly Monogram clearly demonstrate how a filmmaker could use the Poverty Row companies that existed at the margins of Hollywood as a training ground for developing a personal visual style while at the same time helping those companies be taken more seriously by their peers. In this sense, an in-depth examination of these less appreciated Lewis films can assist film criticism in learning much more about the working practices of a particular filmmaker. Perhaps more important, it can also help film critics to understand better American cinema of the classical Hollywood period.

Notes

1. Francis M. Nevins, *Joseph H. Lewis: Overview, Interview, and Filmography* (Lanham, MD: Scarecrow, 1998), xi.

2. Ibid., 99–113. All these figures were taken from Nevins's exhaustive filmography.

3. See in particular James Naremore, *More than Night: Film Noir in Its Contexts*, 2nd rev. ed. (Berkeley: University of California Press, 2000), as well as Alain Silver and Elizabeth Ward, eds., *Film Noir: An Encyclopedic Reference to the American Style*, 3rd ed. (Woodstock, NY: Overlook Press, 1996).

4. A key example here is Jim Kitses's book on *Gun Crazy*. See Jim Kitses, *Gun Crazy* (London: BFI Classics, 1996). For a study of *The Big Combo*, see Tom

Flinn, "*The Big Heat* and *The Big Combo*: Rogue Cops and Mink-Coated Girls," *Velvet Light Trap* 11 (1974): 23–28.

5. See for instance Everson's revised volume on the western. William K. Everson, *The Hollywood Western* (New York: Citadel Press, 1992).

6. See for instance Ed Grant, "Art on a Budget: Joseph H. Lewis," *Time*, October 31, 2000, http://www.time.com/time/arts/article/0,8599,59141,00.html.

7. In *American Independent Cinema: An Introduction* I argued a similar point with relation to the Charlie Chan film series that moved to Monogram around the same time the East Side Kids series was being launched. See Yannis Tzioumakis, *American Independent Cinema: An Introduction* (Edinburgh: Edinburgh University Press, 2006), 77–82.

8. Greg Merritt, *Celluloid Mavericks: A History of American Independent Film* (New York: Thunder's Mouth Press, 2000), 63.

9. Thomas Schatz, *Boom and Bust: American Cinema in the 1940s* (Berkeley: University of California Press, 1999), 64.

10. Douglas Gomery, *The Hollywood Studio System* (New York: St. Martin's Press, 1986), 34, 52, 148, 162.

11. Charles Flynn and Todd McCarthy, "The Economic Imperative," in *Kings of the Bs: Working within the Hollywood System*, ed. Todd McCarthy and Charles Flynn (New York: Dutton, 1975), 13–43.

12. Tzioumakis, *American Independent Cinema*, 69.

13. Richard Maurice Hurst, *Republic Studios: Between Poverty Row and the Majors* (Lanham, MD: Scarecrow Press, 1979), vi.

14. Ibid., 6.

15. Yannis Tzioumakis, "Edgar G. Ulmer: The Low-End Independent Filmmaker *Par Excellence*," in *Edgar G. Ulmer: Detour on Poverty Row*, ed. Gary D. Rhodes (Lanham, MD: Lexington, 2008), 3–23.

16. Matthew Bernstein, "Hollywood's Semi-Independent Production," *Cinema Journal* 32, no. 3 (1993): 41–54.

17. Hurst, *Republic Studios*, 3.

18. Gomery estimates the number of these companies during the studio times at approximately thirty. Gomery, *Hollywood Studio System*, 173.

19. Tzioumakis, *American Independent Cinema*, 68.

20. Ibid.

21. "31 Offices Set Up for Monogram Distribution," *Hollywood Reporter*, March 22, 1937, 12.

22. "New Monogram Ready," *Motion Picture Herald*, March 27, 1937; and "Monogram Sets 42 Features and $4,333,000 Sales Quota for 1938," *Motion Picture Herald*, March 8, 1937.

23. "Monogram Operating at Profit; 70% of Pathe Holders Favor Plan," *Motion Picture Herald*, February 25, 1939.

24. "26 Features and 16 Westerns on Monogram '38–'39 Program," *Motion Picture Herald*, May 7, 1938.

25. "Monogram Operating at Profit."
26. "Monogram $80,000 Picture Returning About $800,000," *Daily Variety*, October 24, 1938.
27. "26 Features and 16 Westerns."
28. Tino Balio, *Grand Design: Hollywood as a Modern Business Enterprise, 1930–1939* (Berkeley: University of California Press, 1995), 280.
29. Gomery, *Hollywood Studio System*, 97.
30. Tzioumakis, *American Independent Cinema*, 78.
31. Ibid., 79.
32. "Monogram Raises Product to 46; Budget and Sales Quota Increase," *Motion Picture Herald*, May 6, 1939, 1, 48.
33. Ibid., 1.
34. Nevins, *Joseph H. Lewis*, 18.
35. "Monogram Raises Product to 46," 1.
36. Ibid.
37. Paul Kerr, "My Name Is Joseph H. Lewis," *Screen* 24, nos. 4–5 (1983): 48–68.
38. Ibid., 50
39. Tzioumakis, *American Independent Cinema*, 83.
40. Ibid., 83–84.
41. "*Boys of the City*," *Variety*, August 17, 1940.
42. Brian Taves, "The B Film: Hollywood's Other Half," in *Grand Design: Hollywood as a Modern Business Enterprise, 1930–1939*, ed. Tino Balio (Berkeley: University of California Press, 1995), 333.
43. "*That Gang of Mine*," *Film Daily*, October 3, 1940.
44. "*That Gang of Mine*," *Weekly Variety*, January 1, 1941.
45. See Nevins, *Joseph H. Lewis*, 14 and 23.
46. "New Production up to Standard: *Pride of the Bowery*," *Hollywood Reporter*, January 15, 1941.
47. Irene Thirer, "*Pride of the Bowery*: On Screen at the Rialto," *New York Post*, January 24, 1941.
48. "At the Rialto," *New York World-Telegram*, January 24, 1941.
49. "*Pride of the Bowery*," *Variety*, January 29, 1941.
50. Wheeler Dixon, ed., *Producers Releasing Corporation: A Comprehensive Filmography and History* (Jefferson, NC: McFarland, 1986).
51. Don Miller, "A Brief History of PRC," in *Producers Releasing Corporation: A Comprehensive Filmography and History*, ed. Wheeler Dixon (Jefferson, NC: McFarland, 1986), 9–37.
52. Ted Okuda, *Grand National, Producers Releasing Corporation and Screen Guild/Lippert: Complete Filmographies with Studio Histories* (Jefferson, NC: McFarland, 1989), 32.
53. William K. Everson, "Introduction: Remembering PRC," in *Producers Releasing Corporation: A Comprehensive Filmography and History*, ed. Wheeler Dixon (Jefferson, NC: McFarland, 1986), 1–7.

2

Hugh S. Manon

Partition and Desire in the Films of Joseph H. Lewis

> If the paths to *jouissance* have something in them that dies out, that tends to make them impassable, prohibition, if I may say so, becomes its all-terrain vehicle, its half-track truck, that gets it out of the circuitous routes that lead man back in a roundabout way toward the rut of a short and well-trodden satisfaction.
>
> Jacques Lacan, seminar 7

> Sometimes I'd only use half a face; sometimes it would be out of focus. But this was me. This was what I saw. This was what I wanted to do and it came across.
>
> Joseph H. Lewis, as interviewed by Peter Bogdanovich

Released in 1945, Joseph H. Lewis's breakthrough film *My Name Is Julia Ross* begins with real temerity, forcing the viewer to contemplate, at great length, the back of a woman's head.[1] It is a rainy afternoon in London and a female figure in a trench coat walks unhurriedly across a dim street. As she drifts into the background, the camera cuts closer, tracking her from behind as she proceeds up six steps to the front doors of a rooming house. Soaking wet, the woman pushes open the doors and enters the front hallway, where a floor-scrubbing housekeeper (Joy Harington) accosts her: "Here—wipe your feet, will ya, and oblige me that has to clean up after ya?" The camera continues to stalk the lodger, admitting nothing of her countenance, and after some catty small talk the housekeeper indicates that there is a letter on the hall table addressed to her interlocutor. "Nobody writes to me," the faceless woman replies. "It must be an ad." Collecting her letter, the woman turns toward the camera, now positioned at waist level, and a cut-in reveals the handwriting on the envelope—"Miss Julia Ross, 51 Carrington Street,

Bloomsbury, London"—providing the identity of the one who holds it. It is a wedding invitation from Dennis Bruce, another resident of the building. The housekeeper contemptuously asks when the wedding will be. Finally, after one minute and twenty seconds of scrupulous withholding, the camera tilts up to reveal the face we have been unable to view. Julia Ross (Nina Foch) appears dazed, her eyes staring off into space as she responds, "It was yesterday."

Appearing in various configurations throughout the mature films of Joseph H. Lewis, the strategy of nondisclosure that dominates this initial scene might most usefully be termed *partitioning*. The term functions here in two ways. First, in spatial terms, the face of Julia Ross has been perfectly obscured, neatly dividing the profilmic space into two parts: a fore-zone that sees (that of the housekeeper) and an aft-zone that fails to see (that of the viewer). Second, in temporal terms, this withholding extends beyond the point at which one would conventionally expect the woman's face to appear. The longer we wait, the more it becomes clear that we are temporarily being kept in the dark so that her identity can be dramatically unveiled at some later point. Our experience of the event is thus divided into two periods: a presumably finite present moment (in which we lack) and an anticipated future moment (in which we will have attained). Crucially, too, the term *partitioning* signals that the viewer is consciously aware that such divisions are at play. Given the camera's reluctance to show, along with the sheer duration of its forestalling, the missing-ness of Julia's face becomes conspicuous in a manner that borders on the self-reflexive. Moreover, when her face is revealed, there is no startling payoff—her face is not scarred, for instance, or bandaged à la Claude Rains. The more we watch, the more we become aware that our desire is being toyed with, that our wishing to see is a direct response to the camera's deliberate obstruction of our view. In other words, instead of compelling his audience to imagine a solution, Lewis foregrounds the obstaculous foreground itself, as if to say, *here, take a look at how your desire works*.

This impulse to spell out the structure of desire constitutes a major current in Lewis's oeuvre, becoming simultaneously more acute and more abstract as his career progresses. To suggest, as a number of auteurist critics have, that Lewis is a "stylist without a theme"[2] misses the point: the director's heavy emphasis on partition—partialized seeing, partialized hearing, partialized knowing—works to confront viewers with the paradox of their own desire, a desire founded on lack, which is to say on the ontologically positive value of obstruction and opacity. It is no wonder, then, that critics find it difficult to locate a sustained theme in Lewis's body of work, since what they are looking for is lack itself. Beginning with this premise, this chapter will undertake a series of close readings of distinctive scenes from Lewis's films in tandem with explications of several key passages from the seminars of Jacques Lacan. In doing so, it will investigate the question of desire in two directions at once. What can Lacan's conception of the *objet petit a*—the object/cause of desire—tell us about the way lack functions in the films of Joseph H. Lewis? And correspondingly, how might certain notable scenes from Lewis's films illustrate, and thus disentangle, the notorious perplexities of Lacan's theory of desire?

The *objet petit a* (abbreviated as *objet a*) is a matter of considerable difficulty for students of Lacanian psychoanalysis; a theoretical aporia, it is difficult by design. But although Lacan insisted that the phrase *objet petit a* "should remain untranslated, thus acquiring, as it were, the status of an algebraic sign,"[3] in his seminars and writings he comments at great length on its structure, value, root causes, and effects. Lacan has described *objet a* as a "privileged object" that is "paradoxical [and] unique" as well as "shaded [and] reserved."[4] *Objet a* is manifest in certain "circumventions" and "cleavages"[5] and can be understood as a "remainder," as in a division problem.[6] It is both "the cause by which the subject identifies with his desire"[7] and "the object that cannot be swallowed . . . which remains stuck in the gullet of the signifier."[8] *Objet a* is at once "absolute and unapprehensible, an element necessarily lacking, unsatisfied, impossible, misconstrued (*méconnu*)"[9] and is discernible in "the presence of a hollow, a void, which can be occupied . . . by any object."[10]

For the purposes of this chapter, however, I want to establish a more succinct definition for the *objet a*, one that will be useful in analyzing certain narrative structures and formal devices in cinema. This definition is as follows: the *objet petit a* is neither the object unperceived, nor the object fully grasped, but rather the object in the process of being revealed. While entirely consistent with the above quotations from Lacan's seminars, this more pragmatic definition admittedly reduces Lacan's conception to its barest form. At the same time, it is important to bear in mind that the cryptic, notational quality of the term "*objet a*" has traditionally been preserved in an effort to designate its status as unnamable—the notion that *objet a* is a pure concept and as such cannot be pinned down in such positivistic terms. According to Lewis Kirshner, in Lacan's later seminars the term "*objet petit a*" "became a quasi-mathematical symbol for a hypothetical or virtual construct: namely the ephemeral, unlocalizable property of an object that makes it especially desirable."[11] Moreover, whereas we can discuss the general structure of *objet a*, we cannot ever definitively say "it is this," because its particular manifestations necessarily vary and are contingent on the unconscious makeup of each individual subject.

In the sections that follow, I argue that the films of Joseph H. Lewis exhibit with striking regularity a desire to illuminate the structure of *objet a*. Considered as a set, the director's post-1940 films represent a theoretical reflection on the allure and evanescence of the half-present object—not simply plot points at which something is missing or lacking, but a schematic, almost metacinematic representation of partition per se. Accordingly, Lewis's best directorial flourishes are really not flourishes at all but instead lockdowns, aversions, excisions, all of which render some aspect of the representation "ephemeral, unlocalizable." The purpose of this chapter is to determine what these shots, editing strategies, and sound manipulations enable, what they prohibit, and finally how this partitioning approach to cinema—one which does not merely deploy lack but actively works to theorize it—has helped to cement Lewis's status as a cult auteur.

Face Off

In a lengthy interview conducted by Peter Bogdanovich, Lewis explains that he "idolized" director William Wyler, watching his films repeatedly, and admits that he "stole from him the same as any other director stole from somebody else."[12] In the course of this discussion, Lewis goes on to identify the specific sequence that clearly inspired the opening of *My Name Is Julia Ross*: "The one scene of his that influenced me greatly was a highly dramatic one with Bette Davis—tremendously dramatic—she walked to the window and he kept the camera on her back and stayed on her back for the entire sequence, allowing the audience to supply the emotion. It was a great lesson I learned and I've never forgotten that one incident."[13] The shot in question does not appear in *The Little Foxes* (1941), as Francis M. Nevins has stated,[14] but instead in an earlier Wyler/Davis collaboration, *The Letter* (1940). Moreover, the same structure appears not in one but in two separate shots from the film: a scene just before the climax in which Leslie Crosbie (Bette Davis) flees a party and bursts into tears in her dimly lit bedroom, and an earlier shot in a doctor's office in which Leslie lies on an examination table as she tries to convince her husband, Robert (Herbert Marshall), to retrieve the incriminating letter. In both instances, the protagonist faces directly away from the camera just as Nina Foch will do five years later in *Julia Ross*. Likewise, in both of Wyler's sequences the camera lingers for quite some time before it cuts away to deliver a reverse shot of the protagonist's face.

There can be little doubt that Wyler's strategy of withholding in *The Letter* (and perhaps other films as well) made a strong impact on Lewis; however, the ways in which Lewis presses the issue of lack are far more exaggerated than anything we see in Wyler's work. Whereas in classical Hollywood such visual enigmas tend quickly to resolve in one direction or another—either we learn who the mystery figure is, or we learn that we will not learn this until the climax of the film—Lewis's withholding of faces is far more tendentious, a pointedly intellectual and even pedantic exercise in style. In various interviews, including the one quoted above, when questioned about scenes in which he refused to show the crux of the action, Lewis repeatedly states that the benefit of such an arrangement is that "the audience supplies the emotion." He also frequently refers to this strategy of halfway revealing as "impression" or "suggestion," presumably in opposition to a more heavy-handed confirmation.[15] Ever the craftsman, Lewis's self-assessments are far too modest, focusing on the need to maximize affect and generate audience involvement. Pressing beyond such practical concerns, in encountering the back of Julia Ross's head we would do better to recall the coldly cerebral, yet oddly cartoonish paintings of Belgian surrealist René Magritte, whose subjects often uncannily face away from the viewer.[16] Lewis's mise-en-scène is similar; it does not set a mood so much as it makes a point. What he stages is suspense distilled to full strength, a surreal display of lack at its most elemental, and this gesture serves no purpose but to raise the crucial question, Where does desire come from, and where does it get us?

Similar faceless shots appear in other Lewis films and produce the same unsettling effect, as if the camera, in refusing to show, were being turned back on the viewer. In *So Dark the Night* (1946), master detective Henri Cassin (Steven Geray) accosts Madame Bridelle (Helen Freeman), the housekeeper at a provincial inn, after he finds her acting suspiciously in his room. The ensuing discussion reveals that she had been comparing one of Cassin's shoes to the plaster cast of an imprint made at the site of a recent murder. Yet despite the fact that Bridelle is the one being interrogated, for over forty-five seconds the two shot reveals only the back of her head, forcing the viewer to guess about what lie-revealing expressions might be crossing her face, potentially betraying her as the real culprit. In *Invisible Ghost* (1941), an identical tactic is employed when Charles Kessler (Bela Lugosi) and his daughter, Virginia (Polly Ann Young), appeal to the governor for a stay of execution for Virginia's fiancé, Ralph Dickson (John McGuire). The role of the governor goes uncredited in the film and his face never appears on-screen, presumably in some contractual effort to limit costs. The viewer is thus forced to deduce the judge's attitude, imagining the disapproving scowl of the law rather than seeing it. Finally, in *Terror in a Texas Town* (1958), the opening sequence is structured around the ominous voice of Johnny Crale (Nedrick Young), whose face is not shown for nearly a full minute, with the camera remaining at hip level, revealing only his holster and gun. In the same way one can speak of the "money shot" in hard-core pornography, in such sequences Lewis delivers the antithesis of a payoff—the "desire shot" of classical Hollywood cinema, but protracted to the point of contentiousness.

Sitting Out

Although it is far from a definitive work for Lewis, the 1942 film *Secrets of a Co-Ed* climaxes in a near-perfect example of the structure of partition that will define his later, more notable works. Like the examples above, the film's most memorable sequence involves the withholding of an expected reverse shot of a character's face and was repeatedly described by Lewis in interviews as a particularly daring ten-minute long take.[17] The truth of the matter is somewhat less impressive—the take lasts for only about six minutes—but Lewis's approach is no less instructive. As the sequence begins, the camera cranes through a courtroom, traveling over the heads of the audience and finally coming to a halt in a high angle shot of defense attorney James Reynolds (Otto Kruger). The lawyer commences delivering the opening argument in the defense of his daughter, Brenda (Tina Thayer), who has been wrongly charged with the murder of a local gangster with whom she was romantically involved. As Reynolds paces back and forth, he appeals first to the gallery (including the reporters who are gathered there), then to the jury box on the right, and finally gestures toward the defendant's table at the far left where his daughter sits. But although the camera tracks him fluidly, missing nothing of Kruger's impassioned performance, at no time does the shot proceed far enough left to reveal Brenda's face. So rigid is this six-minute prohibition that one senses that the camera has excluded not only her reaction but also her very being. In imposing such an unyielding barrier, Lewis creates the sense that the youthful Brenda has already been tried, sentenced, and put to death; the camera's partitioning of space metaphorically "buries" her out of frame. The effect is particularly pronounced when Reynolds says, "That girl is innocent!" and gestures offscreen, yet we see no "girl." The camera has every opportunity to include her—to show that which demands to be seen—yet it steadfastly refuses to do so.[18] It is difficult to think of a sequence from any of the long-take auteurs—F. W. Murnau or Max Ophüls, for instance—that adopts this exclusionary, blinder-like approach. Normally, long takes command our attention on the basis of what we see—an actorly tour de force or a series of difficult camera movements—rather than taunting us with the walled-off proximity of what we are missing, as Lewis's does.

Partition and Desire

To return to my earlier definition of *objet petit a*, the structural center of the courtroom scene is neither an object unperceived (imagine the arrival of a surprise witness who we could not have known was in the gallery), nor an object fully grasped (imagine a sequence that repeatedly delivers shots of Brenda choking back tears), but rather an object in the process of being revealed (what we get: a belabored withholding of what is imminent, yet veiled for the time being). Because we are locked out of it, the space off-screen is effectively advertised as the place to be and the place to see. The paradox of the *objet a* bears on the mutually inextricable relation between presence and absence: what we recognize as absent is nonetheless part of and indeed lends definition and meaning to the field of objects that we see. By failing to go left, where Brenda is seated, Lewis puts her in a conceptual cell, inasmuch as the viewer is made aware of an adjoining space to which he/she has been denied visual access. In this way, in Lacanian terms, she takes up a position as "extimate"; she is the (intimate) structural center of the scene precisely because she has been so rigidly excluded from it. Just as one might digitally remove a detested former spouse from a family photo, the now-empty space within the image remains just as perfectly framed as it was before, looming even larger for its obvious evacuation.

Considered in terms of sheer length, perhaps the most obvious descendents of the long-take courtroom scene in *Secrets of a Co-Ed* are an extended shot of the protagonist's face in *My Name Is Julia Ross* and two long takes shot through the windows of automobiles in *A Lady without Passport* (1950) and of course *Gun Crazy* (1950). In *Julia Ross*, a lengthy conversation on a seaside cliff is filmed in a long take over the shoulder of the apparently psychotic Ralph Hughes (George MacReady). As Julia pretends to question Ralph about her unremembered past life, all we see are Julia's strangely semiexpressive eyes, the lower half of her face having been completely blocked from view. Whereas up to this point we have never questioned Julia's sanity, the partitioning of her expression—partly visible, partly not—creates the sense of a beyond, a sense that we are missing something crucial. We recognize that, at best, we *only sort of* understand what Julia is feeling, and the possibility remains that she will come to believe the spurious history that Ralph and his mother (Dame May Whitty) want to foist on her.

The opening shot of *A Lady without Passport* is similar in structure, if not content. The camera is positioned in the backseat of a moving car as it slowly stalks an average-looking middle-aged man who does not seem to suspect that he is being followed. The camera then pulls back to reveal a passenger in the backseat who shouts, "Ramon!" Responding to his name, the man on the sidewalk turns to face the passenger, and when he tells

The semiexpressive eyes of Julia Ross (Nina Foch).

him to get in the car, Ramon takes off running. The camera pivots ninety degrees to the left, revealing the view out the car's rear window as the fleeing Ramon darts in front of a moving cab and is struck and killed. When the violence comes—an unconvincingly undercranked bump that could not possibly have been fatal—it seems phony because there is no edit to mask the lack of impact. The position of the camera implies that we are along for the ride with someone important, perhaps an immigration agent or a gangster's liaison. But although we see things from this seemingly ideal insider's perspective, our overwhelming sense is one of visual restriction. It is as though we have renounced our human motility and have become the car. The operative metaphor here is again "blinders," so long as we remember that the purpose of blinders is not to prevent a horse from seeing but instead to restrict the *way* it sees, forcing it to look at some things and not others. This is precisely how Lewis operates, assuming that he is helping his audience most—helping them to desire—by restricting what they are able to view. But whereas *A Lady without Passport* misfires, failing to reveal enough of what we cannot see—failing, in effect, to show us enough of the structural blot that is *objet a*—the analogous inside-the-car shot from *Gun Crazy* succeeds by failing, delivering the ne plus ultra of Lewis's cinema of partition.

Partition and Desire

Much has been said and written about the famous Hampton bank robbery in *Gun Crazy*, and justifiably so. Shot entirely from inside the couple's getaway car, it is at once the most mundane and at the same time most exciting holdup in all of American cinema. Although this fully mobile three-and-a-half-minute long take is most often lauded for its endurance, a more remarkable aspect of the shot, as Jim Kitses notes, is that it "locks us inside the car, the robbery happening offstage." Similarly, Paul Schrader understands Lewis's tactic primarily in terms of prohibition, as a taunting of our desire that forces us to look at what we cannot see: "[The camera] sits out the entire robbery like a helpless accomplice forced to watch. The viewer is not thrown into the action, but purposefully held back. As nothing happens, tension builds; the fate of the robbery is being decided just outside one's view, and one occasionally catches a quick glimpse of it." This process of "sitting out" typifies many of the most remarkable sequences of Lewis's oeuvre. The strategy is counterintuitive to say the very least, and although the heist sequence is typically cited as a technical tour de force (owing to Lewis's pioneering use of portable sound-recording devices, an improvised in-car dolly shot, etc.) it must also be understood as a masterful management of perceptual lack. What viewers witness is not a robbery but their own inability to witness, having been forced by Lewis (à la *Julia Ross*, à la Wyler's *The Letter*) to engage with the absent center of their own desire. Or, to state it differently, the bank heist is staged around a nothing, which by virtue of its partial withholding is taken to be a something—something we wish we could access. This investment, based on a rigid but clearly defined proscription, is precisely the function of the *objet a*. It is not, however, Lewis's crafty deployment of the *objet a*, but instead the high degree of abstraction and reflexivity with which it appears, that exposes the director for the Lacanian that he is.

Unsharp Mask

André Bazin famously claimed that the cinematic screen must be understood not as "a frame like that of a picture but a mask which allows only a part of the action to be seen."[19] Nowhere is this axiom more acutely epitomized than in the cinema of Joseph H. Lewis, and many critics have noted that the director's shot compositions are distinctively unbalanced. Counter to classical Hollywood's ideal of an accessible object, positioned front and center and in full view—in short, an object of satisfaction—Lewis's camera delivers an object of desire by pushing his objects to the margins of the screen, as if they were teetering on the edge, perhaps to fall out of view. In such shots, the camera frame produces not an overt sense of disguising or covering but an aura of part concealment that, in its partialness, reorients our relation to what remains visible.

Three examples of Lewis's cinematographic lopsidedness bear a brief mention. First, in the opening of *So Dark the Night* (1946), protagonist Henri Cassin (Steven Geray) is established as an important detective who has gone missing in Paris. Palpably underscoring his disappearance, the camera cuts to a scene in which we see only Cassin's feet as he strolls up and down a bustling street. This prohibition continues for about twenty seconds before the protagonist's face is brought into view, at which point the shot becomes palpably *less* interesting, more clichéd. Second, in *The Undercover Man* (1949), a predominant shot type involves framing the actors with excessive headroom, as if the architecture of the film's shabby interiors—transoms, pendant lamps, grimy ceilings—were more important than its characters. Here, we get a sense not of obstruction but of visual excess, a suffusion of extraneous dead space that might otherwise have been masked off. However, to be clear, the masking effect that Lewis exploits can also be accomplished as a function of depth and distance. In a third example, from *The Swordsman* (1948), a foot chase through a forest is filmed from such a distance that the actors appear "like little mice running." Of this sequence, Lewis remarked to Peter Bogdanovich, "Anybody can shoot a horse running, you know, but to withdraw."[20] The key is to recognize that in pushing the boundaries of framing and scale, the results are not so much views "of" some object but rather partitions that uncomfortably prohibit us from seeing anything resembling completeness.

In Lewis's mature works, such as those I have just described, "to withdraw" becomes a full-fledged modus operandi; his partitioning approach becomes highly abstract and full of intent. It bears mentioning, however, that the director's penchant for abstraction appears as early as 1941 (not coincidentally, just after the release of Wyler's *The Letter*). In *Invisible Ghost*, a Monogram B quickie starring Bela Lugosi, Lewis delivers a series of defocused shots that cannot fail to remind us that we are not seeing the full picture. Highly unconventional for classical Hollywood, the shots are all modified examples of so-called rack focus, a technique wherein the camera operator or "focus puller" adjusts the lens so that, for instance, objects close to the camera gradually become blurry, while formerly blurry objects in the distance gradually come to appear crisp. As with the sequences discussed above, however, Lewis is not content to merely foster desire according to time-tested Hollywood principles but instead overdrives the desire-generating machine, transforming our passive engagement into a surprise rendezvous with *objet a*.

In one scene from *Invisible Ghost*, set late at night, the mysterious

Charles Kessler (Lugosi) looks down from an upstairs window to see his supposedly dead wife (Betty Compson) staring up at him. With an expression of confusion and distaste, Charles turns from the window, blinking his eyes and rubbing his forehead. The camera rack focuses, rendering the entire image blurry, and when focus returns Charles is lit ominously from below with a deranged expression on his face, primed for another kill. The effect is reminiscent of Man Ray's surrealist film *L'étoile de mer* (1928) in which certain scenes are shot through a textured gelatin filter, rendering the entire image blurry, yet not quite entirely nonrepresentational.[21] In other words, the director invites the audience to *see through* the distortion but at the same time prohibits them from freely doing so, suspending viewers in a moment of partial seeing.

Later in the film, Charles accompanies Mrs. Mason (Ottola Nesmith) to the coroner's office to view the body of her murdered husband, Jules (Ernie Adams), the gardener at the Kessler estate. When the corpse unexpectedly revives, Charles asks the dazed Jules if he can identify the man who tried to kill him. We then see Jules's low-angle point of view from the slab, a completely defocused shot of the looming Charles, who we know to be the mad strangler. A look of shocked recognition crosses Jules's face—we imagine

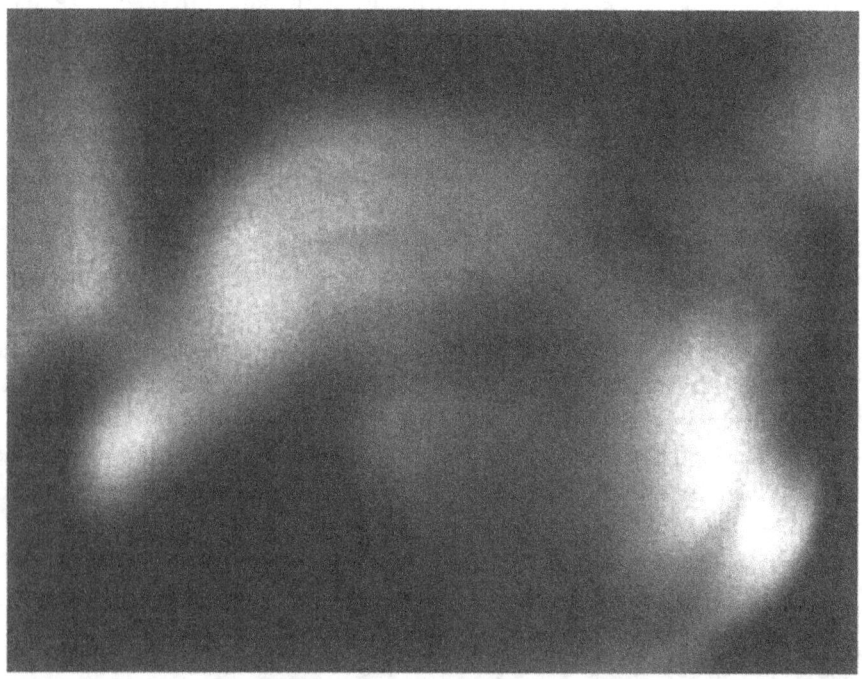

The defocused fugue state of Charles Kessler (Bela Lugosi) in *Invisible Ghost* (1941).

that his own perspective has now "rack focused," revealing Charles standing over him—and Jules dies a second time without having said a word. Such shots are unconventionally abstract for a type of "stunt" shot, delivering an aesthetic rupture that cannot easily be reconciled. By forcing us to look at something we cannot see, Lewis again invites us to consider the desire-generating power of such halfway representation.

In terms of genre, *Invisible Ghost* is largely unclassifiable—a psychological gothic horror detective film in an old dark house? Indeed, even before we have seen the film, the awkward redundancy of the film's title bespeaks a rhetorical circumvention, one of the qualities Lacan associates with *objet a*. Ghosts, by definition, haunt the living by emerging eerily from the darkness, by becoming visible. As such, they alternate between two states: appearance and nonappearance. So what exactly would an *invisible* ghost do? How would it function and what would it entail? Failing absolutely to appear, perhaps an invisible ghost would hold us in sway on the basis of a pure promise, a nonarrival to which we respond accordingly: by waiting as if something important might happen at any moment, all of the time.

The *objet a*, I would argue, is precisely such an "invisible ghost," an empty cipher that by virtue of its emptiness appears full and thus potentially confirmative; it is a worthless shell that we perceive to conceal a satisfying kernel, a signifier of nothing but the beyond per se. It is thus tempting, especially given Lewis's strangely fractional cinematography, to argue that the cause of Charles's psychotic fugues is blurriness itself, a psychic force that, like the *objet a*, is "lacking . . . non-specular . . . not graspable in the image."[22] The fact that the film's titular ghost is so crisply out of focus—at once nowhere and everywhere, invisible and fully embodied—speaks precisely to the point: whether a ghost is absent or present, the real horror lies in its endless vicissitude, the anticipation of it emerging or disappearing, but in either case becoming something else.

Flare Up

The apotheosis of the cinema of Joseph H. Lewis can be found in a single shot from the third act of *Gun Crazy*, a shot that no one seems to notice because it contains no dialogue, no actors, no plot-advancing action, and minimal content. For the five seconds that this unusual shot appears onscreen, Lewis presents us with a sort of schematic diagram for the way desire functions in *Gun Crazy* and in his other mature films. The shot comprises part of a travel montage that features footage of a switching yard, passing railroad crossings, and a rough-looking Bart Tare (John Dall) and Laurie Starr (Peggy Cummins) riding in a boxcar. The two are traveling from Los

Angeles, where they have been spotted by FBI agents, to Cashville, Bart's hometown, where they will hole up at the home of his sister, Ruby (Anabel Shaw). As the montage sequence progresses, we hear engine sounds and a train whistle, mimicked by the percussive chug-chugging of the film's score. Then, as if to blast a hole in the gut of this rather conventional plot-advancing sequence, Lewis delivers an image that looks like two flying saucers passing in the night, but which we quickly realize are refractions produced by the locomotive's headlight as it moves forward. It is arguably the most provocative and thematically relevant use of camera flare in the history of cinema.

The sequence is part of a minor trend in which Lewis shows his audience glaring beams of light on-screen—for instance the smoke-filled beam from the theater movie projector in an early scene from *Undercover Man*, and the climax of *The Big Combo* in which a car-mounted spotlight is shone on Mr. Brown (Richard Conte), leading to his demise. However, in the *Gun Crazy* sequence, the source of light is not oblique but instead pointed directly at the camera, momentarily calling attention to the technology of the film's production. Surrounding the bright headlight of the locomotive appear two undulating ghost images.[23] As the train draws nearer, these waltzing halos of light encounter each other on a diagonal axis, overlap for a brief

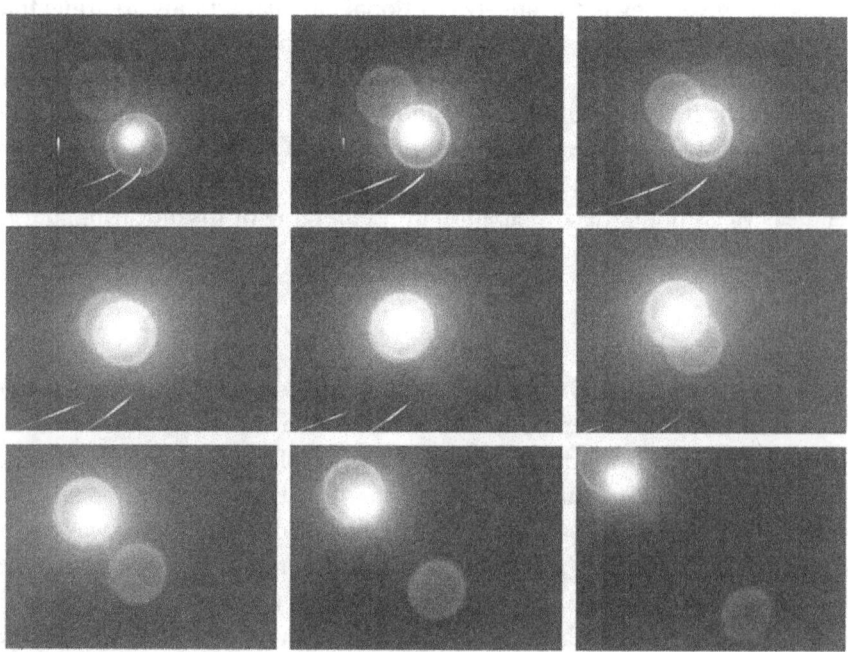

A most provocative and thematically relevant use of camera flare in *Gun Crazy* (1950).

moment near the center of the frame, and then hover together in a virtual eclipse before shooting off in opposite directions.

Predating by twenty years László Kovács's extensive use of camera flare in *Easy Rider* (Dennis Hopper, 1969), Lewis's shot of the locomotive headlight is both dynamic and highly abstract. As such, the shot recalls two other dance-like circulations that appear earlier in the film. In his BFI monograph, Jim Kitses notes that Bart and Laurie circle around each other in their shooting match on the carnival sideshow stage. This initial meeting is at once a "dance" and an animalistic courtship ritual involving "a pattern of alternating and balancing responses":

> Laurie circles slowly around and behind him, he slowly approaches, thoughtfully scratching his nose and smiling at her. It is all glances, gestures, body language and movements, testifying to a couple of cool, amused characters, to a reciprocal curiosity and mutual attraction.... The suspense builds slowly, along with our delicious sense of this couple's perfect fit, of parallel destinies, of a convergence.... Overall the strategy is one that choreographs characters, space, camera moves, and performance, to emphasize the ritualistic, rhyming structure, the ceremonial quality of the event.[24]

The choreography of the carnival stage sequence is reiterated in a scene just after the Armour heist, when Laurie convinces Bart that they should temporarily part ways. Departing in separate cars, they are not even a block apart when neither partner can force themselves to do it. Their respective convertibles loop back around on the pleasant residential street and reunite. It is a rabid, gasoline fueled do-si-do, replete with screeching tires, and when Bart enters Laurie's car their bodies become so intertwined as to be virtually indistinguishable from each other.

The camera-flare shot represents a third allemande, albeit one that appears purely at the level of form. The point of the shot is not to invoke the old cliché of two trains passing in the night but instead to map out in elemental terms the paradox of desire itself, a kind of invisible magnetic pull between two spheres. In his 1971 article in *Cinema*, Paul Schrader notes precisely this dynamic in his discussion of the carnival scene: "Lewis delicately choreographs this ballet of sex and innuendo. Teasing and smirking, Dall and Cummins revolve about each other, like two magnets irresistibly attracted but afraid to get too close."[25] Arguably, however, Lewis's camera-flare shot already makes this point, and more astutely than Schrader does, since the halos of light appear to both attract *and* repel each other in the same arc.[26] As with the intersection of real magnetic fields, there is a median point at which convergence and divergence might hypothetically be kept in balance, yet in practice this point of balance proves impossible to achieve. That desire must perpetuate itself as desire is inevitable, and it can only go one way or another—either collapsing into an unsatisfying stasis or dynamically exploding. Bart and Laurie live in this magnetically supercharged borderland. Their desire is so intense that they can neither "settle in" nor agree to part; they can only teeter on the impossible knife-edge between the two states. In the camera-flare shot, Lewis represents in a highly intuitive way this psychophysics of desire, and he could not be clearer on the point that it is a doomed enterprise.

At the same time, in a truly provocative homology, Lewis's camera flare—at a certain point when the halos partially overlap—resembles nothing so much as a so-called Euler diagram, a basic figure from the field of mathematics known as set theory. By itself, it is difficult to know what to make of this resemblance. However, to any student of psychoanalysis the Euler diagram is well known as the figure Lacan uses to illustrate the problem of the *objet a*. This particular figure appears only once in Lacan's work, during the first meeting of his 1966 seminar titled "La logique du fantasme."[27] However, Lacan appropriates the basic shape of the Euler diagram elsewhere in his seminars and in many instances invokes its logic, which might be summarized as "neither/nor, yet completely."

According to Sarah Kay, in the original diagram from seminar 15, the barred letter S represents "the subject of the unconscious, which Lacan represents as split because it can never pass into consciousness or assume knowledge of itself."[28] The uppercase A is the big Other (in French, *Autre*) of the symbolic order, and the lowercase a is *objet petit a*, the object/cause of desire. Anticipating this discussion by a number of years, in seminar 10 of 1962–63, Lacan makes a statement that speaks directly to the structure of the diagram: "[*Objet*] a as such, and nothing else, is the access, not to enjoyment, but to the Other. It is all that remains, starting from the mo-

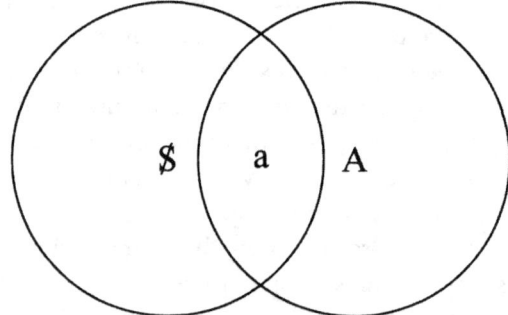

The originary partition: *objet petit a*, Lacan's "little other object."

ment when the subject wants to make its entry in the Other."[29] In this sense, *objet a* can be understood as a functional impasse, a by-product of our ascendance out of the real and into language—into the sensical, rule-bound domain of the symbolic order—rendering all of our worldly desires vexed from the outset. Prohibition is what compels us to move, yet in reckoning this gap we find that it is ultimately illusory, impossible to finally surmount. What we think we want is attainment and satisfaction, whereas what our unconscious wants is the *objet a* itself: partialness, truncation, inconsistency, the approach and not the landing.

Implicit in Lacan's use of the Euler diagram is a paradox, which Sarah Kay explains as follows: "The point of intersection between the two circles of the subject and the Other is . . . not an overlap but a hole which reduces each circle to a crescent. Or rather, each circle now overlaps the other in an empty space, in a space of lack."[30] In other words, the spheres of the subject and the Other do not join up, except in the form of lack itself. *Objet a* is our sole access to desire, yet paradoxically this access comes in the form of a prohibition: *no access for you*! This gap that unites can be understood as the mother of all partitions, and by shading in portions of Lacan's diagram the problem becomes clear. The crucial object in desire is *objet a*, a structure of partiality/linkage between two states, neither one of which is ever totalized, except in the empty-from-either-perspective mirage of the *objet a* itself, which knots them together. The paradox of such an arrangement is that any desire connection between two human subjects—to the extent that such a thing can be said to exist—depends precisely on nonconnection, separation, the gap between the spheres. This is not to say that nothing can ever work out between two subjects, but that nothing can ever *fully* work out, since any engagement always already entails being at odds with one's object of desire.

Strikingly similar to Lacan's Euler diagram, albeit more visually dynamic, is Lewis's camera flare, which does this same theoretical work. I do not, of

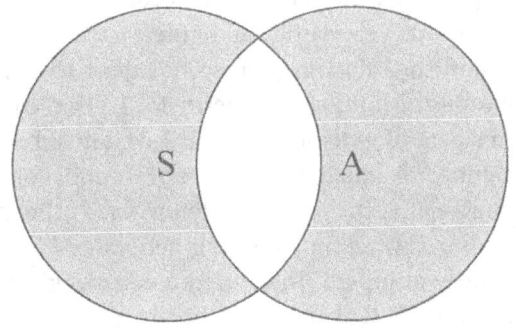

"Not an overlap but a hole": lack as constitutive for the human subject.

Partition and Desire

course, wish to suggest that Lewis considers himself a theorist, or that he ever envisioned this single shot to be the crux of his film (as I do). However, in electing to include the shot, Lewis unconsciously re-presents the problem between Bart and Laurie as a problem in adjustment. Moreover, the shot follows closely on the heels of Bart's most succinct enunciation of their mutual attraction: "We go together, Laurie. I don't know why. Maybe like guns and ammunition go together." In other words, we each lack something, just not the *same* thing. In effect, Bart's statement gets it exactly right, although he does not (and cannot) recognize that the fuel for his strong attraction to Laurie, the ammunition that keeps him firing, is precisely the condition of *not knowing why*. To be able to articulate this unknowable X-factor—this ineffable quality that in a more conventional romantic affair might be described as a "certain special something"—would be to nullify it.[31]

Limping along, always halfway out of step with the Other, the subject's desire is anything but concentric, and in pursuing desire to its fullest, Bart and Laurie discover just this. Can there be any question that this fundamental human problem—that desire entails its own dissolution—is the core of the film's continued appeal? On the one hand, we have the desire of Bart, whose attention to Laurie at the sideshow is duly noted by his compatriots when he cartoonishly pitches forward in his seat. The shot symbolizes Bart's arousal, yet it is clearly the fact that Laurie is unusual—a woman with that certain special "something else," an inexplicable facility with weapons—that turns him on. On the other hand, we have the somewhat more obscure desire of Laurie who, in the words of Jim Kitses, is "at once unscrupulous and innocent, loving and manipulative, sweet and fiercely resentful of authority, hard as nails yet feminine to the end."[32] Both desires are partially unclear, yet in both cases it is opacity itself—the unknowability of what the other wants, and why—that makes each attractive to the other. Hence, as in Lacan's diagram, it is the negative space between the two crescents, a mutually reinforced, highly energized sliver of nothing, that holds the arrangement together. At no point do the subject and the Other connect, except in this negative space. At the same time, according to the more traditional logic of set theory, this very same gap renders each of the parties fragmentary, a lacking (and thus desiring) crescent rather than a complete circle. In the words of Robert Mundy, Bart's desire for Laurie "can only be sustained as he performs acts of violence, and her love for him is only expressed after these moments."[33] As such, the two are profoundly out of sync. All they have in common is each other's inconsistency, each other's incompleteness, and in this gap an overwhelming desire is generated.[34]

If, as Paul Schrader has famously quipped, "there are no excuses given for the gun craziness—it is just crazy,"[35] Lacan would beg to differ: it is just neurotic, which is to say normal and even constitutive for the human subject. Bart and Laurie do not represent a different species of subject, and they are not psychotic. Rather, the intensity of their pursuit (of gun violence, living without working, feeling so alive, or what have you) sets in high relief the fact that any attraction is based on a prohibition, the promise of a beyond that is neither essentially "good" nor even existent. The perfect and perpetual enjoyment we imagine beyond the next obstacle is an illusion produced by the obstacle itself. Bart and Laurie's lawless *amour fou* is forbidden, and although they cannot consciously realize it, this forbidden-ness is what fuels it. Lewis Kirshner describes this dynamic as follows: "Because the *jouissance* we unconsciously pursue is impossible to achieve within the limits of reality, it is 'beyond the pleasure principle' and definitely not conventionally enjoyable. Rather, it has a deadly aspect, in that it operates without regard for the welfare of the individual, of his or her meaning or symbolic identity."[36] Arguably, there is no better work of American cinema to illustrate desire's self-destructive underside than *Gun Crazy*. But why does desire contain the seeds of its own destruction? Lewis's diagrammatic use of camera flare illuminates this problem, too.

Perhaps the most revealing aspect of the camera-flare shot is one that we assume but cannot actually see: Bart and Laurie are both supposed to be riding on the nocturnal freight train whose headlight blares in the direction of the camera. Their restless forward motion is itself what initiates the gap/overlap between the two circling halos of light. The impulse to press on—in its strictest sense a forward *pulsion*, or drive—causes the *objet a* to arise, fomenting the couple's desire. Yet this same chugging *pulsion* is also what makes the arrangement magnetically polarized and thus explosive. If *Gun Crazy* is Lewis's masterpiece, and if a number of his other films are interesting for the part objects they deploy, we might venture the following axiom: the cinema of Joseph H. Lewis is a cinema of the *drive*, a cinema at odds with the mainstream because it satisfies the circulatory imperative of the drive in unexpected ways.

As Slavoj Žižek notes in *The Parallax View* and elsewhere, Lacan insisted that "the true aim of a drive is not to reach its goal, but to circulate endlessly around it," with pleasure deriving from the "repeated oscillation" to and fro. "A drive, as it were, turns failure into triumph—in it, the very failure to reach its goal, the repetition of this failure, the endless circulation around the object, generates a satisfaction of its own."[37] Like a freight train, the only destination for the drive is to continue from one destination to the next, charging and discharging, endlessly continuing the loop. To say this is to go a long way toward reconciling some of the most famous appraisals of the film, for instance Schrader's assertion that "there is no reason for the gun craziness." The drive has "no reason"; it just goes. What do we see in Laurie's crazy eyes, as she barks "I'll kill you! I'll kill you!" into the fog at the film's climax if not the indiscriminate thrust of the drive at its purest? Whereas Bart seems largely to abide by the law of desire, and thus remains frustrated most of the time, Laurie cannot help but short-circuit it. This tendency is there from the outset: Bart (embodiment of desire) *fantasizes about shooting*, whereas Laurie (embodiment of the drive) *shoots to kill*. Even more radical than Vera (Ann Savage) in Edgar G. Ulmer's *Detour* (1945), Laurie is the most uncompromised, stripped-down example of the femme fatale we have, a woman who does not cede in her desire but who "persist[s] in it to the very end when its true nature as the death drive is revealed."[38]

If *Gun Crazy* is, as most agree, Lewis's greatest film, it is also a testament to the director's intuitive grasp (without having read Lacan, of course) of one of the primary insights of psychoanalysis, which could be summed up as follows: although the subject consciously desires to attain satisfaction, the unconscious drives can only be satisfied by attaining lack itself. The paradox of such an arrangement is that the drive simultaneously underwrites and overrules desire. The two processes are wholly at odds yet at the same time indistinguishable from each other inasmuch as one's satisfactions can never be (wholly, permanently) satisfying. The point cannot be shouted loudly enough, nor can it be made too frequently, since the entirety of humanist enterprise (not to mention the ethos of late capitalism) posits satisfaction as a real, achievable goal, when in fact nothing could be further from the truth. Proliferating the illusion of satisfaction at all costs, contemporary Western culture is exactly one half phase out of sync with the reality of desire's loop. The unconscious drive, and not the conscious will to act, will always ultimately win the day. Lewis clearly recognizes this underlying problem with desire and through his off-kilter, out-of-phase approach to the medium of cinema wants to enlighten us about it, too, even if enlightenment is no kind of solution.

Conclusion: "Closer . . . Closer . . ."

From the defocused abstraction of *Invisible Ghost*, to the faceless image of Julia Ross, to a bank robbery sequence in which we see only the exterior wall of the bank, we do not need to wade very far into the Joseph H. Lewis oeuvre to encounter a director who appears more invested in obscuring his scenes than in revealing them. Indeed, Lewis's much-celebrated nickname "Wagon Wheel Joe" refers directly to his penchant for including seemingly unnecessary objects in the foreground of his shots to compensate for weak plotting—in Lewis's words, "to take away from the scene that wasn't really there."³⁹ In his westerns, these objects were often wagon wheels, but in his later crime films and melodramas we see a whole range of other foreground objects and formal devices partially covering over the main subject of the shot, as if to simultaneously invite the viewer into the story world and to bar their entrance, like a velvet rope. Understood as a pervasive structure, and not merely as distracting ornamentation, such diaphanous, lattice-like blockages promise that something lies beyond—that there is something to it—while forming a kind of diegetic shroud that constitutes this beyond zone as such. In this chapter, I have argued that Joseph H. Lewis is preoccupied with a paradoxical part object Lacan calls the *objet petit a*. Through an analysis of several of the director's most distinctive sequences, I have suggested that Lewis does not simply deploy the *objet a* as a route toward viewerly engagement and pleasure but instead seeks to actively confront his audience with the shape of their own desire. I will leave it to the reader to determine to what extent, if at all, the structure of partition I have delineated above appears in Lewis's work beyond the several films I have mentioned.

In conclusion, too, I want to be careful to acknowledge that such deliberate partialization cannot be present in every scene or sequence in Lewis's films, for any such consistency would undermine the wobbly, imbalanced, only-ever-halfway-here structure of *objet a*. As a target of considerable cult devotion, Lewis's oeuvre is in a greater sense a cinema of the "ephemeral" and the "unlocalizable." As such, it is no coincidence that his individual films often appear stronger in parts than as wholes.⁴⁰ In a 1982 article, Paul Willemen described Lewis's inconsistency as follows: "Many avowed auteurists in France, the US and Britain have attempted to claim him as an author. All have failed. Not because it would be impossible to construct a thematic coherence covering a substantial proportion of his work, but because the films appear to resist such efforts, locating their pleasure elsewhere, on a more disturbing though fascinating level."⁴¹ Partially but not completely muddled by questions of authorship, Lewis's body of work makes a bold statement: satisfaction itself cannot be satisfying. In developing what amounts to a cinema of partition, Lewis can be understood as being very much in line with the later Lacan, "striv[ing] to debunk . . . the fantasy of the whole."⁴² To suggest, then, as Willemen does, that auteuristic approaches to Lewis must fail because his pleasures lie elsewhere is quite perceptive. They do. This uncannily fascinating "elsewhere" is the *objet a*, and it never draws any closer for being right there in front us.

In accordance with this logic, I would argue that in Lewis's apparent inconsistencies as a director, something is nonetheless accomplished, as there can be little doubt that the elusiveness of Lewis's style is part of what sustains him as a cult figure. In effect, it is as if the opening monologue in Lewis's final feature, *Terror in a Texas Town* (1958), represents a kind of invitation from Lewis to his potential/future devotees—the cult of Lewis. As the killer Johnny Crale (Nedrick Young) stands on a desolate Old West street, baiting George Hansen (Sterling Hayden) to deliver his vengeance, his ominous words have everything to do with visual nonaccess: "You're too far away for a fair throw, Hansen. Come a little closer, huh? Just a little closer. You wouldn't want to disappoint your friends. They all came here to see blood. Why don't you bring them in a little closer—close, so they can see it, huh? Please, Hansen. Five steps. Two steps. One, Hansen. Just one step. Just close enough so you can get a fair chance with that meat hook. How about it, Hansen?" The irony of the scene depends on its status as a framing device that plays twice for the viewer, repeating again at the film's very end. When this climatic sequence arrives, we already know what's coming—have heard it all before—and when Hansen throws his whaler's harpoon and hits Johnny Crale square in the chest, killing him on the spot, we wish we hadn't seen it. The moment is as hyperbolically sincere, and ultimately as campy, as any in all of cinema. Yet Crale's words linger. Desire has pulled us "closer . . . closer . . . ," but we are unable to finally arrive. Once the object of desire is attained, we are already past it, unsatisfied and unsatisfiable.

It is always a bit disturbing to read the most prestigious commentaries on Lewis's work, many of them from the auteuristic 1970s and seemingly all too ready to gleefully enumerate his shortcomings. Virtually all of these critiques end with a qualifier, however: the majority of Lewis's films/scenes are lousy, but some of them are not. Robert Mundy notes that "it is difficult to pick out wholly satisfying films in Lewis's career,"[43] while Andrew Sarris suggests we might scrutinize Lewis's early westerns, except that "in this direction lies madness."[44] In the pithiest of these critiques, Pauline Kael is willing to praise *Gun Crazy* only for its "fascinating crumminess."[45] Yet is not the real "madness" of Lewis that his films' lapses become strange attractors, that his implausibilities and "crummy" flaws perplex us and thus, in some unspeakable way, manage to coax us out and to lure us in? Neither regularly watched nor entirely watchable, Lewis exists in a strange border region in which a tantalizing occlusion, and not the satisfaction of attainment, is the best that can be hoped for. In other words, like the *objet a*, we can chase this auteur, but we can never have him.

Notes

1. Noted for its technique, the film became "the sleeper hit of the year" in 1945–46. Andrew Sarris, *The American Cinema: Directors and Directions, 1929–1968* (New York: Da Capo Press, 1996), 133. For more on the positive critical reception of *Julia Ross* and the doors it opened for Lewis at Columbia Pictures, see Peter Bogdanovich, *Who the Devil Made It: Conversations with Legendary Film Directors* (New York: Ballantine, 1998), 658–62.

2. Jim Kitses, *Gun Crazy* (London: BFI, 1996), 14.

3. Jacques Lacan, *The Seminar of Jacques Lacan*, bk. 11, *The Four Fundamental Concepts of Psycho-Analysis*, trans. Alan Sheridan (New York: Norton, 1978), 282.

4. Ibid., 257, 268, 134.

5. Ibid., 259.

6. Jacques Lacan, *The Seminar of Jacques Lacan*, bk. 20, *Encore: On Feminine Sexuality, The Limits of Love and Knowledge (1972–1973)*, trans. Bruce Fink (New York: Norton, 1998), 6.

7. Ibid., 136.

8. Lacan, *Four Fundamental Concepts*, 270.

9. Ibid., 154.

10. Ibid., 180.

11. Lewis Kirshner, "Rethinking Desire: The *Objet Petit A* in Lacanian Theory," *Journal of the American Psychoanalytic Association* 53, no. 1 (2004): 84.

12. Bogdanovich, *Who the Devil*, 653.

13. Ibid.

14. Francis M. Nevins, *Joseph H. Lewis: Overview, Interview, and Filmography* (Lanham, MD: Scarecrow Press, 1998), 12. It should be noted that the very end of *The Little Foxes* (1941) features a "highly dramatic" shot of Regina Giddens (Bette Davis) standing at the window of her darkened bedroom, but in this sequence the camera repeatedly cuts back to a close-up of her face, permitting the viewer to read her emotions. On the contrary, Lewis is clearly recalling *The Letter* when he says that Wyler "kept the camera on her back and stayed on her back."

15. See for instance Bogdanovich, *Who the Devil*, 664, 669, 675, 679, 686, as well as Robert Porfirio and Carl Macek, "Joseph H. Lewis," in *Film Noir Reader 3*, ed. by Robert Porfirio, Alain Silver, and James Ursini (New York: Limelight Editions, 2002), 81.

16. I am thinking of such works as *Les rêveries du promeneur solitaire* (ca. 1926), *La boîte de Pandore* (1951), *La decalcomania* (1966), and especially *La reproduction interdit* (1937).

17. Bogdanovich, *Who the Devil*, 657; Porfirio and Macek, "Joseph H. Lewis," 70.

18. As a counterpoint, consider the fact that when Reynolds walks toward the jury box on the right, we actually see one member of the jury, who stands

in for them all. But when he goes to the defendants table on the left, the camera never pans far enough to include the daughter whose life hangs on his every word.

19. André Bazin, "Theater and Cinema—Part Two," in *What is Cinema?*, vol. 1, trans. Hugh Gray (Berkeley: University of California Press, 1967), 105.

20. Bogdanovich, *Who the Devil*, 669.

21. Man Ray, *Self-Portrait* (New York: Little, Brown, 1998), 225. More recently, Martin Arnold's experimental film *Deanimated* (2002) digitally erases various characters from the original *Invisible Ghost*, in some ways completing a process that Lewis has already begun.

22. Jacques Lacan, *The Seminar of Jacques Lacan*, bk. 10, *Anxiety*, trans. Cormac Gallagher (Eastbourne: Antony Rowe, 2002), xix, 12.

23. From a technical standpoint, these artifacts are an example of "camera flare," and not "lens flare," because the artifacts are produced by a very bright light source (here, the locomotive's headlamp) passing close to or directly in front of the lens and reflecting off the interior surfaces of the camera (for instance, the lens barrel). For a technical account of how such ghost images are produced, see Sidney F. Ray, *Applied Photographic Optics Lenses and Optical Systems for Photography, Film, Video, Electronic and Digital Imaging* (Oxford: Focal Press, 2002), 138–44.

24. Kitses, *Gun Crazy*, 29–30.

25. Paul Schrader, "Joseph H. Lewis 1," *Cinema* (US) 7, no. 1 (1971): 43.

26. In his interview with Porfirio and Macek, Lewis explicitly refers to Laurie's powerful hold over Bart as "magnetism." "Joseph H. Lewis," 75.

27. Jacques Lacan, "Le séminaire XIV: La logique du fantasme, 1966–1967" (unpublished manuscript, session of November 16, 1966), http://gaogoa.free.fr/Seminaires_HTML/14-LF/LF16111966.htm.

28. Sarah Kay, *Courtly Contradictions: The Emergence of the Literary Object in the Twelfth Century* (Stanford, CA: Stanford University Press, 2001), 33.

29. Jacques Lacan, *Le seminaire de Jacques Lacan*, bk. 10, *L'angoisse* (Paris: Seuil, 2004), 209. The original quotation is as follows: "A, comme telle, et rien d'autre, c'est l'accès, non pas à la jouissance, mais à l'Autre. C'est tout ce qui en reste, à partir du moment où le sujet veut faire son entrée dans cet Autre." I am indebted to Todd McGowan for this insight, as well as for the translation.

30. Kay, *Courtly Contradictions*, 34.

31. In *Secrets of a Co-Ed*, when the District Attorney (Addison Richards) admits Brenda Reynolds's diary into evidence, he says, "Ladies and gentlemen of the jury, I have here a silent witness. Yes, silent—but a very dynamic and conclusive witness." He then reads a passage that spells out Brenda's engagement with *objet a*: "At last something has happened to take the kinks out of this dull routine. What a man. What a smile. Nick—he's different. Wonder what it is about him? I feel reckless, daring, thrilled."

32. Kitses, *Gun Crazy*, 60.

33. Robert Mundy, "Joseph H. Lewis 2," *Cinema* (US) 7, no. 1 (1971): 45.

34. Recall that in their original shooting contest, which culminates in the "crown of matches," there is one match difference between the two—a visual pun in the sense that the two do not quite "match." It is at this point, and no other, that their *amour fou* commences.

35. Schrader, "Lewis 1," 44.

36. Kirshner, "Rethinking Desire," 85.

37. Slavoj Žižek, *The Parallax View* (Cambridge, MA: MIT Press, 2006), 63–64.

38. Slavoj Žižek, *Looking Awry: An Introduction to Jacques Lacan through Popular Culture* (Cambridge, MA: MIT Press, 1991), 63.

39. Porfirio and Macek, "Joseph H. Lewis," 68.

40. Paul Kerr, "My Name Is Joseph H. Lewis," *Screen* 24, nos. 4–5 (1983): 63.

41. Paul Willemen, "Edinburgh Debate," *Framework* 19 (1982): 49.

42. Bruce Fink, *Lacan to the Letter: Reading* Écrits *Closely* (Minneapolis: University of Minnesota Press, 2004), 166.

43. Mundy, "Lewis 2," 45.

44. Andrew Sarris, "The High Forties Revisited," *Film Culture* 24 (1962): 66.

45. Pauline Kael, *5001 Nights at the Movies* (New York: Henry Holt, 1991), 310.

3

Michael E. Grost

The Joseph H. Lewis Nobody Knows
The Television Films

Joseph H. Lewis's feature film career ended in 1958, but his filmmaking career had only reached its midpoint. By that time, Lewis had made roughly 40 of his 106 known films. The rest of his career would be in television, an area that has been all too often ignored in studies of his work. His television era represents an unbroken extension of his film career; his television programs are films in a sense, not only because his work in the medium was shot on film, but also because the episodes collectively represent such a strong visual, narrative, and thematic achievement. Moreover, the television "films" exemplify a continuation of the personal and individual style that Lewis the auteur had previously stamped onto his theatrical films.

Lewis's career in television was extensive. For example, he directed forty-nine episodes of the series *The Rifleman* (1958–63) in which actor Chuck Connors played Lucas McCain, the title character.[1] Lewis also directed at least seventeen episodes of other television series. The exact number is not known; researchers such as Francis M. Nevins are still discovering new works in Lewis's television filmography. A few of these have not been seen in decades, but fortunately most of Lewis's television work is available in good prints.

Television not only allowed Lewis to continue his filmmaking, it also afforded him artistic opportunities not available in feature filmmaking. US television in 1960 allowed openly political left-wing themes and commentary, and Lewis became one of the most politically outspoken liberal television directors of his generation. His television work is one of the most politically varied, explicit, and detailed bodies of work of any commercial narrative American filmmaker. Indeed, while some of his television films featured straightforward plots (such as "The Deadly Wait" in 1959), many others—"Duel of Honor" (1958), "The Deserter" (1960), and "Pompey" (1964), for example—were far more explicit about politics than much of what is often labeled as "political cinema." Television also served as what biologists call a "refuge" for endangered species of filmmaking. The medium allowed Lewis to direct works in film noir in an era when noir was fast disappearing from theatrical films, and it allowed him to create westerns that built on traditions stemming from his B movie beginnings in the 1930s.

Lewis's television films also represent a major artistic achievement. They are consistently rich from a cinematic standpoint, with complex camera movement, depth staging, and elaborate, geometric composition. He was able to work in black and white and a traditional aspect ratio during a period when theatrical films were in a mass conversion to widescreen and color. Lewis's love of depth staging was enabled by black-and-white television filming, which allowed much deeper focus than most color film technology of the era. Furthermore, Lewis took great advantage of filming on the huge studio set of *The Rifleman*, visually capturing an entire small western town in a kind of studio-created world, working in a tradition that goes back to Murnau, if not earlier.

Indeed, in 1958 Lewis was perhaps more prepared than many Hollywood film directors to work meaningfully in television. Lewis started as a B movie director, and most of his theatrical work is short, often no more than an hour for his low-budget films. As a result, Lewis had a fast-paced, economic approach to storytelling. He knew how to pack in rich details of plot, character, and social commentary in little screen time. Consequently, his twenty-three-minute *Rifleman* episodes seem to have as much narrative, visual, and thematic content as many other directors' feature-length films.

The Rifleman—as well as some other shows for which Lewis would direct episodes, such as *The Detectives Starring Robert Taylor* (1959–62) and *The Big Valley* (1965–69)—was produced by Four Star Productions.[2] Four Star ranked among the highest-quality American television companies of the era. It employed theatrical film directors such as Lewis and also seemed to have either indulged or encouraged the theatrical "look" Lewis brought to his television films. Though Lewis was unable to impose his personal style on the single episode of *Bonanza* that he directed (which was not a Four Star series), his work for Four Star reveals a consistent vision that was different from others who directed *The Rifleman*.[3]

Major Themes and Issues

Joseph H. Lewis: A Personal Filmmaker

How personal is Lewis's television filmmaking? Does it reflect subjects, themes, visual style, and film techniques found in his theatrical work? In my Web book on Lewis (http://mikegrost.com/lewis.htm), I argue that the answers to these questions are very definitely yes. As evidence, I document over 150 subjects and film techniques, identifying how and where they occur in Lewis's work. In most cases, the evidence shows that Lewis's subjects and techniques are first seen in his B movies, recur in his bigger budget 1945–58 theatrical films, and then persist throughout his television work, resulting in a coherent and repeated artistic vision.

For example, Lewis liked to have his camera move through walls, thus drawing attention to the artifice of the cinema. The camera will go from one room of a studio set into another, seemingly passing through the wall. This effect starts in such early Lewis B movies as *The Spy Ring* (1938) and *Blazing Six Shooters* (1940). Twenty years later, Lewis employed it for episodes of *The Rifleman* such as "The Hangman" (1960), "The Actress" (1961), and "The Wyoming Story" (1961), as well as for his episode of *Daniel Boone* titled "Pompey" (1964). Similarly, the circular camera movements that begin in such early Lewis films as *Courage of the West* (1937), *Invisible Ghost* (1941), and *Boss of Hangtown Mesa* (1942) persist in episodes of *The Rifleman* such as "The Deadly Wait" (1959), "Honest Abe" (1961), and "A Young Man's Fancy" (1962). If anything, working in television seems to have only encouraged Lewis's love of complex camera movement.

In terms of mise-en-scène, Lewis enjoyed building backgrounds out of hay. Key Lewis scenes are full of hay stacked in geometric patterns that form visually rich backgrounds for action in the foreground. This seems to begin with Lewis's B western *The Man from Tumbleweeds* (1940), the finale containing an elaborate use of hay. It persists in such Lewis nonwesterns as *So Dark the Night* (1946) and *The Return of October* (1948), as well as in *Gun Crazy* (1950), in which the lovers flee in a train car filled with hay. Lewis had not forgotten such ideas by the time of *The Rifleman*. Part of the town celebration in "The Fourflusher" (1960) is a huge wagon covered with banners and bales of hay, recalling a somewhat similar wagon in *The Halliday Brand* (1957). "The Fourflusher" wagon is first introduced in motion, soon counterpointed by the camera moving in the opposite direction. The hay wagon then shows up in subsequent static shots, covered with cowboys rhythmically swinging their boots. Lewis uses what appears to be a similar hay truck in a later episode, "The Actress" (1961); hay then proceeds to play a major role in such *Rifleman* episodes as "The Pet" (1959), "Heller" (1960), "Baranca" (1960), "Face of Yesterday" (1961), "The Shattered Idol" (1961), "A Young Man's Fancy" (1962), "The Bullet" (1963), and "Old Tony" (1963). In one of Lewis's last television films, "Night of the Wolf" (1965) for the series *The Big Valley*, the climactic murder plays out against bales of hay.

Hay is just one of many visual motifs than run through Lewis's work. These motifs serve as building blocks of Lewis images, making striking geometric compositions. One could write an entire essay about peaked roofs, which run through at least thirty-six of Lewis's films, from his first to his last. The roofs range from single peaks that make dramatic triangles to elaborate buildings with numerous peaked gables, resulting in a kind of visual music. He also relied regularly on two types of fences, field fences with wire strung between short posts and white picket fences around yards. Rooms and small buildings with glass walls, laundry hanging on lines, wells with covers on top, alcoves, and swinging gates/doors all appear in countless Lewis films, usually in beautiful and imaginative ways. These imaginative backgrounds, built up by permutations of Lewis's favorite building blocks, form a personal architectural world. In this way Lewis films anticipate the environments sometimes created by some avant-garde artists that form unusual geometric locales in which spectators can wander, such as Allan Kaprow's *Yard* (1961) filled with tires, Athena Tacha's geometric city park *Connections* (1981–92), Rachel Whiteread's *Embankment* (2005–6) with its rows between boxes, and Carsten Höller's *Test Site* (2006) with its tubular slides.

There are even favorite Lewis foods as well. Coffee is as ubiquitous in Lewis's television work as it is in his theatrical films. A giant coffeepot serves as a phallic symbol in front of Little Joe (Michael Landon) in Lewis's *Bonanza* episode, "The Quality of Mercy" (1963). The Lewis sweet tooth is often in evidence as well. Cake—which appears in difficult, often troubled family celebrations in Lewis features like *Minstrel Man* (1944) and *Retreat, Hell!* (1952)—appears at a tense gathering in the television film "Honest Abe" (1961). Pie, another recurrent kind of food, appeared first in his B movies—*The Spy Ring, Texas Stagecoach* (1940), *The Return of Wild Bill* (1940), *Invisible Ghost* (1941)—before resurfacing in nine episodes of *The Rifleman*. It is a favorite of young Mark McCain, along with his love of candy. One almost has to laugh when, near the end of Lewis's *Gunsmoke* episode "One Killer on Ice" (1965), Marshal Dillon, Doc, and others gather to discuss a mystery case and end up appreciatively eating some pie and drinking coffee.

The Detective Hero

Lewis's television work centers on men who think. The Lewis hero is a man who uses his mind, and who works long and hard at difficult questions. One way the Lewis hero uses his mind is to perform detective work. This is not the image most viewers hold of the "typical western hero." However, there were many books, television films, and comic books about cowboys who are detectives or other kinds of thinkers. When *The Rifleman* was originally being broadcast on television, Merle Constiner was writing his paperback western novels about cowboy detectives, and Edward D. Hoch was creating his cowboy sleuth Ben Snow. Television programs such as *Maverick* often showed their leads solving mysteries, and comic book series such as *Pow-Wow Smith, Indian Lawman* featured a Sioux sheriff solving mysteries in the Old West. However, Lewis predated these efforts in his B movies *The Last Stand* (1938) and *Blazing Six Shooters* (1940), both of which featured cowboys who solved mysteries.

His detective films, whether set in the Old West or modern day, are notable for their rigorous standards of detective work. They resemble the best prose mysteries, with their emphasis on reasoning out solutions to mysteries from clues. The Lewis hero does not guess. He investigates, discovers evidence, and then deduces solutions to mysteries. The Lewis hero follows the same intellectual process as Sherlock Holmes or Ellery Queen.

Such reasoning from evidence is known as "genuine detection" or "real detective work" among prose mystery writers. It is highly prized and often considered a key criterion in separating good mysteries from bad mysteries. Of all film directors, Joseph H. Lewis is likely the most insistent about having such genuine detective work in his films. It immediately separates his films from those of many other directors. A great deal of screen time and character energy in Lewis films is lavished on plot developments involving real detective work, which occurs in at least fourteen of Lewis's theatrical features, and sixteen of his television films.

Lewis detective films are also unusual in terms of their close adherence to aspects of prose mystery fiction. For example, both *Texas Stagecoach* and *The Rifleman* episode "The Pet" (1959) contain "dying messages." These are cryptic clues left by dying characters that have to be interpreted by clever detectives. Dying messages are common in prose mysteries, such as those by Ellery Queen, but rare on-screen. Similarly, "The Bullet" episode of *The Rifleman* is a pure "scientific detection tale" in which lab work and ballistics are used to develop evidence against a culprit. Lewis had already included police lab work in *The Undercover Man* (1949) and carried on this tradition in his television work. "The Bullet" even has a shot framed through a magnifying glass, echoing a similar, earlier shot in *The Undercover Man*.

While the Lewis detective hero is good at thinking, he is not necessarily an impressive figure in the worldly sense. Danny in *Pride of the Bowery* (1940) is a slum teenager, one of the East Side Kids, but his detective work would do credit to Sherlock Holmes. Charles Starrett in *Blazing Six Shooters* (1940) looks like any other B movie cowboy leading man. Mark McCain in *The Rifleman* episode "Surveyors" (1959) is a thirteen-year-old, and a modest, quiet, well-behaved one at that. But his mounting deductions from evidence he encounters bring him closer and closer to the solution of a mystery that no one else in town understands. Even such police heroes as Lieutenant Diamond in *The Big Combo* (1955) and the Marshal in *The Rifleman* episode "The Bullet" face uphill battles and skeptical colleagues as they laboriously reason their way through cases. The unpretentiousness of Lewis's detective heroes might even prevent critical recognition of these films. Can "Surveyors," a gentle detective tale about a thirteen-year-old sleuth, be a major work of cinema?

The Fat Man

Though it was apparently not broadcast, in approximately 1958 Lewis made an hour-long pilot for an unsold television detective series called *The Fat Man*.[4] It might have been Lewis's first work in television. At any rate, *The Fat Man* has many links in plot, character, and setting with two of Lewis's best-known theatrical features, *The Undercover Man* and *The Big Combo*. All three feature determined urban "good guy" detectives who work tirelessly to find evidence that will convict corrupt mobsters. Sympathetic, poor Italians are mob victims in all three films of what we might dub Lewis's detective trilogy. Robert Middleton, who portrayed the police chief in *The Big Combo*, took the lead role as the detective hero in *The Fat Man*.

The detective trilogy is rich in metaphors. The police heroes of *The Undercover Man* and *The Big Combo* are compared to adding machines; *The Big Combo* also compares its sleuth to a classical pianist, whose concert the hero attends. The Fat Man is himself a keyboard musician, and he gets the key clue to his case by analogizing the situation to a sonata he is playing on his harpsichord.

However, *The Fat Man* also reveals some differences with Lewis's theatrical films. It features Lewis's first major private eye detective, rather than a police hero. And, more crucially, the sleuth is apparently the first genuine intellectual hero in Lewis's canon. The private eye plays Bach and Scarlatti on the harpsichord, collects Shakespeare editions, and is a gourmet chef. He is also highly intelligent, one of the most intelligent detective heroes in

Lewis's work. The hero of Lewis's *The Return of October* (1948) was also an intellectual, a professor of animal psychology whose scientific concepts are surprisingly deep and well researched. But the professor is mainly a comic character, one that only gains heroic stature in the courtroom scenes at the film's conclusion. By contrast, the Fat Man is an admired intellectual from the first frames of the pilot.

Nonviolence and Violence

One major strain of Joseph H. Lewis's politics is a commitment to nonviolence. This theme runs through many of his films; for example, *Bombs over Burma* (1943) glorifies nonviolent resistance to the Axis invasion of China, with Chinese peasants building the Burma Road and American volunteers working to keep public services open in Canton. *Gun Crazy* (1950) can certainly be read as a parable about the evils of using force, with the couple's gun violence leading to death and destruction.

Indeed, nonviolent political ideas found renewed visibility in Lewis's television films. The hero of "The Vindicators" (1965) pilot for the series *Branded* makes huge personal sacrifices to prevent warmongers from starting a battle with Native Americans. An episode of *The Detectives Starring Robert Taylor* titled "The Hiding Place" (1959) opens with a sign on a Los Angeles auditorium announcing "Peace Rally 11 A.M." The plot follows the police as they try to track down and defuse a bomb planted by a fanatic opponent of the rally. Additionally, the *Daniel Boone* episode "Pompey" (1964) is a trenchant antislavery drama with Brock Peters in the title role as a slave in eighteenth-century America.

However, Lewis's most remarkable film about nonviolence may well be *The Rifleman* episode "The Deserter" (1960). When an army deserter shows up at the McCain ranch, he triggers escalating resistance from the hero. Few films show such a deep commitment to the philosophy of nonviolence. The episode culminates in a full-scale nonviolent protest of townspeople and features open defiance of the army's commander, thus becoming one of Lewis's most powerful storytelling works. Audacious, politically committed, and original, it is one of Lewis's most important television films and offers an amazing viewing experience.

Of course the other side of nonviolence is an understanding of the havoc wreaked by war and violence. Lewis films are replete with massacres. His early Bob Baker westerns *Courage of the West* (1937) and *Border Wolves* (1938) depict wagon train massacres. He then explored this theme in *Retreat, Hell!* (1952), which depicts a real-life Korean War disaster in which marines were massacred in record numbers. Lewis also directed *7th*

Cavalry (1956), dealing with the massacre of Custer's troops at Little Big Horn. Lewis television work includes two more films in the direct tradition of *7th Cavalry*: The *Rifleman* episode "The Journey Back" (1961) and the *Branded* pilot "The Vindicators." All three films deal with cavalry massacres by Native Americans, all show the aftermath of the massacre (not the battle itself), and all three are critical of white men.

Other Lewis episodes of *The Rifleman* deal with the aftermath of the US Civil War. Like the cavalry films, these focus not on battle scenes but on the bitter aftermath of war, with chilling examinations of its high costs. "Face of Yesterday," "The Prisoner" (1961), and "Honest Abe" are not dull tracts, however. They bring out Lewis's surrealist side, featuring startling events, weird characters, bizarre scenes, and black humor. For example, "Face of Yesterday" invokes one of Lewis's favorite surreal images, the dead man who seemingly comes back to life, a motif that runs through Lewis features from John McGuire in *Invisible Ghost* to Randolph Scott in *A Lawless Street* (1955). The suspense drama "The Prisoner" climaxes with the Rifleman Lucas caged like an animal, a frighteningly literal version of the many shots through iron bars in Lewis's films. And "Honest Abe" centers on a sympathetic man, deluded since the Civil War, who believes he's Abraham Lincoln. The high points of "Honest Abe" include two full-contact wrestling matches, one staged in a saloon with circular camera movements.

Specific Television Films

"Duel of Honor" and the Gay Hero

Lewis's best television work may well be his first episode of *The Rifleman*, which was titled "Duel of Honor" (1958). This episode asks a simple, obvious, but also unexpected question: What would happen if a gay man showed up in a town of the Old West? "Duel of Honor" explores the results with a mix of suspense, comedy, and trenchant political depth. "Duel of Honor" and the theatrical film *Tea and Sympathy* (Vincente Minnelli, 1956) are the only two major works of the period that examine discrimination and prejudice against homosexuals.

While being rejected by some of the townspeople, a visiting count gets strong support from Lucas McCain. In a subplot, the two also form a close personal relationship. At one point in the story, the count takes off his jacket, leaving himself in a pure white shirt and trousers. He becomes one of Lewis's many men in white clothes that are nonconformists. In his feature films, these include the undercover hero of *A Lady without Passport*

(1950) and the determined and independent cop in *The Big Combo*, whose white dress shirt seems to glow in John Alton's cinematography.[5]

"Duel of Honor" also illustrates how Lewis could couple a challenging theme with memorable visuals. This episode contains one of Lewis's most adventurous camera movements, a complex long take showing the stage passengers enter the hotel. This follows a Lewis tradition of camera movements that swing back and forth, from left to right and back. It also continues another Lewis tradition: shots that link the indoors and the outdoors in one unified view. Much of *The Rifleman* was shot on a giant studio set representing the western town of North Fork. This set included both the town's main street and the interiors of many businesses that open onto the street. Throughout the episodes he directed, Lewis created shots that linked the "outdoors" of the street, with its horses and buggies, with the "interiors" of the hotel, the general store, the blacksmith's, or the Marshal's office.

The climactic scene in "Duel of Honor" also represents one of Lewis's best set pieces. It recalls the first meeting of the hero and heroine in *Gun Crazy*, when they take part in the shooting contest. Lewis's films often contain duels with strange weapons and are always upbeat, off-trail, and exuberant. The harpoon duel on a western street in *Terror in a Texas Town* (1958) is famously surreal, and the jujitsu training scene in *Retreat, Hell!* is also memorable because of its comical style. Lewis's television films have a number of such grand contests. They recur in *The Rifleman* episodes "Strange Town" (1960), "Baranca," "Honest Abe," "The Shattered Idol," "Death Never Rides Alone" (1962), and "Sidewinder" (1963), as well as in the *Daniel Boone* episode "Pompey," where the title character, a fugitive slave, unexpectedly fights by attacking people using the manacles in which he is chained. The strange content of the duels are equaled by dynamic filming techniques. For example, the first contest in "Honest Abe" is shot through wagon wheels; the second is filmed with two camera movements that encircle the action, in addition to a pulsating lateral track. The characters and the viewer are caught up in an unfolding process that unwinds like a music box or piece of clockwork.

"Duel of Honor" also combines two themes that show up, separately or together, in many other Lewis-directed episodes of *The Rifleman*. Sometimes the Rifleman speaks up for social outsiders in a liberal crusade for their rights and welfare. In other shows, the Rifleman male bonds with social outsiders. In such episodes as "Shivaree" (1959), "Panic" (1959), "Hero" (1960), and "The Deserter," a social outsider appears in town and is subject to public opposition. Advocating unpopular, liberal principles in his speech, Lucas often risks personal injury, ranging from social opprobrium to violence or governmental arrest, to defend these characters.

Variations on these themes appear in other Lewis-directed *Rifleman* episodes. In "The Deserter," Lucas both speaks up and risks violence for a young cavalry deserter, but Lucas's male bonding occurs not with the deserter but instead with a handsome cavalry officer played by Harry Carey Jr. In "Baranca," Lucas shows courage in standing up for the rule of law against violent opposition. But his bonding is not with a man in trouble but instead with the visiting Baranca, a racial Other. Moreover, the episodes "Strange Town" and "The Bullet" combine defiance against socially powerful criminals with male bonding.

I have been using the words "male bonding," but perhaps these television films could also accurately be described as having gay themes. How can one tell the difference between male bonding and a gay love story? It is not easy. Censorship codes and opposition from film producers, sponsors, and the public made it hard to feature explicitly gay content in pre-1968 commercial narrative film. It is plausible that filmmakers who wished to include gay characters or relationships would avoid explicitly labeling such content as gay, presenting their ideas through more coded narratives and characterizations.

Certainly there are aspects of some of Lewis's films that invite gay readings. The virulence of the town's reaction in "Duel of Honor" makes little sense unless it is motivated by antigay sentiment. In addition, male relationships in Lewis television films can be intensely physical. The Rifleman and the count in "Duel of Honor" share a hotel room overnight, and the Rifleman sits on the count's bed while the count rests on it. The Rifleman and the guest characters of "Baranca" and "Honest Abe" have physical contests resulting in much body contact. In "Closer Than a Brother" (1961), the Rifleman makes an intense speech about how he opened up to the Marshal emotionally. A milder version of this was reprised in a Lewis episode of *A Man Called Shenandoah* titled "Incident at Dry Creek" (1965) in which the sheriff talks about how he learned to trust the hero.

The closest ancestor to the Rifleman in Lewis theatrical features is the hero of *The Man from Tumbleweeds*. Like the Rifleman, the hero (William Elliott) of this B western is a social crusader standing up for unpopular opinions and social change. Also like the Rifleman, he is brilliantly articulate as a public speaker, as well as being determined and masculine in manner. Although there is a heroine in *The Man from Tumbleweeds*, the film depicts no romance between her and the hero. Instead, the hero bonds with a male social outsider. *The Man from Tumbleweeds* may represent the origin of the gay-themed hero in the films of Joseph H. Lewis.

In addition, I would draw attention to the fact that non-Lewis episodes of *The Rifleman* regularly depicted the hero as heterosexual, as in "Milly's Brother" (Richard Donner, 1962). The Rifleman did have steady girlfriends in the last three of his five seasons on television, and they sometimes play heterosexual roles in Lewis episodes, notably in "Sheer Terror" (1961) and "I Take This Woman" (1962). The Rifleman has romances with female guest stars in "The Visitor" and "The Actress," episodes directed by Lewis and partially written by Chuck Connors. Much better are three episodes in which Lucas bonds with dance hall women: "Eddie's Daughter" (1959), "The Wyoming Story," and "The Vaqueros" (1961). These women are all social outsiders, similar to the men Lucas bonds with. Indeed, they recall the hero's dancer girlfriend in *The Big Combo*.

"Surveyors" and Growing Up

Several of Lewis's films show the young hero entering into manhood. Lewis first solo directorial effort *Courage of the West* (1937) has the hero passing into adulthood; as a musical number fades out on his boyish soprano, the film then fades in on his adult voice. This all occurs as he is riding with a group of singing rangers. There is nothing this audacious in Lewis's subsequent work, although the hero's transition to adulthood in *The Jolson Story* (1946) is also represented by his changing singing voice. However, the difficulties of growing up remain a constant Lewis theme. Young Mark McCain is a sharply observed character at the center of many *Rifleman* episodes. He is the archetypal "good kid," similar to most of Lewis's youthful heroes, who are intelligent, determined, moral, polite, and quiet but courageous.

In "Surveyors," young Mark is interested in a possible career as a surveyor on crews that lay out plans for new railroads. The plot echoes early Lewis B movies that glorify those persons who build the nation's infrastructure. For example, there are no less than three early Lewis films about road builders: *Texas Stagecoach*, *Pride of the Bowery*, and *Bombs over Burma*. Those examples are in addition to the company laying telegraph wire in *Boss of Hangtown Mesa* (1942) and the plans for the new dam in *The Silver Bullet* (1942).

"Surveyors" is typical of Lewis's detective films in that much-needed facts do not come easily. People learn truth gradually, after much effort and thought. Young Mark, the detective hero, has to go through many stages in which he reasons out more and more of the truth. Nor does his skeptical father recognize the truth immediately either. Lucas McCain must also go through a huge mental struggle in order to see the light. Truth, learning, and discovery in Lewis's films come only after hard work, persistence through periods of partial success and failure, and deep commitment to thinking, reason, and the life of the mind.

In addition to its story line, "Surveyors" is a work of great visual beauty. The conversation between Lucas and the Marshal on the town streets is highly memorable. Lewis follows the two with the camera while the buildings of the town of North Fork unreel in the background. Beautiful, ever-shifting compositions appear as the architecture is used to create geometric patterns. "Surveyors" also features the single most extreme depth staging in all of Lewis's work. This occurs in the second shot of the film. The setting is outside, with two surveyors talking in the foreground. A third surveyor is seen in the far distant background. He steadily walks toward the camera. Eventually, he reaches the close foreground. His arrival is synchronized with plot events. The whole unbroken long take is like a film structured around a staging technique. It anticipates avant-garde films such as *Wavelength* (Michael Snow, 1966), which is built around a long zoom. However, "Surveyors" was made long before any of the structural films of Snow or other sixties-era directors. Long-take sequences in Lewis in which a character moves either from foreground to background or background to foreground are common in his cinema, a basic building block of his cinematic language. They appear in at least fourteen of his theatrical films and twenty-two of his television episodes.

An earlier camera movement in the episode opens with a deep focus shot down a covered sidewalk: a beautiful architectural image. The camera then begins to move, crossing from one side of a row of pillars to another, a Lewis device that is always visually gripping to watch. The shot then accompanies the villains as they cross North Fork's main street and enter the bank; the camera continues panning outside the bank along a window through which we see the villains move inside. The shot thus moves through five different types of visual imagery or zones, always maintaining its steady propulsive movement. The combination of deep focus sidewalk shots and crossing rows of pillars occurs in *A Lawless Street*, *The Rifleman* episode "Sheer Terror," and *The Big Valley* episode "Night of the Wolf." Pillars are also crossed outside the sister's home in *Gun Crazy*, inside the family living room in *The Halliday Brand*, and in *The Rifleman* episode "The Trade" (1959).

Signs appear everywhere in Hollywood films. But signs play an especially conspicuous role in Lewis's works (appearing in twenty-one theatrical films and twenty television films). In *The Rifleman* comedy episode "Suspicion" (1963), a sign painter (Kevin McCarthy) is even the main character. In "Surveyors," there are signs on the windows of the bank and on the bank's safe that is robbed. The surveyors' wagon has a sign on its side. The

North Fork town buildings are full of elaborate signs. So is a shack out in the countryside, near a long fence that Lewis uses for beautiful perspective shots. Letters from the bank window are projected inside the bank as shadows. They are also used to mask shots through the windows. The signs are a key aspect of Lewis's visual design, which is particularly apt given that the film involves detection.

In "Surveyors," Lucas's final investigation at the bank involves staring into a mirror. Lucas discovers the truth about the mystery while looking into a mirror. Truth emerged in mirrors in early Lewis crime films, such as in *The Spy Ring* and *The Silver Bullet*. Mirror shots also are used for suspense; for example, the heroine of *Gun Crazy* has a confrontation with the carnival owner in front of her mirror. The mirror sequence in "Surveyors" is also notable for its formal complexity. Lucas sees the mirror inside the bank through the window as he stands in the street. Lewis stages this as a point of view camera movement that gradually sweeps through the bank interior till it encounters the mirror reflecting a hidden bad guy. Camera movements staged through windows are a Lewis tradition seen in nine of his theatrical films and seventeen of his television films; this one is unusual in that it is combined with a mirror. The shot is made even more complex by writing on the window that forms an Ophüls-like mask in front of the image and grillwork for the teller's cage inside the bank.

"Squeeze Play" and the Oppressive Rich

The Rifleman episode titled "Squeeze Play" (1962) revisits one of Lewis's most persistent plots: big rich crooks trying to force ordinary people out of their homes and businesses. For Lewis, this plot seems to begin with the B western *The Man from Tumbleweeds* and then gets an in-depth treatment in *A Lawless Street* and *Terror in a Texas Town*. Such films clearly reflect a leftwing skepticism about the vicious, oppressive actions of the rich. However, such Lewis films also tend to depict the victims of the rich as sympathetic small businesses, such as the freight company in *Arizona Cyclone* (1941) and the telegraph company in *Boss of Hangtown Mesa* (1942). In "Squeeze Play," cattle rancher Lucas McCain is the target. Hero Lucas is a landowner, not a peasant farmer or a sharecropper, recalling the landowner victims in *A Lawless Street* and *Terror in a Texas Town*. All of these Lewis films are politically left of center but—with their respect for property owners and small-business owners—still capitalist rather than Marxist.[6]

One of the famous stories about Lewis is that in his early B western days he liked to shoot scenes through the spokes of a wagon wheel; Lewis even became known in the film industry as "Wagon Wheel Joe." Until I saw Lewis's B movies, I thought this was some sort of casual nickname, maybe based on a scene or two in his films. But his movies tell a different story. Wagon wheel shots are prominent in nine of Lewis's early B movies. Moreover, wagon wheels are only one example of his desire to shoot through an array of objects: hanging baskets, chandeliers, ceiling fans, candelabra, clocks, fireplaces, triangles, buggy reins, and steering wheels. Lewis also liked to shoot through architectural features: shelves, the insides of closets or sleeping berths on trains, and blacksmith's shops. This whole style of shooting is preserved and extended in Lewis's television work. The wagon wheels, which largely drop out of Lewis's 1945–58 feature films, make a triumphant return in *The Rifleman* episodes "The Deadly Wait" (1959), "The Stand-In" (1961), "Honest Abe," "The Shattered Idol," and "Long Gun from Tucson" (1961). Similarly, Lewis also framed many shots through trees. Often these are tree branches that arch over the rest of the composition; in other cases, Lewis shot through wiry shrubs. Beautiful images of vegetation are at their richest in "Squeeze Play," a television film that includes shots captured through trees and a lace curtain.

"Night of the Wolf" and the Color of Emotion

"Night of the Wolf" is the best of Lewis's episodes for *The Big Valley*, a tragic story of remarkable emotional power. The hero in "Night of the Wolf" (Peter Breck) has run away from home, just as characters do in at least twenty-nine Lewis films; in six of those, including "Night of the Wolf," children are abandoned. Curiously, however, the hero shares far more characteristics with Lewis villains than he does Lewis heroes. He is one of the first Lewis heroes to be dressed in the gunslinger attire often worn by Lewis villains. He is wealthy and—also like Lewis's bad guys—has lavish living quarters.

"Night of the Wolf" shows visual echoes of earlier Lewis films. The elaborate rope structure used to tie up the horses at the start recalls the one that appears in *Texas Stagecoach*. The finale, with its encounter between actors Peter Breck and young Ron Howard, is staged, right down to camera setups, like the final meeting between Lucas McCain and his son, Mark, in *The Rifleman* episode "The Wyoming Story."[7]

Unlike most of Lewis's television films, however, *The Big Valley* (and thus "Night of the Wolf") was shot in color. Lewis's work shows a distinctive approach to color. The hero's costumes in "Night of the Wolf" are in color-coordinated shades of brown. This "symphony of brown" approach recalls Glenn Ford's 1940s sportswear ensemble in *The Return of October*, as well as his brown suit, and Randolph Scott's outfits in *A Lawless Street*.

Brown costumes for men return in another Lewis *The Big Valley* episode, "The Man from Nowhere." Brown clothes for American men are atypical, both on- and offscreen, and fashion experts often view brown negatively, recommending blue and gray for men instead. In the films of the great color stylist Vincente Minnelli, brown clothes tend to be worn by men behaving badly, such as mob enforcers or sexual oppressors like the coach in *Tea and Sympathy*.

Lewis's color design for individual scenes suggests much about his unique approach. Once again, a contrast with Minnelli can be seen. Minnelli tends to have an overall color scheme for a scene. Everything will be red or green. Or another scene will be in blue and orange. Alfred Hitchcock uses a similar approach in his color films. By contrast, Lewis is unafraid to include nearly every color in the rainbow in a single shot. Whether it is a cityscape of town buildings in *A Lawless Street* or the deep focus geometric composition of sidewalks and porticos seen under the credits of "Night of the Wolf," Lewis will utilize more colors on-screen than typically allowed by Minnelli or Hitchcock. One even suspects that Lewis had the road in *A Lawless Street* painted reddish pink, with some gold mixed in, similar to the way Max Ophüls had the roads painted in *Lola Montès* (1955).

In "Night of the Wolf," Lewis at times color coordinates characters with their backgrounds. When Breck first shows up in his brown gunslinger's costume at the family dining table, we see a hall behind him with brown curtains and red furniture. His loving siblings have no idea yet of Breck's problems, so by contrast, they are in light-colored clothes that coordinate with the cool, serene light-green walls behind them. When Breck goes up to his bedroom, the screen erupts with blazing red furnishings and books, orange chairs and sofas, and brown walls; Breck's bedroom also features brilliant red curtains with elaborate gold trim. Gold, orange, red, and brown: Breck is associated with the colors of fire.

Conclusion

This chapter represents a brief introduction to a very rich body of achievement so large as to be impossible to cover in limited space. For example, this chapter barely mentions important television films such as "Shivaree," an emotionally powerful story that packs a surprising number of ideas and feelings in a brief running time, or "Day of the Hunter" (1960), with its ecological concerns and its portrait of the Rifleman Lucas McCain at his most thoughtful and committed. Nor does it much discuss such works of pure storytelling as the "Sheer Terror" (1961) episode of *The Rifleman*, an old-fashioned suspense thriller that shows what Lewis can do with the "bad guys take someone hostage in their home" plot, a motif that runs through all of Lewis's work.

I have examined all forty-nine of Lewis's *Rifleman* episodes, all of the other Lewis films and television episodes mentioned in this chapter, and many others that space limitations have prohibited me from discussing herein. But there are still Lewis television episodes I have been unable to track down. Where is Lewis's work for *Alcoa Theatre* (1959), *The Investigators* (1961), or *The Dick Powell Show* (1962)? One hopes that all of these survive somewhere. Lewis's work on these television shows might well contain films of substance that will shed new light on his work. Having viewed so many of his films, it is my belief that should "missing" television episodes become available, they would likely support an argument that can already be made: Lewis was an auteur whose work reveals a repeated and coherent vision.

The sheer size of Lewis's output is still not widely understood. Lewis's more than 106 films are among the largest bodies of work of any major film director. He made more films than Josef von Sternberg, Howard Hawks, and Luchino Visconti put together. The more Lewis films one sees, the more one appreciates his artistry as a filmmaker. To be sure, Lewis made outstanding films during all three periods of his work: his B movies, his feature films, and his television episodes.

Most of the films discussed in this chapter are widely available, either through DVD, cable television, or other media. As I stated at the beginning of this chapter, Lewis's television films cry out to be viewed, studied, and understood as a major aspect of his film career rather than—as so often happens with film directors who started or ended up working in television—ignored due to a prejudice against the medium. They are films in every sense of the word; it was just that they were broadcast on television rather than screened in movie theaters. Discovering and appreciating Lewis's full range of achievements is still a work in progress and a work that cannot be understood without exploring his triumphs in television.

Notes

1. For more information on *The Rifleman*, see Christopher Sharrett, *The Rifleman* (Detroit: Wayne State University Press, 2005).

2. A few words on *The Rifleman*: This 1958–63 western television series stars widowed father Lucas McCain (Chuck Connors) and his teenage son, Mark McCain (Johnny Crawford). The McCains are owners and sole workers of a small cattle ranch in post–Civil War New Mexico. They live near the small frontier town of North Fork, where the Marshal (Paul Fix) is Lucas's best friend.

Both father Lucas and son Mark are intelligent and heavy readers; Mark wants to be a writer when he grows up. Both Lucas and Mark are startlingly articulate, having an awesome ability to express ideas in words—reflecting Lewis's long-term emphasis on thinking heroes.

3. Lewis was not alone: the great stylist Jacques Tourneur also produced visually routine footage in his sole *Bonanza* episode.

4. This pilot has survived and has surfaced on DVD.

5. Other *Rifleman* episodes such as "The Deadly Wait" (1959) and "Hero" (1960) also dressed sympathetic individualists in white garb.

6. Lewis also eschews Marxism by glorifying the town bank in *The Rifleman* episodes titled "The Safe Guard" (1958) and "Boomerang" (1959).

7. Both "Night of the Wolf" and "The Wyoming Story" also feature towns that have suffered an economic collapse.

2
Individual Works

4

Gary D. Rhodes

"A House Where Anything Can Happen and Usually Does"

*Joseph H. Lewis, Bela Lugosi,
and* (The) Invisible Ghost

Writing in the May 1, 1941, issue of the *Hollywood Spectator*, a film critic noted his displeasure at attending the premiere of Orson Welles's *Citizen Kane* (1941). "After the first half hour, I began to wonder what the story was all about," he complained. "From there on, I was more bored than entertained." In years to come, of course, his view proved to be in the minority. The critic also admitted that he had not caught the name "Rosebud" on the burning sled at the end of the film; his wife had to point it out to him on the drive home.[1] Not only had he been arguably incorrect in his assessment, but he had also been careless.

Elsewhere in the very same issue of the *Spectator*, another reviewer spoke with even more disdain about Joseph H. Lewis's *Invisible Ghost* (1941): "'[Lugosi] is a finished actor,' he wrote, 'but he will be finished for good if he is obliged to continue frightening little children with such inconsequential roles as the demented murderer in *The* [sic] *Invisible Ghost*. . . . It is only mildly interesting and can please only those who are shrieker fans—for even whodunit fans will not like it because we all know from the start whodunit.'"[2] As with *Kane*, once again we can see the carelessness of a *Spectator* critic: *Invisible Ghost* has no definite article in its title.

The names Orson Welles and Joseph H. Lewis appeared under the same cover again over twenty-five years later in Andrew Sarris's book *The American Cinema: Directors and Directions, 1929–1968*. Sarris considered Welles to be a "pantheon director" and believed *Citizen Kane* had "influenced the cinema more profoundly than any American film since *Birth of a Nation*."[3] While he speaks well of such films as *The Lady from Shanghai* (1947) and *Touch of Evil* (1958), Sarris clearly believes *Kane* was Welles's major contribution to the cinema.

By contrast, Sarris includes Joseph H. Lewis in his section "Expressive Esoterica," and he begins his discussion on the director by quoting from a previous critic who saw any attempt to "awaken the world to the merits of Joseph H. Lewis" as problematic due to the perceived limitations of his early works. "Admittedly, in this direction lies madness," the critic concluded.[4] Sarris continues by citing Lewis's *My Name Is Julia Ross* (1945) as the beginning of a consistent and personal style; he then suggests *Gun Crazy* (1950) was Lewis's "one enduring masterpiece."[5] Here we get a different argument than Sarris offers on Welles: rather than starting with a masterpiece and forever after creating inferior work, Lewis honed his abilities on over twenty apparently unimportant films before directing *Julia Ross*. While he avoids discussion of Lewis's early work, Sarris did offer a brief rejoinder to the critic he recited: "Madness is always preferable to smugness."[6]

Writing about Lewis a few years later, Myron Meisel spoke directly about *Invisible Ghost*, giving Lewis credit for exemplifying "more fluidity of style than is customary" in a Monogram film. Nonetheless, Meisel seemed careful to avoid smugness or madness, noting, "It is almost as easy to overrate his early, ludicrously ephemeral work as it is to underrate it. *The* [sic] *Invisible Ghost* (1941), *The Mad Doctor of Market Street* (1942), and *The Boss of Hangtown Mesa* (1942) are only arguably related to art, yet, given the intractable awfulness of the goings-on, Lewis manipulates his camera and scissors with startling integrity."[7] Meisel's essay provides a more in-depth analysis than Sarris but still offers only vague generalities about Lewis's early work. And he repeats the *Hollywood Spectator*'s mistake of appending a definite article to the title of *Invisible Ghost*.

When I interviewed Lewis aboard his yacht in Marina del Rey in 1996, he spoke in only vague terms about *Invisible Ghost*. Though a wonderful bon vivant, Lewis seemed to have even less interest in the film than either Sarris or Meisel. He grudgingly admitted that he might have learned something from its star, Bela Lugosi, but could not identify what that might have been. Lewis then emphasized the fact that many of his B movies were made in *days*, rather than weeks; his comment seemed an excuse for both his limited memory of *Invisible Ghost*'s production and perhaps its individual merits as he saw them.

But *Invisible Ghost* deserves more individual attention than Sarris, Meisel, or Lewis cared to give it. Certainly it has attained some renewed appeal based on the fact that the cult of its star Bela Lugosi grew much larger and more vocal during the 1990s. However, such attention might force us yet again to consider that *Invisible Ghost* bears no definite article in its title. More than just reflecting carelessness on the part of previous authors, that fact should remind us that there might be many *Invisible Ghosts*, ranging from the one viewed so dismissively by those writing on Lewis in the past to the one viewed in the by Lugosi fans in the 1990s, who very much rechristened it as a Lugosi film.

This chapter will suggest another approach to the film, reclaiming it as a Joseph H. Lewis film, but one that desperately needs to be considered on its own merits, something that has not occurred in the past. In the same way that Welles inherited the "great man" biopic and reinvented that genre in *Citizen Kane*, Lewis attempted a similar kind of reinvention with *Invisible Ghost*. He begins with the premise that he must grapple with and overcome Bela Lugosi's image and the expectations of a typical Lugosi horror film. To consolidate his control over the film, Lewis then exerts authorial intent by use of a roving camera synthesized with a complex use of editing and sound. Those elements result in a horror film that is in many respects ahead of its time, and one that deserves the respect it has not previously been given.

Directing Bela Lugosi

By the time he starred in *Invisible Ghost*, Bela Lugosi had been working professionally as an actor in four different countries over the span of four decades. He had appeared in over seventy films since 1917 and had worked with such important directors as Michael Curtiz, F. W. Murnau, Victor Fleming, Tod Browning, Raoul Walsh, Robert Florey, William Dieterle, and Edgar G. Ulmer. Ten years had passed between his Hollywood breakthrough in Universal's *Dracula* (1931) and the filming of *Invisible Ghost*. In that span of time, Lugosi had lived the life of an American film star.

Immediately following *Dracula*, he was arguably one of the hottest properties in Hollywood, but a combination of problems rapidly changed his fortunes. He mishandled his finances, going bankrupt in 1932. In an apparent effort to avoid typecasting, he did not star in *Frankenstein* (1931), which created another horror film star in Boris Karloff. Lugosi soon began appearing in low-budget films such as Monogram's *Mysterious Mr. Wong* (1935), which hardly bolstered his image as a major actor. Then Hollywood stopped producing horror films in late 1936, due in large measure to a British ban on horror films.[8] Once again, Lugosi faced financial doom, tied to a genre that disappeared off the cinematic landscape until Universal released *Son of Frankenstein* in 1939 immediately after a successful 1938 reissue of *Dracula* and *Frankenstein*. The new film meant the comeback of horror and, of Bela Lugosi.

However, Lugosi—perhaps acting once again out of necessity—repeated his earlier career move of intermingling low-budget films at lesser studios with his work at the majors; it was a problem amplified by ratio, as his work on "Poverty Row" increasingly outnumbered his work at major studios. This resulted in a slow, inexorable decline in the overall quality of his films from the dawn of the 1940s to his infamous work with Edward D. Wood Jr. in the 1950s with *Glen or Glenda* (1953) and *Bride of the Monster* (1955). Indeed, the world of low-budget filmmaking cast a shadow over Lugosi even after his death in 1956 with the posthumous release of Wood's *Plan 9 from Outer Space* (1959), a movie that featured brief shots of Lugosi, as well as of a stand-in wearing a cape.[9]

Aside from his trio of Ed Wood films, Lugosi's most famous and beloved grouping of low-budget movies would be those that have affectionately become known as the "Monogram Nine," a reference to that same number of films he made during the early 1940s for the Monogram Pictures Corporation, one of the more prominent and venerable production companies that constituted Hollywood's Poverty Row.[10] In some respects, the grouping makes sense: Lugosi made all nine of the films at the same company during a four-year period, and—at least to a small degree—they featured repetition of cast and crew and even library music.[11] Most notably of course, they all starred Lugosi, with the phrase "Monogram Nine" privileging stardom (and company affiliation) over, for example, directorial control as a determinant factor in how they should be viewed or discussed.

Under scrutiny, however, the notional grouping suffers; the foundation of the category cracks from the fissures of difference. *Voodoo Man* (1944)—which borrowed somewhat from Lugosi's non-Monogram film *White Zombie* (1932)—is the only one of the group in which the supernatural plays a key role. Indeed, despite a brief use of the supernatural (or mad science) at its conclusion, *Bowery at Midnight* (1942) is more of a crime thriller than a horror film. Two others—*Spooks Run Wild* (1941) and *Ghosts on the Loose* (1943)—are comedies featuring the East Side Kids, neither of which involves supernatural content despite their titles. Four more—*Black Dragons* (1942), *The Corpse Vanishes* (1942), *The Ape Man* (1943), and *Return of the Ape Man* (1944)—are essentially mad scientist films, though *Black Dragons* places more emphasis on a Japanese spy organization in the United States than it does on the (non-"mad") plastic surgery used to make the spies appear less Asian. And overall, these three to four mad scientist films bear greater similarity to some of Lugosi's non-Monogram movies—such as *The Devil Bat* (1940), made at PRC and featuring both a notable actor (Dave O'Brien) and canned library music that would return in his Monogram films—than they do to other entries in the "nine."

That includes *Invisible Ghost* (1941). More than any other entry in the Monogram Nine, it is a film that desperately needs to be wrested from that category. It was the first of the nine films, and as a result it was not affected in any way by its successors. It does not bear narrative similarities to any other Lugosi film, let alone others in the nine; the same could be said of the character that Lugosi portrays. And it was the only film in the Monogram Nine—or indeed, the whole of Lugosi's filmography—to be directed by Joseph H. Lewis.

Much as we might now attempt to remove *Invisible Ghost* from the Monogram Nine (and by extension, from Lugosi's filmography, to the extent the film might be seen as a "Joseph H. Lewis film" rather than—or certainly in addition to—being seen as a "Bela Lugosi film"), Joseph H. Lewis had to contend with the same dilemma in directing the film. How does a young director in the early stages of his career—a director hoping to create a unique film in order to further his career, but one that still remains safely within the remit of what a B movie needed to be so that he could also continue to find work—contend with the weight and breadth of Lugosi's experience as an actor, as well as the sheer power of his image, which was so consolidated by 1941?

The answer to that question came in part thanks to *Invisible Ghost*'s script, written by Al and Helen Martin, and the character Lugosi would portray, Mr. Charles Kessler. A few previous filmmakers had grappled with Lugosi's image by casting him in roles that would defy audience expectations, at least to a degree. Edgar G. Ulmer's *The Black Cat* (1934) featured Lugosi as Dr. Vitus Werdegast, a man who takes revenge on Boris Karloff's villainous Dr. Hjalmar Poelzig by literally skinning him alive but who is at the same time the film's nominal hero. More surprising still was Sol Lesser's tactic of casting Lugosi as the heroic Chandu the Magician in the twelve-part serial *The Return of Chandu* (1934). In it, Lugosi was a hero without the baggage carried by Vitus Werdegast. Lesser's decision was even more fascinating when considering that Lugosi earlier had starred as the villain Roxor in the feature film *Chandu the Magician* (1932).

But *Invisible Ghost* offered Lugosi a more complex character than either *The Black Cat* or *Return of Chandu*. Charles Kessler would not be a hero, which was a rather simple inversion of Lugosi's villainous persona. Plagued by his wife's infidelity as well as her disappearance from his life, Kessler is nearly driven to tears at her memory; he has also developed the annual habit of celebrating their wedding anniversary with a dinner for two, pretending that she is with him even while her seat sits empty. His problems are amplified by the occasional appearance of his wife (Betty Compson) at the window of his home, an event that sends him into a trance. Kessler is neither a hero nor a villain but a cuckolded husband who unknowingly, unwittingly becomes a murderer. He is a victim of tragic proportions.

But at times, Kessler becomes something more complicated still. In two scenes, Lewis has Lugosi subtly parody his association with the horror genre. After his visit to the morgue and discovery that Jules the gardener (Ernie Adams) is not actually dead, Kessler tells his daughter, "It was ghastly." Later, after Kessler discovers the portrait of his wife has been ripped, he announces it was "unquestionably the work of a madman." Both moments represent rich dark humor informed not only by the audience's awareness that Kessler is actually the murderer (something which Kessler does not yet know) but also by the fact that the noted horror film star Bela Lugosi is reciting such unlikely dialogue.

To be sure, parodies of horror films and actors associated with them had a history in America that dated to the 1920s. *The Hollywood Revue of 1929* featured the humorous song "Lon Chaney's Gonna Get You If You Don't Watch Out," for example, and the cartoon *King Klunk* (1933) provided a comic takeoff of *King Kong* (1933). Bela Lugosi had certainly participated in such parodies, time and again. In the short subject *Intimate Interviews* (1932), he played a rather staged version of himself, "scaring" interviewer Dorothy West at the end of their brief encounter. The following year, he played a wax figure of "Bela Lugosi as Dracula" come to life in a 1933 *Hollywood on Parade* short subject in which he bites an actress portraying Betty Boop ("You have booped your last boop"); the following year, he played a comical game of chess with Boris Karloff in a 1934 short subject that parodied a scene from *The Black Cat*. Those were in addition to his acting in such feature-length horror comedies as *The Gorilla* (1939) and *You'll Find Out* (1940).

However, Lewis achieved something different in *Invisible Ghost*, even more so than what the Broadway play (1941) and film version of *Arsenic and Old Lace* (1944) would do with Boris Karloff's image. This is true specifically because neither the overall film nor the overall character of Charles Kessler is a parody of either the horror film or of Bela Lugosi. Rather Lewis inserts two brief moments that offer a sophisticated intermingling of postmodernist humor within a film that otherwise proceeds as an insular and generally serious plotline. Such an approach was largely unique, and it would remain so until later films such as Peter Bogdanovich's *Targets* (1968), Douglas Hickox's *Theatre of Blood* (1973), and—by substituting genre conventions for star identification—Wes Craven's *Scream* (1996).

Directing *Invisible Ghost* (1941), Lewis had to grapple with and overcome Bela Lugosi's image and the expectations of a typical Lugosi horror film.

Controlling the Space

Connected to the question of how to contend with Bela Lugosi was the issue of aesthetic design. For Lewis, that meant determining what kind of visual landscape he could create within the confines of his low budget and—as he underscored in my interview with him—his limited production time. His decision became an effort to impose control over the story line, the other actors, and the set just as he had attempted to do with Lugosi. This meant an emphasis on carefully planned scenes that are shot in such a way as to maximize their effect in editing, as well as an emphasis on moving camera that allows Lewis not only to control the space but to comment thematically on characters who exist within it.

To be sure, *Invisible Ghost* includes some limitations in its visual design of the sort we might expect in a B movie of the 1940s. For example, full-screen newspaper headlines quickly and cheaply convey important narrative information, ranging from the fact that Ralph Dickson (John McGuire) will be put on trial for the murder of Cecile Mannix (Terry Walker) to the announcements of Dickson's conviction and pending execution. The courtroom itself is tiny, with the judge surrounded by darkness, thus preventing the need for a fully dressed set. And when Kessler and his daughter, Virginia (Polly Ann Young), visit the governor to plea for a stay of execution, we do not see the governor's face, thus eliminating the need for anything more than an extra's shoulders.

That is all in addition to an expected use of postproduction effects. To expedite the movement of the story, for example, wipe transitions separate the courtroom testimony of Mr. Kessler, Ralph's onetime landlady (actress unknown), Jules (Ernie Adams), and Evans (Clarence Muse) while Virginia and Ralph observe, allowing Lewis to show them all in a rapid succession of close-ups and medium shots. Similarly, wipes also help expedite the movement of characters; the gardener Jules steals food in the kitchen for Mrs. Kessler, then a wipe transports him outside of the Kessler home. In this instance, the wipe not only condenses narrative time but also conceals what otherwise would have been an awkward edit, one that would not have respected the thirty-degree rule.

Despite the budgetary and time limitations he faced, however, Lewis succeeds in providing an array of more sophisticated images that would not generally be associated with B movies of the period. For example, on a trio of occasions, Kessler is pictured in his home with flames of a fireplace crackling in the foreground, a shot often seen in A-budget Hollywood films of the period but illustrating a kind of added attention that would not mark the average Monogram film. Consider also the shot in which the camera focuses on a Holy Bible as Kessler recites Psalm 23:6, the camera then tilts up to Virginia, then moves back to show an over the shoulder of Kessler just before the phone rings. "Yes? [pause] I see," Kessler says before hanging up the phone and telling Virginia, "It's all over." Here Lewis transforms the budgetary need to limit camera setups into a well-timed and carefully executed single shot that contains the whole of the Kesslers' reaction to Ralph's execution.

More strikingly, when suspicion for the murders falls on Evans, Lewis illustrates his skill at shooting with a specific eye toward editing, which by extension allows him to maintain some control over the postproduction process. We see a close-up of Evans, then the camera tilts upward to show a close-up of Mr. Kessler. The film then cuts to a close-up of Paul Dickson (John McGuire) and then tilts down to a close-up of the psychiatrist (Lloyd Ingraham). The result offers an uncomfortable series of close-ups, one after the other, edited only with straight cuts, resulting in a sequence that is somewhat outside the norms of the classical Hollywood style. In terms of its aesthetic design and thematic purpose, it reminds one very much of a similar sequence in Huston's *The Maltese Falcon* (1941) in which Wilmer (Elisha Cook Jr.) regains consciousness to see that the others in the room have decided he will be the fall guy for the film's murders. But here Lewis has bested Huston, at least in terms of chronology, as his film was released nearly six months before *The Maltese Falcon*.

However, nowhere does Lewis show his ability to shoot a scene with plans toward editing and pacing (and, in this case, the use of postproduction sound) more successfully than when Kessler murders Cecile. In a trancelike state, he approaches her bedroom door in Shot A, the camera panning from screen left to right as he opens it. We hear dance music, though do not yet understand its origin or purpose. As he enters the room in the same shot, Cecile—who is lying in bed under a blanket—speaks his name with surprise. After he shuts the door, Shot B shows Kessler approaching Cecile's bed; he immediately takes off his robe. The setup, shot with the camera adjacent to her bed, has every indication of a sexual crime in the making.

Then a match-on-action cut to Shot C shows Kessler holding his robe with both hands. Lugosi's eyes stare directly into the camera lens, violating the classical Hollywood taboo against doing so. Given the rarity of such an image, we are immediately led to remember a similar image in *Dracula* in which Lugosi stares directly into the camera lens at no one in particular, and—since Lewis has placed his camera in the approximate position of Cecile—we might even more clearly consider *White Zombie*, which includes shots of Lugosi staring into the camera lens with his gaze directly connected to victims like Beaumont (Robert Frazer). But here Lewis will go beyond both films, which had used such a gaze into the camera to suggest the characters' hypnotic power over others. *Invisible Ghost*, by contrast, has him leering lustily at the audience, who have been forced into Cecile's point of view. Rather than hypnosis or mesmerism, Kessler appears to have very physical plans.

Shot D briefly is a medium shot of a frightened Cecile grasping at her blanket, while Shot E offers a close-up of a radio. Only now do we understand that the dance music we have heard since Shot A is diegetic. Then Shot F, a medium close-up, returns us to Lugosi's eyes as he stares into the camera with a devilish grin on his face. More than any prior shot, his hands are holding the robe in such a way as to suggest a pending strangulation or smothering. After Kessler walks closer to the camera, Lewis cuts to Shot G, which again shows Cecile cowering in her bed. Shot H then repeats Shot E, but only for the space of one second, as the increasing tempo of editing tries to suggest Kessler's increasing proximity to Cecile and her increasing fear. Shot I then shows Kessler's staring face in a close-up, and Shot J shows Cecile one last time; each shot is approximately one second long. Then Shot K returns us to Kessler's staring face in what has become an extreme close-up, which itself recalls extreme close-ups of Lugosi in *White Zombie*. He now raises the robe in such a way that the screen goes black. We hear Cecile scream, then Kessler lowers the robe slightly to reveal only part of his face. A quiet groan from Cecile suggests she is still alive, causing Kessler to raise the robe once more, covering the camera (and Cecile's) view of Kessler and ending the scene (and Cecile's life); the blackness of the robe has removed the need for an optically printed fade to black.

While it is important to focus on significant scenes or images in *Invisible Ghost*, we must also recognize that the film is more than just a Poverty Row horror film punctuated by occasional moments of visual sophistication and power. Specifically, we should consider Lewis's ongoing reliance on moving camera throughout the film. Here he controls the space by synthesizing it, much as Kubrick will later do with the Overlook Hotel in *The Shining* (1980). At times this heightens the fact that we the viewers are—at least for the bulk of the film—trapped inside the Kessler home along with the characters. The camera moves behind the Kessler dinner table early in the film; it moves when Cecile enters the kitchen to speak to Evans; and it tracks behind Kessler when Virginia tells him she loves Ralph. The camera then follows Evans as he approaches Cecile's bedroom, it tracks behind Police Lieutenant Williams (George Pembroke) as he investigates Cecile's murder, and it moves through a candelabra to follow Virginia as she goes to bed. In short, the camera follows all of the key characters in the film, imbuing it with the occasional look of a higher budget film, while also simultaneously (and ironically) exploring the movements of persons who cannot escape the Kessler home.

In larger terms, the moving camera also reinforces the fact that Lewis alone controls the space. It is he who allows or does not allow visual access, as his cinematography can choose to reveal or conceal, depending on the scene. For example, at times his camera—by way of passing in front of the set—appears to penetrate through walls as it moves from room to room without need of a door or other passageway. By contrast, while Lewis uses moving camera to show Evans approach Cecile's bedroom the morning after her murder, he does not allow the camera to move inside her room; we are only allowed to see her dead body from the hallway, pictured at a distance as framed through her bedroom door.

His moving camera can also proceed slowly. After stylishly showing and simultaneously not showing Jules's apparent murder by letting it play out as shadows on the wall, Lewis forces us to observe Jules's dead body (or what we presume to be dead, as he later reawakens in the morgue) with a close and lingering scrutiny, building up the event with a very slow camera move downward from a table to the floor. Lewis then reveals Jules's body in a carefully planned and executed move, rather than a cut or even a tripod-bound tilt. Here again we see Lewis working against a tight schedule to include a shot that was unnecessary to complete the shoot, but wholly necessary to his planned regimen of moving camera.

Lewis's moving camera also reveals important narrative and thematic information as well, such as when it accentuates the curious link between Mr. Kessler and Mrs. Kessler. Her reappearances provoke his murderous trances, and at the climax of the film, Kessler's awareness of that fact seems to cause Mrs. Kessler's death. The two are psychically linked in a manner that is reminiscent of Svengali and Trilby in Mayo's *Svengali* (1931) and of Legendre and Madeline in *White Zombie*, a film that, as previously noted, had starred Bela Lugosi. Visually we understand the Kesslers' bond from the very first shot in *Invisible Ghost* when the camera shows a painting of Mrs. Kessler in the entrance hallway of their home before moving backward and to screen right to reveal Mr. Kessler descending the stairs and then approaching the painting.

At the end of the film, that opening shot is repeated but reversed, as if it is a mirror opposite. It begins by showing Kessler (and his police escorts) descending the stairs. The camera pans to screen left to follow Kessler to the painting. Lewis cuts to a close-up, the edit allowing us to see Kessler by himself, apart from the police. He looks up at the painting and speaks to it as if it really is Mrs. Kessler. The camera then tilts upward to reveal her likeness. Lewis shows her portrait in a close-up that echoes how he has just pictured Kessler. Even after her death, the two remain linked, as Kessler's closing dialogue suggests.

In addition to connecting the Kesslers by use of camera movement, Lewis also visually emphasizes their shared mental problems. For example, in the film's first scene, he shows Kessler seated at a table as reflected in a mirror, after which—thanks to a camera pan—we again see the painting of Mrs. Kessler hanging in the hallway. And then there is our introduction to Mrs. Kessler, during which she recounts her traumatic car crash to Jules; when she finishes her story, the camera pans to a nearby mirror to show her bemoaning the fact that she cannot go home. But nowhere are their problematic mental states more clear than when they appear in the frame together. On four occasions, Kessler and his wife examine each other through window glass just as if they are looking into mirrors, the result of which triggers his murderous trances.

Kessler's visual transformations from kind businessman to unwitting murderer are very much worthy of notice. He undergoes the transition five times, the first four of which rely on the camera lens racking out and then back into focus. During that time, Lugosi changes his expression into an intent but controlled rage. The first two transformations also feature a shift in lighting from high-key to low-key that coincides with the shift in focus. Here we see the reliance on a camera trick to create a character's on-screen transformation into a monster. Mamoulian's *Dr. Jekyll and Mr. Hyde* (1932) had previously done the same in an arguably most sophisticated manner; certainly it also employed the use of makeup as well as a shift in the actor's expression. However, the camera-based transformation was generally rare in usage until Waggner's *The Wolf Man* (1941) and subsequent appearances of the same character throughout the 1940s. Once again, Lewis was somewhat ahead of the game, as *Invisible Ghost* appeared in theaters nearly seven months before *The Wolf Man*.

Moving from the Past to the Future

In constructing *Invisible Ghost*, Lewis directed a film that in many ways was ahead of its time. The use of the camera to visualize Kessler's transformation is but one example, and it may well be the least interesting. While in some respects *Invisible Ghost* is in a dialogue with the horror film's past, Lewis uses its tone, setting, and characters to infuse the horror film genre with what years or even decades later would become new codes and conventions.

For instance, the aforementioned use of humor surrounding Lugosi's identification with the horror genre is not the only way in which Lewis brings a comic sensibility to the film. At times, he draws on the same kind of comic relief that pervaded the horror film of the 1920s and 1930s—that is to say, brief comedic interludes to relieve the horror inspired by other scenes. Immediately we might think of Martin (Charles Gerrard) in *Dracula*, for example, or Albert Conti and Henry Armetta as the police sergeants in *The Black Cat*. Within *Invisible Ghost*, that means some unfortunate and decidedly unfunny dialogue given to African American actor Clarence Muse, whose character Evans asks Jules if he "look[s] pale" after the arrival of Ralph's brother, Paul. It also means Detective Ryan (Fred Kelsey) cornering Evans and demanding to know where he was on the night of January 13, a date that has no meaning to the story; rather than answer, Evans offers him coffee, which Ryan gladly accepts. Their interplay is little more than the reworking of a similar joke from *The Laurel-Hardy Murder Case* (1930), which featured Fred Kelsey as a detective interrogating Stan Laurel.

Rather than depend solely on comic relief as used in previous horror films, Lewis also includes moments of some rather sophisticated dark comedy. Certainly James Whale had previously explored dark comedy within the horror genre, particularly in such films as *The Invisible Man* (1933) and *Bride of Frankenstein* (1935). Lewis does the same with the unexpected reawakening of Jules's "lifeless" body at the morgue, which prompts his wife to shout, "Get him out of here! He isn't dead!" The dialogue is rife with comedy embedded in an otherwise horrific moment of the type that one can imagine having appeared in Whale, screamed perhaps by Una O'Connor, or appearing decades later in the cinema of Sam Raimi.

But Lewis also offers an even darker form of comedy with the discovery of Cecile's corpse. Evans tries to rouse Cecile by knocking on her door while her radio plays inside, as it apparently has been all night long. Rather than dance music, it is an exercise program. The announcer's voice prepares his listeners with instructions, and then has them begin exercising; he is relentless in his rhythm of "One-Two-Three-Four, One-Two-Three-Four." Evans opens the door to find Cecile lying stiffly in her bed; he touches her and realizes that she is dead. The oblivious radio announcer continues, his directions to the exercising listeners providing a marked contrast to Cecile's lifeless body. Here the black comedy is arguably more unsettling and more subtle than anything ever constructed by Whale. Indeed, it seems decidedly out of place in 1941, smacking more of the hotel bathroom scene in Jean-Luc Godard's *Alphaville, une étrange aventure de Lemmy Caution* (1965) and the "Singin' in the Rain" rape sequence in Stanley Kubrick's *A Clockwork Orange* (1971), both of which would also play sound against onscreen action to achieve uncomfortably dark humor.

As Cecile's murder suggests, *Invisible Ghost* presents a house under siege, the killer's identity unknown to the other characters who are trapped within its four walls. Certainly that places the film into the "old dark house" tradition, bringing to mind such films as Leni's *The Cat and the Canary* (1927) and Whale's *The Old Dark House* (1932). *Invisible Ghost* even includes the requisite stormy night and shots of a lightning bolt striking in the night sky.

And yet *Invisible Ghost* appropriates those few elements from the old dark house films and transforms them into something different. After all, the murders at the Kessler home take place over a much longer period of time than those in a typical old dark house film. Early in the narrative, Cecile inquires about the murders and notes that there had been "a lot of them." An undetermined number of deaths over an unknown period of time, all of which occur before the film's running time has started; the murders we do witness proceed to take place over a series of many days, if not longer. In other words, it is not as if the characters are forced to stay in the Kessler home for only one single night due to the reading of a will (*The Cat and the Canary*) or a terrible storm (*The Old Dark House*).

Instead, characters are trapped in the Kessler home without an end in sight, either due to family obligation (Virginia) or to employment (Evans, Jules, Cecile, and Marie). We learn that a court has tried to shut the house down, but that Mr. Kessler, who "carries a lot of weight around here," has not allowed it to do so. "Sentimental reasons" and the hope of his wife's return anchor him to the property. With few exceptions—such as Ralph's trial and execution, the Kesslers' visit to the governor, and Jules's recovery at the morgue—the majority of the film's running time traps the audience at the Kessler home as well.

Here again *Invisible Ghost* seems to point the way to the future as much as it does to the past. Horror film landscapes of the future—sleep-away camps, small towns under threat, and houses without bad storms or washed-out bridges—will smack of the Kessler home in that the pending victims can easily leave; they just choose not to do so, even as murders occur. And—much like the horror films of the 1970s and 1980s—Lewis places emphasis on the depiction of those murders, as well as on the discoveries of the victims' bodies. That means taking great pains to stage each one of them differently.

Not only are the characters trapped in their geography, two of them—Mr. and Mrs. Kessler—are trapped by the past, though it is a past that Lewis largely conceals from us. We understand that she has cheated on him and that she was in a bad car crash, but we hear no concrete information. Locked somewhere in the recesses of Mr. Kessler's mind, and in the shadows within the Kessler home, are hidden details about the affair and Mr. Kessler's reaction to it. However, Lewis gives us only a negative narrative space of the sort that Val Lewton will employ in such films as *The Seventh Victim* (1943) and that film noir will exploit in the postwar period. The result means the audience must supply the film's most lurid, debased content on its own.

And then there is the lovely young couple. As in so many horror films of the 1930s, ranging from Browning's *Dracula* and Halperin's *White Zombie* to Ulmer's *The Black Cat* and Landers's *The Raven* (1935), we have a young hero and heroine that are thrown into a dangerous and horrifying situation. Certainly Virginia Kessler seems innocent, but—in marked contrast to prior films in the horror genre—that is hardly the case with Ralph Dickson. Even when we first meet Ralph, he is easy to dislike. Because it is her father's wedding anniversary, Virginia intentionally asks Ralph not to come by the Kessler home, but he ignores her wishes. Admitting him into the home, Virginia admonishes him and invites him into a sitting room, but

Ralph again ignores her wishes, lingering at the dining room door to spy on Mr. Kessler speaking to a wife who isn't there.

But being rude and insensitive is not Ralph's major crime. Instead, it is that he represents a breed of young horror film victims that would proliferate in the splatter film era of the 1970s and 1980s. What we learn soon after his arrival at the Kessler home is that he and Cecile know each other. Later, when Ralph begins to walk home, Cecile confronts him, threatening him that Virginia will have to learn "sooner or later" about their prior relationship. Though he implores her to remember that he "never said he loved [her]," Cecile argues that she would make Ralph a good wife. Later in the film, Ralph recounts their sexual liaison in coded language: "I knew Cecile a couple of years. She offered me the companionship I needed." Later, Ralph's onetime landlady underscores the sexual side of their relationship by noting to the court that she "thought they were married." The court's verdict seals Ralph's fate: he will die in the electric chair.

Invisible Ghost cannot allow the standard horror film plotline of the 1930s and 1940s to proceed. Of course the governor cannot prevent Ralph's execution, because Virginia cannot reunite with Ralph, as, say, Mina and Harker do at the conclusion of *Dracula*. Officially, Ralph is put to death for a murder that Kessler committed, but that is incidental rather than central. Ralph dies for the same reason that Cecile dies: their sexual promiscuity dictates it. After all, the same is true for Mrs. Kessler; the fact that she has had an affair with another man leads to her eventual demise. It is in their deaths that *Invisible Ghost* most clearly points the way to the future of horror films, to the 1970s and 1980s when premarital sex or adultery leads to punishment meted out by torture and then death.

Conclusion

During his investigation, Police Lieutenant Williams quite rightly refers to the Kessler home as a "house where anything can happen and usually does." Lewis's emphasis on the speed at which he made films like *Invisible Ghost* was also a well-founded observation, as *Invisible Ghost* is hardly perfect. For example, a careful viewer cannot help but notice that when Detective Ryan's stiff body falls forward, actor Fred Kelsey's open eyes shut midway to the floor. The moment hardly inspires the seriousness or the shock that Lewis intended.

Nor does *Invisible Ghost* overall show the maturity and consistency of vision of later Lewis films such as *Gun Crazy* (1950), *The Big Combo* (1955), or *Terror in a Texas Town* (1958). It would in fact be easy to argue that it suffers by comparison to such Lewis films as *My Name Is Julia Ross* (1945) and *So Dark the Night* (1946). And yet such comparisons are finally unproductive; *Invisible Ghost* can and should stand on its own merits.

The May 1, 1941, issue of the *Hollywood Spectator* was indeed lacking judgment in its observations about *Citizen Kane*, as the passage of time has shown. But—even if its review of *Invisible Ghost* represents a much lesser affront to our sensibilities—the *Spectator* review of it bears revision as well. Much the same might now be said of Sarris and Meisel, both of whom offered more nuanced views of Lewis than the *Spectator*, but both of whom remained overly skeptical of his early films. Investigating *Invisible Ghost* in 2012 reveals a unique film worthy of being removed from simplistic categories of Lewis's "ephemeral" work, as well as from the so-called Lugosi Monogram Nine. After all, Lewis had grappled successfully with Bela Lugosi's image and the expectations of the typical Lugosi horror films, including those he made at Monogram. While we should of course remain open to many interpretations of *Invisible Ghost*, if a definite article must be forced in front of its title, it should be in singular recognition that (*The*) *Invisible Ghost* is one of Lewis's important achievements, as at its best it possesses a sophisticated visual style and a prescient artistic vision that deserves ongoing inquiry, even more so than Lewis himself believed.

Notes

1. W.B., "Comments on Current Pictures: *Citizen Kane*," *Hollywood Spectator*, May 1, 1941, 6–7.

2. "Comments on Current Pictures: *The* [sic] *Invisible Ghost*," *Hollywood Spectator*, May 1, 1941, 14.

3. Andrew Sarris, *The American Cinema: Directors and Directions, 1929–1968* (New York: Dutton, 1968), 78.

4. Ibid., 133.

5. Ibid.

6. Ibid.

7. Myron Meisel, "Joseph H. Lewis: Tourist in the Asylum," in *Kings of the Bs: Working within the Hollywood System*, ed. Todd McCarthy and Charles Flynn (New York: Dutton, 1975), 81–103.

8. For more information on the British ban, see Tom Johnson, *Censored Screams: The British Ban on Hollywood Horror in the Thirties* (Jefferson, NC: McFarland, 1997).

9. For more information on the life and career of Bela Lugosi, see Gary D. Rhodes, *Lugosi* (Jefferson, NC: McFarland, 1997); Gary D. Rhodes, *Bela Lugosi: Dreams and Nightmares* (Narberth, PA: Collectables, 2007).

10. For more information on the Monogram Nine and other low-budget horror movies of the 1940s, see Tom Weaver, *Poverty Row Horrors! Monogram,*

PRC, and Republic Horror Movies of the Forties (Jefferson, NC: McFarland, 1993).

11. For example, actor Vince Barnett appeared in *The Corpse Vanishes* (1942) and *Bowery at Midnight* (1942); John Carradine appeared in *Voodoo Man* (1944) and *Return of the Ape Man* (1944); Louise Currie appeared in *The Ape Man* (1943) and *Voodoo Man*; J. Farrell MacDonald appeared in *Bowery at Midnight* and *The Ape Man*; Wanda McCay appeared in *Bowery at Midnight* and *Voodoo Man*; Wheeler Oakman appeared in *Bowery at Midnight, The Ape Man,* and *Ghosts on the Loose* (1943); Dave O'Brien appeared in *Spooks Run Wild* (1941) and *Bowery at Midnight*; George Pembroke appeared in *Invisible Ghost* and *Black Dragons* (1942); Angelo Rossitto appeared in *Spooks Run Wild* and *The Corpse Vanishes*; Minerva Urecal appeared in *The Corpse Vanishes* and *The Ape Man*; and Terry Walker appeared in *Invisible Ghost* and *Voodoo Man*.

In addition, William Beaudine directed *The Ape Man, Ghosts on the Loose,* and *Voodoo Man*; Wallace Fox directed *The Corpse Vanishes* and *Bowery at Midnight*; and Phil Rosen directed *Spooks Run Wild* and *Return of the Ape Man*. Gerald Schnitzer contributed to the story for *The Corpse Vanishes* and the screenplay for *Bowery at Midnight*; Marcel Le Picard shot *Invisible Ghost* (along with Harvey Gould), *Spooks Run Wild, Voodoo Man,* and *Return of the Ape Man*; and Carl Pierson edited *Bowery at Midnight, The Ape Man, Ghosts on the Loose, Voodoo Man,* and *Return of the Ape Man*.

LANCE DUERFAHRD

B Is for Belief

*Joseph Lewis's Experiments with
the* Mad Doctor of Market Street

The phone book of cinema has numerous entries under mad doctor. The listings include some of the most eminent names in film history: Caligari, Frankenstein, Mabuse, Rotwang, and lesser luminaries such as Phibes, Moreau, Soberin, not to mention their numerous "assistants." Our affinity for the figure of malpractice can be explained by the way he overcomes divisions in the film production process: he combines the activities of director (materializing his visions), editor (stitching new life from old scraps), actor, and spectator.[1] Embodying projector, screen, and even advertisement (the tireless promotion of his mad projects bridging the gap between prophesy and tagline), the mad doctor anthropomorphizes the cinematic apparatus.[2] Above all, the mad doctor is a generator for the hypnotic authority that singularly characterizes the film medium. Observing how fascination in the movie theater prepares spectators for actual political subjection, Siegfried Kracauer draws a line from Dr. Caligari to Hitler and places the doctor figure within what he calls the "procession of tyrants." Like the mad doctor, cinema seems less interested in the cure of the spectator than in stimulating the addiction to shock, maintaining that precious illness called cinephilia, and guaranteeing a return. Cinema owes its most spectacular moments to the destruction of the Hippocratic oath.

More than a set, the mad doctor's laboratory is the site of a movie's production. Here experiments *in the film* become experiments *in film*. These two experiments convene in the special effect in which our awe overlaps that of the spectators within the fiction. The last outpost of the miracle in our jaded era, the special effect compels belief, immersing us in the false immediacy of the spectacle. In the context under discussion here, we can call these special effects by their medical name, *placebo effects*, which refers to the way patients respond positively to medications that are in fact pharmacologically inert (dummy pills, for example).[3] Our belief in the film helps incarnate its effects. The way in which we speak of being moved, touched, or violated by film (a medium that nevertheless requires distance from the spectator in order to work) testifies how even casual discourse about cinema bears the mark of film's placebo effect. *Placebo* comes from the Latin meaning "I will please" (as opposed to "I will cure"). In this way it resembles the promise uttered by every film, the reality of which is animated by our conviction.

From Caligari to Benson

What happens when the grandeur of the mad doctor collides with the shoestring budget of the B film? How are we to understand the coupling of the fabulous claim to immediacy of the one with the awkward theatricality of the other? Clearly the B film makes its declaration to please (its placebo) differently, and at times so inaudibly, compared to its A counterpart. Since its artifice is always intruding on the proceedings, the B film tests (rather than depends on) our capacity to believe. Lewis's *The Mad Doctor of Market Street* (1942; hereafter *Mad Doctor*) interrupts our fascination with the mad doctor. Lewis's strategy isn't, however, to make just a more inexpensive version of the august madmen that preceded his. We can find a parable for this in Lewis's decision to use the set of Verona Square, built in 1936 for MGM's *Romeo and Juliet*, for the bordertown in *Lady without Passport* (1950).[4] Lewis turns to Shakespeare not to redo Shakespeare but to find Tijuana. Similarly, *Mad Doctor* turns to the legacy of movie medicine to supply us not with a mad doctor of reduced effect (a weaker placebo) but with one of questionable effect. Lewis inserts a quack into Kracauer's "procession of tyrants." The pleasure offered by *Mad Doctor* emerges not through our conviction that what we see "is really happening" but in a more circumambient exploration of the gap between what its images are saying and what they are doing.

We need to start with a synopsis of the film because it is clear that not many people have *seen* this film. In the critical literature on Lewis, *Mad Doctor* takes a very distant seat to the masterpieces *Gun Crazy* (1950) and *The Big Combo* (1955) and to the celebrated smaller noirs *My Name Is Julia Ross* (1945) and *So Dark the Night* (1946). The mention it does receive is negative and pithy: "a low voltage horror," "beyond salvage," "subjuvenile dialogue." A synopsis interestingly reveals how its plot seems to advance as if in quest for an audience who will find Benson credible: from a liner packed with gossiping socialites who believe everything whispered to them (and then repeat it, even to Benson), to a lonely island populated with B film primitives who superstitiously see Benson's work as magic, naming him god of life.

Lionel Atwill plays Dr. Ralph Benson in the title role. He explains to his first test subject how he keeps his patients in suspended animation until all traces of disease have been removed. He revives them, newly immortal. Something goes awry in the experiment, and Benson flees as the police break down the door. A disguised Benson is next seen on a cruise ship, his whereabouts providing rich gossip material for the socialites (Una Merkel, Claire Dodd) on board. After the ship sinks, Benson and a few other passengers arrive in a lifeboat on a small island. They are about to be put to death by the natives when Benson claims he can reanimate the recently deceased princess Taneo using his equipment saved from the wreckage. Benson revives her and, dubbed "god of life," grows increasingly tyrannical. Fearing for their lives as his test subjects, the other castaways seek to debunk Benson by presenting him with the corpse of Barab, one of the villagers. The chief gives Benson one night to bring Barab back to life. Benson can't, and the villagers throw him into a fire. A passing plane sees the smoke and picks up the remaining castaways.

The Forlorn Sign of the B Picture

The key to understanding a B film is not its plot but its feel. To grasp how Lewis proposes a different type of credibility and authority for his mad doctor (and consequently for his film), it helps to remark its aesthetic environment. The doctor's laboratory is traditionally the place where the horrifics convincingly unfold before our eyes. Yet in *Mad Doctor* the lab is in recession: everything is scaled back, truncated, the details grayed out by dim lighting (without acquiring, however, the ominous mood of a film noir). One of the curious aspects of Benson's laboratory is the absence of *work* happening there. The test tubes are placed high atop the cabinet out of consideration for their value as shadows rather than for their useful availability. There are no experiments either completed, botched, or in progress. Lewis confines Atwill's doctorliness to a few gestures, an attitude, a lab coat, and one menacing close-up. Talking to Saunders, Benson says, "My findings will not be accepted in the medical world until they have first been demonstrated on . . . [track camera in] a human being." But where are these "findings"? In similar films, the condition of the caged animals would bear the entire superstructure of Benson's evil: they would incarnate the demonstration for us. But these animals seem strangely unaffected by the doctor, who playfully puts his index finger through the grillwork of the cages as he talks. Their pathos derives not from being the doctor's victims but from the way they seem on display, as in a pet shop, and as such seem exposed to an uncertain fate. This uncertain fate owes itself less to the despotic authority of the mad doctor than to the exposure to mortality that comes from not knowing where they will find a home.[5] The animals seem part of a kennel rather than a lab. These animals mirror the spectator's own state of underinfluence by the doctor, the spectator detained (rather than fascinated, subjected) by the authority of the film.[6]

This *forlorn* status of the animals makes them emblematic of the B film aesthetic. One of the great informal definitions of a B movie is a film in which the sets shake when an actor slams the door.[7] This definition, beyond the question of decor, suggests a film system that does not securely establish its signifiers. The loose arrangement of the B film allows its components to independently and unintentionally resonate. The "nonpsychological style" that critics attribute to Lewis seems rooted in this way in which objects resonate on screen but not with the spectator.[8] Let's think about something that literally shakes (a doorbell) when Sanders enters the doctor's lab after he has decided to submit himself to Benson's experiments. Sanders fixates on the bell ringing above the door: his whole body freezes, he cannot step through, and the film seems to freeze up too. Pregnant for the on-screen character, this pause feels somewhat vacant to the spectator, who has no way to grasp what Sanders sees or hears in this ringing. Does Sanders see the bell tolling his death (an omen) or simply his presence, his literal entry into the lab (thereby awakening him to the nature of his choice)? To restate this in Pavlovian terms, the audience has not been sufficiently conditioned by the film so as to grasp the fictional significance of this bell. Instead of salivating, we are left questioning. This breaches one of the fundamental codes of the "mad doctor film": the audience is estranged from the character's surprise. Paradoxically, his fear scatters, rather than coalesces, our attention.

Myron Meisel writes that *Mad Doctor* is "hardly terrifying, but on any other level than the dramatic, it is a desultory marvel."[9] Rather than following a line, the film aimlessly drifts through a series of incomprehensible leaps and repressed enigmas, such that any synopsis of the film must be punctuated by question marks placed within parentheses. For example: following his close escape from the police, Benson is shown in tuxedo on a cruise ship(?). We see him seated at a table alone, in full view(?). The detective on board stands facing Benson but seems to take no interest, possibly because he is distracted by all the movement on the dance floor between them(?). The detective leaves the dance hall with the captain, who asks, "Do you think he's still on board?" To which the detective replies, "He must have dyed his hair or shaved his beard. He might be a little difficult to identify but we have over a week before we get to New Zealand, so that gives us time to identify him. You see, an ordinary killer is easy to catch, but this fellow Benson is clever. Very clever." We scratch our heads at this official praise of Benson's cleverness: not only has the detective accurately predicted that Benson has shaved his beard, but this doesn't really alter Benson's identity. A fine line exists in this film between an incognito and an identity. Close-ups of Benson's face are strangely incriminating not to Benson but to us, the audience, as if we could be doing more to assist the detective's destitute powers of perception. "Desultory" literally describes the turtle pace of the thinking, a mental torpor matching the dim sets: the investigation literally takes the leisurely cruise as its time frame ("We have over a week before we get to New Zealand"). In pursuit of a suspect who has barely disguised himself and who seeks asylum in the closed system of the cruise ship, the detectives endow their work with all the urgency of a vacation.

Benson, or the Wind in the Trees

After the credit sequence in which we see the film's title, the film begins with a sign that says Market Street. Squarely transposing half of its title into its fictional world, the film precipitates a rush of questions: Where is the other half, the "mad doctor"? Will his madness be as clearly inscribed within the image as the street sign to which he is linked?[10] Instead of satisfactorily answering these questions, the film promotes our internal quest for a certifiable incarnation of the madman, who will exist more in our guesswork than on the screen we are watching. The phrase *mad doctor* is uttered by the police dispatcher sending out an alert for his arrest. The very mode in which the phrase is announced lets us hear how the title is applied with force. But does the title stick? Will this movie live up to its own title?

On screen Benson is spectralized by his ambition. A thoroughly bombastic figure, he recalls what D. W. Griffith claims to be missing in modern film: the wind in the trees.[11] His capacity to project gives him a strangely liminal presence, as if he were trying to envision himself out of his modest film surroundings. "How long will you want me that way [in suspended animation]?" asks Benson's concerned patient. "Oh," replies the doctor nonchalantly, "Only so long as to substantiate my theories." The world will wait for Benson's theories, for that elusive instant in which they decide to appear. Speaking of himself as a supercancellation, Benson declares, "Some day because of me there will be no death." This claim outbids those of Greek myth in which not a single hubris-riddled figure claims to conquer death permanently. Exceeding the traditional mad doctor ambition for his own immortality, Benson wants immortality for everyone. We are surprised at the modest size of the chest into which Benson has fit all the components for his laboratory work. Not since Robert Aldrich compressed a nuclear reaction into a leather case at the bottom of a gym locker in *Kiss Me Deadly* (1955) has such vast power been made so fabulously portable. Lewis, however, isn't settled with the reduction of scale and seeks the reduction of its value. As the ship sinks, Benson tries to get his Lazarus kit into a lifeboat, only to be actively pushed away by the passengers waiting to be lowered into the sea: Benson gets into the next lifeboat. Lewis creates a curious situation in which the immortality recipe is actively rejected by people who are trying to save their own lives. Their gesture subdues the mythic powers of the crate, stamping it with the status of a luxury item, something disposable and inessential.

This gesture is one way in which Lewis leads us to question the demonstrable utility of Benson's medical experiments. Even more shocking than the mad experiments in this film is the variety of interruptions that befall them. Benson claims he has conquered death. In the process his own event takes on something of Death's reluctance to appear at the appointed hour. On four different occasions, he conducts his experiment of inducing suspended animation in his subjects before reanimating them with their diseases "purged." During each experiment, Lewis lets a different grain of sand fall into the film apparatus. The smooth unfolding of cinematic illusion is interrupted so that we not only question Benson's medical degree ("Genius or fiend?" asks the film's tagline) but reevaluate our relation to the screen. Lewis does more than show us a potential quack: he pursues a quack cinema. His experiments are experiments on our perception: each issues a new challenge to our capacity to suspend disbelief. In place of the special effect, Lewis proffers a more indeterminate event. Consequently, cinema's (and Benson's) Lazarus powers are not instantiated but cast into rumor and become phenomena that can be neither verified nor dismissed.

Accidental Experiments / Experimental Accidents

The first experiment begins with an unremarkable question. Expressing his fear of dying during the test, Sanders requests that Benson give his wife the money "should anything happen." Benson replies, "Oh, nothing will happen. Here, let me take your coat." Benson's chilly offer to take Sanders's coat only makes the initial question hang in the air: What exactly *should* happen? Did it happen, in the sense suggested by the patient, or did nothing happen (as predicted by the doctor)? As Benson approaches the patient (whose point of view we inhabit) with a cloth covered with chloroform, the screen gradually blacks out. This unconsciousness is the only vicarious experience afforded by the movie, and we are unable to see the experiment.

The next morning Benson approaches Sanders's body, which lies just below frame and out of our vision. Benson tests the pulse and then listens with his stethoscope. We are forced to guess the test's outcome through the intense yet unclear expressions on Benson's face. Does his surprise suggest the shock of failure or rather the realization that he has succeeded in horrible fashion (the living death of suspended animation)? The more we are given just the face, the less we can employ it to ascertain what is actually happening. Making matters more confusing, Lewis intersperses Benson's reaction shots with images of a police car approaching Benson's lab. Lewis hijacks the Kuleshov effect in order to make Benson's face react to something other than his experiment. His looks of surprise seem inspired by the arriving vehicle rather than by the body in front of him. Benson's stethoscope seems to pick up the sound of the siren rather than the heartbeat of his patient. The montage momentarily achieves an incredible effect: it cues our belief in Benson's telepathic powers. We understand his face as a response to what is magically imminent rather than to what is scientifically at hand.[12] The editing *unconfirms* any assessment of the outcome. Benson rushes out the window when the police knock down his lab door. This concludes the experiment. But we don't know how the experiment concluded.

The second experiment takes place after Benson and other survivors wash ashore and are about to be put to death by the "natives." Their execution is interrupted by the death of Princess Taneo, announced by a shrill scream. "I can make Taneo live again," says Benson, speaking to the natives in telegraphic English from which all articles and most verbs have been subtracted: *Black case in boat. Bring it quickly.* Boat? *Boat we came in. On beach. Must have black box. Hurry.* Benson takes a bottle marked Adrenaline from his black box. Seen in close-up, this label invests the content of the bottle with the same fabulous potential for causality as labels marked Poison in films from the silent era. So Lewis initiates our anticipation for a logical unfolding of events, the chemical inevitability of the adrenaline that will revive Taneo.

Yet an almost imperceptible disruption takes place. During Benson's ministrations, our attention is hooked, scandalized, by a detail within the frame showing us the dead Taneo. Before Benson begins to revive her, we become gradually aware that her seashell necklace is already heaving. The alarming brevity of these shots of "dead" Taneo seems a strategy by Lewis to abbreviate this life movement so drastically as to reduce our ability to perceive these breaths. That is, Lewis uses film editing in order to suspend the actor's animation. Yet the images are not truncated enough to convince us of her deathlike stillness. Our suspicion is confirmed as we gradually realize that the shot through which we have been observing Taneo's "corpse" is the same that reveals her recovery from death. The impression left on us therefore is not of a distinctly separate "before" (death) and "after" (reanimation) for which Benson's intervention is the fulcrum but of strips of film that have migrated backward; the director hopes we won't notice the difference. The use and reuse of shots destroys any effective sense of temporal progression: Taneo seems to be recovering *before* she's been treated.

In his discussion about belief in the cinema, Christian Metz asks, "Who is it who is credulous and must be maintained in his credulousness by the perfect organization of the machinery (by the machination)? This credulous person is, of course, another part of ourselves, he is still seated beneath the incredulous one, or in his heart, it is he who continues to believe, who disavows what he knows."[13] Through the temporal disorganization of its images, the second experiment breaks the illusion and refuses to "maintain our credulousness." The sequence under discussion won't let us suspend disbelief and instead pointedly asks, What are we to believe? Do we believe the images or the fiction for which they are the messenger? How many frames of recycled film do we have to deny in order to believe the fiction of the film? Answering these questions makes it impossible for us to "disavow" knowledge of the film's machinations (as Metz claims). The sequence instead baffles and fragments our knowledge along several lines. It teaches us to separate not only image and fiction but image and editing. Seamlessly unified in the special effect, these elements are here at cross purposes. There seem to be two films happening at once, a kind of double bill within the same B feature. One film is the story of the application of legitimate medicine (adrenaline), which invites the superstitious response from the islanders watching. There is also a second film, a *Making of Mad Doctor*, overlaying the first. This second film shows us the accidents that emerge within the film's construction, the recycled piece of footage that botches the editing of the fictionally successful medical experiment. We watch these films simultaneously yet differently. If Metz claims that ordinary fiction films force the credulous spectator to sit buried below the incredulous spectator (or in his heart, where belief continues no matter what), Lewis's film allows these two halves of the duplex spectator to sit beside each other, on a level.

It is not clear whether the sequence is interrupted by chance or by decision. Yet such mishaps are strangely consistent with the editing in Lewis's other work. In *Invisible Ghost* (1941) Jules the gardener "awakes" from his death in the morgue. His wife, alone in the room with him, screams. After the others run in to see the cause of her shock, Lewis refuses to show us Jules alive on the slab. The two shot, then the three shot, each show us Jules, dead as ever, even though the fiction (his wife's reaction and one peculiar insert of Jules's eyes opening) tells us something to the contrary. The transition from death to life here, as in *Mad Doctor*, becomes a challenge to the spectator to examine the image separately from the story. In both films, Lewis makes us mindful of these tiny disruptions to the "bigger picture." Both films cue an event, but the particular frames evince a reluctance to see it through. Particular images are inserted to obstruct our expectation; they refuse to react to the spectator.

Experiment three begins with Benson impatiently shaking a test tube over a Bunsen burner as Taneo walks in with a tray of flowers. It's never clear what Benson is *doing*. He begins to lecture Taneo about this work, "Nothing must interrupt my research" and, after explaining he has conquered Death, "That is why I must go on with my great work." We want to affirm this guardedness of Benson's labor, but differently: his work cannot be interrupted because it is never really begun. We find depressing confirmation for this when, before experiment four, Benson declares, "That cave will be perfect for my first experiment!" We are three-fourths through the movie and Benson is still talking about his first experiment? We feel briefly susceptible to the doctor's amnesia, for in light of all the interruptions to his work, Benson does seem to be a kind of perpetual novice for whom every experiment is his first. Proof of his madness is always about to begin but is never in process. Will it ever arrive?

Experiment three provides another manner of interruption to Benson's experiment. As he sees Taneo inhaling the flowers, Benson decides to contaminate one with chloroform. He prepares the flower with his back to her and the camera; the ominous music begins. He turns and walks toward the camera with the anesthetized flower. This scene evokes the first experiment and we expect a similar editing structure that sutures the viewer alternately into the point of view of Benson (approaching Taneo) and then Taneo (seeing Benson approach). Yet the experiment sabotages this symmetry. Instead of looking at Taneo through Benson's eyes, Lewis cuts to a shot of Taneo looking languidly askance at Benson. This shot halts our vicarious participation. The sudden introduction of a third perspective distracts us from the horror of the moment, making us ask, through whose eyes are we viewing her?[14] The camera foregoes the reaction shot and evacuates the space of the patient-doctor relation. The shot gives us something rarely seen in the mad doctor film: this third-person perspective is the equivalent of a second opinion. No mad doctor survives a second opinion.

Near the conclusion of the film one of the castaways, fearful of becoming a test subject, says aloud, "If there was only some way we could break down their [the islanders'] blind faith in Benson." What is it that will *undo* the belief of the primitive? The counteragent to credulity is, paradoxically, also its source: they propose a final experiment. After they find Barab washed ashore, the castaways bring his body to Benson's lab. As if they have been spectators to their own film, they acknowledge that the opportunity for Benson's demonstration (the corpse) will also be its scandal. They want to change the disposition of the spectator just by telling Benson, "Get to work!" The chief gives Benson until dawn to revive Barab.

This demonstration of Benson's hoax status is strangely ambiguous. Benson literally starts to work, pulls an all-nighter, but doing what? How many variations are there in that little chest of tubes and stirring sticks? The sweat that covers his brow and douses his shirt is the very icon of the scene's ambiguity. Is it the sign by which his labor shows itself? Or is it merely a sign of his show labor? Or the heat of the approaching sun, his deadline? Is this man really trying to discover a cure for mortality under the threat of his own death? The sunrise is pointedly announced by Benson's defeated shrug: we do not know whether this gesture signals defeat at the proximity of the cure (if he only had more time!) or at the inevitability of his own dying.

Sunrise is the moment of reckoning in Murnau's *Nosferatu* (1922). Whereas the vampire evaporated in the sunlight like an overexposed photograph, Benson merely shrugs. The undead are not far from Lewis's thinking in this movie where the dead touch the living through ambiguity. But what really dies in *Mad Doctor* when the sun comes up? According to the story, dawn disperses our belief in the cinematic demonstration. Sunlight murders that credulousness of the spectator that, according to Metz, is buried like a corpse under the spectator. (Put differently, sunlight makes it harder for us to understand what movies do to us in the theater.)

Questions Raised by the Interruption of Benson's Work

There is startling ingenuity to the breaks and cuts that intercept the cinematic transmission of Benson's work. Each moment stutters in a different way. How are we to account for these obstructions cast in the path of the special effect? Benson's project calls to order one of the fundamental fantasies of the cinematic medium: the illusion that the undead can have a second life.[15] Lewis's work is rife with bogus resurrections because they are rife with bogus deaths. The subtle shocks put to Benson's Lazarus project are the way *Mad Doctor* takes up the theme found more overtly in *Minstrel Man* (1944; the falsely reported death), *Invisible Ghost* (the return of the twin brother), and *A Lawless Street* (1955; the prematurely assumed death).

Questions of evidence and identity are recurring themes in Lewis's work. Our difficulty in assessing either the competence or the madness of doctor Benson's projects resonates with all the broken identities dramatized in Lewis's film titles: *My Name Is Julia Ross*; *Undercover Man* (1949), *A Lady without Passport* (1950); *The Halliday Brand* (1957). We will recall that Lewis gets his start in the film industry courtesy of a disguise: out of work, Lewis lays claim to his brother's identity, an editor at MGM, to get hired at Mascot Pictures.[16] Whereas Lewis's films and biography narrativize this disruption to identity, *Mad Doctor of Market Street* relocates the problem within the space between viewer and screen: instead of a character falling short of her identity, we have here a film falling short of its own title. Later works will seemingly interiorize the problems we have in gathering a case for or against Benson. The authority of Mr. Brown in Lewis's more celebrated *The Big Combo* derives from a stipulation that he obsessively repeats: violence, he says, should leave no trace. Spokesmodel for mafia pedagogy, Brown insists on demonstrations of power that leave no traces that could implicate his hand. When he asks the boxer he manages (and who has just lost the bout) to hit him, the boxer's nonresponse demonstrates his subordination to Brown, even though nothing has technically happened. The dysfunctional boxer is one of the telling resonances between *The Big Combo* and *Mad Doctor*. In the earlier film we first see the boxer (Nat Pendleton) on board the cruise ship, where he performs frantic footwork across the deck but without ever throwing a single punch. He noisily practices the boxer's evasive movement but cannot rehearse the uppercut. Throughout the film, the boxer refuses to do anything that would allow us to characterize him as a boxer. Given the opportunity to enter a fight, he instead moves sideways toward his shipmate who predictably restrains his arm. The boxer arrives always after the fight is over: his response in frustration is to punch the palm of his hand. If *The Big Combo* features a boxer stymied by the request to punch, *Mad Doctor* turns the boxer inside out so that he mirrors the figure of Benson, whom the film does not allow to fully defend his title (neither his madness nor his medical degree): Pendleton plays a quack boxer. An auteurist reading of Lewis's work would have to begin with this vacated site of the boxer, a visual namesake. Is it not inevitable that a director named Joe Lewis would give us two characters who are the mere *projections* of boxers, beefy characters lacking the pugilist instinct, and who are boxers only *in name*?[17]

Are these accidents truly accidental or are they willful in nature? B film flaws are usually attributed to the economic conditions of their production: the pressure from low budgets ("gargantuan cheapness of produc-

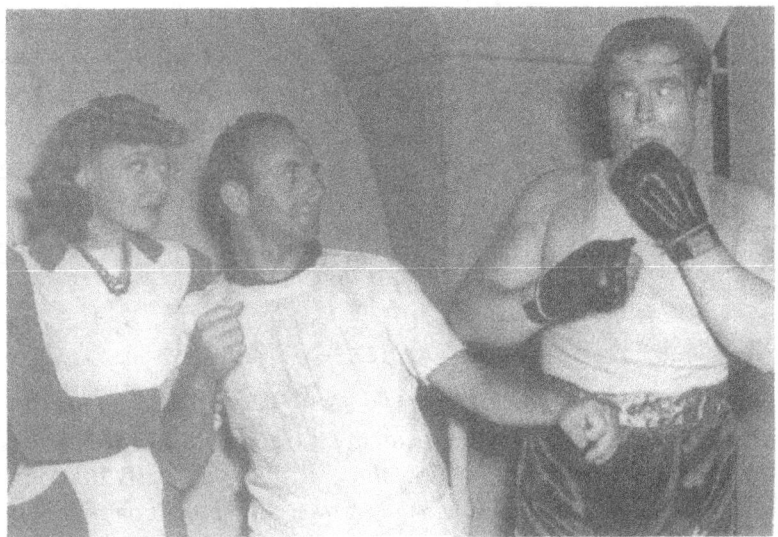

"Shadowboxing": On the set of *Mad Doctor of Market Street* (1942), Joseph Lewis impersonates Joe Louis while Una Merkel and Nat Pendelton watch. (Courtesy of Lance Duerfahrd)

tion values") and tight schedules ("an editorial policy of fast, fast, fast").[18] Makeshift, slapdash, clapboard, slipshod, mockup are some of the compound words describing the glued-together look of the B film. Juxtaposed to this image of a hand forced by the conditions of production is the image of Lewis as skillful and steady-handed craftsman. Critics unanimously praise the way Lewis's style ameliorates his movies. Charles Tesson describes Lewis as a Midas figure who "behaves like an alchemist-director, a forger of genius—*pine always looks like oak in his work, thanks to the polish of his style.*"[19] Lewis's style is the transformative agent converting image-trash into image-treasure. Yet *Mad Doctor* has no place in Tesson's discussion. In this film we are dealing with (or are dealt) a very different hand. We do not encounter magical sleights that successfully turn dreck into gold but rather a clumsy hand that obstructs and actively compromises the film material.

The limits of auteurism and the director's supervisory authority are evident in Lewis's description of his work. Speaking with Peter Bogdanovich, Lewis states, "I signed my name to every frame of film."[20] Referencing older image technologies such as lithography and printmaking, Lewis suggests a craftsman's control over the production process that never exceeds the vision, the marks, or the scale of the artist. Yet we reach an impasse as we bring these terms for the director's singularity up to cinematic speed. Since each frame is sacrificed to create the illusion of motion, Lewis's name ceaselessly withdraws from our perception. Technically speaking, Lewis's signature would not be visible to us. Intended to assure Bogdanovich that his films preserve the imprint of his tireless and idiosyncratic labor, Lewis's claim ironically gives us the contrary sense of a haunting directorial presence whose sign is elusive rather than monumental, more like a mote than a signature.

Madness

The most frequently cited praise of Lewis's films is Ado Kyrou's comment about *Gun Crazy* that "alone of all cinema it clearly marks the road which leads from *l'amour fou* to *la revolte folle*."[21] Instead of clearly marking the path of or to madness, *Mad Doctor of Market Street* exerts a mildly maddening influence on the spectator: the madness promised by the film takes place in our relation to it. Our attention is split between what is happening in the film and what seems to be happening to the film. The core experiments in the film prove to be untenable events. The film encourages mis-seeing and pulls our focus away from the diegesis. The film induces a strange dissociated state in the spectator. Our mind starts to resemble a B picture as our thoughts grow asynchronously with the story and as we actively dub a new tale over the one we are told. Myron Meisel aptly describes Lewis as a "tourist in the asylum." This suggests that Lewis didn't care about having us experience madness vicariously, only to see it from the tour bus. Madness seeps into us through our witnessing.[22]

The maddening quality of *Mad Doctor of Market Street* comes from not knowing what kind of film it is. If *Gun Crazy* is hailed as "an almost unclassifiable work," *Mad Doctor* forces critics to actively misclassify it in the process of critical integration.[23] The film invites new and bizarre taxonomical distinctions. Noting the unconscious quality of the acting and plotting, Rick Thompson writes that "the film operates on zombie level between Ulmer's perversely minimal *Club Havana* (1945) and Buñuel's compulsively catatonic movies about people caught in the same room, such as *The Exterminating Angel* (1962)."[24] Meisel adds, "The moronic repetitions and zombie performances function as a metronome that beats lugubrious cadences for the film's implacable visual staging."[25] He also describes how Lewis "infuses a ludicrous project with enough personal involvement and pure zombie audacity to pull off something even Allan Dwan might have scanted."[26] Another critic calls the film a comedy since everything in it is laughable "except the comic relief."[27]

What are we to call this monstrous genre, this hybrid of zombie and comedy film in which neither zombie nor comedian technically appear? The zombie effect seems generated by the film's unmotivated accidents and bursts that seem edited in rather than edited out, combined with its plodding momentum. The B film actor showcases the questionable status of consciousness in movie acting (and perhaps movie watching). The actor is essentially a zombie: cued by external sources, he is an agentless agency. We will recall how Lewis bemoans having to use real cowboys in making his first feature, *Courage of the West* (1937). In an awkward phrase suggesting the distance between these actual figures and Hollywood images of them, Lewis refers to the leading man as "a cowboy whom we made act."[28] The made-to-act actor is hired because he can ride a horse and work a lasso. An adjunct to the props he owns, the real cowboy becomes a prop and introduces reality into the film not as illusion but as liability. His performance—indistinguishable from his audition—blends in with the inanimate decor.

How Do B Films Haunt Us?

No one can ever have the last word on this haunting subject.

Andrew Sarris, Beatitudes of B Pictures

What is it that makes B films—even those without ghosts—haunting? Sarris's observation partially addresses the ways in which we remember B films differently from A films. The latter garner all the burial ceremonies: the award shows, the critical eulogies, the reverent attention of film restorers. (Would anyone *dare restore* Lewis's *Mad Doctor of Market Street*? Wouldn't the effort to "doctor the film up," as they say, curing it of all the surface scars and editing hiccups, be just a misguided attempt to restore the doctor to the film?) The B film by contrast *drifts* and verges on disappearance.[29] It hasn't suffered institutional anchoring in the same way.[30]

The B film is not officially recognized because we have a hard time recognizing it. It does not sustain a reciprocal relation to the viewer and seems, often, to unfold apart from us. With its emphasis on the interruption of illusion and with its artifice loudly clanging, the B film repeatedly issues extradition papers to the audience. Every frame persistently reminds us that we are in front of a screen, rather than "in" it. Yet in ceasing to act as a window, the screen of the B film acquires a strange and indeterminate presence. Let's consider the strange hybrid of genres critics summon in describing what happens in *Mad Doctor*. What is this but testimony to the way in which, ghostlike, the B film *conjures* cinema, without itself embodying any recognizable cinematic shape? In blocking vicarious participation, the B film invites projection and rehallucination from the audience.

Films haunt us through our obsession with them. We rewatch B films no less compulsively, obsessively, than we do great films. I paused, rewatched, even watched in reverse, each of Benson's experiments just to make sure what I was seeing. The film's supreme moments are also its most interrupted and questionable ones, as they find ever-resourceful ways to fail our vision. Our fascination with the film, as with a bad magician, alights less on the trick than with the abundance of subtle accidents that the act trains our eye to see. Since Lewis makes such wagers with his camera, he invites chance into the image. Orson Welles claims that the director is one who "presides over accidents." One of the eeriest indices of this accident is the sudden appearance of the shadow of Lewis's camera. The fan of Lewis becomes accustomed to the double take at the sight of the camera's shadow projected accidentally onto a figure walking in the foreground, or the sound of the camera tracking through the fake underbrush, or the way a chair trembles slightly when Lewis's camera taps it after one of its ornate choreographies.[31] Long conceived as the device through which the world leaves its imprint on the film negative, the camera in Lewis's films imprints its own shadow on the world it records. Lewis enters his films not as an extra or through momentary and scripted cameos à la Hitchcock, but furtively, as a shadow/ghost, in the space between the accidental and the wholly contrived. Lewis explores this space through the urgent mobility of his camera that, ghostlike, famously moves through walls, goes from room to room without the need of a door or an editorial cut.

Through this abundance of slight tears in its fabric, the B film imposes a definite phenomenological response on the audience: it makes us rub our eyes, as if the sabotage of the cinematic illusion had become a problem with our depth perception. If we review an A film to undergo once again the vision of its director, the B film takes a different route to repetition: we rewatch it in order to reacquaint ourselves with our own eyelids. We blink.

Notes

1. Soviet filmmaker and theorist Sergei Eisenstein discusses editing as if it were a biological experiment. "The shot," he claims, "is a montage cell. Just as cells in their division form a phenomenon of another order, the organism or embryo, so, on the other side of the dialectical leap from the shot, there is montage." Sergei Eisenstein, *Film Form/Film Sense*, trans. Jay Leyda (New York: Meridian Books, 1967), 37. For mad doctor as actor, see Lotte Eisner's remark

that Dr. Mabuse is "less of a superman figure than a product of the inflationary period, a kind of tireless Proteus [that] constantly changes his appearance." *The Haunted Screen* (Berkeley: University of California Press, 1990), 240.

2. Siegfried Kracauer notes how the hypnotic utterance within the film, "You must become Caligari," finds its way onto posters imploring audiences to see *The Cabinet of Dr. Caligari*. See *From Caligari to Hitler* (Princeton: Princeton University Press, 1974).

3. The placebo effect has other connections to the cinema. The term *placebo* has an earlier meaning that refers to a person who appears at a funeral, claiming (often a false) connection to the deceased in order to obtain a handout. The placebo is a stand-in for the ghost, the revenant, and so on.

4. For a discussion of this in light of Lewis's auteur status, see Paul Kerr, "My Name Is Joseph H. Lewis," in *Auteurs and Authorship: A Film Reader*, ed. Barry Keith Grant (London: Blackwell, 2008), 241.

5. Everything on a Lewis set wordlessly repeats two utterances from *Invisible Ghost*. Mrs. Kessler's "I want to go home," followed by the daughter's rationale about why the family doesn't vacate the home after all the murders that have happened there: "We can't leave."

6. An example of how a film's semiotic system successfully integrates animal life: Ridley Scott's *Blade Runner* (1982) creates a future in which the animal kingdom has been replaced by genetically engineered replicants. Cutting to a marketplace in which these animals are sold, the film successfully inspires spectatorial wonder for the craftsmanship (and exchange value) of peacocks, ostriches, and camels. We even begin, possibly, to appreciate the make of these animals. The film so adequately integrates us into its world that we assume its premise as our own, and the (real) animals seem to demonstrate the fabrication of life as a spectacular industrial product, as manufactured commodities that prepare us for the arrival of the replicants.

7. Charles Flynn and Todd McCarthy, "The Economic Imperative: Why Was the B Movie Necessary?" in *Kings of the Bs: Working within the Hollywood System*, ed. Charles Flynn and Todd McCarthy (New York: Dutton, 1975), 13.

8. Myron Meisel observes that "the lack of psychological depth inhibits our identification with the protagonists." "Joseph H. Lewis, Tourist in the Asylum," in *Kings of the Bs: Working within the Hollywood System*, ed. Charles Flynn and Todd McCarthy (New York: Dutton, 1975), 89.

9. Ibid., 82.

10. On this score Lewis's *Mad Doctor of Market Street* has much in common with Aldrich's *Kiss Me Deadly* (1959). In that film we hear the voice and see only the lower legs and feet of the evil Dr. Soberin but do not actually see him on-screen until the final scene of the movie (at which point he is shot by his assistant). Lewis seems to work much more radically. Whereas Aldrich links Soberin's authority to a partial embodiment (an offscreen voice that dies as soon as the speaker is incarnated on-screen), Lewis gives us a doctor who is entirely visible but whose status (and authority) is maddeningly unclear and in question.

11. Quoted in Gilbert Adair, *Movies* (New York: Penguin Books, 1999), 40.

12. One of Lewis's favorite tactics, most prominently displayed in *Invisible Ghost* and *A Lawless Street*, is showing us witnesses instead of letting us witness (for ourselves). This detour prolongs our wonder about the disruptive event, given curious afterlife in the face.

13. Christian Metz, *The Imaginary Signifier*, trans. Ben Brewster (Bloomington: Indiana University Press, 1982), 72.

14. In his essay "The Tutor Code of Classical Cinema" Daniel Dayan describes these sudden jolts that desuture us from the film as a "discovery of the frame" (rather than an enjoyment of what lies within it). "[The Spectator] discovers that he is only authorized to see what happens to be in the axis of the glance of another spectator, who is ghostly or absent. This ghost, who rules over the frame and robs the spectator of his pleasure, Oudart proposes to call 'the absent-one.'" *Film Theory and Criticism*, ed. Leo Braudy and Marshall Cohen (Oxford: Oxford Press, 1997), 127.

15. André Bazin famously claims that a "mummy complex" and the "insurance against death" lie at the heart of cinema. This point is matched by a writer from 1895 who speaks of cinema in a way that almost echoes Dr. Benson's promise: "When these cameras are made available to the public, when everyone can photograph their dear ones, no longer in a motionless form but in their movements, their familiar gestures . . . *death will have ceased to be absolute.*" See Noel Burch, *Life to Those Shadows* (Berkeley: California press, 1990), 21 (my italics).

16. "I called up Mr. Levine at Mascot and said: 'Mr. Levine, my name is Lewis, I'm in the M-G-M editorial department, I would like to come in and see you. . . . Nat Levine saw this list of credits, thinking I was my brother, and so assigned me to head the editorial department." Francis Nevins, *Joseph H. Lewis: Overview, Interview, Filmography* (Scarecrow Press: London, 1998), 9.

17. One of the production stills from the film shows Lewis "winding up" as if to punch a scared-looking Pendleton.

18. See Flynn and McCarthy, "Economic Imperative."

19. Quoted in William D. Routt, "Better Than Good—a Tribute to Joseph H. Lewis," no. 10 (2000), http://www.sensesofcinema.com/2000/10/lewistribute/ (my italics).

20. Peter Bogdanovich, *Who the Devil Made It: Conversations with Legendary Film Directors* (New York: Knopf, 1997), 695.

21. Quoted in Rick Thompson, "Joseph H. Lewis," no. 10 (2000), http://www.sensesofcinema.com/2000/10/lewis-2/.

22. It is possible that one can only be a tourist to madness, since it is a territory so foreign that we can only experience it secondhand, even when it is our own. Sam Fuller's *Shock Corridor* (1963) bears out this insight.

23. Raymond Borde and Etienne Chaumeton, *A Panorama of American Film Noir*, trans. Paul Hammond (San Francisco: City Lights Books, 2002), 94.

24. Thompson, "Joseph H. Lewis."

25. Meisel, "Tourist in the Asylum," 82.

26. Ibid., 102.

27. Jean-Pierre Coursodon, "Joseph H. Lewis," in *American Directors*, ed. Coursodon with Pierre Sauvage, vol. 1 (New York: McGraw-Hill, 1980), 220.

28. Lony Ruhmann, "Gun Crazy, the Accomplishment of Many, Many, Minds," *Velvet Light Trap* 20 (1985): 21.

29. See Arthur Lyon's fascinating account of lost B film noirs in *Death on the Cheap: The Lost B Movies of Film Noir* (New York: Da Capo Press, 2000).

30. Sarris suggests a more idiosyncratic way to remember B films: "Perhaps if we all pool our memories without shame or snobbery, we can see to it yet that nothing of merit in the movies is ever completely forgotten or completely undiscovered." Adair, *Movies*, 145.

31. We are alerted to the camera's presence throughout Lewis's work, through what it does (mutely) but also through what it does visibly, loudly. The camera emerges conspicuously on the backs of extras in the crowded saloon scenes in *A Lawless Street*, where the camera has a particularly stalking force; the sound of the camera going through the bushes is audible in *Mad Doctor*; a chair is tapped by the apparatus as it moves in for a close-up of the main figure in *So Dark the Night*.

BRIAN TAVES

Joseph H. Lewis, Anna May Wong, and *Bombs over Burma*

When Joseph H. Lewis received the task of writing and directing *Bombs over Burma* in early 1942, his work was influenced by several factors above and beyond simply the setting of World War II. First, there was a whole tradition of movies over the previous decade depicting conditions in China, both as impacted by paramilitary groups and in terms of the life of the people. Second, the star of *Bombs over Burma*, Anna May Wong, had been the preeminent Asian American performer for two decades. Despite the history of films set in China and Wong's previous roles, Lewis's directorial sensibility intervened to create a film that is distinct from others. The fact that this is Lewis's only screenplay credit makes his narrative interventions in Wong's persona and existing patterns of Chinese settings all the more important.

During the 1930s, the inevitable topicality of the strife in China spawned a whole cycle of movies. The land was depicted as ravaged by unrest that affected men and women of many races, offering only slight reasons for hope. On occasion, a melodrama such as *The Good Earth* (1937) attempted to delineate the Chinese people, and other films looked at missionary work (particularly after the Communist takeover). These went beyond the typical colonial genre of the white character trying to adjust to life in the East, such as in *The Painted Veil* (1934), to concentrate on Chinese bandits (including *Barricade* [1939]).

The most frequently seen cinematic stock figure in these films was the Chinese warlord, invariably enacted by Caucasian actors in yellowface. Warlords ranged from the menacing (Warner Oland in *Shanghai Express* [1932], Akim Tamiroff in *The General Died at Dawn* [1936], Boris Karloff in *West of Shanghai* [1937]) to the romanticized (Nils Asther in *The Bitter Tea of General Yen* [1932]). At least once, too, the warlord role was transformed into a renegade Russian, enacted by C. Henry Gordon in *Roar of the Dragon* (1932). While China's Nationalist government could not help but be displeased by the unflattering representation of conditions and did all it could to discourage such movies, the fact remained that this background appeared regularly in both B and A films.

With the coming of World War II, certain plot elements of films set in China shifted, while others were unchanging. Throughout the 1930s the Chinese peasant, whether in the foreground (*The Good Earth*) or background (the warlord cycle), was heroic and sympathetically treated. With the coming of war, this remained constant, although the figure of the missionary as outside beneficiary tended to be replaced by the American helping in the struggle for freedom. The warlord himself, the bane of his people, was replaced by the Japanese army of occupation.

Apparently the first major studio release, at the beginning of February 1938, using the Sino-Japanese conflict as a major portion of the background was *International Settlement*. While initially based on a 1936 novel, Twentieth Century Fox altered *International Settlement* to focus on a reporter caught in the midst of the hostilities; the film became an espionage tale of a soldier of fortune (George Sanders) running munitions with a strong romantic subplot. The studio was determined to avoid explicitly dealing with the "controversy" between China and Japan, despite an opening montage by Lowell Thomas to add verisimilitude and the narrative twice depicting the bombing of Peiping (as Beijing was known at the time). The only Asian player billed was Keye Luke as a Chinese physician in a supporting role.

Overt sympathy for the Chinese against the Japanese was first in evidence in *North of Shanghai*, released in February 1939. The working title was *Life Is Cheap*, apt for a plot wherein the Chinese characters lose their lives in a morass of betrayal and enemy action. Keye Luke as a newsreel cameraman is tempted to enter battle when he sees the fate of his countrymen and is eventually killed when investigating the murder of a missionary sympathetic to the Chinese cause. Another half dozen Asian actors had featured roles in this Columbia B.

North of Shanghai retained its primacy in cinematic treatments of the conflict even as the real fighting escalated. Several films made in 1941 centered on the Burma Road. First was Universal's *Burma Convoy*, released in October 1941. While involving spies around Lashio, *Burma Convoy* curiously manages to avoid mentioning the Japanese. The Metro-Goldwyn-Mayer B *A Yank on the Burma Road* was filmed before Pearl Harbor and released in February 1942. An American is hired to lead trucks filled with medical supplies from Rangoon to Chungking. Along the way he becomes involved with a woman whose German-born husband is helping the Japanese without her knowledge. Inspired as well by two heroic Chinese played by Keye Luke and Sen Yung, the American's motives soon change from the mercenary to the altruistic and eventually the patriotic as the United States enters the war.

Emerging at this time, Lewis's *Bombs over Burma* must be understood not only as a genre film but as a starring vehicle for Anna May Wong. In scripting *Bombs over Burma*, Lewis was aware he was creating a movie for not only a durable star but one who had assumed special status as an active woman on behalf of her ancestral land.

Wong was the first Asian American to become a star of the Hollywood cinema and was a top-billed player for over twenty years, working not just in Hollywood but also in England and Germany. She was also a star of the international stage and a frequent guest performer on radio, and would headline the first American television series concentrating on an Asian character, *The Gallery of Mme. Liu-Tsong* (Dumont, 1951). Her remaining roles were sporadic over the final years of her life, and she died at a relatively youthful age, in 1961.

Born in 1905, Wong was the daughter of a Chinese immigrant who owned a Los Angeles laundry. A career in the movies began in the typical manner of the time; she saw a local film crew at work and knew at that moment the life she wanted to pursue. She overcame family opposition and by 1922 had played the lead role, a Madame Butterfly part, in *The Toll of the Sea*, the first Technicolor feature.

As simultaneously a star, yet one whose roles were necessarily limited, at least in Hollywood's view, by ethnicity, Wong's career oscillated between major roles and character parts or exotic bits in Chinatown or Far Eastern scenes. While much of her work on the silent screen is lost today, typical extant roles include her playing a seductive spy opposite Douglas Fairbanks in *The Thief of Bagdad* (1924) and a barmaid temptress in *Across to Singapore* (1928).

No less phenomenal than her performances was the widespread coverage given her career in the fan press. Wong embodied a Chinese beauty that was new to Hollywood films and beguiled spectators in Europe and the United States, who accepted her in any type of role, whether playing hero, villain, or victim. The frequency of portraits and articles about Wong appearing in magazines, despite many relatively small roles and secondary billing, demonstrated the incredible popularity she had with the mainstream, Caucasian audience. Wong was typically described as an intelligent, independent woman whose life was suspended between the two worlds of East and West, invoking the racial mythology of the time. Nonetheless, she frequently found herself losing roles that should have been hers to white performers. The dictates of the economy of a studio system with contract players who had to be kept busy regardless of the roles led to their frequent casting in the occasional Oriental characterizations available. The evidence of press coverage strongly suggests that moviegoers had more progressive inclinations than the conservative studio chiefs and producers who made the casting decisions.

At the end of the 1920s, Wong was invited to star in a series of films for German director Richard Eichberg and quickly became a star in Europe. She spent the 1930s oscillating between movies in the United States and England. After a widely publicized trip to China, she starred in a series of vehicles designed around her persona, the first such in her Hollywood career. In *Daughter of Shanghai* (1937), Wong uncovers the alien-smuggling racketeers who killed her father. The plot admittedly resembles a screen serial by placing the heroine in a series of perilous predicaments, but this was also one of the few forms available at the time for a woman to display her own courage and self-sufficiency. Wong again played a sleuth, using astrology, in *When Were You Born* (1939).

China itself increasingly played a role in the evolution of Wong's persona, beyond the implicit suggestion of such titles as *Daughter of Shanghai*. In *King of Chinatown* (1939), she plays a Chinese American doctor who accepts the gift of a reformed Caucasian gangster, whose life she had helped save, to help found a Red Cross hospital with her husband in China. In *Island of Lost Men* (1939), she travels into the jungles north of Singapore to clear her father, a Chinese general whose name has been besmirched by a gunrunner. In *Ellery Queen's Penthouse Mystery* (1941), Wong plays a contact for a shipment of gems from China to be sold in New York to raise funds for much-needed supplies for the war effort.

During these years, as Hollywood's highest-profile Chinese star, she recognized that her public standing and status gave her a unique opportunity to speak out against Japan's invasion of China, earning publicity that was at least as effective as her screen appearances. Laboring for this cause came to assume a greater priority in her own life than movie roles; as the *Christian Science Monitor* noted in November 1940, she "has given up her motion picture career to aid the cause of China."[1] By that year, Wong had embarked on a formidable public appearance schedule that saw almost daily activities, hosting films, giving speeches, and organizing fashion and theatrical shows, all on behalf of China's cause. In addition, she still found time for numerous radio broadcasts, with a few acting appearances on stage.

With Pearl Harbor, Hollywood at last lost its reluctance to portray the Sino-Japanese War. In March 1942, Wong signed with the Producers Releasing Corporation (PRC), resulting in two movies that would bring her to the movie screen as a star for the last time.[2] "It's about time we got Anna May Wong back on the screen again," noted Hollywood columnist Hedda Hopper.[3]

Bombs over Burma and the other Wong film, *Lady from Chungking*, are two of the best-remembered movies from PRC. PRC had emerged as many of the small production companies gradually merged in the late 1930s into the B studios of Republic and Monogram. PRC evolved from the bankruptcy of one of the remaining entities, Ben Judell's Producers Distributing Corporation, which had sponsored mostly westerns directed by Sam Neufeld. One exception was *Hitler—Beast of Berlin* (1939), an early example of anti-Nazi propaganda at a time when it was still avoided by most studios. During the 1940s, PRC emerged as a prolific producer of low-budget fare that occupied a niche below Monogram on the scale of production values. Most PRC movies were shot in six days or less, with low expenditures guaranteeing profitability, and concentrating on westerns, as well as comedy, horror, war, jungle, and film noir. By employing a variety of talent not otherwise working at the moment, PRC attracted some skilled names in front of and behind the camera, resulting in a number of memorable low-budget masterpieces along with the routine fare. The company continued until the end of the war, when it was absorbed by Eagle-Lion Films. Because the copyright of PRC films was not renewed, this ensured that they still would be widely seen decades later.

For the first and only time in her career, Wong was able to forcefully express her own political views about China and the war effort. In a direct and unequivocal manner, she became the ideal cinematic incarnation of Chinese resistance to Japanese aggression. To demonstrate her purpose in making the PRC movies, she donated her $4,500 paycheck to the China War Relief Fund.[4]

Wong appeared in some 50 features; paradoxically, just a half dozen of these had Chinese settings: *Shame* (1921), *The Toll of the Sea, Drifting* (1923), *Streets of Shanghai* (1927), and *The Crimson City* (1928). Only one had been made during the sound era, *Shanghai Express*, and simultaneously with the production of *Bombs over Burma*, Paramount was remaking the Harry Hervey story that served as the basis for *Shanghai Express*, this time with the title *Night Plane from Chungking*. In so doing, Paramount drastically reconfigured the narrative of *Shanghai Express* to make it topical and give it propaganda value, avoiding any of the characterizations that had caused Nationalist offense back in 1932. Oland's portrayal of a warlord who seizes the express and Wong's characterization of the raped prostitute who kills him had embodied the spiral of mutual destruction reflecting a China torn by civil war in the 1930s.

Lewis may also have been aware of this remake in the process of writing and directing *Bombs over Burma*, and as the *New York Times* review noted, *Bombs over Burma* bears a resemblance to *Shanghai Express*.[5] In contrast with the Paramount movies, however, Lewis had to create his film with minimal resources, starting production on March 30, 1942, the same month Wong joined PRC. Filming lasted two weeks, more time than given to most PRC product, on a budget of $25,000.[6]

Just as *Night Plane from Chungking* deleted the rail journey from *Shanghai Express*, Lewis substituted it with a bus trip. The journeys serve to highlight the various characters of the fellow passengers, the crisis bringing forth their true natures. A patriotic portrayal of China would eliminate the problematic depiction that had caused *Shanghai Express* to be banned by the Nationalist government, which criticized Wong for the role when she visited China in 1936. In *Shanghai Express*, the Asian characters had been marginalized in favor of the romance between leads Marlene Dietrich and Clive Brook. *Bombs over Burma* reverses this approach, a similar structure this time serving the opposite goal, to foreground the Chinese and their heroism. Without the necessity for a love story between the leading players, Lewis was able to take an entirely different approach to China and also to tell a story more purely endemic to the nation at the time.

Wong in particular is shifted from victimized, vengeful supporting player in *Shanghai Express* to starring, self-sufficient hero in *Bombs over Burma*. This new role is one commensurate with her new profile as public champion for China; the role of the prostitute she had played in *Shanghai Express* was no longer appropriate. The new image Lewis provided in *Bombs over Burma* was almost as true of Wong's PRC follow-up, *Lady from Chungking*.

Lewis was credited as coscreenwriter on *Bombs over Burma* (with Milton Raison, who also coscripted the other PRC Wong vehicle, *Lady from Chungking*). Therefore, a detailed plot synopsis, which will also note the highlights of the film in the press book's advertising campaign, is necessary to fully understand the extent of Lewis's intervention in the conventions of the genre. *Bombs over Burma* opens in Chungking, where, after stock footage of the streets, the scene becomes an idyllic classroom. Wong is Lin Ying, a teacher, in whose charge is China's future, both literally and metaphorically. Among the eager students is Ling (Hayward Soo-Soo), who must be sent to the corner for disrupting the class, earning himself a dunce cap. Though mischievous, he is also an innocent.

Seriousness intrudes when a merchant stops by the classroom, ostensibly carrying sweets for the children. However, written in code on a candy wrapper is a message for Lin Ying. His enigmatic status is signaled by the first of several key shots through foreground objects that signal pivotal points in the narrative (although not necessarily high moments of drama). Lin Ying calls on a mysterious weaver, who gives her, in Chinese, her mission. He is Colonel Kim, played by Richard Loo, most typically seen during these years cast as a malicious Japanese character in war films. (Loo was actually a native of Hawaii.) Much of the approach to espionage in these scenes is found again in Lewis's *Criminals Within*, made in 1943 for PRC.

Returning to her class, the students sing "Yankee Doodle"—the first intrusion so far of English into what has been strictly Chinese dialogue. The children's melody indicates simultaneously that China's next generation relies on America, as well as the rebellious spirit that won the United States its own revolutionary war against colonialism, no less than China's struggle against Japan.

The song begins to be drowned out by the sound of approaching Japanese planes. Lin Ying must lead her class to the air-raid shelter as the bombs begin to fall. Ling, still in the corner, hides and stays behind to watch the airplanes above. Singing "Yankee Doodle," he imagines he is shooting antiaircraft fire at the planes. Soon real bullets from strafing planes replace those he imagines firing. Contrasted with his youthful, uncomprehending view of the growing devastation around him, the audience feels increasing anxiety about the peril of his untenable position. It will be too late; Lin Ying only finds his body after the bombs have wrought death.

> CRASH! And a Jap bomb snuffs out the life of a little Chinese schoolboy . . . who thought they were playing for fun![7]

This ends the first act, thirteen minutes into the movie. The characterization of the conflict has been laid out in stark terms, the Japanese bringing death to the defenseless Chinese. Meanwhile, Lin Ying must embrace the responsibilities of her dual role as teacher and spy—occupations that are not contradictory but interdependent—if she is to succeed in her wartime mission and create China's future.

The use of stock footage of bombs and airplanes and the studio set of the classroom during the Chungking portion function acceptably within the typical discursive mode of such combinations in war films. Although there is an obvious contrast between studio shots and news footage, despite the obvious visual disjuncture of two types of filmmaking, a sense of realism has been gained. This will become evident during other portions of

Bombs over Burma in which both are readily edited together. A far more jarring contrast ensues when Ma Sing, a Chinese woman taking the bus tickets enacted in an annoyingly sing-song voice by Connie Leon, appears in the same frame with Wong.

Act 2, signaled by another foreground shot, begins in the depot of Lashio. The bus journey unfolds in what could have been a variety of settings, including a stagecoach in the Old West—no surprise considering Lewis had already directed some dozen westerns. The bus driver in *Bombs over Burma* could easily be a stagecoach driver, particularly as his role unfolds in the narrative. There is little to mark the atmosphere, and the road unfortunately resembles precisely the back lot that it is. Indeed, the trip resembles the journey of redemption undertaken in Lewis's *Border Wolves* (1938), where the journey west to the wealth of California proves wrought with danger and mistaken identity, leading the heroes to have to go outside the law, infiltrate a gang, and bring them to justice.

> The convoy's off! . . . With its bus-load of Americans and Chinese . . . ready to die that China might live!

Mysterious music is in the background as the various passengers on the bus are introduced. There is a slick Englishman, Sir Roger Howe (third-billed Leslie Denison), seated next to Lin Ying. A fat, oily Portuguese, Pete Braganza (Dan Seymour), observes a Hindu, Hallam (Frank Lackteen), suspiciously. A young couple serve as the expected ingenues and are the only obvious red herrings, Judith Gibson and Dennis Moore (Lucy Dell and Tom Whitley). Lewis hoped to cast perennial heavy Marc Lawrence as the driver, hard-boiled American Slim Jenkins, a role eventually taken by Nedrick Young.[8] Lawrence's persona would have given the part more uncertainty and potential menace.

Lin Ying is traveling incognito, as she is placed in a new position, the audience uncertain of the role to be played by the character so succinctly revealed in the opening of *Bombs over Burma*. She comments to Roger on the unceasing labor of the Chinese to maintain the roads that bring supplies to their country, foreshadowing the conclusion in act 3.

The key locale of the movie is the monastery where the bus pauses overnight. Except for brief scenes with the basket weaver, this is the only elaborately decorated set of the movie, befitting the centerpiece of a series of machinations that reveal the character and plot motivations. The monastery exterior posed a potential problem, considering the budget. Lewis recalled, "All we did was take a winding dirt road, put a pair of gates in front of it on hinges—which opened into it—and that was the monastery. We shot it through the eyes of a person within the monastery itself." In this way the effect was achieved without expense.⁹

> What terrifying intrigue goes on behind the quiet monastery doors? As a ruthless Jap spy sends his secret code message to the bombers!

Leading the monastery is the priest Me-Hoi (played by second-billed Noel Madison). Early on, Lin Ying sees Me-Hoi go into a secret chamber behind the basement statue of Buddha to which he prays. Concealed behind the Buddha is a radio room where Me-Hoi receives and transmits messages. Initial suspicion points to him as a possible Japanese spy. This seems more than likely when the bus's engine distributor disappears, and the Japanese pinpoint bombing destroys the road ahead during the night. Lin Ying looks up at the skies with hatred as again stock footage is used, as in the opening shots in Chungking, to reveal Japanese devastation.

Initially, Lin Ying's mission, and the status of Me-Hoi as a traitor or patriot, is uncertain, and typical of the espionage genre. From the outset the narrative of *Bombs over Burma* sets itself to unraveling these mysteries, in a manner similar to other Lewis films, whether the illegal alien smuggling of *A Lady without Passport* (1950) or the family and neighbor feuds that unfold in retrospect in *The Halliday Brand* (1957). Like these films, or *A Lawless Street* (1955) and his *Big Valley* television pilot, "Boots with My Father's Name" (1965), much of the plot interest in *Bombs over Burma* lies in the gradual unveiling of concealed identities. While evident in these varying genres, whether melodrama or western, it is a device seen most purely in the form of a detective case in Lewis's *The Falcon in San Francisco* (1945). Following this pattern, there is similar uncertainty in *Bombs over Burma* as to how Lin Ying's dual identity as schoolteacher and spy will evolve, and precisely what her mission is. Equally questionable at this stage is how Me-Hoi fits in.

At last the real identity of the monk is revealed. He is the contact agent for Lin Ying, although initially they distrusted each other. As Hollywood columnist Edwin Schallert had noted in announcing the casting of Madison in the role, while he had played a villain in some eighty films, here he changes "completely by enacting a kindly Chinese priest."¹⁰ Me-Hoi is the rare Hollywood incarnation of a clever, patriotic Buddhist monk.

> That Buddhist Monk Is a Holy Man . . . A Holy Terror to the Japs!

Me-Hoi reveals that the actual convoy, containing the most important supplies, awaits his radio signal that the spy has been exposed. The pairing of Lin Ying and Me-Hoi, who address each other as "father" and "daughter" in a way that is far more than either literal or purely honorary, reveals the essential role of both in the birth of a new China united in opposition to its invaders. By implication, education, faith, and subterfuge must be combined on the front lines of China to defeat the latest enemy of an ancient civilization. With its commentary on Chinese resistance, uniting the teacher and the monk, a guide for the children and one for the spirit, *Bombs over Burma* presents a symbolic portrait of a nation at war.

No less symbolic is the role of the driver, Slim, the American expatriate in charge of modern industrial technology in the truck, and the one who realizes Howe's use of the razor for radio communications. Lin Ying had learned that Slim is an exile from New York City and a child of its streets, toughened, she notes, as China has become. Slim's emerging importance returns to the parallel between China and America set in the opening with the students singing "Yankee Doodle." Slim, like his country, has been searching for a way to contribute to the war effort.

Hence the spy must be an outsider whose motive is purely mercenary. Pete the Portuguese is ready to betray China, along with the East Indian. However, most important, it is the Englishman who betrays the Allied cause and knifes Pete in the back when he is about to name the culprit. Flash shots of each of those present at Pete's murder are reminiscent of early sound technique. Indeed, much of *Bombs over Burma* is in a style more typical of a decade earlier; for instance, the editing rhythms imposed by the two insertions of extensive stock footage force a more sedentary approach during the first and second acts. By contrast, the second PRC Wong film, *Lady from Chungking*, is rather more contemporary in its overall style but lacks the impact of the final crescendo of the violent close of the third act of *Bombs over Burma*.

Howe finally comes to the fore as he and Hallam trick Me-Hoi into revealing his hiding place and the radio. Howe and Hallam turn Me-Hoi and Lin Ying over to Slim, convincing him that China has been betrayed by its own people. Lin Ying reveals to him the truth when he hears the staccato sounds of Howe's electric razor, a secret transmitting device. (World War II espionage films often had code machines hidden in the least credible manner.) With this twist, *Bombs over Burma* follows the pattern of so many Lewis films and pivots on the discovery of identity. Just as in such generically distinct fare as his *Invisible Ghost* (1941), *My Name Is Julia Ross* (1945), or *The Big Valley* episode "The Man from Nowhere" (1966), the narrative revolves around the revelation of an individual's character against circumstances and adversaries that have obscured it. In the case of

Lin Ying (Anna May Wong) and Slim (Nedick Young) hold the signaling device concealed as an electric shaver, used by the traitorous Englishman Howe (Leslie Denison, *left*). (Courtesy of Brian Taves)

Bombs over Burma this is true not only of Howe but of Lin Ying, Me-Hoi, Braganza, and Hallam.

> On the Road to Chungking... an innocent looking Chinese school teacher spots the Jap spy... and clears the Burma road for the supplies to come through!

Act 3 returns to the road, this time the convoy instead of the bus, with Lin Ying volunteering to ride with Howe in the first truck, driven by Slim. Tension builds as the line of trucks snakes through the hills, and the sound of airplanes is gradually heard. Suspense is enhanced by uncertainty, arising from Anna May Wong's persona, as to whether she will lose her life as in the climax of so many of her previous films. Instead, Howe panics and tries to flee the anticipated bombing. Lin Ying whistles after him, summoning the peasants working on the road that had been seen in the initial journey of the bus.

In the following sequence, *Bombs over Burma* offers a completely distinct climax from Wong's sacrificial death in *Lady from Chungking*. Instead, in *Bombs over Burma* the Chinese people take vengeance on the man who betrayed them. They may lack the technology of Howe and his allies, but they have the numbers, determination, and weapons, which will suffice. Peasants line the hillside, circling Howe. There is silence as the camera shows the pitiless faces and simple implements of farmers and road builders. Lewis recalled the action as emphasizing Howe's own torment from his realization of guilt. "Standing in front of him he saw one Chinese peasant holding a stick; then he looked in another direction and there were two Chinese peasants, one holding a pitchfork; then he looked at another and there were groups of two and three."[11] They close in around him as he goes on his knees, mutely imploring mercy, finding none. Denison's performance as Howe is at its best in these wordless moments. A pickax is raised, then others. The striking blows are not seen; only Howe is heard crying out. His grisly end is left to the imagination, as the peasants walk away, justice done.

As in Lewis's *Deadly Is the Female / Gun Crazy* (1950), it is this scene of unusual and unexpected violence that supplies the most memorable element of surprise in *Bombs over Burma*. The style of the climax with its farm and road implements as weapons would be echoed in Lewis's *Terror in a Texas Town* (1958), where again modern technology wielded by evil is overcome by a simpler, more primitive weapon. There the contrast is emphasized by having the teaser opening hint that the heroic whaler will not use his harpoon—only heightening the surprise when it is cunningly thrown at the conclusion of the draw.

> A spy! But those loyal coolies on the Burma Road took care of the Jap spy!

With the death of Howe, Lin Ying reveals to Slim that the airplanes overhead are not Japanese at all. Howe's fears were the manifestation of his own guilt. In fact the planes are American, returning from a raid on the Japanese. Symbolically, while the Americans have aided importantly in the war effort, in *Bombs over Burma*, unlike many films, it is the Chinese themselves who hold the ultimate knowledge and provide the solution. Slim provides assistance, as do the offscreen American planes, but it is the wisdom of Lin Ying and Me-Hoi, along with the strength of the Chinese peasants, that serves the future of the country. Back at the monastery, the priest pronounces that the road is open and once more the journey can resume. China's representations of father and daughter, Me-Hoi and Lin Ying, so address each other for a final time as she, Slim, and the remaining passengers board the bus for a final time.

The role was one of Wong's relatively few films to involve extensive Chinese dialogue. According to the press book, the Nationalist government desired that all Chinese in Hollywood films be shown speaking Mandarin. Wong, whose family dialect was Cantonese, had to be coached in Mandarin for the movie by Miss Shu Ying Loo, a native of Beijing, an area where Mandarin is spoken (Wong's father was a native of southern China).

The opening night reviewer in Los Angles commented that Wong "does very fine work, besides looking beautiful."[12] Wong wore a unique hair style in *Bombs over Burma*, one unlike any of her other roles. While retaining her characteristic bangs, a "muy phom" drew her hair into twin plumes at the top rear of her head. As described in the press book, "Miss Wong parts

The unity of Chinese tradition, faith, and family defend the homeland, whether the teacher Lin Ying (Anna May Wong) or the Buddhist monk Me Hoi (Noel Madison). (Courtesy of Brian Taves)

her hair in the middle above Chinese bangs. Then she winds it into muffins, netted in black mesh. These two muffins create a distinct hair arrangement that is both striking and exotic." The coiffure was featured in *Harper's Bazaar* as one that dated back over 2,000 years to the Tang dynasty and was offered as a tie-in with beauty shops. A suggested slogan was "Modern China shows the way in raw courage! And ancient China shows the way in ultra-modern Chic . . . exotic Anna May Wong, appearing in *Bombs over Burma*, wears this novel arrangement." This duality was also reflected in her use of the hairstyle at China relief functions.

In Los Angeles, *Bombs over Burma* premiered Thursday, July 9, 1942, at the independent Vogue Theater on Hollywood Boulevard. It led another PRC release, *Prisoner of Japan*, on a double-billed "Slap the Jap Week." The *Los Angeles Times* headlined that Wong was playing the starring role. The opening night was announced to include appearances by Wong, Madison, and Gertrude Michael and Alan Baxter of *Prisoner of Japan*, but actually only included Michael, Corinne Mura, and Billy Moya (both also of *Prisoner of Japan*), with Madison as master of ceremonies. (Wong left just before the performance to go to San Francisco for Chinese war relief.[13]) The program was reviewed as "good ones both."[14]

In New York, *Bombs over Burma* opened at the Central Theatre on Broadway on Saturday, August 8.[15] By September 30, it was in Chicago at the Grand, leading a double bill of "2 hits" with, ironically, another Lewis film for PRC, this one about a crooked lawyer's imprudent daughter, *Secrets of a Co-Ed*. *Bombs over Burma* had moved to the suburbs by late fall, playing three times a day on the lower half of a double bill in Boston, and Wong was given sole listing as star in the Chicago and Boston schedules.[16]

Wong's two PRC films, *Bombs over Burma* and *Lady from Chungking*, are distinct from each other, but a comparison is revealing, particularly to highlight Lewis's contributions as writer and director of the former. *Bombs over Burma* was the first, and its Poverty Row origins and relatively simple tale are always apparent but concealed in fast pacing. (Today, the technical quality of both of Wong's PRC films appears even poorer because of the battered copies in circulation.) In *Lady from Chungking*, an espionage mission requires Wong's underground leader to become the mistress of a Japanese general. After revealing the invader's troop movements to the Flying Tigers, she is executed by an enemy firing squad. Even as her character transcends bullets to incarnate the immortal spirit of China, the climax is commensurate with the frustration Wong expressed with many similar roles that also ended in her death.[17] By contrast, *Bombs over Burma* followed the more recent trend of Wong as a survivor, as in *Daughter of Shanghai, King of Chinatown, When Were You Born, Island of Lost Men,* and *Ellery Queen's Penthouse Mystery*. Ironically, while Wong biographers have often valorized *Lady from Chungking* and its A film pretensions, they have dismissed *Bombs over Burma* as a formula B without recognizing that it does not require the sacrifice.[18]

To succeed in her career, Wong had to become an expert at circumventing the standard Hollywood formula—classical filmmaking with its emphasis on a middle-American milieu and yellowface casting in its occasional Oriental forays. To find a place in Hollywood, Wong had to learn to work in its sidelines and fissures. This was no less true in her work on the war; despite her status as a leading spokeswoman for the Chinese war effort in America, she was, in the words of Hedda Hopper's column, "more than slightly slighted by our picture makers when Madame Chiang Kai-Shek was here, [but is] going right ahead working for China relief."[19] Throughout her career, Wong was able to use nuances of performance, whether supporting roles or particularly "Bs," along with taking advantage of press coverage, to establish the place of a Chinese American star in Hollywood. Similarly, Lewis, as a director emerging through "B" filmmaking, had to be equally adept at using the slightly greater freedom found in the margins of Hollywood to create a distinct style and narrative. In that respect, the two made an ideal combination as star and director, creating a unique war movie in *Bombs over Burma*.

With *Bombs over Burma* and *Lady from Chungking* Wong made a contribution to the war effort and to a positive screen depiction of China, not facilitated by Hollywood in the previous two decades of her films. Typically her career is framed by commentators through absence, as the actress who was passed over for *The Good Earth* in favor of white performers.[20] The sole canonized film for which she was recognized for many years was *Shanghai Express*, because of its significance in Josef von Sternberg's Dietrich cycle. (Yet this was an important film for Wong only in retrospect; the press book includes not even the smallest story on her, which costar Warner Oland at least merits. Rather all attention is given to Dietrich and Brook as the white romantic leads.) While I would argue that discussing Wong primarily in light of the studio system's yellowface practices is a seriously misguided and reductive approach to her career, it is clear that *Bombs over Burma* and *Lady from Chungking* stand in contrast to the prevalence of this approach. They offer a way to recognize an alternative, if the possibility is accepted that B films may be as important as their big-budget counterparts, such as *Daughter of the Dragon* (1931) or *Limehouse Blues* (1934). I believe that such Bs are as vital, and ultimately it is the full range of Hollywood production that must be examined to recognize that there was indeed a way in which figures such as Wong and Lewis could bring China to the screen at a crucial time. In both PRC Bs, *Bombs over Burma* and *Lady from Chungking*, Wong became the screen symbol of Chinese resilience and rebirth. While these films served this function, she, like many other stars, chose to continue her own wartime labors as well as spending months entertaining the troops, joining the USO, and traveling as far as Alaska.[21]

Unlike so many movies of the time seen today, there is nothing about *Bombs over Burma* that reflects a patronizing attitude or which will make modern audiences wince. By contrast, when another Pearl S. Buck novel was brought to the screen by MGM in 1944 as an obvious follow-up to *The Good Earth*, it was the epic, big-budget *Dragon Seed*, with all the leads played in yellowface in a paternalistic, heavy-handed family saga. *Dragon Seed* is distinct from the direct, courageous portrayals Wong gave in *Bombs over Burma* and *Lady from Chungking*. *Bombs over Burma*, running sixty-seven minutes, may not have lasted over two hours or been derived from a prestigious novel, but it was one of the first Hollywood films in the wake of Pearl Harbor to bring to the screen a timely story of China, espionage, and resistance to invasion and fifth columnists. It is, in its own way, a *Good Earth* for wartime, but unlike *Dragon Seed*, we actually are favored with a Chinese lead.

There is a realism about *Lady from Chungking* and especially *Bombs over Burma* and their portrayal of the Chinese people both in the lead roles to the smallest bits that is refreshing, honest, and uncompromised. Moreover, *Bombs over Burma*, released June 4, 1942, was not a spark soon forgotten, but was rereleased in 1948, and on numerous other occasions overseas well into the next decade and beyond.[22] Joseph H. Lewis as writer and director was able to facilitate these innovations, breaking the existing patterns of movies with Chinese settings, and composing for Wong one of her most unique roles.

NOTES

For their assistance, the author would like to thank Hye Seung Chung, Conrad Doerr, Philip Leibfried, Frances Nevins, and his Library of Congress colleagues Zoran Sinobad, Larry Smith, and George Willeman.

1. "Chinese Actress Visits Saltonstall," *Christian Science Monitor*, November 18, 1940, 9.

2. A contract for three movies, with only two made, is given in Philip Leibfried and Chei Mi Lane, *Anna May Wong* (Jefferson, NC: McFarland, 2004), 9. The figure of four movies was in the announcement, "Signs New Contract," *New York Times*, March 13, 1942, 22, where the title of the first movie was announced as *The Devil's Sister*.

3. "Hedda Hopper's Hollywood," *Los Angeles Times*, March 14, 1942, 9.

4. Karen Janis Leong, "The China Mystique: Mayling Soong Chiang, Pearl S. Buck and Anna May Wong in the American Imagination" (PhD diss., University of California, Berkeley, spring 1999), 165, cited in Anthony Chan, *Perpetually Cool* (Lanham, MD: Scarecrow, 2003), 263, 269. Chan gives the figure as $4,000 on page 149.

5. T.S., "*Bombs over Burma*," *New York Times*, August 10, 1942, 15.

6. The shooting schedule is given in Karen J. Leong, *The China Mystique* (Berkeley: University of California Press, 2005), 101–2, and the budget by Lewis in his oral history in Peter Bogdanovich, *Who the Devil Made It: Conversations with Legendary Film Directors* (New York: Alfred A. Knopf, 1997), 655 and repeated in Francis M. Nevins, *Joseph H. Lewis: Overview, Interview, and Filmography* (Lanham, MD: Scarecrow, 1998), 23.

7. These advertising slogans are found in the movie's press book.

8. Quoted in Francis M. Nevins, *Joseph H. Lewis*, 23.

9. Quoted in Bogdanovich, *Who the Devil*, 656; Nevins, *Joseph H. Lewis*, 23.

10. Edwin Schallert, "Edward Robinson Will Do Newspaper Comedy," *Los Angeles Times*, April 3, 1942, 13.

11. Bogdanovich, *Who the Devil*, 656.

12. G.K., "Thrillers Share Bill," *Los Angeles Times*, July 10, 1942, p. 17.

13. Ibid.

14. "Advertisement and Independent Theaters Daily Guide," *Los Angeles Times*, July 9, 1942, 12; "Chinese Player Stars in New Vogue Picture," *Los Angeles Times*, July 9, 1942, 12; G.K., "Thrillers Share Bill," 17; Independent Theaters Daily Guide," *Los Angeles Times*, July 10, 1942, 16; Independent Theaters Daily Guide," *Los Angeles Times*, July 11, 1942, 6; Independent Theaters Daily Guide," *Los Angeles Times*, July 12, 1942, B2; Independent Theaters Daily Guide," *Los Angeles Times*, July 13, 1942, 9; "Independent Theaters Daily Guide," *Los Angeles Times*, July 14, 1942, 12.

15. "Of Local Origin," *New York Times*, August 8, 1942, 14; "Films of the Week," *New York Times*, August 9, 1942, X4.

16. Theater schedules in *Chicago Daily Tribune*, September 30, 1942, 22; *Chicago Daily Tribune*, October 1, 1942, 28; *Chicago Daily Tribune*, October 2, 1942, 24; "Entertainment Timetable," *Christian Science Monitor*, November 11, 1942, 5.

17. These include *The Toll of the Sea, Old San Francisco* (1927), *The Chinese Parrot* (1927), *The Devil Dancer* (1927), *Song / Show Life / Wasted Love* (1928), *Grosstadt Schmetterling / The Pavement Butterfly / The City Butterfly* (1929), *Piccadilly, Hai-Tang / The Flame of Love / The Road to Dishonour* (1930), *Daughter of the Dragon, Tiger Bay* (1934), *Limehouse Blues, Java Head* (1934), *Dangerous to Know*, and *Lady from Chungking*.

18. For instance, see Karen J. Leong, *The China Mystique* (Berkeley: University of California Press, 2005), 101–2. Similarly, Anthony Chan, *Perpetually Cool* (Lanham, MD: Scarecrow, 2003), gives only cursory treatment to *Bombs*

over Burma, while *Lady from Chungking* receives extended analysis.

19. Hedda Hopper, "Looking at Hollywood," *Chicago Daily Tribune*, April 23, 1943, 29; Hedda Hopper, "Miss Bergman Again!," *Washington Post*, April 28, 1943, 16.

20. This proclivity is true not only of historians but particularly of journalists and others who have told Wong's story, such as playwright Elizabeth Wong in *China Doll*. It is also the case in more incidental tellings of her story, such as in the documentary *Hollywood Chinese* (2007), which again places *The Good Earth* at the center of Anna May Wong's career.

21. Hedda Hopper, "Looking at Hollywood," *Chicago Daily Tribune*, January 4, 1944, 14; Hedda Hopper, "Just Like Hedda's Hats," *Washington Post*, January 10, 1944, 12; "Anna May Wong Leaves on U.S.O. Tour," *Los Angeles Times*, March 30, 1944, A1; "Anna May Wong Tells of Alaska Camps Tour," *Los Angeles Times*, July 25, 1944, 7.

22. *Bombs over Burma* was the subject of a *Star cine vaillance* comic book as *Mission Burma* published August 3, 1963, in Italy but written in French and distributed to French-speaking countries and regions, including Switzerland and Canada.

7

Marlisa Santos

"People Can Think Themselves into Anything"

The Domestic Nightmare in
My Name Is Julia Ross

Joseph Lewis is marked, as Andrew Dickos points out, by his "noir sensibility, among the strongest in its appeal to violence and sex as the raison d'être in noir filmmaking."[1] Years prior to films such as *The Big Combo* (1955) and *Gun Crazy* (1950), however, Lewis began flexing his noir muscles on more subtle films, such as *So Dark the Night* (1946) and *My Name Is Julia Ross* (1945). Though *Julia Ross* may seem tame in some respects when compared to Lewis's other films, it can be seen as actually more disturbing because of its subtlety and comparative restraint. Julia Ross, the film's heroine, is terrorized by a banally evil mother and her psychopathic sexual predator son in a *Gaslight*-type situation, one in which she is being forced to believe that she is an amnesiac with a different identity. The film is psychologically charged, employing dream imagery, forced identity assumption, persecution, and psychopathology. Indeed, it can be argued that most of the film itself can be seen as a dream, a surreal representation of Julia's thwarted romantic hopes and wishes. She finds herself in a nightmare that questions her very existence and makes a mockery of the prospect of true female independence in the postwar world.

From the start of the film, Julia Ross (Nina Foch) is presented as an unusual female character in noir, one who is independent, not sexually sterile, and yet is not a femme fatale. She does, however, find herself in a typical noir predicament, alone in an unfamiliar city and soon in danger arising from the most innocent of circumstances. She hails from rural Sussex but is now in London in need of a job as she is recovering from an operation. She is without family, friends, or romantic love, and the Vacancy sign outside her boarding house speaks to more than the house's rental availability. From the opening shot of the film, Lewis underscores her anonymity and isolation. This slightly askew shot shows Julia clad in a raincoat as she makes her way across the windy, stormy street to the boarding house; her drenched figure is barely distinguishable in the torrential rain. Even as she enters the house, she is shot from behind and her face is not seen for several minutes, though she carries on a conversation with the housemaid. This visual manifestation of her isolation foreshadows the imminent threat of her lost identity. Nicholas Christopher argues that noir often reflects an "urban dreamscape—often nightmarish . . . always symbol-laden, and sometimes so starkly black-and-white (literally and figuratively) in its depiction of city life, and of the innermost conflicts and struggles of the human spirit in the city, that it shocks us into moments of recognition and epiphany."[2] The situation established by the film's first few moments posits Julia Ross at a crossroads, captured by the chaos of nature juxtaposed against the anonymity and harshness of city life. The camera only pans up to reveal her face when she discovers a wedding invitation from her estranged boyfriend, Dennis (Roland Varno). Thus, the revelation of Julia's identity to the viewer comes at the moment she discovers that a door has been closed on her prospects of a love relationship that would likely have led to a safe and protected domestic life. Her position is underscored by her conversation with Bertha, the maid, who scoffs at Julia not trying to get Dennis back: "If you had, you wouldn't have to worry about the three weeks rent you owe Mrs. Mackie." From the outset, Lewis presents Julia Ross as a woman whose attempts to rebuild her life after physical illness and financial straits are slowly failing her, an echo of the displacement of wartime and postwar individuals in the face of changing social conditions.

It is Julia's desperation and need to support herself as an independent woman that lead her, seemingly under these most innocuous of circumstances, to Mrs. Hughes (Dame May Whitty) and her son, Ralph (George Macready), who are in search of a live-in secretary. As Foster Hirsch argues, the film "is a clever variation on the *noir* theme of unstable identity; who you are can be altered, or eradicated, by the simplest act—by something as mundane as a job interview."[3] What the Hugheses are searching for is a young woman with no family or boyfriend, and Julia fits this description; she tells them, "I'm absolutely alone." What Julia does not know is that the job search is a cover; even the job agency is a front for what they are really seeking: a look-alike for Ralph's first (and murdered) wife. They are pleased that Julia seems like the right choice—"perfect," Ralph says, "even a small resemblance." Julia has become a doppelgänger of a dead woman, as her relatives become their own doppelgängers to Julia's real, but absent, family. By closing her eyes to her own doubts (the "live-in" nature of the position and the immediacy of its start), she has entered a surreal world of nightmare, but this entrance is framed as salvation, a gift, like a poisoned apple to an unwitting fairy-tale victim.

Lewis's typical long takes and tight close-ups characterize Julia's late-night arrival at the Hugheses' home as being fraught with suspense and disorientation. The square is shrouded in darkness and the shadow of the front door passes ominously over her face before she enters, signifying the imminent threat behind it. The camera initially moves in for a close-up of a menacing lion knocker on the front door, fading into a silver tea set in the bedroom of the sleeping Julia, after which a male hand is seen removing her purse from the nightstand, this image finally dissolving into a crackling fire. This fire becomes the repository of her belongings and, symbolically, the crematory of her identity. "For Lewis," according to Myron Meisel, "the frame's foreground is where we reach inside his characters, who in turn are tortured by forces reaching out from the hard-focused background."[4] The scenes of Julia's arrival fit this characterization, as they signify Julia's visual erasure once she walks through the front door, as she will soon become physically and psychologically erased. Drugged by the Hugheses, Julia Ross and her identity are completely eradicated, as they destroy all her possessions and identification. These possessions are not simply destroyed, though, but violently torn to shreds as Ralph cuts them up with a knife, rather than just discarding them. His mother tells him to put away the knife, adding, "Remember that if it weren't for your temper, we wouldn't be in this awful trouble today." The "awful trouble" turns out to be the fact that the psychotic Ralph has murdered his wealthy wife and now the Hugheses must cover up the crime by creating her double in Julia, moving to a new town and systematically planning a realistic scenario for her "suicide." Julia sleeps upstairs, oblivious to the fact that she is becoming another person; a medium shot of Julia's photo being consumed by flames, another violent symbol of the erasure of her identity, shows that she is being murdered without bloodshed. The characterization of noir violence by Borde and Chaumeton as an "incoherent brutality, something dreamlike" is evident in this scene and in others to follow later in the film.[5] Julia Ross has entered a situation in which she assumes security and protection, the substitution of the romantic loss of a life with Dennis; however, when she falls asleep in the Hugheses' house, she enters a surreal nightmare in which these hopes are perverted into danger and cruelty.

The feeling of the film as a dream is most evident upon Julia's initial awakening in her alien surroundings. Though she is Julia Ross when she falls asleep, she is a blank self when she awakens, her independence transformed into helplessness and her identity subsumed into that of a dead

Mrs. Hughes (Dame May Whitty) feeding Julia Ross's identity into the fire.

woman. She finds herself in a different bed than the one in which she first fell asleep, and a glance at a calendar further reveals that some time has been lost. The measured ticking of a small elephant pendulum clock on the table is an ominous symbol of what has been stolen from her. As the camera leisurely pans around the room, emphasizing the unfamiliarity Julia has with her surroundings, the monogram of "MH" appears everywhere, including on the nightgown she is now wearing; her body itself has therefore even been violated, as her most intimate clothing has been removed and replaced. Both her view from the window and the subsequent shot of the secluded large house on the rocky terrain overlooking the water reinforce the enormity of her isolation and contribute to her disorientation upon awakening in a new world. Her confusion is compounded when a maid enters, calling her "Mrs. Hughes," expressing concern over her health, and commenting that this is her "new home" in Cornwall and how worried her husband has been about her. The fact that the Hughes family has created this transformation through sleep is disarmingly effective; Julia's identity has been removed upon her awakening, as if her previous life had been a dream, except that to Julia, the present is actually the dream. The lack of certainty about reality one feels when dreaming is conveyed when Julia finds herself, when she opens her eyes, in another life, one that is completely foreign to her. Christopher asserts that "noir films are the only films in which the presentation of dreams is consistently identical to the presentation of straight narrative action. One might miss the cutaway to a dream in film noir by blinking at the wrong moment."[6] Here, the viewer might experience the same dream disorientation as Julia herself without close attention; it may seem as though the reality is that Julia Ross never existed and that she is indeed the true Marion Hughes, brought back to her true identity. And from the opposite perspective, the vulnerability of the self when surrendered to sleep is underscored as Julia awakens to find her old name and her old life obliterated. As much as she believes herself to be Julia Ross, the various elements that contradict this belief give her enough pause to doubt her most fundamental certainties and give her the sense that she is indeed stuck in a surreal nightmare rather than her "real" life.

The Hugheses' plan is to attempt to convince the outside world that "Marion," Ralph's wife, is mentally disturbed, after which they can stage an "accident" in which she appears to have killed herself, an event no one would then question. In this respect, *Julia Ross* prefigures Hitchcock's *Vertigo* (1958) in its marital murder and cover-up plot. In *Vertigo*, however, the "fake wife" character of Judy is in on the deception and is in no real danger (from the murdering husband, at least). Julia Ross, however, is an unwilling prop in the Hugheses' plan, and her movements and thoughts seem hollow and dreamlike, as she is being forced to assume another identity. Her dreamlike environment is further emphasized by the middle of the night scene in which she is awakened in fright by Ralph's shadowy threat. The scene begins in darkness as a disembodied male hand, similar to the one that removed her handbag on her initial night with the Hughes family, stops the pendulum on the elephant clock. This hand becomes a great dark shadow moving, Nosferatu-like, over her body. Desperately fearful, she screams and throws an object from her nightstand across the room, shattering the dressing-table mirror. Julia's reaction to the shadowy threat is a symbolic rejection of the identity being projected onto her: there is no need for a mirror to exist to reflect the persona of "Marion Hughes" in the room in which Julia Ross is living a false life.

The sudden intrusion of this shadow molester, and the jolting awakening it provides, again underscores the film's liminal dream/waking state. The maid and the Hughes family, in fact, try to convince her that she had a nightmare; they say it must have been a dream. To this, Julia agonizingly cries in response, "Why did you bring me here? Are you trying to drive me crazy, is that it? Tell me what you're planning to do with me!" This exchange is an example of James Naremore's characterization of violence and disorientation in noir, as he asserts that noir narratives "are often situated on the margins of dreams, as if to intensify the surrealist atmosphere of violent confusion, ambiguity, or disequilibrium."[7] Julia is desperately trying to hold on to the remnants of her own identity by fighting to seek answers that explain the mystery of her predicament; the stark reality of her bleak life as an unmarried woman in financial straits has transformed itself into a surreal domestic nightmare in which she is a "wife" surrounded by "family" whose singular goal is her destruction.

Julia Ross lacks some of the intrigue of true *Gaslight* noirs, such as André de Toth's *Dark Waters* (1944) and Roy Rowland's *Witness to Murder* (1954). In these films, the protagonist is in true doubt of her sanity due to the machinations of others. In *Julia Ross* the actions of Ralph and Mrs. Hughes are less about truly convincing Julia that she is actually insane and more about outside appearances, but part of this plan does involve treating Julia as though she were Marion, so that her denials of her identity seem part of her psychosis. Oddly, even when Ralph and his mother are alone, they both refer to Julia as "Marion," rather than "Julia" or even the neutral "she"; for instance, when Ralph sees Julia running from the house, he reports to his mother, "Marion is going toward the road." Though they may do this to stay in "character" for the benefit of the servants and outsiders, it seems that they in part truly see her as a reincarnated Marion, and their comfort with enacting the charade reinforces the dreamlike atmosphere of the film. And with the same futility that one may try every resort for escape when in danger in a dream, Julia tests every inch of her environment, looking for a way out, including pressing on the bedroom walls for a secret panel and enlisting (unsuccessfully) the help of the maid. The maid reassuringly—and ironically—says that she has "a beautiful home, nice relations, pretty clothes: everything a woman would want." This false life in which Julia finds herself is one that is antithetical to the one she had left—of wealth and privilege, marriage and security, which is, of course, "everything a woman would want." The dark underside to all of this is the fact that it also, for Marion Hughes, came with a psychotic and violent husband and transforms the conventional domestic fantasy that women are supposed to desire into a sinister nightmare. Sylvia Harvey argues that "[it] is the representation of the institution of the family, which in so many films serves as the mechanism whereby desire is fulfilled, or at least ideological equilibrium established, that in *film noir* serves as the vehicle for the expression of frustration."[8] Likewise, Christopher asserts that the noir portrayal of the family is "something to be exposed, compromised, or fractured in the course of the individual's struggle for *self*-preservation. In short, the family is presented as something wholly unsuited to the stresses and strains of a disintegrating social structure."[9] The perverse version of domestic fulfillment that Julia finds with the Hugheses is typical of the noir distortions of family life. The maid tries to reassure Julia further by saying, "You're letting yourself be took up by illusions . . . letting it gnaw at you and gnaw at you. It's all in the mind. People can think themselves into anything." The "illusion" is, of course, the reality—who Julia used to be—and despite Julia's determination to maintain her identity, the position she is in makes clear how easy it might be to convince someone that she is a different person. Though she exists in this new reality, she is a "shadow," as we often personify ourselves in dreams—able to see things happening to us but helpless to affect the outcome.

Ralph Hughes is a noir "homme fatale," the villain in Julia's nightmare and the antithesis to Dennis, the kind of man with whom Julia might have imagined finding love and peace. As the film progresses, it becomes more and more clear that Ralph not only is a murderer but has genuine psychotic tendencies; in his psychosexual violence and torturous impulses, he prefigures *The Big Combo*'s Mr. Brown. Ralph is portrayed as a violent and destructive child, one who remains under the thumb of his mother, but who is capable of losing control. There are numerous scenes in which Mrs. Hughes admonishes him about his temper and must stop him from using knives or glass in destructive ways, and she locks up assorted sharp instruments that she has confiscated from him. The mental instability that is being projected onto Julia is actually fully realized in Ralph, whose violent impulses are the cause of Julia's captivity. Not only has he killed his wife, but he has done so in the most violent of ways. Contending to his mother that "it was Marion's fault; she shouldn't have cried," Ralph even relives the murder, violently slashing the couch on which he is sitting. His violence was so great, according to Mrs. Hughes, that no police could be called, lest anyone see "the marks of [his] fingers on her or see the scratches on [his] face." Interestingly, the breakdown of Ralph's relationship with Marion was caused by her discovery that he was penniless and that he had married her for her money. The dynamic of her financial independence and his violent aggression ended in her destruction; this is reenacted in the charade that the Hugheses construct with Julia.

This dynamic is further highlighted during an illuminating encounter between Ralph and Julia after one of her escape attempts. She decides to take a walk with Ralph around the grounds, in an effort to get him to reveal information that could help her escape. She plays along with the deception, saying that perhaps Ralph and his mother are really right about her, that maybe she has been ill and asks for his help in remembering. This dissemblance is reminiscent of what Elizabeth Cowie explains as other devices in noir for discovery and fact-finding pursuits, including flashback and detective work. She argues that these pursuits are analogous to the distinction in psychoanalytic theory between what is latent and what is manifest, following "the same division Freud describes for two aspects of the dream-work whereby the latent meaning of the dream is discovered indirectly through the associated thoughts and memories of the analysand as he or she recounts the manifest text of the dream."[10] This kind of unintentional discovery is seen in noir generally, especially in amnesia narratives, such as Joseph Mankiewicz's *Somewhere in the Night* (1946), in which the amnesiac is on a quest to discover the truth of his or her identity but ends up pursuing his own self in the process as a criminal accomplice to the mysterious loss of memory. Lewis's own *So Dark the Night* exemplifies this pursuit as well, as police detective Henri Cassin (Steven Geray) is himself the murderer that he is pursuing. He muses, "I've always been able to outguess the murderers. . . . I don't know where to turn," the reason for his confounding being that he himself is the murderer he is seeking. In *Julia Ross*, Julia knows who she is, but she is trapped in a hostile environment that will not acknowledge her identity. Therefore, she seeks information from Ralph to gain knowledge about her "shadow" self and thus attempts to talk her way out of her dream while she is still dreaming. She is trying to navigate with an Ariadne thread a path through the labyrinthine nightmare she is experiencing by gathering clues from her tormentor.

Julia's symbolic captivity is crystallized by Lewis's brilliant claustrophobic camerawork in the scene on the cliff overlooking the crashing waves. Meisel argues that Lewis favored the insertion of incongruous "open-air" shots that "indicate the presence of a normal world existing completely beyond this seamy underlife . . . he insists on preserving his reasonableness for all his fascination with dementia."[11] However, in this scene, it is apparent that the natural world is infused with this unnatural "dementia," making the dementia seem all the more "natural," and thereby terrifying. Likewise, for all its seeming fantastical elements, a nightmare seems nonetheless all too real to the dreamer, and this surreality is evident in Julia's encounter on the cliff with Ralph. As they stand on the cliff, Ralph turns away from Julia, musing about the beauty of the sea. As he speaks, the camera shoots him from behind as he looks at the sea, while she faces the camera. Ralph tells her, "[The sea] doesn't say anything, does it? That's what I like about it. It never tells its secrets. But it has many. Many, many secrets . . . ," and the shot moves into close-up on the upper part of Julia's face, so that only her eyes and nose are seen looking over his shoulder. She appears to be looking at his face and at the camera at the same time, but the viewer only sees his shoulder and her eyes over it. The effect is incongruously claustrophobic—though they are standing in the open air, she appears completely surrounded by his body and has become shrunken into a pair of eyes. His enormous presence in the frame signifies the threat of her slow disappearance from the world as she fights to hang on to her reason, signified by her gaze. This kind of dynamic is explained by Mary Ann Doane, who argues that "what is particularly interesting about *film noir* for a feminist analysis is the way in which the issue of knowledge and its possibility or impossibility is articulated with questions concerning femininity and visibility. The woman confounds the relation between the visible and the knowable at the same time that she is made into an object for the gaze."[12] Julia has put herself into harm's way, making herself an object for Ralph's destructive gaze, ironically to find out knowledge about her doppelgänger in order to free herself from that link. It is an incredibly disorienting moment for the viewer, who almost experiences a kind of vertigo on the cliff along with Julia Ross, her entire identity at risk. Julia is trying to turn Ralph's psychotic tendencies against him, while delicately balancing her own sanity and life in the process.

In this, however, Julia is foiled at every turn. Every attempt she makes at escape or even communication of her plight ends in greater frustration and failure. Cassandra-like, the more she attests her sanity and identity, the less she is believed. These repetitive attestations of her true identity and attempts at escape are usually presented in the same kind of visually claustrophobic scenes, most of which, as already noted, are ironically outside the prisonlike environment of the house in the open air. In this way, her frustration at being unable to free herself feels surreal, as if her captivity follows her wherever she goes, much as in a dream, sensations of fear or imprisonment pervade the literal action of the dream, however incongruous it may seem. Freud comments that "in dreams the ideational content is not accomplished by the affective consequences that we should regard as inevitable in waking thought."[13] In other words, the level of emotion one experiences in a dream is often at odds with the literal action therein, and the kind of incongruity that is felt by Julia as she tries to fight her way out of her predicament is typical of the disconnect in dreams that Freud describes. After a failed attempt to convince the estate's gatekeeper of her true identity, she scribbles a note describing her plight (on the back of a newspaper crossword puzzle, a fitting metaphor for her own mysterious dilemma) in order to throw it outside the gate in the hopes that someone will find it. The shot of her writing frantically is captured in a tight worm's-eye view shot that feels intensely "interior" and closed in. A similar effect is produced after she fails to make herself believed by a group of visitors to the house, her protests about being kept prisoner again only reinforcing the claim by the family that she is mentally disturbed. She attempts to hide herself in the backseat of the visitors' car when they depart, and the shots of her crammed into the small space on the car's backseat floor have an extremely claustrophobic effect; though she is outside of the Hugheses' estate, she is still within their extended grasp, as is soon proven when she is recaptured by Ralph. One further example of this exterior "closeness" is evident in the scene in which Ralph drives Julia to town to post a letter. She is going to extreme lengths and machinations to send this missive to Dennis, and her efforts almost seem as though she is acting in slow motion, the time taken for such a simple endeavor disproportionate to its reality. Though she and Ralph ride in his open-air convertible, the atmosphere is powerfully suffocating, in Julia's tension and the close-up shot of her hands switching the letters surreptitiously out of Ralph's sight. These scenes synthesize the nature of the nightmare that Julia is experiencing; her flight from the pain of isolation plunge her into a spiral of terror and confinement that is the antithesis of the domestic fantasy that she might have imagined.

Julia's last hope rests on reaching out for her original romantic savior, Dennis, to awaken her from the nightmare she is experiencing. He is the only possible restorer of order in what has become a chaotic alternate universe. It is in pursuit of this savior that Julia experiences the ultimate disorienting experience that will either ensure her destruction or restore her identity. In yet another middle of the night abrupt awakening, she hears a whispering voice call "Julia . . . Julia Ross . . . Hurry." Thinking it is Dennis, she obeys the voice, actually Ralph's, which says he will wait for her downstairs. Julia's figure is shrouded in shadow at the head of the stairs as she queries, "Where are you, Dennis?" her face in full darkness as she seeks the illumination of rescue and restoration of her true self. But her realization of the voice as unfamiliar, and thus a false representation of her hopes, brings into sharp relief the conflation of the various identities in her confusing dream—Dennis is mixed with Ralph, as she is mixed with Marion. Julia has awakened in darkness to the call of her name, and she seeks to reinforce her own identity by following that call and refinding her own identity. Following this call would mean her own death, however, as Ralph has tried to orchestrate her demise by removing steps from the staircase. Though she does not fall, her restoration, ironically, can only be realized by her death, or at least the faking of her bodily death, insofar as her body belongs to the identity of the phantom Marion Hughes. Her scream after the staircase incident leads Ralph and Mrs. Hughes to her room to find the bars opened on her window and what seems to be a white-clad body on the cliff below. What they believe to be her dead body is only her empty white robe, the final symbolic nod to the empty identity that she was made to assume.

Bringing Ralph's crime to light, and thereby ensuring her own rescue, is the only way that Julia can break the spell of her own nightmare and awaken to the "real" world. Julia's faking of her own death may seem not to meet this end, since this orchestration appears to spell good news for the Hughes family: the "suicide" that Mrs. Hughes calls their "best alibi." However, Ralph's need to violently ensure Julia's death proves to be his undoing and thus secures Julia's freedom. Andrew Dickos argues that "women in the film noir are created and seen through the eyes of men, and the perception of them stems, as has often been written, though the power they wield in disorienting the male object."[14] Julia Ross succeeds in making Ralph Hughes relive the murderous scene of power and frustration that he experienced with his real wife Marion, and his making of Julia into a surrogate Marion only leads to his downfall, as he must confirm Julia's actual death and perhaps gain some final satisfaction in potentially finishing the job himself (he lifts a rock to bring down on her head for extra insurance). The real Marion haunts him, and he cannot believe that the death of the faux Marion will put his mind at ease without him actually performing the final violent deed of killing her. Though he killed her before, she did not die a "public" death and this therefore prevented his freedom.[15] But unlike the real Marion, the faux Marion is not truly alone. Julia has escaped, but not without the help of men—including both Dennis and a doctor. The denouement of the film shows Dennis offering Julia another "job"—as his wife, encompassing the duties of "secretary, nurse, companion." The terms of her rescue involve another kind of captivity; though she is awakened, Sleeping Beauty–like with a male kiss, from the nightmare of this kidnapped existence, it is not to her restored independence. The reiteration of the film's title holds true, as Julia can reassert her own identity, but only for a time, as her salvation depends on her "new job" as Dennis's wife. Ironically, she will soon assume a new name and a new identity, although one presumably not at the hands of a violent psychopath.

My Name Is Julia Ross is a compelling precursor to what became the psychologically complex films Lewis was best known for and shows his willingness to explore the dark, pathological recesses and hidden vulnerabilities of the human mind. Julia Ross's nightmarish journey both affirms and undercuts her identity, as her efforts for security lead her directly into the most helpless of situations, one in which conventional domestic fantasies are twisted into life-threatening perils. When Julia falls asleep in the Hugheses' house, she enters a dream in which her entire identity and existence is at risk, and can only be awakened into peace and safety by the intervention of male authority that will transform her fledgling independence into marital subservience. Christopher asserts that a noir film, "like the dream in psychoanalysis, may be an explanation in itself, through it symbolism, its juxtapositions, and its story, however fractured."[16] In *Julia Ross*, then, the machinations and eventual success of escape from the torturous dream only prove that there is no escape; the visual expressions of captivity speak louder than the eventual plot resolution. The titular affirmation that her "name is Julia Ross" rings hollow; the name is merely a placeholder for the next identity she will assume. Though Julia never really believes that she is someone else or that she is really insane, Lewis does a masterful job of painting the terrifying portrait of alienation and identity crisis that is particular to female independence in the postwar noir universe.

NOTES

1. Andrew Dickos, *Street with No Name: A History of the Classic American Film Noir* (Lexington: University Press of Kentucky, 2002), 151.

2. Nicholas Christopher, *Somewhere in the Night: Film Noir and the American City* (New York: Henry Holt, 1997), 43–44.

3. Foster Hirsch, *The Dark Side of the Screen: Film Noir* (New York: Da Capo Press, 1981), 182.

4. Myron Meisel, "Joseph H. Lewis: Tourist in the Asylum" in *Kings of the Bs: Working within the Hollywood System*, ed. Todd McCarthy and Charles Flynn (New York: E. P. Dutton, 1975), 102.

5. Raymond Borde and Etienne Chaumeton, *A Panorama of American Film Noir, 1941–1953*, trans. Paul Hammond (San Francisco: City Lights Books, 2002), 10–11.

6. Christopher, *Somewhere in the Night*, 221.

7. James Naremore, *More than Night: Film Noir in Its Contexts* (Berkeley: University of California Press, 1998), 21.

8. Sylvia Harvey, "Woman's Place: The Absent Family of *Film Noir*," in *Women in Film Noir*, ed. E. Ann Kaplan (London: BFI, 1998), 36.

9. Christopher, *Somewhere in the Night*, 196.

10. Elizabeth Cowie, "*Film Noir* and Women" in *Shades of Noir: A Reader*, ed. Joan Copjec (London: Verso, 1993), 155.

11. Meisel, "Tourist in the Asylum," 97.

12. Mary Ann Doane, *Femmes Fatales: Feminism, Film Theory, and Psychoanalysis* (New York: Routledge, 1991), 103.

13. Sigmund Freud, *The Interpretation of Dreams*, trans. James Strachey (New York: Avon Books, 1965), 497.

14. Dickos, *Street with No Name*, 156.

15. He also seems as though he would not eschew the by-product satisfaction of actually bashing in Julia's skull as repayment for her rebuffs of his sexual advances.

16. Christopher, *Somewhere in the Night*, 207.

8

BRIAN HOYLE

"A Matchless Stylist Exercise"

Joseph H. Lewis and So Dark the Night

No study of Joseph H. Lewis's career would be complete without an appreciation of *So Dark the Night* (1946). While it is perhaps a minor work in comparison to his best-known films, *Gun Crazy* (1950) and *The Big Combo* (1955), it should nevertheless be seen as "the first major film in the Lewis canon" and the one which premiered the director's fully developed style.[1] It was the second assignment Lewis completed at Columbia and the biggest production he had yet been involved in, but it is still very much a B movie, made quickly and with limited resources. The film is marked by low-budget production values, a rather mediocre script, and variable performances. However, these shortcomings are offset by Lewis's direction. Indeed, with the possible exception of Edgar G. Ulmer, Lewis was the quintessential B movie stylist. His films are often remembered for their distinctive directorial touches rather than the quality of the writing or any profundity of meaning. *So Dark the Night* remains one of the finest examples of this phenomenon. As Tony Rayns writes, "This is what Joseph H. Lewis is all about. The script is a perfunctory and frequently silly murder mystery. . . . However, none of this matters. The film is directed like a million bucks . . . it has more cinematic ideas and effects per square foot of screen than any number of contemporary 'A' features. In other words, it's a 'typical' Lewis movie: low on thinks, but with enough style to send lovers of cinema reeling."[2] The plot of the film is indeed rather implausible. An obsessive and single-minded Parisian detective, Henri Cassin (Steven Geray), is sent by M. Grande, the commissioner of police, to recuperate in the countryside as he teeters on the edge of a nervous breakdown. While in the country he meets and falls in love with Nanette (Michele Cheirel), the young daughter of an innkeeper, M. Michaud. Nanette dreams of the glamour of Paris and flatters the older detective into proposing marriage. She nevertheless maintains an affair with a local man, Antoine, to whom she was previously promised. On the eve of the wedding her father begs the detective to allow Nanette to marry Antoine. Soon after, the two young lovers are found murdered. Cassin investigates. After some anonymous threats, the young lady's mother is also killed. The detective assembles all the evidence and begins to suspect himself. He returns to Paris and explains his theories to Grande and the police psychiatrist, Dr. Manet. Cassin asks to be placed under guard. The doctor explains to Grande that it could be a case of split personalities and argues that the strain of his job and the implication that he was too old to marry Nanette has caused the violent personality within Cassin to emerge. Meanwhile, Cassin "changes," kills his guard, and boards a train back to the village to murder M. Michaud. At the inn, the two men fight but before Cassin is able to kill Michaud the commissioner arrives and shoots his friend. As he is dying Cassin sees a reflection of his former self reflected in the window. He smashes it with a fire poker, thus killing his "good" half just before his "bad" half also dies.

The film's doppelgänger theme is reminiscent of numerous gothic novels; the presence of a schizophrenic murderer seems to prefigure Alfred Hitchcock's *Psycho* (1960); and the idea of a detective searching for himself would be developed in Alan Parker's neo-noir, *Angel Heart* (1987). However, such connections are rather misleading. *So Dark the Night*'s explanation of its protagonist's split personality is "equal parts cod-Freud and O Henry" and extraordinarily glib.[3] What is far more interesting is the way that Lewis visualizes the character's dual nature through a complex series of mirror images throughout the film. Therefore, those seeking a psychoanalytical reading will need to look elsewhere. This chapter will rather offer a close examination of the film's key attribute, Lewis's cinematic technique.

Stylistic analysis of this kind has been labeled as formalist and criticized for its lack of ideology.[4] However, as David Bordwell has argued, "Style is not simply window-dressing draped over a script; it is the very flesh of the work."[5] This is statement is particularly applicable when considering Lewis, whose reputation largely rests on his ability to transform scripts of dubious merit by virtue of his strong visual sense. Lewis was not an auteur, and his work is rarely "personal." Rather, as Jim Kitses has argued, "Lewis is essentially a stylist without a theme," and his "hodgepodge of a filmography absolutely resists reduction to any consistency."[6] For him, a project such as *So Dark the Night* was a "stylistic exercise";[7] therefore, a formal analysis such as this is in keeping with the spirit of the work. While this chapter will largely focus on this one film, it will refer to others by Lewis and his con-

The inspector (Steven Geray) investigates the scene of the murder he has unwittingly committed in Lewis's noir-thriller *So Dark the Night*.

temporaries in order to situate it (and Lewis) within the wider context of Hollywood studio filmmaking before going on to assess *So Dark the Night*'s place within a more specific style of film noir.

"From the opening, [*So Dark the Night*] shows complete visual control,"[8] and an examination of the first reel provides a textbook example of Lewis's economical style while demonstrating some of the eccentricities that make him such a distinctive director. As in his previous film, *My Name Is Julia Ross* (1945), Lewis places the opening titles over a few "postcard" shots, which use instantly recognizable landmarks as an inexpensive shorthand to establish location. In *Julia Ross*, London had been implied by a single shot of the Houses of Parliament (complete with Big Ben) and London Bridge. In *So Dark the Night* Lewis makes the obvious but effective move of including the Eiffel Tower in the background of the first two shots. The third shot is of a building on the banks of the Seine. There is then a dissolve to a close-up of a sign that reads, "Prefecture de Police: Bureau de la Sûreté." This is easily dismissed as a simple establishing shot and part of the title sequence (the name of the film's producer, and "prefect," Ted Richmond, is laid over this sign). However, it must be noted that this sign acts as a mirror. It is also significant that it is filmed on a slightly dutch angle. Therefore, the first reflective surface in a film full of mirrors and reflections is slightly distorted by both the words written over it (including the word *police*) and this skewed angle.

The shot of the sign dissolves into a close-up of a telephone. Both objects are placed in the exact center of the frame and fill the same space. The dissolve that links the two economically tells us that this telephone belongs to the commissioner of police himself. Lewis places his own title card over the close-up of the telephone. It begins to ring as the camera dollies in, and then moves up with Commissioner Grande's hand as he answers it. He asks about the whereabouts of Henri Cassin, his finest detective. He orders the man on the phone to "search the city" for the missing man and then asks to see Dr. Manet, who quickly enters the room. In next two shots the commissioner tells Manet what kind of man Cassin is. He establishes his honesty and reliability, saying that Cassin would "turn in his own mother if he thought she was guilty." He also says that the detective is "so single-minded that he can appear sluggish and even stupid at times," however, he says it is unlike Cassin to forget an appointment, and the commissioner's chauffer was scheduled to drive the detective into the country for a well-earned rest. This single-mindedness, coupled with this sudden onset of forgetfulness and the need for a vacation, sows the seeds of the mental breakdown that will cause Cassin to become a murderer. However, the Cassin the audience first encounters seems slightly bumbling, just as the commissioner implied, but he is also affable and charming.

The second shot in this sequence, in which the doctor is seen entering the room, is a high-angle shot that looks down on the action from the ceiling. The foreground of the top left corner of the screen is dominated by an electric fan, which is slowly turning. There is something unusual about the placement of this fan. It is both too high up and too far away from Grande's desk to be of any practical use. It seems rather to have been placed there for aesthetic reasons. This composition, in which we must look *through* the blades of the fan at the action below, is reminiscent of dozens of shots in Lewis's B westerns where the action was framed through the spokes of a wagon wheel placed in the extreme foreground. In fact these shots were so prevalent (and infamous) that they earned the director the nickname "Wagon Wheel Joe," as the director himself explains, "I carried a box filled with different wagon wheels, different spokes, wide ones, narrow ones, curved ones . . . whenever I'd come to a scene which was just disgraceful in dialogue and all, I'd place a wagon wheel in one portion of the frame and make an artistic shot out of it, so by the time the scene was over you only saw the artistic value and couldn't analyze what the scene was about."[9] This overhead shot (which is itself another typical Lewis camera placement) is in essence the master shot in this short sequence, as it gives the viewer a coherent sense of space and the distance between objects and characters. However, Lewis does not return to it. The reason for this is simple: the remainder of the scene will be played out in a single take, lasting just under one minute.

In this shot, the camera is placed on a track on the floor, slightly below eye level. At first all three men are in shot. The camera then tracks past the chauffer and closes in on Commissioner Grande and the doctor who are now framed in a medium shot by the commissioner's desk, perpendicular to the camera. From this point on, through a few simple tracks and careful choreography of the actors (the commissioner paces between the window and his desk, twice turning his back on the camera, while the doctor remains stationary, pivoting to face Grande as he moves), Lewis creates the appearance of an over-the-shoulder shot / reverse shot pattern without cutting.

There is nothing virtuoso about this shot. In fact it is framed and blocked in a way that does not call attention to itself. However, it is a fine example of a director choosing to rely on movement rather than editing when filming a conversation. Of course, Lewis was not the only director to use this technique. Bordwell notes a more sustained example of the same phenomenon in the middle of Otto Preminger's *Fallen Angel*, released one year earlier, in 1945. He writes, "Preminger's four-and-a-half-minute *plan sequence* needs no shot/reverse shot. Characters take turns assuming an over-the-shoulder stance with utter naturalness, and the tightly confined camera movements present constantly changing foregrounds that hold or deflect our attention."[10]

One should not assume that Lewis is borrowing this technique from Preminger. Indeed, there are several examples of the same technique in *My Name Is Julia Ross*, made the same year as *Fallen Angel*, such as the minute-long conversation between Julia and the maid, Alice, about thirty minutes into the film. Rather, the stylistic similarity points to a wider trend among some notable directors working within the Hollywood studio system. It is fair to say that the sustained take is common in the work of stylists such as Sam Fuller, Ulmer, Preminger, and Lewis, who all did some of their best work in B and low A genre movies, and major studio directors such as Vincent Minnelli, John Stahl, William Wyler, Howard Hawks, John Ford, and Orson Welles as well.

Barry Salt suggests that the average shot length in a Hollywood film made between 1940 and 1951 is about nine or ten seconds,[11] whereas the average shot in a Lewis film is likely to be higher, and in some cases substantially so. Even in his some of his more rapidly cut films, such as *Gun Crazy* and *My Name Is Julia Ross*, there are notable long takes, and the average shot length is around eleven seconds in both cases. Similarly, the average shot lengths in *Invisible Ghost* (1941), *So Dark the Night*, and *Terror in a Texas Town* (1958) are between fourteen and fifteen seconds, and *Secrets of a Co-Ed* (1943) and *The Big Combo*, in which many scenes are composed of only one or two shots, approach nineteen seconds each.

The reasons for employing long takes were varied, but one could argue that there were three main reasons for consistently utilizing them. The first is simply a matter of style. Hollywood films were conventionally made up of a decoupage of short shots assembled together using the rules of continuity cutting, and the directors listed above used longer takes as a way of going "against the tide."[12] Also, as Salt notes, "directors were becoming bored [with the rules] and were inclined to welcome a different method of scene dissection."[13]

Second, a carefully conceived long take was an invaluable way to make up for lost time in a shooting schedule,[14] especially one as tight as those Lewis was used to. For example, the celebrated robbery sequence in *Gun Crazy* was shot in a mere three hours and managed to condense seventeen pages of the script, scheduled to be shot over four days, into a single three-and-a-half-minute take filmed from the back of a car. Speed was also the primary motivation behind another famously sustained take in Lewis's oeuvre, the courtroom climax to *Secrets of a Co-Ed*. Lewis recalls,

> I remember I made a film in six days . . . in which I shot a courtroom scene that ran a full ten minutes in one shot. Now, it's true, it took me the entire morning of rehearsal; and I'm sure my producer was pulling his hair out because I hadn't made a shot. Every 15 minutes or so the 2nd assistant [director] must have been calling him and saying, "This guy's crazy, he hasn't made a shot." But by noon we had 10 minutes, 10 minutes in one scene; and I never shot anything to protect it.[15]

The fact that Lewis remembers not shooting anything to "protect" this long take is another indication of the time constraints he was working under, which would not allow for something as seemingly fundamental as shooting coverage. However, it also points to the third reason why many notable Hollywood filmmakers employed longer takes: a long take, especially when shot without coverage, was hard for editors and producers to manipulate in postproduction. At a time when few, if any, directors had the right of final cut on their films, this style of filmmaking allowed directors to preserve their vision of the material.

Perhaps the most notable exponent of this style of filmmaking was John Ford, who "took the precaution of 'cutting in the camera.' That meant that he shot as little nonessential footage as possible, avoiding repeated takes or 'covering' the scene from many angles as most directors did in that era." This, claims Robert Parrish, "was Ford's own guarantee against possible butchery by front office executives.... Ford left them no extra footage to play around with."[16] Similarly, as the only footage of Kruger's final speech in *Secrets of a Co-Ed* was this single extended take, the editor would be left with no choice but to include it unbroken and in its entirety.

Before returning to *So Dark the Night*, the courtroom climax of *Secrets of a Co-Ed* is worth examining in more depth. The sequence is commonly used as an example of Lewis's directorial invention and virtuosity in studies of his work and has taken on near-legendary status. Surveying Lewis's career in *The Film Handbook*, Geoff Andrew writes that "*Secrets of a Co-Ed* ends with a ten minute courtroom scene constructed astonishingly from a single take."[17] Francis M. Nevins is more elaborate in his description: "Five years before Hitchock's experiment with ten-minute takes in *Rope* (1948), Lewis chose to shoot the court-room scene in a single take that incorporates close-ups, long shots, medium shots, over-the-shoulder shots, and just about everything else in the repertory."[18]

However, a close examination of the sequence reveals something quite different. The final courtroom sequence in fact lasts about twelve minutes, and the first part is conventionally shot and edited. This half features around thirty shots taken from what appears to be six different camera setups. There is a two shot of Tina Thayer and Otto Kruger (as the accused and her lawyer father); medium shots of the judge and the witness chair; a single tracking shot across the faces of the people watching the trial; and two complex crane shots, the first beginning on a close-up of the Prosecutor before pulling back dramatically to cover the entire courtroom from above, and the second surveying the proceedings from behind the jury box. The legendary long take, which lasts six minutes, not ten, takes up the entire second half of the trial scene in which Kruger defends his daughter by confessing his own guilt. Here, Lewis reverses the earlier crane shot with the Prosecutor. He begins with an extreme long shot, which dwarfs Kruger's character. It then moves closer, framing him in a medium shot. *Pace* Nevins, this shot does not contain "everything . . . in the repertory" and the camera remains at roughly the same distance from Kruger for the remainder of the shot, as it follows him pacing in front of the jury. If this shot is not quite as long or as complex as many descriptions have made out, it does not greatly detract from Lewis's achievement. It is still a very long and complicated shot and one that is a good deal more sober than many critics give it credit for. In a direct contrast to the Prosecutor, who was filmed with a level camera, Lewis consistently films Kruger from a high angle, so that the audience looks down on him. However, we also come to sympathize with his plight, and Lewis's camera sticks close to Kruger to give us the full power and emotion of his very committed performance, rather than distracting us with bravura camerawork.

The slightly exaggerated descriptions of this shot perhaps stem from the fact that Lewis's early films were rarely screened and many critics had to rely on memory, word of mouth, and the director's own somewhat inaccurate recollections when writing about them. But the tendency toward exaggeration is also indicative of the mystique that cineastes have formed around Lewis's movies. Another such example is the re-creation of the French village in *So Dark the Night*. The legend goes that the "illusion of a French village was so convincing that Lewis was attacked in some quarters for taking production money and jobs out of the country."[19] Lewis remembers that "there was terrible criticism from most every newspaper, claiming that Columbia was trying to put one over on them by buying a picture that was shot in Europe and pretending that it was made here in the United States, which pleased me to no end."[20] It is hard to take Lewis's version of the events entirely seriously. The re-creation of France is hardly convincing enough to fool most reviewers into thinking the film was actually made there. On the contrary, Rayns goes as far as to argue that the film is "set in a ludicrous evocation of France, most embarrassing in the opening scenes in Paris, but still irritating when the plot takes the police inspector hero . . . into the country."[21] Certainly, at first glance, the depiction of Paris bears Rayns out. The budget clearly did not stretch to anything close to an authentic re-creation of the city, but Lewis responds with typical pragmatism. A review from *Variety* perhaps comes closest to the reality when it says that "despite the obvious budget limitations, the layout of the streets, interior decorations and landscape shots define France as it exists in our imagination."[22] For example, the sole exterior scene set in Paris (after the credits) lasts only one minute and is divided into two shots. The first of these is a tracking shot that keeps the camera at a low angle, following Cassin's feet. By keeping the camera focused on the pavement, Lewis hides the fact that he has little set to show. However, when the camera tilts up slightly, Lewis does reveal a sign for a sandwich shop written in French. Even if the set is minimal to say the least, Lewis is careful to try to give an impression of authenticity. The second shot, which places the camera closer to eye level, is less convincing. It is all too apparent that the set consists of little more than half a street containing two or three shop fronts, with a few café tables and patrons placed in the foreground to give the illusion of offscreen space. However, as Lewis tracks left he places a flower stall in the foreground of the shot and things begin to seem more believable again. The flowers, which now take up the bottom third; the frame of the stall; and the awning disguise the set's lack of depth.

The tracking shot that follows the detective's feet shares a stylistic affinity with the (subsequent) work of the French filmmaker Robert Bresson, whose films contain countless shots of this kind. For example, in a costume drama such as *Lancelot du lac* (1973), Bresson includes tracking shots of his actors' legs and feet, often clad in full armor. By often filming only portions of his set and his actors, Bresson is able to create the impression of medieval France with great economy of means. Lewis has always demonstrated a similar ability to create something out of very little, and it was not his intention to re-create Paris or a French farming village in *So Dark the Night* so much as to create the *impression* of them.

In this regard Cassin's arrival in the village is worth examining. Again, this sequence contains only a handful of shots taken from very carefully chosen angles. The first unmistakably bears Lewis's signature. The car is seen driving down a dirt road. To one side of it are three small buildings and a church with a small bell tower, on the other side only one building is visible. This one street is all Lewis has to work with in order to create his village. However, Lewis again places objects in the foreground to give the viewer a sense that there is more here than meets the eye. On the right there is a sign telling us the name of the village, St. Margot. The left side of the screen, perhaps unsurprisingly, is dominated by a straw-filled cart complete with wagon wheel. Lewis then presents Cassin's arrival "into the town from the viewpoint of how the town sees him, and not the other way around."[23] Lewis explains how he does this:

> A peasant woman is looking out the window as the car drives by, and we had nothing to shoot. So we found a black velvet drop . . . because we had no set; we put this woman in front of the black velvet—looking out the window—and shot into the window, reflecting the dirt road, and showed the car come winding all the way down, through the eyes of this woman, as reflected in the pane of glass. Impressions again: you'd swear you were in a French village.[24]

In fact, there are two shots of the peasant woman watching the car. The second shot is exactly the way Lewis remembers, with the woman standing in front of a black background and the car reflected in the window in front of her. However, in the preceding shot the camera is placed inside the house, looking out the window at the car. What is more, the window frame is visibly different in the two shots. In the first, the horizontal muntin toward the top of the window is far larger than in the second. Yet it is highly unlikely that this is a simple continuity error. Rather, it more likely that Lewis shot two different windows as one offered a better view of the small village set and the other a better angle to film the reflection of the car. Also, if one examines the two shots carefully, one can see that some care has been put into making them match. The second shot, showing the reflection of the car is shot from a slightly lower angle than the first. The reflection of the church bell tower, which features prominently in the top left and then top right corner of the successive shots, creating another mirror image, is here elongated and on a slight angle. This was perhaps done in order to make the tower appear in the correct corner of the window. This admirably demonstrates Lewis's pragmatic approach to filmmaking. The slight discrepancy between shots is excusable if it means that the scene will play better as a whole.

Lewis was not merely a great pragmatist, and several scenes demonstrate a rare understanding of the medium and its conventions. A fine example of this comes in the scene depicting Cassin's arrival at the inn, when he first sees Nanette. It begins with a long shot of the chauffer-driven car pulling up outside the inn. This is followed by a close-up of Nanette peering at it from behind the blanket she is hanging out to dry. There is then a medium long shot of Cassin, who is stretching after his long journey. He is looking off to his right before turning and catching sight of Nanette. He smiles. There is then a return to the close-up of Nanette; she is looking more intently than before, her eyes wide. Logically, an audience would then expect a cut back to Cassin meeting Nanette's gaze. However, Lewis instead cuts to an extreme close-up of the shining chrome headlight of the car. This is rapidly followed by close-ups of the car's front grill and emblem. There is then another close-up of Nanette, who seems almost hypnotized, followed by a pair of shots of a (rather phallic) door handle and a hubcap. Following this shot-reverse shot between Nanette and parts of the car, Lewis finally returns to a shot of Cassin, who seems equally entranced by the sight of the young woman.

This, of course, is subversively playing on the convention of the "eyeline match," a cut between two shots in which the first shows a person looking offscreen in a certain direction and the second shows who or what it is that the person is looking at. However, the meaning of this scene cannot be missed. Cassin clearly sees Nanette and is charmed. But she does not see him; she sees the car and the possibility of money, excitement, and escape it represents. Also, by breaking the car down into component parts, emphasizing its curves and glinting surfaces and having a woman desire it, Lewis is inverting the male gaze. Laura Mulvey argues that "pleasure in looking has been split between active/male and passive/female. The determining male gaze projects its fantasy on to the female figure which is styled accordingly."[25] Here however, the tables have been turned and it is the woman who actively desires and it is her gaze that objectifies. Without a word, Nanette's predatory nature is established.

Lewis then shows Cassin and the commissioner's chauffer walking into the inn. As they approach the entrance the camera moves behind the side wall and is temporarily obscured. One would then expect there to be a cut or dissolve, which would relocate the action inside. However, Lewis does not cut but rather continues to track, and the camera moves from the exterior to the interior through the wall. If the minimalist evocation of the French setting can be favorably compared to the work of Bresson, this kind of graceful camerawork has drawn comparison to the work of Max Ophüls.[26] It is a testament to Lewis's distinctiveness and abilities as a director that he can bear comparison to two such divergent talents. If Bresson is synonymous with austerity, especially in regards to mise-en-scène, Ophüls rather antithetically implies an "uncommonly elaborate visual style."[27] However, Paul Kerr does not note any contradiction in these comparisons and argues that "the much commented-on 'Bressonian' sparseness of Lewis's settings and yet the fluid 'Ophülsian' manner of his shooting style both originate precisely in the industrial constraints under which the film was made."[28] In short, the Bressonian elements have been imposed on Lewis's film by financial restrictions. For Bresson, synecdochical images in which a part represents a larger whole, such as "a wheel instead of an automobile, a doorknob instead of an apartment"[29] are an aesthetic (and ascetic) choice. For Lewis, however, a synecdoche such as having four buildings and a dirt road represent a village is born of necessity. Out of this imposed austerity, where production values are almost nonexistent, grows Lewis's more elaborate visual style. With nothing particularly lavish to show an audience in terms of setting or design, the camera itself must be employed in an imaginative way.

Perhaps the most overtly Ophülsian elements in *So Dark the Night* are these shots where the camera tracks "through" walls and Lewis's propensity to frame shots through windows and doorways. Ophüls utilized the former technique in several of his American films of the 1940s, including *Letter from an Unknown Woman* (1948); however, it is most prevalent in his 1949 noir-melodrama *Caught*. The latter technique is most noticeable in Ophüls's final American film, *The Reckless Moment* (1949). However, Salt notes that this was a new trend for Ophüls, and while it would reappear in his later French films, especially *La plaisir* (1952), "this had never happened to this extent in Ophüls's films before."[30]

Despite the stylistic similarity, Lewis is not borrowing from Ophüls here. On the contrary, *So Dark the Night* predates Ophüls's Hollywood films and Lewis had been passing his camera through walls and framing through windows as early as *Invisible Ghost*. Rather, the connection again speaks to a wider trend in Hollywood filmmaking of the late 1940s. As Salt writes, "When Ophüls finally returned to film-making in America in 1947, the stylistic context had radically changed. Long takes had become an accepted part of the scene again, and extensive camera movement had been used by Minnelli and Preminger and others from 1945 onwards. . . . The immediate outcome was the increase in take length and in tracking and craning visible in the camera movement."[31] Therefore, Ophüls is merely doing what a good many other Hollywood-based directors, such as Lewis, are doing and is experimenting with longer takes, unusual camera angles, and complex camera movements made possible by technological advances such as the crab dolly. What is more, *Caught* and *The Reckless Moment*, unlike the slightly more personal *Letter from an Unknown Woman*, "represent Ophüls' struggle to make something stylistically interesting out from rather unpromising melodramatic material."[32] Therefore, these two genre films, which are now seen as being among Ophüls's finest works, can also be seen as "stylistic exercises" that show him working in a manner similar to Lewis on *So Dark the Night* and a dozen other films, imbuing potentially unpromising material with his directorial signature.

While Lewis worked across many genres, he is probably most associated with two, the western and the film noir. While, hour for hour, he directed more westerns, it is the noir films that Lewis is best remembered for. Indeed, as Paul Schrader has argued, selected randomly, "a Joseph H. Lewis 'B' film noir is [likely to be] better than a Lewis 'B' western."[33] The decade between 1945 and 1955 represents both the golden age of film noir and Lewis's peak as an artist. As Kerr points out, of the dozen films he directed in this period, nine can be considered noirs.[34] It goes without saying that *Gun Crazy* (a hybrid noir-western) and *The Big Combo* are considered by many to be among the finest examples of this particular style of American filmmaking. However, *So Dark the Night* must also be counted as "one of Lewis' purest *noir* achievements."[35]

This may not be apparent upon first viewing, as it is in many ways a rather unconventional film noir. As Kerr notes, in most noir films, "the main action has a habit of occurring in shadowy rooms, dingy offices, overlush apartments, and rainwashed streets. In such settings both actors and décor are often partially obscured by the foregrounding of oblique objects—shutters or banisters, for instance, casting horizontal or vertical grids of light and dark across faces and furniture."[36] Aside from the placing of objects in the foreground of the frame, a Lewis trademark that extended far beyond wagon wheels, *So Dark the Night* at first seems to have very few of these qualities. First, the film is set in the bucolic French countryside, not the "rainwashed streets" of an urban metropolis. Even more importantly, while there are a few notable sequences, such as Michaud walking alone through the dark streets of the village after the murder of his wife, that are dimly lit and full of deep shadows, Lewis and cinematographer Burnett Guffey often eschew the chiaroscuro lighting effects that are synonymous with film noir in favor of lighting in a high key. Even scenes that may perhaps call for darkness, such as the scene in which Cassin discovers the body of his murdered fiancée, are brightly lit.

There is however a good reason for the film's atypical lighting scheme, and there is a tradition of noir films that feature scenes with high-key lighting designed to contrast with more recognizably noir elements. As Kerr notes, "*Noir* sets are often only half or quarter lit, with the important exceptions of those brief scenes in the *blanc* (that is, 'normal') world."[37] A fine example of this is Fritz Lang's *The Big Heat* (1953), which uses high-key lighting in the scenes depicting the hero's happy home life and low-key lighting in the scenes depicting the dark underbelly of the city. In *So Dark the Night* this contrast between light and dark (and what they represent) becomes apparent in almost every scene.

For example, the sequence in which Cassin examines Nanette's corpse begins with a shot of the villagers gathered on the footbridge across the river, watching the detective at work. At first, the camera is tilted down and shows the reflection of the villagers in the water. The image is darkened by the shadow of the bridge and distorted by the ripples from the water. Lewis then tilts the camera upward and frames the villagers against the skyline. The image is now light. Dark and light here coexist within the same shot, just as two distinct personalities, one gentle, one deranged, coexist within Cassin. The distorted nature of Cassin's personality is also underscored when we see him standing over the boat in which Nanette's body was found. Although the river is visibly behind him, a light reflecting the ripples of the water shines clearly on his face when Lewis cuts to a close-up. This shot "further develops the visual link between [Cassin's] repressed realization and images of him reflected in water, mirrors and the like."[38] Both the shot of the crowd on the bridge and the distorting light reflected on Cassin's face also refer back to an earlier sequence in the film that takes place in the same location in which Cassin discusses the possibility (and problems) of an older man marrying a younger woman with the local doctor. Here Lewis tilts up from Cassin's image reflected in the murky water to Cassin himself, "emphasizing the separation within [him] between a submerged murderous identity and a gentle, sympathetic character."[39] This demonstrates the rigor of Lewis's direction. He does not merely include numerous shots of mirrors and reflections to emphasize the dual nature of the hero; rather he goes further and actually has shots mirror each other, thus making doublings part of the formal fabric of the film. However, Meisel leaves out one small but essential detail in this scene. The sequence does indeed begin with Cassin's image reflected in the water; but, just before Lewis tilts up to show the "normal" Cassin on the bridge, the doctor enters the shot. For a split second the reflections of two men can be seen in the water, and as Meisel rightly points out, it is the "challenge of marriage to a much younger woman [which is about to be discussed] that forces the hidden identity out into the open."[40] Therefore, fleeting appearance of a second figure reflected in the water can be viewed as Lewis's visual announcement of the emergence of Cassin's murderous personality.

Sometimes, Lewis's depiction of Cassin's dual nature is strikingly simple, as in the scene in the village post office. While at the counter, the detective is filmed behind bars, a clear visual metaphor for his guilt. He then walks across the street to speak to the local inspector. Lewis follows him with a simple panning shot on a noticeable dutch angle. As he crosses the street, from his "criminal" side to the police station, he moves from shadow into the light. A more complex example and a scene that "exemplifies much of the film's visual method" is that in the farm yard where Antoine's body is found.[41] In one particularly notable shot, which shows the detective's arrival at the scene, Lewis places the camera inside the barn where the body lies and shoots Cassin and the local policemen thorough the window. The vertical muntin divides the screen into two unequal halves. The smaller of these, on the left, is dominated by a wagon wheel. The larger frame, to the right, is slightly distorted by a fault in the glass and it is here that we see Cassin. As he approaches the barn he moves from a pool of bright sunlight into the shade created by the farm house, and the shadow can be seen moving up his body until it covers him. The camera pans right and focuses on the door knob as Cassin tried to open it (he cannot as it is blocked by Antoine's body). Lewis then pans back to the window as Cassin, now in close-up and totally in shadow, looks through it. In the background, M. Michaud calls out, having found something. As Cassin turns, Michaud can be seen behind him in deep focus. Cassin goes to him, moving out of the shadow back into the light. Within a single shot, Lewis visualizes the split nature of the character as he moves from light into darkness and back again. Even later, when the body is found, Cassin cannot enter the barn. It marks the boundary between the dark, shadowy self he does not yet know exists and the lighter self he still believes himself to be.

The moment in the film in which Cassin's dark half takes over is simply but elegantly visualized by Lewis in a manner that again harkens back to *Invisible Ghost* (which can in many ways be seen as a trial run for *So Dark the Night*). In the earlier film Bela Lugosi's character is another unwitting mass murderer who kills when placed under a hypnotic spell. Each time the character is hypnotized, Lewis frames Lugosi in a close-up with high-key light and then suddenly drops it to a low key, casting a shadow across Lugosi's face. In *So Dark the Night*, the effect is even more dramatic. Cassin sits at his desk, writing. A guard paces in the hallway behind him. Both the foreground and background of the shot are evenly lit in a high key. Suddenly, the key light in the foreground is extinguished, while the background remains unchanged. Cassin's body instantly becomes a silhouette. Only a very small fill light remains on him, hitting the right side of his face from an upward angle, enabling us to see that he is ominously looking directly at the camera.

There is nothing realistic about this lighting. On the contrary, it is theatrical, expressionist, and quintessentially B noir (Ulmer uses a similar lighting change before each flashback in *Detour* [1945]). This expressionism, which has been kept at bay for so much of the film, is brought to the fore in the final sequence, which shows the director at his most baroque. Here Lewis brings together the film's "complex motifs of framing, objects in the foreground, reprised bells on the sound track, deep focus, mirror images, and ratcheted light."[42] The sequence is perhaps too complex to discuss in depth here, however, a few outstanding moments require examination.

First, when the two men grapple, Michaud at first has the upper hand, he is on top of Cassin and beings to throttle him. Lewis cuts to a dramatic composition with the camera positioned inside the fireplace. Cassin seems to be engulfed by the flames that now dominate the foreground of the shot. However, when Cassin turns the tables on Michaud and their positions are reversed, Lewis "lets us see the placid, respectable [Cassin] imagistically burned up as his submerged character emerges."[43] Meisel calls this "perhaps the only justifiable camera-in-fireplace shot in cinema."[44] However, it is far from being the first instance of such a camera placement in Lewis's oeuvre. The same angle makes several appearances in *Invisible Ghost*, where it is indeed little more than an interesting camera angle designed to enliven the film. However, the final shot of *Secrets of a Co-Ed* is more meaningfully shot from the fireplace. Here, the heroine's diary (representing her old life) burns in the foreground, as she and her beau walk off to a new life in the background. But even this is a far cry from the symbolic complexity of the equivalent shot in *So Dark the Night*. Indeed, as this comparison so readily makes apparent, "Fireplace" Lewis was forever refining his style.

Seconds later, Commissioner Grande shoots Cassin as he is about to kill Michaud with a poker. This leads to what is perhaps the most startling image in the film. As Cassin turns to the window he sees not his reflection but an image of himself as he was when he arrived in the village. This is a projection of his former self, at once the same person, but also different. For the first time in the film, the two halves of Cassin's personality meet face to face, just before their mutual destruction. When Cassin smashes the glass it is at once the murderous Cassin destroying his good half and also the original Cassin, France's finest detective, bringing his final case to a close.

So Dark the Night is a "matchless stylistic exercise" in which style becomes substance.[45] The film's formal qualities and increasingly dark lighting scheme reflect the changing personality of the protagonist. The film literally grows more noirish as it progresses and Cassin's murderous personality begins to dominate. It is this careful modulation of light and darkness, *blanc et noir*, that gives the film its power and makes it one of Lewis's finest achievements.

Notes

1. Myron Meisel, "Joseph H. Lewis: Tourist in the Asylum," in *Kings of the Bs: Working within the Hollywood System*, ed. Todd McCarthy and Charles Flynn (New York: E. P. Dutton, 1975), 86.

2. Tony Rayns, "*So Dark the Night*," in *The Time Out Film Guide*, ed. by John Pym (London: Penguin, 2003), 1116.

3. Ibid.

4. David Bordwell, *On the History of Film Style* (Cambridge: Harvard University Press, 1997), 5–8.

5. Ibid., 8.

6. Jim Kitses, *Gun Crazy* (London: BFI, 1996), 14.

7. Meisel, "Tourist in the Asylum," 86.

8. Ibid., 84.

9. Francis M. Nevins, *Joseph H. Lewis: Overview, Interview, and Filmography* (Lanham, MD: Scarecrow Press, 1998), 14.

10. Bordwell, *History of Film Style*, 233.

11. Barry Salt, *Film Style and Technology: History and Analysis* (London: Starword, 1983), 282.

12. Ibid., 307.

13. Ibid., 308.

14. Orson Welles recalls using long takes for this reason while shooting *Touch of Evil* (1958). See Orson Welles and Peter Bogdanovich, *This Is Orson Welles* (London: HarperCollins, 1993), 308.

15. Robert Porfirio and Carl Macek, "Joseph H. Lewis," in *Film Noir Reader 3: Interviews with Filmmakers of the Classic Noir Period*, ed. Robert Porfirio, Alain Silver, and James Ursini (New York: Limelight, 2001), 70.

16. Jim McBride, *Searching for John Ford* (London: Faber and Faber, 2001), 251.

17. Geoff Andrew, *The Film Handbook* (Harlow: Longman, 1989), 171.

18. Nevins, *Joseph H. Lewis*, 23.

19. Ibid., 32.

20. Ibid., 33.

21. Rayns, "*So Dark the Night*," 1116.

22. "*So Dark the Night*," in *The Variety Film 1995*, ed. Derek Elley (Hamlyn: London, 1994), 835.

23. Meisel, "Tourist in the Asylum," 84.

24. Peter Bogdanovich, *Who the Devil Made It: Conversations with Legendary Film Directors* (New York: Ballentine Books, 1998), 664.

25. Laura Mulvey, "Visual Pleasure and Narrative Cinema," in *Popular Television and Film*, ed. by Tony Bennett, Susan Boyd-Bowman, Colin Mercer, and Janet Woollacott (London: BFI, 1981): 209.

26. Meisel, "Tourist in the Asylum," 84.

27. Andrew, *Film Handbook*, 203.

28. Paul Kerr, "My Name Is Joseph H. Lewis" *Screen* 24, nos. 4–5 (1983): 55.

29. Gilbert Adair, *Flickers* (London: Faber and Faber, 1995), 144.

30. Salt, *Film Style and Technology*, 371.

31. Ibid., 265.

32. Virginia Wright Wexman and Karen Hollinger, eds., *Letter from an Unknown Woman* (New Brunswick: Rutgers University Press, 1986), 20.

33. Paul Schrader, "Notes on Film Noir," in *A Film Noir Reader*, ed. by Alain Silver and James Ursini (New York: Limelight, 1996), 61.

34. Kerr, "My Name," 55.

35. Rayns, "*So Dark the Night*," 1116.

36. Paul Kerr, "Out of What Past? Notes on the B-Film Noir," in Silver and Ursini, *A Film Noir Reader*, 111.

37. Ibid., 111.

38. Meisel, "Tourist in the Asylum," 85.

39. Ibid.

40. Ibid.

41. Ibid.

42. Ibid., 86.

43. Ibid.

44. Ibid.

45. Ibid.

9

DAVID J. HOGAN

The Undercover Man and the Police Procedural

> I came to borrow some books. Here's my library card.
> Treasury agent Frank Warren, while seizing criminal financial ledgers

Although the main preoccupation of John Huston's *The Asphalt Jungle* (1950) is the planning and execution of an audacious heist by a variegated group of professional criminals, the film includes a significant scene with a police inspector (John McIntire) who switches on a phalanx of police radios simultaneously, so that gathered reporters will be reminded of the ceaseless challenges to a big-city police force. Dispatchers recite the latest particulars of crime and other trouble: robbery, assault, missing persons, domestic arguments. Officers in radio cars calmly acknowledge. The voices blend and overlap in a chorus of potential disaster and solutions. Huston wanted us to understand that police officers are on duty every day—all day and all night. When we need help, they are there. Only the police separate us from the perpetrators of anarchy. In this, *The Asphalt Jungle* suggests the "thin blue line" that documentary filmmaker Errol Morris brought to our attention a generation later.

This perception of police as a narrow but broad bulwark against societal collapse is possibly the ultimate logic, and truth, of the police procedural film genre. Society is grounded in the necessity of order and systems. Methodology, whether practiced in a factory, a sales office, or a police station, is the constant that allows our world to function. Systems, rules, protocol, patience. This is procedure, this is safety, and this is where we meet Frank Warren, the highly trained Treasury agent of Joseph H. Lewis's 1949 procedural gem, *The Undercover Man*.

The March to Realism

Although this chapter begins with a nod to *The Asphalt Jungle*, that film does not concern itself chiefly with police procedure. Jules Dassin's 1948 classic, *The Naked City*, is typically cited as the initial example of the procedural subgenre, and while a strong case can be made for its importance (and will be, in this chapter), Henry Hathaway's 1945 semidocumentary *The House on 92nd Street* must be acknowledged as the breakthrough picture. The narrative retells the true story of German spies based in an anonymous house in New York City during World War II, whose mission was to ferret out A-bomb secrets. Hathaway shot on the streets and in the buildings where the real drama played out, and while his protagonists are FBI agents, as opposed to the municipal cops whose presence characterizes many of the archetypal procedurals, Hathaway's emphasis on the frequently mundane realities of fact gathering, and on refined principles of procedural conduct, certainly contributed to the development of the subgenre of which Lewis's *The Undercover Man* is an important part.

Despite the suggestion of investigative tedium that informs moments of *The House on 92nd Street*, the film merely *pointed the way* to true procedurals rather than fully *defined* them—probably because of the presumed glamour of FBI agents and the extraordinarily high stakes of their investigation. "Classic" procedurals, as we'll see, are more closely tied to neighborhoods, small businesses, and everyday people.

Henry Hathaway came back, in 1948, with another picture that predates *The Undercover Man*, the quasi-procedural *Call Northside 777*. This is a tense drama about an inherently skeptical newspaper reporter who comes to believe in the innocence of a condemned man and mounts a step-by-step investigation that he hopes will lead him to the true perpetrator of the crime. As with the FBI agents of *92nd Street*, the sleek reporter (played by James Stewart) is a bit removed from viewers' everyday experiences, so *Northside* is another direction marker to procedural style rather than a true example.

A Pair of Key Precedents

In narrative structure and tone, *The Undercover Man* occupies midground between Anthony Mann's *T-Men* (1947) and Jules Dassin's *The Naked City*, two highly significant procedurals that preceded the Lewis film into theaters. *T-Men* is the archetypal noir, with moody photography by preeminent noir cinematographer John Alton and a pair of professionally and emotionally linked deep-undercover Treasury agents, one of whom must literally stand by and watch as gangsters murder his partner. *T-Men* is a noir thriller overlaid with elements of the then-new police procedural, most notably in the training undertaken by the agents as they prepare to pass themselves off as criminals.

Mann's use of melodrama and exaggerated stylization (such as the hideous death of a man locked inside a steam room) suggests a heightened sort of reality rather than an effort to suggest reality itself. The agents' preparation before they begin their assignment is matter of fact but leads them into a claustrophobic house of horrors that could exist only in the movies. Ultimately, the protagonists find themselves in completely untenable situations: brutally physical for the agent who is killed, and mercilessly existential for the one who must look on.

For *The Naked City*, Jules Dassin eschewed extreme stylization. Instead, he shot exteriors entirely on location in New York with documentary-style cinematography that avoids familiar noir stylistics. If any single element of *The Naked City*, other than its colorful locations, characterizes the picture's aesthetic, it is Dassin's reliance on natural lighting—occasional bright sunlight, but most often the diffuse light of mildly overcast days. The blah summer weather—neither here nor there—is a perfect trope for the unavoidably dreary nature of the investigative process.

The narrative focus of *The Naked City* is on murder, an everyday sort of crime that is considerably more dramatic than the intentional accounting irregularities of *The Undercover Man*. The Dassin film (and another significant release from the same year, Alfred L. Werker's *He Walked by Night*) suggests that criminal activity is not uncovered and punished by enormous strokes of luck or climactic confessions of hysterical killers but by dogged, routine legwork of detectives and uniformed officers. Their efforts are complemented back at headquarters by the quiet persistence of fact gatherers and crime-lab technicians. One thread leads to another, and after a while—sometimes days, sometimes weeks, sometimes longer—the threads become a piece of cloth. In *The Naked City*, the pieces finally reveal the killer, who desperately scales a New York bridge, briefly holds police at bay, and then is (literally) shot down. This denouement is visually exciting and in keeping with the persistence of the police and the nature and skills of the murderer (he's not simply violent but an expert wrestler and acrobat).

Still, criminals are not usually gunned down from bridges or other spectacularly visual places. *The Undercover Man*, by contrast, climaxes in an alley, during some brief and not improbable gunplay between the protagonist and minor hoodlums. The story concludes, satisfyingly, with a series of simple arrests. In this, the Lewis film is even more closely linked to real life than *The Naked City*.

However, the young detective of *The Naked City* experiences a crisis of confidence as the murder investigation goes on and on. He has to walk around too much. His feet hurt. He's frustrated and bored because he hasn't come to terms with the actual nature of police work. He grows agitated when big breakthroughs—like those in the movies—don't happen. Along with the procedural details of *The Naked City*, the unhappiness of the young detective is among the film's most believable elements.

The young cop's partner is a much older detective who evaluates the meager results of each day's work with philosophical patience. He understands criminals and knows that they leave clues, even if the clues amount simply to an assemblage of the criminals' habits. The older cop's experience tells him that elusive criminals are usually tripped up by something of an everyday nature—a past profession, a fondness for a particular type of clothing or companionship, peculiarities of diet or address.[1]

Frank Warren of *The Undercover Man* is at least twenty-five years younger than the veteran cop of *The Naked City* but shares that character's willingness to endure tedium. Warren occasionally becomes frustrated but never doubts himself or his methods. His training has taught him to develop a usefully patient mind-set that sets him on a path to ultimate success. The unendurable that must be endured, of course, is time. Investigations take time.

Although Warren carries a revolver, a typical day at work involves knocking on doors or working through mounds of subpoenaed ledger books. Those ledger books are filled with numbers—columns and columns of them. Unfortunately for the local arm of the syndicate, no two people write numbers in precisely the same way. Warren knows this, and so does the handwriting expert back at the lab. Eventually, handwriting on an envelope is matched to ledger entries, and the investigation begins to pay off.

INTENSITY AND FLAW

Undercover Man screenwriter Sydney Boehm came to movies relatively late in life, at age thirty-eight, following a career as a newspaperman. His first screenplay was for the 1947 crime drama *The High Wall*. From 1947 to 1955, Boehm wrote such superior, tough-minded pictures as *Side Street, Union Station, Mystery Street, The Big Heat, Rogue Cop, Violent Saturday,* and *Hell on Frisco Bay*. (He later became a reasonably successful writer-producer and remained active in the business until 1971.)

Boehm's screenplays are marked not just by attention to procedure and to deeply flawed protagonists (see the obsessed cop in *The Big Heat* or the prepossessing young man who slips into thievery in *Side Street*) but by an overriding notion that even the innocent among us are rarely innocent at all. If they're in trouble, it's probably because they have given in to their own worst instincts, or, perhaps even more damagingly, done nothing at all to thwart the corruption that surrounds them. In *The Big Heat*, passive complicity of the city's police commissioner and other officials allows the local crime lord to dominate the system. The blonde babe of *Mystery Street* has a physical relationship with a cynical older man, becomes pregnant, and makes the fatal mistake of blackmailing him. The victim's landlady, who is even less well equipped to deal with a killer, subsequently tries a giggly sort of blackmail herself and ends up just as dead as her former tenant. And in *Violent Saturday*, Boehm, working from a splendid novel by W. L. Heath, suggests that the seeds of America's destruction lie within each of us: when a small town is invaded by a trio of killers intent on robbing the local bank, most of the locals are powerless to resist, as they've fallen prey to petty thievery, adultery, alcoholism, even window peeping. (Change "trio of killers" to "Reds," by the way, and you have an intelligent and uncompromising Cold War parable, perfect for the period in which Lewis and Boehm worked most successfully.)

Lewis himself explored the theme and consequences of personal flaw when he combined erotic attraction with neurosis and fashioned Bart Tare, the male protagonist of *Gun Crazy* (1950). Bart's obsessive interest in guns takes physical form in murderous sharpshooter Annie Laurie Starr, and very quickly Bart is spiraling to his doom.

Brainwork, Footwork

The only obsession displayed in *The Undercover Man* is the zeal with which Treasury agent Frank Warren (Glenn Ford) attacks ledger books that have been subpoenaed and seized by the government. Throughout the city, countless ordinary people spend their nickels and dimes to play the numbers. That money, in turn, finances the syndicate's more unpleasant activities: loan sharking, prostitution, drugs, labor unrest, organized murder. Because the syndicate's members, large and small, are understandably reluctant to reveal the sources of their incomes, men like Frank Warren dig out the hidden money and build cases of tax evasion. The government's primary target is the local crime boss, "the Big Fella," who owes the government $3 million in back taxes. (A real-life 1927 ruling by the US Supreme Court held that income derived from criminal activities is subject to income taxes.) Along the way, the Treasury men must cultivate (or coerce) informants. Stripped to its most basic narrative, *The Undercover Man* is a lesson in the methodology of forensic accounting mated to street-level legwork. Its clear and linear plot reflects the neat columns of figures in the ledger books that preoccupy Warren and his companions.

The Undercover Man is firmly grounded in the workaday reality it chronicles and celebrates. The credited source material is "Undercover Man: He Trapped Capone," an article by former Treasury agent Frank J. Wilson, which was serialized in *Collier's* in 1947. *The British Film Institute Companion to Crime* suggests another possible source, Elmer L. Irey's 1948 book *The Tax Dodgers: The Inside Story of the T-Men's War with America's Political and Underworld Hoodlums*.[2] In any event, the "undercover" of *The Undercover Man* is only nominally accurate: neither the real-life Frank J. Wilson nor the movie's Frank Warren goes undercover in the common melodramatic sense (as in *T-Men*). Wilson merely traveled to Chicago with his wife and posed as a tourist holed up in a hotel, while in the movie Warren shows up for work in a new city, his wife exiled elsewhere.

Some previously published synopses of *The Undercover Man* identify Chicago as the story's setting, though the film makes no mention of that city, either in voice-over narration or dialogue. (No city is named at all.) Writers of earlier pieces are likely to have assumed the city is Chicago because "the Big Fellow" is clearly Chicago mobster Al Capone (though the roman à clef narrative moves the circumstances of Capone's bookkeeping mischief and subsequent downfall forward in time more than fifteen years). Sharp-eyed viewers will identify Chicago from a few establishing shots, but in the main the film's "feel" is strongly suggestive of New York, perhaps Brooklyn or Manhattan's Lower East Side.

Lewis and Boehm utilized the T-man's daily drudgery to develop character and a counterintuitive but satisfying sort of suspense. Key to the narrative's development is the notion that ordinary people are frequently complicit in their own miseries. *The Undercover Man* repeatedly underscores the truth that the Big Fella and his stooges could not exist if ordinary citizens did not allow them to. Agent Warren is frequently disgusted, but seldom more pointedly than when he walks into a grocery or candy store and observes the owner encouraging customers to risk a nickel or a dime on the numbers. The customers know that the game is illegal, and that winning is a long shot, but they also reason that it's all in fun, it's harmless—so they hand over their coins, and the Big Fella's operation grows stronger. A more powerful syndicate means a broader pattern of corruption, more money for bribes, and a less effective police force. Flip a dime on the candy store counter and you're not really playing a game—you're undermining your hopes.

Luckily for the forces of justice, the syndicate expects even the owners of candy stores to keep financial books of the transactions—books that can be seized by Warren and other agents.

As one might imagine, however, the mob is reasonably clever about hiding its fiscal footprint. Whole sets of dummy books exist for no other reason than to lead snoopy investigators into dead ends. How will Warren locate the ledgers he needs in order for the government to prosecute? Who's lying to him? Does anybody really want to help him, or will he get his break serendipitously, as in someone's offhand comment or a carelessly discarded scrap of paper? Can the syndicate (an entity whose cleverness we grudgingly admire) stay a step ahead of Warren and the other T-men? Is it possible for Warren to be bribed? All of this contributes to the paradoxically low-key but acute suspense of *The Undercover Man*.

Speaking with Images

Visually, *The Undercover Man* is neither as dramatic nor as stylized as Lewis's other major crime films, *Gun Crazy* and *The Big Combo* (1955). The reason for the difference is reflected in the films' titles: *The Undercover Man* follows the activities of a Treasury agent—a civil servant—as he goes about his work. The other films revolve around the criminal, and thus anarchic, activities of society's outsiders. Because those people, particularly the sadistic gangsters of *The Big Combo* and Annie Laurie Starr of *Gun Crazy*, are society's dangerously unpredictable random elements, they invite a director to work with shadows, unusual angles, peculiar settings (such as the misty, weirdly claustrophobic swamp of *Gun Crazy*), and frequent, intense close-ups.

Frank Warren, by contrast, works according to carefully codified protocol. He may himself be occasionally surprised by the activities of others, but he never surprises himself. Unlike many criminals, he's tightly disciplined. He dresses like a midlevel businessman. He spends parts of his days in plain, government-issue sedans, and he's married (happily, no less). Because Warren is a man of mental action, Burnett Guffey's camera examines him with slow, easy pans and occasional, restrained dolly-ins during especially meaningful moments.

In one visually intriguing setup, Warren's head and shoulders occupy the bottom third of the frame; above is nothingness, a negation. Warren is like an aerialist or a man temporarily lost at sea: he's intrepid, but he has few handholds. His best asset is his mind.

A protracted sequence that plays out in various parts of a movie theater begins in the dark upper balcony, as a film unspools on the screen below.

Warren and his coy informer, Zanger (Robert Osterloh), slouch beneath the smoky wedge of light thrown from the projector. The edges of their faces are sharply illuminated, but the rest of the tableau is in near blackness. This momentous, long-awaited meeting was reduced by Lewis to a pair of faces floating in the void. As such, it's a sort of landscape of the mind and a perfect visualization of Warren's intensity of focus. The sharp edge of Warren's (and the government's) energies and the unavoidable, queerly companionable moments when order and crime must meet are captured memorably in that inky balcony.

Lewis, however, was nothing if not a stylist fond of contrast. Agent Warren goes about his legwork on the city's streets not in darkness but beneath brightly overcast skies. An early sequence in which Warren sits in a train station waiting for somebody who never shows up suggests the larger, airier aspects of urban existence: the station has enormously high ceilings, capacious windows, and floors that stretch on forever. But the train station doesn't at all reflect Warren's usual base of operations. He spends hours in a tiny government office that is more like an anteroom—a poorly illuminated architectural afterthought. This room has no window. The walls are very close together, and Lewis angled his camera so that we frown at the low ceiling. Here, with his partner (James Whitmore) and, frequently, one or two other agents all shoved together virtually shoulder to shoulder, Warren pursues his unambiguous agenda.

Because the DC-based Warren is working out of town, his expense-account hotel room mirrors his awful workspace: small, dim, and confined. (He's also a young man alone in a hotel room without the companionship of his pretty wife.) Warren's conversations with his coworkers, though spiked once in a while by mordant wisecracks, are mainly perfunctory. His most compelling dialogues are with people involved, to varying degrees, in the syndicate. When he finally has a useful exchange with his informer, Zanger, the meeting is in the movie theater's men's room. With its low ceiling and bleak functionality, the place is a visual reiteration of the thematic implications of Warren's office and hotel, but with a key difference: because the agent and the criminal occupy the bathroom space together, the sequence (like the earlier scene in the balcony) forces a certain equivalency between them. The feeling is almost subliminal, but you infer that Warren has had to conduct such meetings many times before, in cheap diners, in tobacco shops, in doorways, in other men's rooms.

Although Warren verbalizes few frustrations to his coworkers other than his discontent with the forced, six-month separation from Judith, his patient and intelligent wife (Nina Foch), he must surely resent having to perpetually exist on the level of the punks he wants to put away or, as in the theater, barter with for information. In a beautiful throwaway bit that was smartly directed by Lewis with the camera tilted at a slight upward angle and brilliantly played by Robert Osterloh (one of the most believable and prolific character men of his generation), the informer pulls a paper towel from the men's room dispenser after rinsing his hands, looks at it in distaste before allowing it to fall to the floor, and then pats his hands dry with his own handkerchief. *He's* the low-life, *he's* the criminal, and *he's* the one who's offended by the shortcomings of the venue where he's come to bargain with one of his betters.

The Poisoned Fruit of Corruption

A corrupt mob lawyer, Ed O'Rourke (Barry Kelley), has similar pretensions. Warren sees O'Rourke for the first time at the police station, and although Warren has no idea who the man is ("I never saw him before," Warren says later), O'Rourke emphasizes on the spot that *he* knows precisely who Warren is, making it apparent to Warren and to us that the mob has procedural skills of its own.

A later sequence set at O'Rourke's rolling estate plays out in brilliant sunshine. The place is manicured and beautiful, and Warren's brief, polite interaction with the lawyer's (apparently oblivious) wife suggests an innocuous sort of graciousness. But when Warren and O'Rourke get down to cases, a clumsily offered bribe illustrates that you can't dress a toad in a tuxedo. In just a minute or two of dialogue, the gracious setting becomes not just ironic but distasteful (and personally aggravating to Warren, too, because he's still denied his wife's companionship while the well-fed attorney is required to make no such sacrifice). Back in the city's neighborhoods, ordinary citizens survive on Crackerjack, bad coffee, and foolish hope. In their stores and apartments they stare at grimy walls, narrow hallways, and those inevitable low ceilings. Each of them is alone, victimized by childlike greed and the larger forces that swallow the nickels and dimes.

Lewis and Boehm painted the city as a landscape of crooks, grifters, and fools. When an agent notes aloud that the local syndicate employs five thousand people, the vulnerability of ordinary citizens is pathetically obvious. Meanwhile, Warren and his fellow agents continue to ruin their eyes examining ledger books and struggle to remain calm when eyewitnesses who have been intimidated by syndicate hoods claim sudden memory loss. In one maddening sequence, an eyewitness to the machine gun murder of the informer Zanger shamefacedly pleads amnesia.

Worse, some police officers have been intimidated, as well. When the mob attorney O'Rourke barges into the police crime lab, he obliquely but brazenly threatens an inspector and completely cows a middle-aged desk sergeant who had been a detective until he defied the mob the previous year. The leash of somebody high in the police chain of command was given a sharp tug, and the detective was busted in rank. As the mob views things, cops must be (and *can* be) neutralized with bribes or otherwise rendered impotent. This must happen in precinct after precinct, until the entire city is an unfenced vista of corruption. The Big Fella and his army are in jeopardy on the tax beef, but in other ways the syndicate remains a potent (if reckless) power, laying its heavy hand on the city's "thin blue line."

Breakthrough

Warren continues to toil over slim leads and those damnable books. His wife, Judith (his muse and his chief source of encouragement), is never far from his mind. A particularly interesting double exposure overlays Judith's face atop a shot of Warren and others as they struggle to decipher seized ledgers. An instant after Judith says, "Something will break any day now," an adding machine is punched too hard and promptly refuses to work anymore. In a single moment, then, Lewis and Boehm illustrated the emotional toll and work-related drudgery suffered by Warren and all the other underpaid proceduralists.[3]

Later, a police roundup of mob bookkeepers seems routine, but Warren announces that anybody who expects to see his lawyer must write his name and address. What are ledger books, after all, but collections of handwriting? This is a clever gambit that promises to give Warren and the others additional hours and days—perhaps weeks—of numbing comparison work. The growing shame of the disgraced desk sergeant moves him to give Warren the scribbled-on card of a bookkeeper he arrested while still a detective. This lead, like any other, must be chased down and takes Warren to the gloomy basement apartment of a low-level syndicate bookkeeper named Salvatore Rocco. The little girl who answers the door looks at Warren's photograph of the murdered informant and says, "That's Mr. Zanger, Daddy's friend." After a few moments the child's angry mother rushes to the door and hustles the kid back inside. Mrs. Rocco—an attractive but careworn woman of about thirty-five—glares at Warren and spits that the child is mistaken. But Warren knows he has a solid lead. When he returns to the apartment, Salvatore's mother (Esther Minciotti) convinces her daughter-in-law to cooperate because it's the only way Salvatore can be saved. Mrs. Rocco agrees. She explains to Warren that her husband has gone away. He sent money for a while, but no longer. He's hiding, and his wife is worried. She gives Warren a sample of her husband's handwriting on an envelope she removes from a ledger book. (We see the book but Warren does not.) The crime lab quickly ties the business card to the envelope. Salvatore Rocco is the man Warren needs to find. With Mrs. Rocco acting as an intermediary, and with some encouragement engineered by Warren and Salvatore's mistress, the fugitive bookkeeper (Anthony Caruso) comes out of hiding.

Of all of Lewis's greatest films, *The Undercover Man* is the most measured and careful. There is not a sharply emotional close-up until the camera studies the face of Salvatore Rocco. He's a handsome man who now resembles a fretful animal, simultaneously relieved and wary about being out in the sunlight once again. On a bright, crowded sidewalk he happily embraces his daughter (the soulful child actress Joan Lazer), proudly signs her report card (an honest and poignant moment), and tells her about a special book in a trunk in the cellar. Then Rocco makes ready to turn himself in. But in the full glare of that reassuring daylight, before his daughter's eyes, Rocco is accosted by mob torpedoes and shot dead.

Fresh Resolve

To kill a T-man is probably the ultimate mistake, but because the syndicate learns that Warren is getting close, it has to do *something*, so goons ambush Warren in his hotel room and give him a sound beating. After he comes to, Warren soothes his damaged head beneath a stream of tap water that pulses like blood from a torn artery. A day or two later, a duplicitously convivial O'Rourke finds Warren and obliquely threatens his wife.

The disgraced desk sergeant commits suicide.

For the first time, Warren feels doubt. He wants to quit, to forget all of it. He's not afraid, but he feels like Sisyphus. He's tired. But then Rocco's mother and daughter find him at his hotel room when Warren is packing a suitcase. The little girl says, "Grandmother wants to know if you're leaving your post of duty." Warren stops what he's doing. The child relays the old lady's story of her husband, a good man who was murdered in Italy by "the Mafia, the Black Hand" when he refused to be extorted.

"Grandmother says it's very beautiful in America." With that, Salvatore's grieving mother produces her son's secret ledger book.

Warren is visibly moved, not by schmaltz, but by how close he has come to forgetting a fundamental part of his training: When you're intimidated, keep plowing forward. And oh, yes: Be more determined than ever. This is procedure that's good for the public, and good for Warren.

The suitcase goes back on the shelf.

The fearless young daughter (Joan Lazer) and principled immigrant mother (Esther Minciotti) of a mob bookkeeper prepare to literally hand federal agent Frank Wilson (Glenn Ford, *far left*) what he needs to nail "the Big Fella." Wilson's wife (Nina Foch) and a fellow agent (James Whitmore, in suspenders) quietly wait for the big moment.

Throw Away the Key

Encouraged by street chatter about the government's investigation of the Big Fella, a young accountant named Gordon (Leo Penn) comes forward with his forthright wife (Patricia White, later Patricia Barry) and offers to cooperate. He explains that he became a syndicate accountant as a callow kid. Now he's ashamed of himself. He hates the syndicate's system. He wants out, and he'll help the government however he can.[4]

In a meaningful touch, the Gordons are never filmed in shadow. Lewis emphasized the couple's good looks and earnest demeanor. Still, we're not meant to admire them, because these young people represent two worlds: the criminal life and the gullible but essentially decent life of the broader public. The youngsters link one world with another and bring the law's fist down on the Big Fella, who is indicted and bound over for trial.

When Warren subsequently serves O'Rourke with a subpoena, he makes sure it's in broad daylight, at the racetrack and in clear view of mobsters who have been keeping an eye on their cocky attorney. The serving of a subpoena is routine procedure, but Warren's pitiless method turns the tables on O'Rourke. Suddenly desperate, and no longer the blustering bully we've observed earlier, O'Rourke becomes just another sweating fat man, desperate to make a deal. Later, when alone with Warren, he spills that the mob has identified the Big Fella's jury panel, and bribed one or more of its members. This is O'Rourke's last throw of the dice, and it works. Warren tears up the subpoena. He can live with it: you get the reptiles where you want them, they give valuable information, and sometimes you tear up a subpoena. Procedure.

Significantly, O'Rourke makes his plea not in his plush office, or on his fabulous estate, but while walking with Warren beneath overcast skies in a grimy industrial area. The lawyer is in Warren's world now.

A corrupt syndicate lawyer (Barry Kelley) makes the mistake of gloating as an unswerving federal agent (Glenn Ford) recovers from a mob assault. Shortly, the tables will be turned.

This is also the ugly world of the syndicate, revealed: A car follows Warren and O'Rourke as they talk. Warren palms his revolver. Then, in a perfectly brilliant three-or four-second sequence that unfolds with rapid-fire edits and all the miserable reality of a Weegee photograph, O'Rourke is run down by the car and crushed in the mud. Warren dodges aside. As the speeding sedan continues forward, a brutal swish-pan from the driver's point of view wrenches our gaze leftward to Warren, who fires while hugging a wall. The car crashes noisily. The whole of *The Undercover Man*, then, has been a carefully prepared prelude to this moment. The Treasury Department, with its quiet, incorruptible agents who usually work with pencils and ledgers, is every bit as remorseless as the mob.[5] The government doesn't give up. If you ask for it, the system will crush you. In practical terms, Warren has fired on and killed the driver (and, by extension, the Big Fella's schemes), but metaphorically he unloads on us, in a sharp reminder that his brand of procedure is as potentially violent, and conclusive, as the syndicate's.

In a satisfying coda, a fresh jury sends the Big Fella to prison for twenty years. At the train station days later, Warren is one of many observers who crowd the platform to get a glimpse of the deposed crime lord as he begins his journey to prison. A uniformed cop gives Warren a gentle tap with his nightstick. "C'mon buddy," the cop intones, "this doesn't concern you."

Step by Step to Greatness

By 1949, Joseph H. Lewis had directed about ten movies over the course of a decade. His imagination and high level of craftsmanship were already beyond doubt, and *The Undercover Man* established him as an important director—although Hollywood didn't necessarily care to acknowledge it. In the 1940s and 1950s, genre pictures had no hope at all of achieving the stature they now enjoy. Studio heads assumed that people who directed low- to moderately budgeted thrillers were exactly where they deserved to be in the Hollywood pecking order. In a just world, Lewis would have achieved stature and career longevity similar to that enjoyed by his star, Glenn Ford, who became a major figure despite his subtlety, unconventional looks, and resolute intelligence. Then again, Anthony Mann, another director of potent genre pictures, did finally make the leap to A-level films—only to bow beneath the crush of enormous budgets and big stars. Mann's final films are among his least interesting.

That Lewis remained in genre filmmaking is, in retrospect, a stroke of great good fortune for people who watch and study movies. He knew film grammar as thoroughly as Frank Warren knows the steps that must be taken to catch a criminal. Tight budgets forced Lewis to hone his gifts for tough, concise storytelling and sharp, frequently merciless character development that would quickly engage viewers. Lacking the luxury of fat budgets, he knew he had to ration his best effects and knock an audience back in its seats at moments of his choosing, for maximum impact. See the U-turn and car-to-car embrace of the murderous lovers in *Gun Crazy*, the soundless execution of the deaf crime boss in *The Big Combo*, and that devastating swish pan in *The Undercover Man*.

Lewis didn't game the Hollywood system, because he was too talented to have to do that, but he did develop an impeccable understanding of the system's limits and expectations. He made his pictures efficiently, on time and on budget, with an artistry grounded in plain, beautiful craftsmanship. Lewis was one of Hollywood's great procedurists.

Notes

1. All of this—the unhappy young detective with an older, even-tempered boss who understands the revealing habits of criminals—informs much of Akira Kurosawa's great Japanese procedural, *Stray Dog* (1949). In it, the young cop searches the length and breadth of a miserably hot Tokyo for the thug who stole his service revolver.

2. Phil Hardy, *British Film Institute Companion to Crime* (London: Cassell, 1997), 3.

3. Another 1949 release, Raoul Walsh's quasi-procedural *White Heat*, gives its clever lawmen considerably more sophisticated investigative tools, including a complex radio-tracking device that would seem only barely plausible in the more realistic world of *The Undercover Man*.

4. In this, the Gordons are similar to the foolish dilettante played by Howard Duff in *The Naked City* and the young couple of *Side Street*, all of whom mount desperate efforts to extricate themselves from the consequences of bad decisions.

5. Although *Dragnet*, Jack Webb's remarkable, long-running radio show about police procedure and the incorruptible Sergeant Joe Friday, premiered in 1949, the year of *The Undercover Man*, the Lewis film is one of the last hurrahs for Hollywood's immediate postwar notion that every urban lawman is dead honest. Shortly, as in *Rogue Cop* (1954), *Pushover* (1954), *Private Hell 36* (1954), and *Tight Spot* (1955), easy money would seduce police officers into reckless, cynical criminality.

10

Robert Singer

The "How Big Is It?" Combo

Noir's Dirty Spectacles

The Big Combo (1955), Joseph H. Lewis's film noir narrative of criminal intrigue, expressive and repressed sexualities, and their causalities, appears toward the end of the film noir's primary cycle in American production history (1941–58), yet this film remains curiously underappreciated, especially when compared with two competing noir narratives released in 1955, Stanley Kubrick's *Killer's Kiss* and Robert Aldrich's *Kiss Me Deadly*. Lewis's *The Big Combo* particularly suffers when critically evaluated alongside his earlier gangster narrative of *amour fou* and phallic obsession, *Gun Crazy* (1950).[1] Although James Naremore refers to *The Big Combo* as a "studioish throwback . . . it looked dated even when it was released . . . [and] relatively antiquated," especially when compared with Kubrick's *Killer's Kiss*, there is a significant case to be made for a revised look at *The Big Combo* as a calculated study of violence and unconventional sexuality.[2] A rereading of Lewis's film will clarify some of these pronouncements and persuasively move the critical assessment of *The Big Combo* beyond what one author refers to as the film's "psychological quirkiness."[3] As Laura Mulvey notes, "Ways of seeing do not exist in a vacuum. The 'Gaze' . . . is a key element to the construction of modern subjectivity, filtering ways of understanding and ordering the surrounding world."[4] As the now-familiar gaze affects the observer as a signifying experience both inside and outside the frame, she or he confronts interpretive and moralizing mechanisms that signal sets of meaning, but *The Big Combo* refutes such gendered expectations. Like Lewis's earlier noir narrative *Gun Crazy*, *The Big Combo* is also exceptional as a study in anxiety, violence, and desire. Two years before *The Big Combo* was released, Raymond Borde and Étienne Chaumeton's landmark study of the film noir, *Panorama de film noir Américain* (1941–53), expressed an overview of the noir aesthetic that could be applied to *The Big Combo*: "All works of this series present a unit of an emotional nature as well: it is the state born of tension, for the spectator, of the disappearance of his psychological reference marks. The vocation of black [noir] film was to create a specific uneasiness."[5] More specifically, the "malaise" that unsettles the observer in Lewis's film involves the unvarnished representation of historicized notions of sexual desire and degeneracy as violence-engendering causalities.

The Big Combo, a noir narrative of sexual outlaw practices, invokes and critiques the sexual mores of its time—the postwar, post-traumatic, urban, male-centered naturalist milieu of the compromised noir figure—in the awkward, repressive, and controlling decade of American conservatism and sexual conformity, the 1950s. Despite an active and destabilizing counterpresence to the conformist social and sexual practices of this decade, a sense of imposed structure was maintained.[6] According to Jody W. Pennington, "Throughout the 1950s and into the early 1960s, community leaders . . . promoted conformity with traditional sexual values and emphasized the importance of the family . . . transgressive sexual practices were disparaged. . . . Most states had had laws against sexual offenses, including *sodomy* (which varied in definition from state to state but which usually included reference to heterosexual and homosexual anal-genital contact and oral-genital contact)."[7] When read as a historically unique narrative of gender-specific sexual craving and humiliation, *The Big Combo* assumes a place in American film history and culture as a result of its ingeniously subliminal and overtly expressive shot sequences of unambiguous on- and offscreen taboo erotic spectacles: homosexual longing and a play of cunnilingus. *The Big Combo* examines the naturalist social circulus of the repressed: the violent, sleazy varieties of the urban loser and the women who love them all. As Borde and Chaumeton suggested about earlier noir narratives, "It is often about a naturalism close to Zola, sometimes re-examined by Freud,"[8] and this observation is especially applicable to *The Big Combo*. Complete with noir's stylistic visual tropes—fog, police stations, bottles of booze, boxing rings—*The Big Combo* deploys historicized, contextual images of psychosexual aberration and obsession and remains as playfully subversive as it is genuinely violent to a contemporary audience.

In *The Big Combo*, the compositional strategy of the opening shot sequence, run over the film's credits, involves an aerial, floating perspective as the camera traverses the city at night. The travel shot will land somewhere, on someone, but the anonymous buildings, streets, and intrusive lights create reflections of objects that illuminate nothing in particular. This could be anybody's story. John Alton's status as a legendary director of photography has been amply commented on, but his exceptional work in *The Big Combo* begins in the initial, representative frames of noir's alienating night town, and it will conclude in the film's final frames of human forms passing into the foggy images of elaborately mannered dark and light in an airport hangar that recalls the final romantic images of Michael Curtiz's wartime *Casablanca* (1943).[9] But *The Big Combo* is a seditious study of desire and conflict; it could not be described as romantic. Alton and Lewis's stylized, omniscient, introductory perspective is complemented by a brassy, somewhat sordid jazz sound track composed by David Raksin, featuring a slurred clarinet.[10] Throughout *The Big Combo*, the visual and sound design, along with screenwriter Philip Yordan's sexualized, playfully insubordinate script, are compositional elements that impose a structure creating the space for what Carlos Clarens has described as the noir narrative's "psychological terrain."[11] However set in the menacing, urban experience of postwar human detritus, the physical landscape in *The Big Combo* reflects noir's wounded interior, an emotionally and sexually decentered landscape in a stylized neonaturalism that reveals the experiential process both defining and degrading the individual.

Lewis establishes the signifying presence of a focused yet multi-character-driven narrative via this initial framing and motion of descent into the city at night; as the wide shot continues to lower onto the street, anonymous people and a policeman directing traffic focalize the viewer's perspective to lead to the entrance of a stadium, thus enabling the noir narrative trajectory.

Although Lewis's introductory motion shots cut to a boxing match inside the stadium, it is a somewhat false lead; the fight is elsewhere. *The Big Combo* appropriates the recurring noir fight/boxing trope to lead into familiar images of the imperiled, chased female, similar to Aldrich's introductory, frenzied car chase of the fleeting female on a lonely road in *Kiss Me Deadly*. In these noir narratives, when women run, they flee. But *The Big Combo* leads this running female into new, precarious directions that advance noir formulations of female identity in conflict with the immediate social order. According to R. Barton Palmer, "Aldrich's film [*Kiss Me Deadly*] prominently features a hatred of women, responding like many film noirs to an increasingly insistent theme in American popular culture";[12] in contrast with this misogynistic staple, *The Big Combo* suggests an alternative and pervasive core noir precept that may read as the domineering male emotion: the anxiety generated by the need for obsessive control of both the body and the mind of a woman. In *The Big Combo*, this measure of control is represented by two distinct heterosexual males of urban America celebrated in the media and on all cultural levels in the 1950s, the gangster and the policeman. These men are in actuality so much the same man when the female is desired and taken, and then she is perceived as a marker for their blood rivalry. This is an enhanced expression of noir's functional misogyny.

Throughout Alton's neo-expressionistic contrasting shots of light, dark, and resulting shadows, an attractive, well-dressed woman sprints away from two men in dogged pursuit. This shot sequence suggests directionless and irregular images of entrapment. As the woman, Susan Lowell (Jean Wallace), flees from the legitimized spectacle of violence people pay to see, the pursued and her pursuers pass by a luncheonette seemingly lifted from the sketchbooks of Edward Hopper's pictorial studies of urban loneliness. Finally, this alluring blonde figure is stopped by two men, Mingo (Earl Holliman) and Fante (Lee Van Cleef), gangsters with their own story. After an emasculating slap across Mingo's face, she temporarily calms down, and as the audience discovers, Mingo and Fante, two "apparently homosexual goons," both play important supportive roles maintaining the illicit empire of their gangster boss, Mr. Brown.[13]

"I've Taken Some Pills; I Think I'm Dying"

Who is Susan Lowell, and why does she run? Despite two "strong" noir leads who serve as near-oppositional figures of postwar male heterosexual careerism, the anxiety-driven and blustery police lieutenant Leonard Diamond (Cornel Wilde) and Susan's gangster lover, the sleazy and successful but oddly charming Mr. Brown (Richard Conte), along with supporting characters such as Mingo and Fante, in *The Big Combo*, the noir narrative's energy—its generating presence—is not based on capital or criminal intrigue but more specifically on the body of Susan Lowell (Jean Wallace) and who controls it. She is desired by both of these formidable men; she is nearly destroyed and often humiliated by them, and she conversely alternates between destroying and humiliating each. In the pathetic world of noir relationships, Susan is not the traditional femme fatale who kills as she touches; she is a far more complex sexual magnet who wounds as she suffers.[14] Like Zola's naturalist love machine, Nana, Susan expresses her amorous inclinations, and there are causalities.

In *The Big Combo*, the presence of a menacing, expressed female sexuality confronts and unhinges the more dominant male psychology of possession and control. Unlike Lieutenant Diamond's part-time lover, the burlesque dancer with a heart, and therefore expendable, Rita, or Mr. Brown's problematic and sequestered wife fresh from the therapeutic snake pit, Alicia, Susan Lowell, the "classy" and well-educated former pianist, as a symbol of old WASP America gone awry, remains the focal point of desire for both men as each contrives to rid himself of the other. Susan Lowell is the gendered enigma to be resolved by both male competitors and the audience; the question is not why she is desired, her shapely, quasi–Grace Kelly looks and comportment, when she is not passing out or nearly hysterical—the latter, a trait she shares with her pursuer, Lieutenant Diamond—speak for themselves. Behind her fluctuating icy stare into space, she appears to the audience mostly as a lovely package of damaged goods, an oddly troubled vessel. As an image of distraught 1950s charm, Susan represents an image that might be saved or at least controlled by one of the two men who desire her. In *The Big Combo*, according to Grant Tracey, "the narrative drive embodied in John Alton's moody photography and Joseph Lewis's direction, seeks to suspend female pleasure, to contain her sexuality and to recoup her into the boundaries of the socially acceptable."[15] Tracey's reading is correct to a point, as the film does observe noir conventions and reestablish an uneasy sense of surface domestic order for the 1950s audience; however, *The Big Combo* also reveals an unconventional female sexuality in close-up shots of erotic fulfillment. Few in the audience genuinely picture Susan returning home to a sink full of dishes and a station wagon full of children. Susan as spectacle-image is a naturalist trope; she is noir's fallen woman who does not understand the nature of her desire but who acts on her desire as she struggles between herself and two contrasting images of men: the traditional, sexually procreative Lieutenant Diamond and the nontraditional, creative, "dirty" mobster Brown for whom sex is an expression of power-pleasure. To understand more fully the conflicted identity formation that is Susan, and, inferentially, *The Big Combo*, I will examine the principal characters inhabiting, and often penetrating, Susan's distressed immediate social and sexual life. And then there are Mingo and Fante.

"You're Fighting a Swamp with a Teaspoon"

Lieutenant Diamond, as hard as his name implies, has a crack, a flaw that threatens to ruin his career and especially his investigation into the criminal empire controlled by Mr. Brown, who presides over a money-lending and money-laundering underworld banking system, the "combo," that is so lucrative it might be viewed as an antimodel of corporate success, with Brown allegedly killing his way to the top by eliminating his enemies and replacing his first wife for the chic trophy Susan Lowell. Lieutenant Diamond's obsessive drive to bring down Brown is not only professional but genuinely personal, since both men desire the same woman. Nevertheless, she has chosen the gangster, thus leaving behind her former respectability and social status for something else. As Diamond's superior in the police force the sympathetic captain (Robert Middleton) reminds him, Susan has spent "a lot of days and nights" with her gangster lover. Although Lieutenant Diamond knows that Brown is nearly untouchable, like detective Sergeant Dave Bannion's (Glenn Ford) efforts to ruin the crime boss, the successful, outwardly respectable "businessman" Mike Lagana (Alexander Scourby), in Fritz Lang's *The Big Heat* (1953), Lieutenant Diamond is personally driven beyond professional expectation to annihilate the man and his empire.

Lieutenant Diamond is a traditionally flawed, unsympathetic noir male, a violent, often hyperemotional heterosexual who, although sexually active, remains clueless about the nature of female desire. He was not alone; according to Stephen J. Whitfield, the 1950s in America were "scarred by repression . . . social control left little breathing space for the cultivation of difference. . . . Sex roles were supposed to be sharply circumscribed: men were men, and women were housewives."[16] Lieutenant Diamond "desires" but does not understand the inner nature of what or whom he covets, his unhappy Susan. She is not a typical noir female, complete with gun in hand like the pistolera Annie Starr (Peggy Cummins) in *Gun Crazy*. Susan destroys by enacted states of desire and the lure of possession as it plays out in the literal sexual politics of the 1950s.

Lieutenant Diamond loves Susan in an almost pathetic manner; she is his idealized image of fallen grace to be saved, of course, by him, from nefarious clutches. Neither he nor others can comprehend her attraction to his rival, Mr. Brown. Lieutenant Diamond is so driven that he nearly ruins his career, gets beaten and tortured, threatens others, and accepts varieties of warnings, setbacks, and humiliations in this noir antiromantic quest. Lieutenant Diamond scathingly refers to his rival throughout *The Big Combo* in memorable and revealing dialogue, as he insists to his captain, "Brown's not a man; he's an organization"; fervently warns Susan, "Save yourself; leave him"; and basically admits to himself, "Nobody knows how another person feels." These three revealing statements suggest a psychological overview of Lieutenant Diamond's frustrated and compulsive nature; Lieutenant Diamond wants to have another man's woman as possession even as he fails to understand how much he has in common with his rival. One area of distinction between the rivals is sexual.

In one illustrative shot sequence, as Lieutenant Diamond leaves the hospital after visiting Susan, he exits into a uniquely modeled series of neo-expressionistic squares and frames, passing from dark into light, in pursuit of something he thinks he understands—Susan's "salvation"—but cannot recognize because he never becomes familiar with the other side of Susan's personality and the nature of the Brown-Lowell relationship. Lieutenant Diamond's lack of understanding of himself and others, an expression of unabated egotism, leads to his appalling punishment. A quickly delivered punch to his face from an offscreen assailant, Mingo, temporarily stops Lieutenant Diamond and enables a violent coming together of the male players, although Lieutenant Diamond manages to get off a shot from his gun and hits Mingo in the wrist, thus leaving him limp and whining in pain, facilitating stereotypical moments of noir emasculation.

In a compelling and sadistic follow-up shot sequence, Lieutenant Diamond is tied down to a chair and tortured by a delighted Mingo, Fante, and McClure (Brian Donlevy), an older, almost deaf gangster deposed by Brown in an earlier power struggle for corporate control. However violent and ambitious he may remain, McClure also experiences various humiliations at the hands of Brown, and McClure will later be eliminated in Lewis's infamous execution sequence after McClure's failed treachery to regain power and enlist the aid of Fante and Mingo is exposed. McClure's hearing aid is turned off by a mocking Brown before Fante and Mingo, in phallic poses, machine gun McClure in total silence for a horrifically quiet death. But before this, McClure and then Brown administer the torture and beating to Lieutenant Diamond.

In Lieutenant Diamond's torture sequence, in a crowded medium wide shot, his tormentors surround him as an overhead lamp provides key lighting to illuminate their conspiracy in a realistic noir compositional design suggestively revised by Kubrick in his noir masterpiece, *The Killing* (1956). The gangsters first meet as a team in a seedy room to discuss the plan for the racetrack robbery, and the two lovers, Val (Vince Edwards) and Sherry (Marie Windsor), also conspire, after their adulterous liaison, to betray other low-end criminals, in shots illuminated by Kubrick's signifying lamp/lighting as a diegetic noir staple. After Brown arrives at Lieutenant Diamond's torture-bondage sequence, Brown places the earphone from McClure's hearing aid into Lieutenant Diamond's ear to inflict maximum pain without leaving a sign of its administration, but Lieutenant Diamond gives up nothing.

Before he is released, Lieutenant Diamond is forced by his assailants to "swallow a load" of an alcohol-laced liquid to suggest to the authorities that Lieutenant Diamond is the arrogant, uncontrollable problem, and that, perhaps, his crusade against Brown was also abusive. Lieutenant Diamond does prove to be as inflexible as his name implies; even after his part-time girlfriend, Rita, is mistakenly murdered in his place, Lieutenant Diamond seems unalterably fixed on the idea of destroying Brown, using Rita's death, however upsetting, as one more excuse to go after Brown. Ironically, Rita

Lieutenant Diamond's violent beating.

actually warns Lieutenant Diamond about the dangers he faces but it is she who dies instead; because she is a consumable image of less respectable working class desirability, she can be used in the cause to save Susan—her "better." Along with a bullet-ridden body, all that remains of Rita is a performance poster on an alley wall, indicating a different type of "wanted" to the paying public. Lieutenant Diamond's crusade for the possession of Susan's body leaves a trail of bodies in its wake.

Mr. Brown, the corporate-model gangster, is arguably the more interesting of the two battling men. As portrayed by Richard Conte, Brown is detestably suave and elegantly violent. Well dressed, intelligent, usually soft spoken, Brown provides the perfect foil for Lieutenant Diamond's rough, eruptive, déclassé behavior. When Brown articulates his capitalist ethos, the timely 1950s for-profit message "first is first, and second is nobody," he is speaking to Lieutenant Diamond in particular and the audience in general; those who "do," will, and those who "do not," like the outdated, outsmarted McClure and fiercely disordered Lieutenant Diamond, remain as potential carrion in the struggle to survive and thrive. Brown embodies the postwar noir deceptive image of the outwardly respectable gangster, like Fritz Lang's previously cited crime boss Mike Lagana, and in a nearly archetypal, romantic representation, like Michael Corleone in Francis Ford

Coppola's *The Godfather* (1972); *The Godfather, Part II* (1974); and, especially, *The Godfather, Part III* (1990).

Brown's gangster lineage has its roots in his capacity to express and value violence; in an early shot sequence, as Brown talks over an unsuccessful boxing match with his boxer as chattel, another example of Brown's depersonalization of the body as property, Brown slaps the bruised boxer across the face to test his ability to channel his humiliation and rage. Because the boxer cannot hate him enough to hit him back, Brown voids their contract. There is always more flesh available in the noir landscape to mold for violent or sexual purposes. *Hate* is the key; Brown literally states this as his visionary password toward success. According to Grant Tracey, in both *The Big Combo* and *The Big Heat*, principal characters share in the expression of this requisite noir emotion: "Bannion [in *The Big Heat*] exists in a disruptive emotional state, one of alienation and despair. Following this scene, the narrative spins inexorably to its violent climaxes, as Bannion slips into the dark realm of hate, attempting to purge his and the world's demons."[17] *The Big Combo* is also an exceptional study of the human capacity to hate, and the recognition of this emotion is the compulsive display of violence. Brown, Diamond, Mingo, and Fante, as well as Bannion in *The Big Heat*, are predatory naturalist beasts, bearing a brutish similarity to Zola's transgressive, corrupt, and corrupting creatures engaged in a struggle for survival, whether sexual or social. Even Susan, like the physically scarred Debby in *The Big Heat*, is an angry, wounded survivor. The aforementioned characters hate others, but unlike them, Susan must stop hating herself because she expresses her sexual desires in an era that labels them as immoral, or she must plausibly give up performing these transgressive acts in exchange for a more ordered life.

The capacity to hate defines Brown as he, whether as an abstract concept or quite literally, invokes its presence by his overall feeling of superiority and general detestation of others. Brown controls hate's expression toward others by deploying fear and intimidation as business practices, or by committing aggressive and brutal acts, or by endorsing this behavior in his subordinates. In the interior impassioned world of Brown's personality, in true noir postwar Freudian fashion, aggression and sexuality are thus endemically linked and expressed as a totalizing, focalized energy. After Susan is released from her earlier hospital stay, in the privacy of an upscale apartment, Brown violently grabs and kisses her because he can. There is no real struggle, although she indicates surfacing feelings of repulsion and anxiety. Even when Brown taunts Lieutenant Diamond with the declaration, "The only thing wrong with you is that you want to be me," Brown is not overstating their similar violent tendencies and desires; he is articulating why he has succeeded and Lieutenant Diamond still struggles. Lieutenant Diamond must learn how to hate enough to act, because desire alone is insufficient for resolving conflict, but he will come to learn this lesson. The conclusion of Edgar Ulmer's *Detour* (1945) frames a shot of a guilty man walking into the open road at night, leading to a deterministic space that entraps. In *The Big Combo*, gangster and combo boss Mr. Brown loses all because he has left too many bodies, some wretchedly alive, in his rise-and-fall career. As he passes in and out of shadows at night, Brown is also entrapped by his own destabilizing desires.

Brown actively controls all the minor transgressive players in *The Big Combo*: thugs Mingo and Fante, who worship him; aging thug McClure, who resents but obeys only to pay later for his aborted rebellion; and pathetic Alicia, his self-interned ex-wife, hiding in an asylum for protection from his machinations.[18] Although playing a minor role in *The Big Combo*, Alicia (Helen Walker) is an important symbol of the socially silenced housewife of the 1950s who no longer fits the needs of her enterprising husband and is thus eliminated from his social and professional sphere. Like Susan, Alicia is a woman fooling herself; both women are part of a substantial, ever-present cultural censoring of female identity and desire. As Brown's former wife, Alicia is the last living link to his past. As a former prison guard who abandons his life and identity via the possibilities that violence offers the enterprising male, Brown, a more socially adept figure than the fascist prison guard Captain Munsey (Hume Cronyn) in Jules Dassin's *Brute Force* (1947), nevertheless still enjoys watching or administering a good beating and practicing vicious intimidation. Alicia's alcoholism and mostly posed mental illness, which enables her silence, links her to an entire generation of unhappy women, as illustrated in Betty Friedan's *The Feminine Mystique*, in which the asylum and the home are depicted as all too similar in the deployment of male-female power relations. Alicia's silence buys her more life; she literally lives by leaving, and as Nicholas Christopher notes, Alicia survives "[in] an isolated country cottage, looked after by a permanent housekeeper, where Brown has ensconced [sic] her for many years."[19] As Alicia knowingly confesses, "I'd rather be insane and alive than sane and dead."

The thugs Mingo and Fante, two models of historicized latency at the edge of representation and beyond, are as fascinating as they are plausibly iconic. Mingo and Fante arguably have the strongest romantic relationship in *The Big Combo*. They are openly devoted to each other, share a bedroom, and are almost always in the same shot. In their "hideaway," Mingo longingly expresses his feelings to Fante when he declares, "Let's never come back," and suggests they run off together. Fante, the more solidly "butch" of the two partners, proves his fidelity to Mingo when he presses McClure to pay not only him but Mingo as well for the pleasure of beating Lieutenant Diamond before Brown arrives. They will kill, torture, and even die together, although Mingo outlasts Fante when the bomb left by Brown to dispose of them after they serve their function explodes. In a morgue-like setting, when Lieutenant Diamond begins to press Mingo for information, the policeman reveals Fante's mutilated, dynamited body, literally, what is left of Fante's head and face, to a severely wounded Mingo, who cries and becomes almost hysterical.[20] This is the one true expression of love and loss in the film.

In a review of Richard Barrios's *Screened Out: Playing Gay in Hollywood from Edison to Stonewall*, Brett Abrams states, "During the politically conservative 1950s *The Big Combo* featured a vice czar with two henchmen. The two, who were not labeled homosexual, appear as loving men sharing the same bed."[21] Technically, these men do not appear in the same bed but in the same bedroom, itself an unusually suggestive image for the 1950s cinema in America. One recalls the two-bed solution for the already married Lucy (Lucille Ball) and Ricky (Desi Arnaz) in the *I Love Lucy* (1951–57) television series. These are similar living conditions to Mingo and Fante's

Gangsters Mingo and Fante.

sleeping arrangement, but Lucy and Ricky did manage to produce a baby. The Mingo-Fante bedroom sequence is one of several compelling but not overtly risqué moments in *The Big Combo*, because it indicates a *probability* of forbidden intimacy that would invoke a censorial response to its perceived pornographic content had the depiction gone further or been more visually suggestive. As John Gagnon and William Simon note as late as 1968, "There is no form of sexual activity that is not deviant at some time, in some social location, in some specified relationships, or with some partners," and in particular, "As sexual activity is elaborated, it moves beyond an exclusively or nearly exclusively genital focus and, consequently, increasing numbers of essentially conforming sexual actors find themselves doing things that many others still consider 'unnatural acts'; indeed, doing things that most state jurisdictions define as 'crimes against nature' . . . mouth genital contact, or oral sex, is an excellent case in point."[22] The condemnatory, inflammatory rhetoric that labels such suggested behavior as deviant, unnatural acts, or crimes against nature, may be one plausible explanation why Lewis limits the more explicit representation of the Mingo-Fante relationship, but the evidence for this relationship is there. Lewis leaves images of male-to-male sexual desire to the imagination; to the audience, Mingo and Fante are encoded as more than friends. Although they die together, it just takes Mingo a little longer to get ready. Director Lewis's linkage of Mingo and Fante's personal pleasure at a show of violence, although the product of a corporate decision, generates some expression of revenge for them against a system that would label them as sexual subversives. Each directs anger toward and holds momentary control over a totemic 1950s figure, the "tough cop." Each punch and insult Mingo and Fante take satisfaction in delivering to others may be viewed as a response to experiential, milieu-specific humiliations they presumably have endured. There is also a passing resemblance to other expressions of power-revenge fantasies of the formerly powerless now in control of the "enemy"; I would suggest that Mingo and Fante, idiots with guns, bear a disturbing likeness to the sadistic guards who gleefully humiliated their prisoners in Abu Ghraib, all that is missing in *The Big Combo* are the fetishistic photographs.[23] Whether abusive power is manifest in the form of a forced earplug or a pointed hood, it is easier to execute disturbing orders when they please the inflictor.

Who are all these violent men and struggling women? Each is a variation on a genre precept; these men and women are naturalist spectacles engaged in the grinding, experiential process that strips bare the imposed social and moral order to reveal its repressed violent and sexual layers, the hidden and often "dirty" world underneath the prosperity and stability of any society. Naturalism's deterministic ethos rediscovers itself in the noir formula and its sadistic power struggle for control. In *The Big Combo*, Lewis's narrative links naturalist precepts with the noir aesthetic to reveal the essential subversive. I would also suggest that Harold Pinter's less-than-clever thugs, Gus and Ben, in *The Dumb Waiter* (1957), bear an intertextual linkage with their violent but subversively engaging predecessors, Mingo and Fante. Although Gus and Ben are nominally heterosexual, their unique friendship also culminates in an exceptionally strong bonding that leads to an intense conclusion; they are "married" in their murderous career and its violence, alienation, and shared levels of anxiety. This is especially evident as Gus and Ben, like Mingo and Fante, keep waiting for their superior to show up with instructions for a soon-to-be delivered "hit":

BEN: You'll have to wait.

GUS: What for?

BEN: For Wilson.

GUS: He might not come. He might just send a message. He doesn't always come.[24]

Both the hyperactive Gus (like Mingo) and the slightly more intelligent and commanding Ben (like Fante) just keep talking and waiting:

GUS: Why doesn't he get in touch? I feel like I've been here for years. (*He takes the revolver out of the holster to check the ammunition.*) We've never let him down though, have we? We've never let him down. I was thinking only the other day, Ben. We're reliable, aren't we?

He puts his revolver back in its holster.[25]

Pinter leaves these two men in a compelling silence, facing each other, and Ben, with a gun ever ready, must act against Gus. In *The Big Combo*, Brown acts against both Fante and Mingo with a box of dynamite. In *The Big Combo* and *The Dumb Waiter*, characters wait not for Godot's deliverance but for instructions about the next violently fulfilling moment. Are these all acts of "homosocial bonding"? In *The Big Combo*, Lewis's shot of a physically drained, still impassioned, but mortally wounded Mingo beholding Fante, his mangled love interest, in an emotionally unadulterated series of glance-reaction shots is evidently a distraught lover's expression of pain. Alton's noir lighting design is most angularly expressionistic in its deployment of stylized shapes and shadows generated by a contrasting placement of multiple bodies in the frame in this makeshift morgue. The chiaroscuro and geometrics outwardly suggest Mingo's interior, overwhelming pain revealed as a noir landscape of anguish. In contrast to this, the more traditional heterosexual relationship between Brown and Susan is depicted both on- and offscreen, but it is no less a startling or sexually transgressive expression of desire.

"You're No Longer a Bright, Respectable Girl"

In an interview of Joseph Lewis by Peter Bogdanovich, after the traditional homage paid to *Gun Crazy*, Bogdanovich specifically discusses *The Big Combo* with Lewis and refers to it as "not just an average gangster movie," to which Lewis not only offers insight into the nature of the Brown-Susan relationship but also indicates what is artistically and historically unique about his noir narrative. Lewis states, "I asked Jean [Susan] why her character—a society girl looking like herself—would throw herself at a character like Richard Conte's gangster, a known murderer. And she couldn't come up with the answer."[26] Susan doesn't even seem to like Brown, and when he states before his most spirited effort to arouse Susan, "I'll give you anything at all," her response is mute.

After a series of semiwaffling evasions in the interview, Lewis describes the revelatory process he utilized with Jean Wallace to provide insight into

Expressionist anxiety and Mingo's hysteria.

the dynamic and fulfilling fiction informing the psychosexual makeup of her character: "Has it ever occurred to you that you're attracted to this man because of his lewdness, because of his sex relationship, which was so crude? . . . No respectable man is going to love you the way this gangster's going to love you."[27] Perhaps feigning a degree of cluelessness or simply ignorant of the implications of Lewis's real meaning, Wallace had to be pressed further by Lewis to understand what her motivation was predicated on and exactly what kept these disparate lovers together, since it was obviously not idealized love or romance. Lewis led Wallace on by describing a love and lovemaking process "that you will deny, but in your wildest dreams, yearn for," but the evidently still obtuse Wallace needed further prodding. "When this man takes you in his arms, he doesn't stop kissing you on the lips, he doesn't stop at your earlobe, he doesn't stop at your neck, he doesn't stop at your tummy. He covers you all."[28] The actress bristled with a mixture of fear, resentment, and perhaps even loathing since this suggested act her husband and costar, Cornel Wilde, would obviously have to witness. This was the other love, the sexual practice that dare not speak its name, especially in the 1950s: cunnilingus. Evidently, as if to explain it all, Brown goes down.[29] Perhaps he can perform this taboo sexual practice because of his outlaw status; the camera frames in close-up shots these moments with the detailed focus of a safecracker at work.

Like Fritz Lang's troubled "dame" Debbie (Gloria Grahame) in *The Big Heat*, Susan has two sides. Whereas Debbie is déclassé and brash, Susan is elegant and reserved; both women *act on* their desires, although Debbie has her face scarred and ruined by her thuggish lover, and Susan lapses into a pill-induced catatonia endemic to troubled women of her class and generation. Whether Debbie is framed in Lang's mirror shot or in a two shot with Glenn Ford, Borde and Chaumeton note that Debbie's transgressive behavior indicates more than its effects: "The half destroyed face of Gloria Grahame concretizes with wonder the duality of its heart."[30] Debbie's "better side" is finally exposed as a product of her brutally ruined profile, but she retains both sides. Lewis's revelatory shot sequence of an orgasmic Susan suggests the duality informing her being; her other sensual side is uncovered in the controversial cunnilingus sequence, and she too is both women.

Why is classy Susan Lowell with the suave but violent gangster Brown and not the "safe," traditional, and heterosexual "catch" Lieutenant Diamond? When Lieutenant Diamond's burlesque dancer girlfriend, Rita, reveals to him that, as far as women are concerned, they "only care how he makes love," her comment has two applications: one involves romantic fulfillment and the other involves sexual performance and satisfaction.

Even Susan refers to "a girl's first love," but is it a romantic or physical need? When Susan meets and dances with her former instructor, she appears to be ashamed of herself and aware of her socially and legally compromised predicament; she hardly ever seems happy. Lewis must clarify for the audience the (abnormal) psychology behind Susan's unbalanced, meandering, and noxious relationship with Brown. To propose the "why" behind Susan's predicament, Lewis exposes her sexual desires more explicitly than previously indicated. In *The Big Combo*, Lewis feasibly represents "the connection between degradation and eroticism" on concomitant levels: Susan's social descent from her former class and position, an obvious humiliation, and unseen acts of sexual disrepute.[31]

Susan's act of sexual "slumming" might suggest that she is actively confronting a repressive power structure, and the resulting conflict it creates for her is enormous, but she never seems happy or in control of herself and only occasionally fulfilled. This is not her quest narrative, or that of any other character in *The Big Combo*. According to Grant Tracey, "Diamond loves her; and his narrative quest seeks to ascertain her guilt and to reign [*sic*] her back into the bounds of the acceptable. . . . This brooding, seedy . . . thriller obsessively portrays a fear of women and the need to interrogate and contain her sexuality."[32] I might suggest an alternative perspective on this issue; there is no romantic, courtly, or genre-specific quest narrative functioning in *The Big Combo*. The numerous displays of violent behavior in pursuit of a "goal" are linked to survival schemes and expressions of voracious sexuality; one "beast" wants to control or possess another beast. Lewis's quasi-naturalist narrative essentially explores Susan's conflicted identity in relationship to two atypical male pursuers via the discourse mechanism endemic to noir technique in a 1950s urban milieu, revealing both her and society's values and discontents.

As if to reestablish after the cunnilingus shot sequence that moral order is restored, the shot cuts to a police precinct. For the audience, the cut comes too late; Lewis's noir narrative has expanded into a new area of expressed desire and sexual practice. In several later edifying interviews, Lewis describes the expressive yet concealed lovemaking shot sequence to interviewers: "As Conte kisses her eyes and mouth, the camera keeps coming closer and closer until finally Conte's head disappears from the shot and we are left to imagine what he's doing below the frame by the ecstasy on Wallace's face."[33] The medium close-up shot moves from on- to offscreen. For the audience, the impression and image are indelible. Like Lewis's suggested but not explicit representation of homosexual intimacy between Mingo and Fante, there is a plausible explanation why this oral sex shot sequence continues its movement to an offscreen framing: according to

Gagnon and Simon, "Cunnilingus, among other sexual practices is categorized as one of several 'particular forms of sexual deviance' and labeled as an act of 'normal deviance.'"[34] For the 1950s culture of sexual repression, the provocative and operational word is *deviance*. By the 1970s, in films such as Hal Ashby's *Coming Home* (1978), the moral stigma placed on heterosexual oral sex had mostly dissipated due to numerous social factors, contraceptive advances, and the rise of the soft-core and hard-core pornography industry.

Of course, the censors had a strong indication of what socially forbidden pleasure Lewis was surreptitiously incorporating into the narrative. His response was slyly honest to an angry husband/actor Cornel Wilde, the censors, and, inferentially, the audience: "I left it to your imagination,"[35] which is partially true. The image of the enraptured, sexual female, with a male head descending in the shot, could leave only one impression, but as the sequence goes on just long enough for the head to disappear, any question of intent could be debated, however disingenuously. As Lewis defiantly stated to the censors in his clever, defensive posturing about this sequence: "You supply me with the emotion: that's why I left it to the audience. But don't tell me I'm filthy, or a filthy director."[36] In *The Big Combo*, the offscreen cunnilingus shot sequence is historic.

Even when contemporary film gangsters reminisce about their gendered heritage, the controversial, taboo impressions remain. In Martha P. Nochimson's article "'Waddaya Lookin' At?' Re-Reading the Gangster Genre through *The Sopranos*," she notes that "at the end of the first season, Tony Soprano tells his wife Carmela . . . 'Cunnilingus and psychiatry brought us to this' . . . for the viewer, 'this' is the possibility inherent in modern life for a new understanding of the ambiguous charm of the gangster."[37] Of course, gangster Tony Soprano omits any consideration of female desire and instead focuses on his limited sense of moral and sexual status in his specific milieu. To maintain the rigors of the traditional gangster ethos and to avoid being ridiculed, as Tony's uncle Junior endures by a knowing circle of friends, Tony acts as if he never saw a psychiatrist, which he does, or engage in occasional bouts of oral sex, which he also does. Only outlaw "combo" boss Brown, in the 1950s, has the open, practiced courage to act on the strength of his sexual convictions, for whatever the misogynist purpose. The fall of gangster Brown, the lure of Lieutenant Diamond, and the safer world he represents win over Susan and the censors, and Susan is "redeemed" by her newly found place in the heterosexual mainstream.

Lieutenant Diamond retrieves his emasculated pretensions to the throne, Susan's seat of power, by breaking down a deserving thug, thus closing off her exposure to the gangster social circulus but replacing it with the

The foreplay without precedent.

Noir erotica.

sexually traditional rigidity and related gender and historically applicable social formations they both face in the mid-1950s.

Were there times during that decade when Susan missed Brown?

Notes

I wish to express my gratitude to Elizabeth Dill and Enid Stubin for their invaluable contributions to this project.

1. This critical assessment of *The Big Combo* is most evident in James Naremore's comprehensive study of film noir, *More than Night: Film Noir in Its Contexts* (Berkeley: University of California Press, 1998), which favors the other films listed for comparison's sake. I may disagree with Naremore's classificatory status of *The Big Combo*, but *More than Night* remains the best contemporary reference for the analysis of film noir. For an overview of Lewis's *The Big Combo*, I recommend Rose Capp, "First Is First and Second Is Nobody: Hoodlums and Heroines in Joseph H. Lewis's *The Big Combo*," no. 25 (2003), http://www.sensesofcinema.com/2003/cteq/big_combo/.

2. Naremore, *More than Night*, 156.

3. Francis M. Nevins, *Joseph H. Lewis: Overview, Interview, and Filmography* (Lanham, MD: Scarecrow Press, 1998), 44.

4. Laura Mulvey, "Unmasking the Gaze: Some Thoughts on New Feminist Film Theory and History," *Lectora: Revista de dones i textualitat* 7 (2001): 5.

5. Raymond Borde and Étienne Chaumeton, *Panorama de film noir Américain, 1941–1953* (Paris: Flammarion, 1988), 24. "Toutes les oeuvres de cette série présentent bien une unité d'ordre affectif: *c'est l'état de tension né, chez le spectateur, de la disparition de ses repères psychologiques.* La vocation du film noir était de créer *un malaise spécifique.*" All translations from this text are mine.

6. The reader may think of Betty Page's pinups and photos, Allen Ginsberg's poetry, *Playboy* magazine, soft-core 16mm "underground" films, and various other cultural personalities and products as examples of a functional countertradition.

7. Jody W. Pennington, *The History of Sex in American Film* (Westport, CT: Praeger, 2007), 36.

8. Borde and Chaumeton, *Panorama*, 152. "Il s'agit souvent d'un naturalisme proche de Zola, quelquefois revu par Freud."

9. Among the more famous film productions John Alton is credited with as director of photography are Anthony Mann's *T-Men* (1947), Alfred L. Werker's *He Walked by Night* (1948), Harry Essex's *I, the Jury* (1953), and Richard Brooks's *The Catered Affair* (1956). Alton's artistic pedigree is rightly recognized as seminal to noir's cycle of classic production.

10. Composer David Raksin is a legend in the American film industry. Among his credits are the scores for Chaplin's *Modern Times* (1936), Otto Pre-

minger's *Laura* (1944), Vincent Minnelli's *The Bad and the Beautiful* (1952), Lewis Allen's *Suddenly* (1954), and Richard Wilson's *Al Capone* (1959).

11. Carlos Clarens, *Crime Movies: From Griffith to the Godfather and Beyond* (New York: W. W. Norton, 1980), 233.

12. R. Barton Palmer, *Hollywood's Dark Side: The American Film Noir* (New York: Twayne, 1994), 95.

13. Nevins, *Joseph H. Lewis*, 44. These are *solely* Nevins's words.

14. See Nicholas Christopher's *Somewhere in the Night: Film Noir and the American City* (New York: Henry Holt, 1998), 197, where he makes a similar point about Susan's unconventional noir identity.

15. Grant Tracey, "Covert Narrative Strategies to Contain and Punish Women in *The Big Heat* (1953) and *The Big Combo* (1955)," in *Film Noir: Reader 4*, ed. Alain Silver and James Ursini (New Jersey: Limelight, 2004), 119.

16. Stephen J. Whitfield, "Sex and the Single Decade," *American Literary History* 12, no. 4 (2000): 771.

17. Tracey, "Covert Narrative Strategies," 122.

18. Alicia might be viewed as an early example of the "first wives' club" syndrome.

19. Christopher, *Somewhere in the Night*, 196.

20. I cannot help recalling the final image of the exploding Roman candle held in a crotch shot by the young man in Kenneth Anger's seminal gay film, the violent and hilarious avant-garde narrative *Fireworks* (1947).

21. Brett Abrams, review of *Screened Out: Playing Gay in Hollywood from Edison to Stonewall*, by Richard Barrios, *Journal of the History of Sexuality* 14, no. 4 (2005): 463.

22. John Gagnon and William Simon, "Sexual Deviance in Contemporary America," *Annals of the American Academy of Political and Social Science* 37, no. 6 (1968): 107–8.

23. "Disturbing New Photos from Abu Ghraib," *Wired*, February 8, 2008, http://www.wired.com/science/discoveries/multimedia/2008/02/gallery_abu_ghraib and "Torture Scandal: The Images That Shamed America," *Guardian*, n.d., http://www.guardian.co.uk/gall/0,,1211872,00.html are two websites that illustrate the nature of these abusive practices. The film still of Lieutenant Diamond's beating and humiliation could be retrofitted.

24. Harold Pinter, *The Dumb Waiter*, in *Complete Works: One* (New York: Grove Press, 1994), 144–45.

25. Ibid.

26. Peter Bogdanovich, *Who the Devil Made It: Conversations with Legendary Film Directors* (New York: Alfred A. Knopf, 1997), 685.

27. Ibid.

28. Ibid., 685–86.

29. Perhaps Lewis even considered such an erotically charged, taboo scene between Mingo and Fante.

30. Borde and Chaumeton, *Panorama*, 127. "Le visage a demi détruit de Gloria Grahame concrétise à merveille la dualité de son âme."

31. Gagnon and Simon, "Sexual Deviance," 114.

32. Tracey, "Covert Narrative Strategies," 125–26.

33. Nevins, *Joseph H. Lewis*, 44.

34. Gagnon and Simon, "Sexual Deviance," 109.

35. Bogdanovich, *Who the Devil*, 686.

36. Ibid.

37. Martha P. Nochimson, "'Waddaya Lookin' At?' Re-Reading the Gangster Genre through *The Sopranos*," *Film Quarterly* 56, no. 2 (2002–3): 7.

11

Tony Williams

The Halliday Brand and *Terror in a Texas Town*
Western Allegories of the Blacklist

> I wanted as well to highlight how the rubric of practices includes the institutional forces at work, like production and projection routines, and the technology employed such as standardized reel lengths. A further lesson here is that practices include informal relations among personnel, such as the urge to show one's skill. Filmmakers may address their work to their peers as well as to their public. No historian of painting would be surprised to learn that artists compete in displaying their virtuosity. We can explain important aspects of how movies work by considering filmmakers as creative agents working with craft practices within a community. Members of that community may be sharply aware of traditions and trends. They may replicate well-tried norms or explore emerging ones. They may solve problems in routine ways or pose new difficulties in order to triumph over them. And some of the most ambitions and gifted creators are likely to treat constraints as opportunities.
>
> David Bordwell, *Poetics of Cinema*

The epigraph, from a recent book aiming to defining cinematic practices more precisely than has been the case in the past, also relates to two films by Joseph H. Lewis. Constraint and opportunity may also involve creative interaction with not only stylistic practices operating within an industry at a particular time but also social and historical factors. *The Halliday Brand* (1957) and *Terror in a Texas Town* (1958) are works of stylistic virtuosity revealing significant opportunities low-budget constraints offered Lewis. But they are also films belonging to a particular social and historical context in Hollywood cinema influencing a particular combination of style and meaning.

My first and only meeting with Lewis occurred on April 29, 1994, when he spoke to film production students at Washington University, St. Louis. Then in his late eighties, Lewis impressed me not only as that "tough little guy" Larry Cohen met in 1965 to discuss the pilot episode of *Branded* Lewis directed but also as a talent fully conscious of the wide range of craftsmanship practices displayed in his Hollywood career as well as creative aspects involving "making meaning." He also generously offered advice to film production students and took a sincere interest in what they were doing. When veterans such as Lewis depart, we later regret missed opportunities of asking them more detailed questions about their work. In two major interviews Lewis says relatively little about directing *The Halliday Brand* (1957), but he was more forthcoming about his last film, *Terror in a Texas Town* (1958). These were westerns, a genre Lewis was familiar with since his prolific activity in the 1930s and early 1940s but one to which he had not returned until his collaboration with Randolph Scott in *A Lawless Street* (1955) and *7th Cavalry* (1956). According to Francis M. Nevins, these films are less interesting than the two black-and-white westerns that concluded Lewis's career as a film director.[1] In an earlier interview with Peter Bogdanovich, Lewis spoke about *Terror in a Texas Town*. He regards it with pride but vaguely refers to its predecessor offering a "wonderful opportunity to work with Joseph Cotten."[2] Lewis also mentions the role of blacklisted screenwriter Nedrick Young who acted in *Terror in a Texas Town* and worked on the screenplay uncredited. By contrast, Lewis mentions that the script of *The Halliday Brand* was already completed after producer Collier Young had collaborated "with a writer" and that all he had to do was "prepare it."[3] Credits mention two writers, George W. George and George F. Slavin, who worked on *The Woman on Pier 13* (1949; earlier titled *I Married a Communist*), *City of Bad Men* (1953), and *Big House USA* (1955); their other work was routine. Collier Young was the former husband of Ida Lupino. After their divorce, he produced her 1950s films as director, *Outrage* (1951), *Hard, Fast, and Beautiful* (1951), *The Hitchhiker* (1953), and *The Bigamist* (1953), as well as Don Siegel's *Private Hell 36* (1954) that Lupino both acted in and cowrote.[4] Young's role on *The Halliday Brand* may have involved more than producing. He may either have written the screenplay himself or employed a blacklisted screenwriter using these two other names as a "front." Young and Lupino collaborated on films indirectly questioning the conservative ideology of the 1950s; he appeared uncredited as a Mexican peon in *The Hitchhiker*. Racial overtones within *The Halliday Brand* and *Terror in a Texas Town* reflect the era's growing awareness of civil rights issues also seen in *The Searchers* (1956), *Man in the Shadow* (1957), and *Touch of Evil* (1958).

These two westerns are also allegories of the blacklist, suggesting that Allan Dwan's *Silver Lode* (1954) was by no means exceptional in the 1950s. Raoul Walsh's *Pursued* (1947) and André de Toth's *Ramrod* (1947)—as well as Anthony Mann's *Devil's Doorway* (1950) and *The Furies* (1951)—amalgamated film noir with the western in narratives dealing with social injustice. Mann's films treated issues of racial oppression. Samuel Fuller's *China Gate* (1957) and *The Crimson Kimono* (1959) also examined issues involving miscegenation. Within this context, these two Lewis films are by no means unique. However, they operate as explicit western allegories of the blacklist where casting plays a crucial role.

Consciously or not (and Lewis was certainly aware of the blacklisting affecting his friend Nedrick Young whom he featured in *Terror in a Texas Town*), the director cast several actors associated with both film noir and the blacklist in *The Halliday Brand*.[5] Joseph Cotten not only was associated with film noir but was also a friend of Orson Welles and a key player in the New Deal era of the Mercury Theatre. He was a well-known star and had escaped the blacklist. Before appearing in *The Halliday Brand*, Cotten acted in Budd Boetticher's little-known crime drama *The Killer Is Loose* (1956), costarring with anti-Semitic Hollywood actor Wendell Corey.[6] Jeanette Nolan played the role of Lady Macbeth in Orson Welles's Republic film version of *Macbeth* (1948), while Betsy Blair had suffered from the blacklist at the time of her appearance in *The Halliday Brand*.[7] Ward Bond's associations as a rabid blacklister are well known, and Lewis's casting of him as Big Dan Halliday develops Nicholas Ray's subversive strategy of "shaming Ward Bond" as seen in *On Dangerous Ground* (1951) and *Johnny Guitar* (1954). The first film casts him as a violent patriarchal thug little different from his role in *The Halliday Brand*. *Johnny Guitar* is well known for its allegorical treatment of the blacklist. As Marc Lawrence points out in his memoir of the blacklist *Long Time No See*, Bond had not mellowed with the passing of time but still maintained his red-baiting.[8] If the future Major Adams of *Wagon Train* saw red on the set of *The Halliday Brand*, no record exists of it, and we can assume that Lewis controlled him in the same way that John Ford had.

The Halliday Brand is interesting not only in terms of its historical context but also as the work of a talent fully aware of key traditions within the industrial system that he would utilize in subversive ways. Lengthy long takes and above-average shot ratios occur in certain scenes far above the norm for the era. Although Lewis never shot any of his films in CinemaScope, several compositions in *The Halliday Brand* reveal many of those classical staging options David Bordwell finds so significant in a Scope era that allowed "a cluster of classical staging options one final run-through."[9] Lewis utilized options such as deep focus, wide-angle cinematography, characters in foreground and background compositions, mobile camera movement, and tableau framing shots. Other talents such as cinematographer Roy Renahan and coeditor Michael Luciano collaborated on the film. Luciano also edited several films by Robert Aldrich such as *The Big Knife* (1955), *Kiss Me Deadly* (1955), *Attack!* (1956), *Autumn Leaves* (1957), and the Aldrich-produced western *The Ride Back* (1957) that also deals with issues of race and sexuality. Luciano would likely have recognized Lewis's long-take strategies after editing *Kiss Me Deadly*.

Although not a film noir, *The Halliday Brand* contains several expressionistic shots, including the lynching of Jivaro. At the time the style indirectly influenced films such as Nicholas Ray's *Johnny Guitar* (1954), *Rebel without a Cause* (1955), and *Bitter Victory* (1957).[10] In an interview originally conducted by Robert Porfirio and Carl Macek on February 7, 1975, Lewis expressed indebtedness to his own "creative community," specifically mentioning *Citizen Kane* (1941) and the films of William Wyler.[11] But artists are also innovators. As Robert Keser notes, "Not one of Lewis's films can be dismissed as unworthy of viewing, not one lacks artistic imagination, and not one behaves completely according to the rules."[12] *The Halliday Brand* and *Terror in a Texas Town* employ mise-en-scène and visual style in a self-conscious manner in their allegorical treatments of the Hollywood blacklist.

Whether seen against classical Greek tragedy or Emily Brontë's *Wuthering Heights*, *The Halliday Brand* depicts a divided family struggling with issues of class, race, and sexuality.[13] Tightly constructed with a running time of seventy-nine minutes, the film begins with a prologue set in the present. It employs a long flashback and concludes with an epilogue attempting to resolve the drama. But as Nevins points out, nothing is really resolved since too many loose strands remain incapable of resolution. The film's narrative structure resembles Edward Dmytryk's *Broken Lance* (1954), a film that also depicts a dysfunctional family with patriarch (Spencer Tracy) married to an Indian wife and opposed by his younger son (Robert Wagner). An extended flashback also occurs in it, though *The Halliday Brand* features a more accomplished usage of the technique. It opens with older son Daniel (Joseph Cotten) returning to the bedside of his dying father. The flashback reveals family disunity originating in Dan Halliday's racist feelings against the half-breed suitor Jivaro (Christopher Dark) of his daughter, Martha (Betsy Blair). Halliday uses a lynching mob to remove the threat of miscegenation. History appears to repeat itself in the growing affection between Jivaro's sister Aleta (Viveca Lindfors) and Daniel until Halliday provokes a violent confrontation with her father, Chad (Jay

C. Flippen), resulting in another deliberately motivated institutional murder. Daniel rejects his father and threatens to remove his sheriff's badge (his symbol of authority) from him. Like Vance Jeffords in *The Furies*, he engages in economic and institutional emasculation. But Daniel operates outside the law and in a more vengeful manner than Vance and Diamond in *The Big Combo* (1955). Using his younger son Clay's (Bill Williams) engagement to Aleta to entice Daniel home, Halliday attempts to kill him but his death resolves the struggle between father and son.

The Halliday Brand resembles many 1950s dysfunctional family westerns, but its allegorical treatment of the blacklist is distinctive. Like Ethan Edwards in *The Searchers* (1956), Dan Halliday is a violent racist. His methods resemble those used against victims of the blacklist whether they belong to acceptable or unacceptable racial groups. As in *The Searchers*, Ward Bond plays a law enforcement figure but one sharing Edwards's pathological racism.

Space does not permit a detailed treatment of every scene in this film. But several sequences employing the use of the long take with mobile cam-

From *left to right:* Clay Halliday (Bill Williams), Big Dan Halliday (Ward Bond), and Daniel Halliday (Joseph Cotten) in *The Halliday Brand* (1957).

era and choreographed character movements suggest Lewis's intuitive awareness of the real issues within this film that contain a particular "structure of meaning" influencing the entire narrative.

After an establishing shot showing Clay Halliday riding on horseback moving from long to mid-shot, the second sequence lasts approximately two minutes and fifty seconds. It begins with a mid-shot and Daniel's off-screen voice ordering his brother to dismount. A hand holding a gun enters left of frame. It points toward Clay in the right background. As this deep focus long take continues, Daniel and Clay move within the frame until Clay gets the drop on his brother who remarks, "You pulled a gun on me once before." Although news of his dying father makes no impression, Clay's engagement to Aleta (with his father's approval) does. Daniel decides to ride back with Clay. The sequence ends with Clay extinguishing Daniel's campfire before dissolving to a close-up of Martha's hands tending flowers. The camera tilts up to show her responding to her father's offscreen summons. This shot lasts some twenty seconds; it cuts to a fifteen-second long shot showing Martha going to the house. It ends after the camera tilts down to show an ax embedded in a fallen tree. This final image also concludes the film.

These opening shots exhibit not only economical direction but also enigmatic elements. Why are the brothers disunited? Why does Daniel not care about his father dying? Why is Martha wearing black? What is the significance of the ax buried in the tree trunk? We eventually learn answers to all these questions. The ax symbolizes the peace treaty Halliday made with Indians who once occupied the territory. But, despite this truce, another racial war continues. The master race wishes to maintain racial purity. Family members are not to contaminate the brand by mixing with an inferior race, especially those having mixed blood. As Reynold Humphries notes, from the time of the 1947 hearings of the House Un-American Activities Committee (HUAC), racism played a key role in the blacklist.[14] The ailing Halliday tells Martha, "What I did, I did for your own good." She looks at him, then gazes offscreen: it is the first of many offscreen looks in this film. Martha also suggests that her prospective sister-in-law Aleta may be waiting not only for Clay. The future groom notes how she welcomes Daniel in a later fifty-second shot. "Can't you take your eyes off him? Can't you? Can't you?" Before Daniel pauses before the door of his father's room, Martha tells him, "He wants to forgive you, to go back to the way it was." The repetition of these lines echoing in Daniel's mind leads to a dissolve introducing the flashback. However, preceding scenes contain enough evidence of tensions that may never be easily reconciled.

The flashback's first shot lasts just under three minutes; it begins in

Dan's room. Father and son have a seemingly amicable relationship. Despite Dan's presentation of a pair of silver-plated Colt pistols to a son he sees as having the same "stubborn streak" as himself, Daniel prefers to work at the ranch rather than join his father "wearing a badge" on a posse. The camera moves back and forth during this scene showing father and son occupying different areas of the bed. Guns placed there foreshadow those violent methods Halliday later employs to remove the miscegenation threatening the racial purity of his family. Daniel disapproves of Halliday's methods of beating confessions out of strangers that later turn out to be false. When Dan hears that his half-breed Indian worker Jivaro may have a squaw, he fears overpopulation by mixed breeds and decides to investigate.

Following two establishing shots of Jivaro carrying a lamb outside a shack, an extended scene occurs lasting about three minutes and fifteen seconds ending with Halliday's disruptive offscreen voice. It begins with a cut to the interior. Jivaro enters the door in long shot and moves toward center frame. As he kneels with the lamb, a woman dressed in white enters from screen left. When Jivaro returns to the door to let the lamb outside, the woman turns her back to the camera until she turns to face the audience. It is Martha. This long take also involves them dancing, reminiscent of the dance between Johnny and Vienna in *Johnny Guitar*, and it includes such significant dialogue such as Jivaro's "This is our world. We are safe in it as long as we are not seen" and Martha's "Even out here, we have to close the door." When Halliday's angry face appears in the next shot, he abruptly closes the door. References to doors opening and closing are not accidental. They demonstrate the existence of separate spaces characters inhabit believing themselves to be free from pressures of the outside world. Halliday chooses to exist in his own private space on his ranch. Jivaro and Martha's private space does not survive the outside pressure of racism, which results in Jivaro's murder and the "widowhood" of a daughter Halliday expects to continue to keep house for him.

After Jivaro's lynching, the longest take in the film occurs. It lasts for some five minutes and thirty seconds following a nineteen-second shot of Jivaro's last moments of life and others showing Martha discovering his body hanging from a tree. The former sequence depicts the dark, noir-like jail interior. Clay and Daniel try to free Jivaro too late. A rope thrown by a lynch mob removes them leftward out of frame. The camera then tracks into a mid-close-up of the terrified Jivaro, passing the shadow of a noose on the wall and stopping at Daniel's shadow protesting to no avail, "He's done no wrong. He's innocent." A hand moves from left frame to grab Jivaro and pulls him away.

The long shot begins with the Hallidays grouped around a buckboard containing Jivaro's body. Camera movement emphasizes key portions of the dialogue. Halliday rejects any responsibility for Jivaro's murder as well as past illegal actions. "Maybe a few innocent men got killed but I got things done. Once in a while this kind of thing happens. A man gets himself killed before he can get a fair trial. But you've got to weigh these things for the common good." Daniel not only condemns his father's torture of innocent and guilty suspects but also confesses his own responsibility for what has happened. "Maybe, that's why I never rode with you because on the spread. I could turn my back on this. Your kind of law and order!"

Up to this point, Daniel resembles a spineless Cold War liberal who deliberately ignores ugly historical events as long as they do not affect him. Cotten's casting is crucial toward understanding Daniel's character. Although criticized for his performance as seeming uncomfortable appearing in the western, Cotten often excelled at playing weak characters, whether in the epic western *Duel in the Sun* (1946) or as the hack western writer who betrays his friend in *The Third Man* (1949).[15] Despite intending to take revenge on his father, Daniel struggles with two conflicting tensions: superficial liberalism and a violence derived from his father that will not only contaminate him but ruin any possibilities for a union with Aleta that could have replaced the failed one between Jivaro and Martha. Daniel's role confirms that Lewis deliberately intended to avoid any easy resolution by revealing how *everyone* became contaminated by the blacklist. Like Jesse in *Duel in the Sun*, Daniel's well-intended liberalism proves ineffective in the first part of *The Halliday Brand*. The second part reveals that he is also contaminated by his father's pathological violence. Daniel combines the characters of Jesse and Lewt in *Duel in the Sun* within his persona, but he displays more neurotic anxiety than amoral brother Lewt. Accusing his father of pistol-whipping "the innocent as well as the guilty," Daniel rejects his aggressive methods. He also understands that the Halliday ranch was "just a place to hide" and can no longer ignore his father's virulent racism. Remaining means that he will become just like his father and compliant younger brother. The sequence ends with Halliday looking offscreen left refusing to acknowledge the implications of his action while Daniel kisses Martha good-bye. She decides to remain with the family, as Clay stands in the background. Before Daniel rides away, Lewis groups this dysfunctional family in a revealing tableau composition emphasizing disunity rather than unity.

The final major long take in the film occurs after Halliday has provoked Chad Burris (Jay C. Flippen) into a gunfight and killed him. Halliday's aggressive look during this confrontation reveals that racism really motivates him. Burris is the white man who has "gone native" by marrying an Indian woman and fathering two half-breed children. Finding Aleta sick due to losing her father and brother, Martha takes her home to recover. This three-minute-and-thirty-second sequence begins with Halliday entering his room and sitting down at his desk. The camera moves around to frame the actions of various characters during the scene's duration. After panning left to show Halliday going to his desk, it dollies right as Aleta enters the room through the very door he did and then dollies left to show her face in a mirror above his desk. Ignoring another victim of his racism, Halliday swivels his chair to avoid looking directly at her. He denies her status as a "human being," something his son Clay criticizes him for when he enters the room. This carefully composed sequence utilizes meaningful mise-en-scène that emphasizes the door separating an enclosed inner space within the Halliday ranch. Significant dialogue also complements camera movement and spatial composition. Halliday contemptuously describes Aleta as just "like any other squaw." He condemns Clay's treatment of her as a "country belle," evoking the racist Senator McCanles's attitude toward Jesse and Laurabelle's humanity toward Pearl in *Duel in the Sun*. Father and son argue. Martha then enters the doorway in center frame to support Aleta while Halliday stubbornly articulates a conservative philosophy of an American way of life encompassing not only the Old West but blacklist racism common at the time of the film's production. "The Halliday Brand has stood for certain things. It always has and it always will. And as long as you and Clay are part of this ranch, you will respect such things. Nobody like her has any part in our lives." Martha expresses hope that Daniel will return to humiliate him for his viciousness. Halliday continues to stare offscreen left in the same way he did before Jivaro's body in the earlier sequence. Clay and Martha exit through the door, and the image fades to black.

Other sequences reveal how *The Halliday Brand* is much more than an average western, stylistically and thematically. It is a sophisticated allegory of the blacklist emphasizing hideous consequences affecting everyone. Violence taints everybody in one way or another. No positive resolution appears possible. Aleta rejects Daniel when she sees that his vengeful activities make him little better than his father. She turns to Clay on the rebound. But Clay also recognizes that her former feelings for Daniel are by means absent. Daniel has already removed his father's badge. The dying Halliday suffers another form of symbolic castration when Martha takes away the gun he concealed in his bed to kill Daniel after luring him back by the announcement of an interracial marriage he never intended to happen. She remains at the ranch like a black widow until she can finally witness her father's humiliation. Making one final attempt to prevent his family leaving, Halliday dies in the arms of the son he intended to murder.

Lewis uses camera movement and mise-en-scène tableau composition creatively in this penultimate shot. The camera moves to the left and stops to show Halliday cradled in Daniel's arms in low-angle foreground. Aleta, Clay, and Martha stand in the background near the exterior door. "You're too much like me, Daniel. It would be like shooting myself." Halliday finally dies. However, the film does not end positively by resolving the personal dilemmas of surviving family members. Instead, it dissolves to an exterior shot of the Halliday ranch. The camera tilts down to show the ax embedded in the tree trunk that first appeared in the fourth shot of the film. Like the original agreement between Halliday and original Native American inhabitants that failed to prevent more racial violence, any future treaties will also fail to prevent later occurrences of institutional violence against those existing outside American conservative definitions of family, especially if they belong to the wrong racial category.

Although lacking the frequent long-take tableau compositions of *The Halliday Brand*, *Terror in a Texas Town* has several other distinguishing features. Like *The Halliday Brand*, it operates allegorically, utilizing significant strategies, especially casting. Although official credits list Ben L. Perry as scenarist, he acted as a front for blacklisted writers Dalton Trumbo and Nedrick Young. In his interview with Bogdanovich, Lewis mentions that neither he nor his producers approved of the blacklist.[16] Lewis also told Nevins that Nedrick Young approached him with the proposition of directing a script based on "group collaboration" as a means of returning to Hollywood. He also warned him of possible repercussions involving blacklisting. The director decided to accept the challenge despite the fact that it would involve a grueling ten-day shooting schedule because of a small budget.[17]

Terror in a Texas Town represented a challenge for Lewis in more ways than one. He had recently suffered a heart attack and signed a contract with Four Star for a television series that could have been affected by knowledge of his involvement with Young who not only worked on the screenplay in an uncredited capacity but also played a leading role in the film. The year 1958 was not only that of Lewis's last film but also of *The Defiant Ones* (1958), which Young wrote uncredited due to the blacklist. Defiantly casting Young in a major performance meant that Lewis was taking a calculated risk that also anticipated the later much-publicized role of Kirk Douglas in hiring Trumbo for the screenplay of *Spartacus* (1960) written under his own name.[18] Lewis suffered no repercussions from his action, which may explain why *Terror in a Texas Town* concludes more optimistically than *The Halliday Brand*.

Sterling Hayden's casting was also significant. In 1951 Hayden had capitulated to HUAC and "named names" as a friendly witness. He bitterly regretted this and apologized later in his autobiography, *Wanderer* (1963), earning the respect of blacklist victims such as Abraham Polonsky. Hayden had also previously paraded before a building with a banner asking people not to testify.[19] After *Terror in a Texas Town* Hayden left Hollywood for Europe and next appeared as paranoid Cold War general Jack D. Ripper in Stanley Kubrick's *Dr. Strangelove* (1964).

Terror in a Texas Town begins and ends with a climactic sequence paralleling *The Halliday Brand*'s long flashback. Credits employ shots that will occur in later parts of the film making it quasi-Brechtian by stimulating spectators to analyze the implications of the narrative, unlike an average western. Since Trumbo and Young would be familiar with Brecht's theatrical work and his summons before HUAC, they possibly attempted to employ parts of his methodology in their screenplay. As Thierry Kuntzel points out, the beginning of a classical Hollywood narrative often parallels its end. This axiom significantly applies to Lewis's last film, where personal stylistic traits of authorship complement a highly charged political meaning.[20]

As Keser notes, the opening preview of the climax leading to credits glimpsed through a wagon wheel represents Lewis's reference to credit sequences of his 1930s Mascot westerns and his trademark wagon wheel shots.[21] Nine shots lead to the credits, the eighth of which is the longest, beginning with riders arriving in town. George Hansen (Sterling Hayden) bears a harpoon. He walks right to left as the camera follows him. Townspeople move in the same direction. The shots conclude with a mid-close-up of Hansen stooping toward the ground. The eighth shot is the most visually significant. This long shot begins with Johnny Crale emerging from the hotel as the camera moves toward the right before it stops to frame his left hand near his holster in the right foreground of the frame while George occupies center left background. We do not see Crale's face, only his black outfit. He taunts Hansen concerning the distance he occupies. "Come a little *closer*. You don't want to disappoint your friends. *Closer, closer*, so they can see it. Five steps, two steps. One, Hansen, just one step." The screenplay often repeats lines evoking not only *The Halliday Brand* but also rhetorical devices used in scripts by Abraham Polonsky and others during the blacklist era attempting to incorporate dramatic aspects of classical verse into Hollywood genres. Such a strategy may not be accidental.[22]

Ruthless capitalist McNeil (Sebastian Cabot) employs gunslinger Crale to terrorize farmers to sign over to him their land that contains oil. One man stands up to the bad guy and achieves victory. This is the basic plot of the film. But casting, visual technique, and dialogue complicate this easy reading. The casting of Hayden and Young in *Terror in a Texas Town* parallels similar strategies occurring in *The Halliday Brand*. But here the main difference involves the screen presence of two Hollywood blacklist victims facing each other in the final confrontation full of significant contemporary and historical associations.

Young's Johnny Crale wears black, the iconographic western outfit of the bad guy. McNeil employs him to wage a terrorist campaign against those belonging to different class and racial groups. His costume also ironically symbolizes a blacklist that had affected Hayden, Trumbo, and Young himself. Crale has lost his right hand and wears gloves to conceal this. Far from being a bizarre touch to spice up a low-budget narrative shot in ten days, Crale's iron hand evokes that of Rotwang, the inventor who creates the robot Maria to control workers in a future state, in Fritz Lang's *Metropolis* (1926). As a film belonging to that influential era of Weimar cinema closely associated with the visual style of German expressionism contributing to American "film noir," *Metropolis* influences *Terror in a Texas Town*. Rotwang and Crale both resent their capitalist masters. They inhabit a past world now being overtaken by modernity. Rotwang lives in an incongruous medieval house in the futuristic world of Metropolis. Crale is an anachronistic remnant of an old world of frontier violence no longer appropriate to McNeil's new era of business and capitalist exploitation. As Crale's mistress Molly (Carol Kelly) states, "Your days are all over. I mean it. A gun can't make it anymore."

Crale's murder of Pepe Mirada (Victor Milian) results in McNeil paying off his hired guns and telling them, "It appears we've come upon new times in Prairie City. Violence is passé." Disturbed by Mirada's heroic reaction to imminent execution, Crale ignores the money offered him by McNeil and begins his final descent into madness. In *Metropolis*, Rotwang and the robot Maria also eventually lose control of themselves. With his black costume and iron hand, Johnny Crale conflates the roles of Rotwang and robot Maria in once character, the exception being that Crale succeeds in murdering his boss while Rotwang attempts to kill the boss's son. Crale is no bizarre camp creation. Young's role connects that old world of Weimar cinema influencing American "film noir" with Lewis's 1958 subversive blacklist western.

What makes Johnny run? This dark figure who exhibits an aura of robotic violence becomes disturbed when he finds that Mexican farmer Mirada will not submit to his terror. Mirada will not run scared like a blacklist victim and sign a document handing his property over to McNeil. He will not cringe and submit in the same way that brave victims of the blacklist refused to recognize the illegal and unconstitutional role of HUAC.

Unlike Sterling Hayden and Larry Parks, Mirada refuses to crawl; he refuses to swear that he will not testify against Crale. Mirada will not kneel down before him. "You will kill me because you must kill me. If I swear you will kill me. If I agree you will kill me. If I stand as a man you will kill me. Well, I stand as a man." Mirada realizes that being a friendly witness will not save him. He dies a heroic death at the hands of Crale.

Casting Victor Milian as Mirada was significant. It echoes his other role as the victimized Mexican Sanchez, who may or may not be guilty of the crime Captain Hank Quinlan accuses him of, in Orson Welles's *Touch of Evil*.[23] Quinlan's methods of interrogation parallel those used by Sheriff Dan Halliday whose racism echoes other characters played by Welles in *Man in the Shadow* and *The Long Hot Summer* (1958). James Naremore sees these roles within the context of contemporary American civil rights issues. Welles actively opposed racism over a decade before.[24] Jonathan Rosenbaum and Catherine L. Benamou notice allegorical references to McCarthyism in both Welles's *Othello*, filmed during the introduction of the Hollywood blacklist, and *Touch of Evil*.

Just as easily, one can read these films as referencing first, European or American colonialism, along with racial discrimination in the US armed forces (*Othello*), and second, racially motivated suspensions of human and civil rights in the criminal justice system (*Touch of Evil*, produced in the aftermath of the McCarran-Walter Act, which led to the arrest and arbitrary deportation of countless Mexicans and Mexican Americans during the 1950s). In some cases, the allegory creates a parallel register of representation and interpretation, as in *The Lady from Shanghai* when O'Hara's shark story resonates with his observation, after witnessing a group of American tourists, that there is something altogether too "bright and guilty" about Acapulco.[25]

Dan Halliday and McNeil aim at dispossessing and deporting whatever ethic minority gets in their way whether for reasons of racial purity or capitalist acquisitiveness. Characters turn on each other like sharks whether in the Halliday family or in the uneasy employer-employee relationship existing between Crale and McNeal. They attempt to devour each other emotionally or physically. Dan wishes to murder his son. Crale murders his gourmet boss. These parallels show that *The Halliday Brand* and *Terror in a Texas Town* belong to a specific historical context. Both these westerns oppose illegal and unjust practices of the blacklist, especially those used against racial minorities.

Like Johnny Logan of *Johnny Guitar*, George Hansen is a "stranger here" himself. Here Hayden's character is a foreign national who fortunately has the right documents to save him from deportation should his presence prove too much of a threat. Operating under McNeil's payroll, Sheriff Stoner (Tyler McVey) tells George, "No foreigner is going to come in here and tell me how to do my job." When Crale later asks, "Are your papers in order?" George replies, "If they are not in order, I'll hear about it before long." Crale informs him of the death of his father at their first encounter, leading to George's indignant response. "What kind of country is this that something like this happens and nobody knows about it, nobody does anything?" Crale replies in a manner echoing Dan Halliday, "Things like that happen around here *all the time*," a response confirmed by his henchman, "Yes, *all the time*." Rhetorical repetition dominates this film. Note Crale's later response to the death of Mirada, "I want to tell you about *somebody* I saw this morning, *somebody really remarkable*. What I saw this morning was *really remarkable, really remarkable*. I saw a man who wasn't afraid to die."[26]

Terror in a Texas Town may not contain the same amount of long takes as *The Halliday Brand*, but it reveals unique stylistic and thematic qualities suggesting a deliberate strategy on the part of the director. A low-angle close-up showing Crale on horseback right of frame parallels the type of close-up experiments Bordwell documents as being a part of contemporary Hollywood professional craftsmanship in this era.[27] However, one sequence does involve a long shot combining significant aspects of style and meaning seen in *The Halliday Brand*. It begins with a close-up shot of a champagne bottle McNeil pours into a glass. The camera tracks out to reveal Crale left of frame seated at a table with his back to the camera. It then tracks in to reveal Crale putting the glass into his right hand with his left hand. He wears gloves constantly throughout the film. The camera moves emphasizing key elements of the dialogue such as Crale's pleasure in his deadly work and McNeil's warning that times have changed. Crale's appearance here emphasizes physical infirmity and his desire to conceal this professional "lack." The long shot ends when McNeil gets up from his chair. A series of edited scenes emphasizes their dialogue. Crale asks, "What kind of *business* is this?" to which McNeil responds, "My *business*," leading Crale to comment, "You mean it will be when you get your *example*." The cautious McNeil replies, "Johnny, I never discuss *examples* when there are three people in a room [italics mine]." The dialogue contains significant repetitive rhetorical tropes emphasizing "business" and "examples" linking capitalism and violence in the same manner Polonsky does in his screenplays for *Body and Soul* (1947) and *Force of Evil* (1948) recalling lines similar to those spoken by Roberts to Charley Davis in the first film: "You gotta be businesslike, Charley, and businessmen have to keep their agreements."

The final confrontation between George and Crale evokes comments

George Hansen (Sterling Hayden) in *Terror in a Texas Town* (1958).

ranging from describing the scene as one of the most unique features in a western to absurd and silly.[28] But when seen in terms of an allegorical and subversive treatment of the blacklist, it is actually quite significant. Not only does the imagery anticipate R. G. Armstrong's well-known description of Sam Peckinpah's *Major Dundee* (1965) as "Moby Dick on horseback," but it also takes on a symbolic resonance involving casting.[29] George is nothing of Herman Melville's Captain Ahab figure. He marches heroically on his own to confront Crale and faces overwhelming odds. It is almost as if Hayden receives a second chance to perform that heroic act of defiance he once fell far short of. By contrast, Young portrays a revealing representation of those who harassed him. The actor depicts the cowardice and vulnerability hiding beneath aggressive, bullying, and patriotic blacklisters such as Ward Bond. Lewis also exposes the psychopathological tendencies lying beneath the patriarchal figure of Halliday, who lies to achieve his goals. Crale is the insecure Ahab figure in this narrative. Mirada accelerated Crale's feelings of redundancy affected by his recognition of changing times that will now reject him. Right-wing elements in the 1950s abandoned the bullying McCarthy when his methods became too outrageous and began to represent more of a threat to rather than an aid of their reactionary politics. Crale turns against McNeil in the same way that friendly witnesses turned on their former comrades. He now finds himself abandoned and ostracized in the same way as those who named names did during the blacklist era. Crale is no white whale but a dangerous dark-clad beast whose time has passed. He now faces the vengeance of George and a new alliance of formerly terrorized townspeople. Like the robot Maria he has gone out of control and become self-destructive. Lewis and his collaborators not only subvert the rules of the typical western in *Terror in a Texas Town* but also turn *Moby Dick* on its head. Crale's dark-clad figure is both the enemy outside and the enemy within, the latter being his western incarnation of Herman Melville's paranoid Captain Ahab threatening both himself and others. The film combines Ahab and his adversary within the same persona. During the blacklist the real enemies were those who feared the "other," not the "other." Red-baiters were the Ahabs of their era. This film subversively conflates those who believed themselves victimized by un-American forces with the "white whale" they feared. In *Terror in a Texas Town*, the white whale becomes dark-clad Johnny Crale. He eventually becomes a fearful and insecure figure using an empty shell of a terrorizing figure to face an adversary and a community that no longer fear him.

Against all odds, George wins the battle. The final image shows him kneeling on the ground as townspeople walk past him. Hayden did not act like a brave man when he named names, but he bitterly regretted his actions, apologized, and demonstrated outside the hearings bearing a banner anticipating the harpoon he would carry in his final confrontation. Black-and-white duality works in a particular sophisticated manner. Both actors participate in a symbolic ritual confrontation within the allegorical dimensions of this particular western. Blacklisted Nedrick Young plays a villain while unheroic (at least as far as his original actions go) Sterling Hayden plays the hero. Their characters are not one-dimensional but complex cultural and historical constructions relevant to this particular era. Crale now takes the place of the psychopathological Ahab of Melville's original work becoming pierced by the harpoon wielded by foreign-born George Hansen who acts as an avenging avatar of oppressed minorities belonging to despised political and racial groups. By killing this western version of Moby Dick, George closes a chapter on a dark page of American history. The actor who portrays him receives a pat on his shoulder. Although he has acted at the last moment, his gesture is appreciated by the hand of an unseen figure symbolically representing those he once wronged, affirming his action in the same way that Abraham Polonsky and other victims did.

This chapter began with a quotation from a key work dealing with the issue of historical poetics in cinema. But meaning, as well as style, can represent a key axiom in this concept in which the solution of problems can extend beyond artistry and into the realm of political meaning. Sometimes there are no easy solutions, as in *The Halliday Brand*. By contrast, *Terror in a Texas Town* depicts the symbolic closing of that particular American nightmare involving not just one man standing up against the oppressor but also a formerly terrorized population who decides that it has now had enough and unites behind somebody who will champion its cause. These two films represent Joseph H. Lewis's final and finest achievements as a director. But they also illustrate a concept suggested by Reynold Humphries deserving of further exploration—namely, the demolition of the dominant idea that 1950s Hollywood was a place of mediocrity and the recognition that it may really be "with the exception of the 1940s . . . the richest and most complex decade in the history of Hollywood and, with the benefit of the contribution of the blacklistees, would have been the greatest decade."[30] *The Halliday Brand* and *Terror in a Texas Town* support such a proposition. They also reveal that those affected by the blacklist and directors opposed to it such as Joseph H. Lewis could make a difference. Rather than being regarded as impoverished B movies with inadequate performances by leading actors, these westerns deserve reevaluation in both their original historical context and today's more subtle operation of a blacklist preventing challenging works in literature, film, and television from reaching wider audiences.

Notes

I wish to thank Francis M. Nevins for supplying me with a copy of *The Halliday Brand* for this article.

1. Francis M. Nevins, *Joseph H. Lewis: Overview, Interview, and Filmography* (Lanham, MD: Scarecrow Press, 1998), 45–48.

2. Peter Bogdanovich, *Who the Devil Made It: Conversations with Legendary Film Directors* (New York: Ballantine Books, 1997), 687. This is based on two conversations the author had with Lewis during 1968 and 1994.

3. Ibid.

4. For a recent analysis of the complex role of Ida Lupino as actress and director in this period see Martha Orgeron, *Hollywood Ambitions: Celebrity in the Movie Age* (Middletown, CT: Wesleyan University Press, 2008), 170–203.

5. For Nedrick Young, see Reynold Humphries, *Hollywood's Blacklists: A Political and Cultural History* (Edinburgh: Edinburgh University Press, 2008), 112, 153–54. This indispensable study also mentions that, despite being known as a "friend of the Left," Lewis "suffered no harassment" (ibid., 157).

6. For Corey's anti-Semitism, see Kirk Douglas's autobiography, *The Ragman's Son* (New York: Simon and Schuster, 1988), 128.

7. See Betsy Blair, *The Memory of All That: Love and Politics in New York, Hollywood and Paris* (New York: Alfred A. Knopf, 2003), 314–16. Despite her misgivings about working with Bond, she found that he behaved professionally both on and off the set. However, she adds that *The Halliday Brand* was her last Hollywood film. In a newspaper interview in the *Times* on July 31, 2008, Blair mentioned that her ex-husband Gene Kelly was also known for his left-wing sympathies at the time but MGM regarded him as too valuable a property to be given up to the blacklist.

8. Marc Lawrence, *Long Time No See: Confessions of a Hollywood Gangster* (Palm Springs, CA: Ursus Press, 1991), 144. By contrast, he speaks warmly about John Wayne despite their political differences but adds that he never took up the friendship offered to him. "I didn't think his friends would make me comfortable" (ibid., 116).

9. David Bordwell, *Poetics of Cinema* (New York: Routledge, 2008), 325. Although Bordwell does not cover these two Lewis westerns, he does include a still from *Gun Crazy* (1949) to illustrate the baroque extremes of deep focus size and position sometimes found in 1940s cinema. See Bordwell, *Poetics of Cinema*, 298, figure 10.18. For antecedents to Lewis's use of fluid camera movements during long takes in 1940s films such as *Citizen Kane* (1941), *The Magnificent Ambersons* (1942), *The Lady in the Lake* (1947), and *Rope* (1948), see ibid., 294. Lewis's two films often employ recessional staging placing one character notably closer to the camera than others (ibid., 297). Halliday's foreground look offscreen while other members of his family are situated in the background during one scene in *The Halliday Brand* is one such example. See ibid., 308, figure 10.52 for an example of a Scope offscreen look, the most no-

table exception being that Halliday is much more destructive than Demetrius in *The Robe* (1953). Furthermore, in terms of group compositions, Lewis's staging also parallels contemporary CinemaScope spacious horizontal staging (ibid., 308) while other scenes in these two films reemploy old Hollywood silent film tableau conventions. See ibid., 312–20, but in less elaborate and simpler ways due to budget constraints. The positioning of father and son on opposite sides of the bed during one point of the first long-take mobile camera flashback sequence in *The Halliday Brand* also illustrates Bordwell's argument that "norms of earlier decades were not so much overthrown as adjusted" (ibid., 323) while shots of the staircase leading up to the jail not only employ horizontal and vertical space (ibid., 324) but evoke conventions of "film noir." These examples reveal how much Lewis was a superb craftsman in his profession and how easily he could have adjusted to the scope format within which many westerns were shot during this era. Finally, the low-angle mid-close-up of Johnny Crale on horseback threatening Mirada during their first encounter both parallels and anticipates the type of extreme close-up used during this era and in the Italian westerns of Leone. See ibid., 302, 322–23.

10. Several students in my Nicholas Ray English 307i Core Curriculum Fall 2008 class noticed noir elements operating as indirect stylistic and thematic components in these films that suggested noir never entirely left the creative consciousness of talents associated with this area. I'm grateful to them for many observations here.

11. Robert Porfirio and Carl Macek, "Joseph H. Lewis," in *Film Noir Reader 3: Interviews with Filmmakers of the Classic Noir Period*, ed. Robert Porfirio, Alain Silver, and James Ursini (New York: Limelight Editions, 2002), 83. Robert Keser also notes Lewis's "baroque visual stylization that transcends mere realism, his command of deep focus and long takes, his recurrent visual motifs and his players' intense performances: all these paint Lewis as a kind of Orson Welles of the B-movie, though he rarely originated projects and never worked in theatre like Welles." "Joseph H. Lewis: Great Directors," *Senses of Cinema*, no. 41 (2006), http://www.sensesofcinema.com/2006/great-directors/lewis_joseph/.

12. Keser, "Lewis." He also notes that Lewis worked on all his scripts, as did Alfred Hitchcock. They often oppose the realms of private security to public duty. These contrasts occur in different ways in *The Halliday Brand* and *Terror in a Texas Town* with the community finally deciding to play a more active role in the second film rather than being passively influenced by the individual agency of Daniel Halliday in the first.

13. Nevins suggests the first influence (*Joseph H. Lewis*, 46) and Mike Grost the second. Grost also notes that "considerable political issues are directly embodied in the family's struggles: in *Wuthering Heights*, class warfare; in *The Halliday Brand*, race relations." See Mike Grost, "The Films of Joseph H. Lewis," 89, http://mikegrost.com/lewis.htm. Class and racial issues also occur in both *Terror in a Texas Town* and Anthony Mann's *The Furies* (1951), which also employs aspects of Greek tragedy in its narrative as does *The Man from Laramie* (1955).

Like *The Halliday Brand*, both Mann films deal with the fall of an authoritarian patriarchal figure. Myron Meisel also notes the significant visual style employed in the film, especially in giving Dan Halliday "a fixed motion that doesn't alter despite the camera's adjustment for another character's entrance or speech. For example, Bond is set pacing back and forth in the foyer, facing forward into the camera, which pans to show Cotten entering the room, interposing Bond's to-and-fro motion between us and Cotten.... In *The Halliday Brand*, there is a proper place for everything within a shot." See "Joseph H. Lewis," *Kings of the Bs*, ed. Todd McCarthy and Charles Flynn (New York: E. P. Dutton, 1975), 102.

14. Humphries, *Hollywood's Blacklists*, 10–15, 133, 142.

15. For a criticism of Cotten's performance see Meisel, "Joseph H. Lewis," 102 and the review by FilmFlaneur at "*The Halliday Brand* (1957)," IMDb, http://www.imdb.com/title/tt0050481/. This, of course, ignores certain relevant aspects of Cotten's star persona that often contained elements of masculine insecurity and a type of agency strongly limited by prevailing historical circumstances illustrated by his roles in *Citizen Kane* (1941), *The Magnificent Ambersons* (1942), *Journey into Fear* (1942), *Duel in the Sun* (1946), *Under Capricorn* (1948), *Beyond the Forest* (1949), *The Third Man* (1949), *Niagara* (1952), and *Bottom of the Bottle* (1956). The "jarring nature" of this character that bothers FilmFlaneur may be derived from the character of Daniel as a former "liberal" choosing to ignore the illegal activities of his father and deciding to oppose him by using the same type of illegal methods that part of him resents while his other half becomes too close to his father, as the final lines in the film articulate.

16. Bogdanovich, *Who the Devil*, 688.

17. Nevins, *Joseph H. Lewis*, 47.

18. Keser also recognizes this and comments that as a result of this commitment "Lewis was taking a substantial risk."

19. Humphries, *Hollywood's Blacklists*, 133. Polonsky commented on Hayden's change to *Look Magazine* in 1970 mentioning that Wanderer admitted "what an awful mistake he had made. He did better than beg the pardon of the people he had hurt. He changed." See "Abraham Polonsky," in *Creative Differences*, ed. Barbara Zheutlin and David Talbot (Boston: South End Press, 1978), 89. Two other victims of the blacklist also commended Hayden's recognition of his shameful action. Karen Morley stated that she never forgave any informer, "except maybe Sterling Hayden, who apologized publicly to everybody" while John Wexley mentioned that the actor "was one of those who tried to undo the mischief." See Patrick McGilligan and Paul Buhle, eds., *Tender Comrades: Backstory of the Hollywood Blacklist* (New York: St. Martin's Press, 1997), 479, 717.

20. Thierry Kuntzel, "The Film-Work 2," *Camera Obscura* 5 (1980): 7–69.

21. Keser cites Nevins, *Joseph H. Lewis*, 14 here and then remarks that "these became a bone of contention with producers who preferred a self-effacing director with an invisible style." Again, as with *The Halliday Brand*, I would suggest that style is not entirely devoid of meaning here.

22. Such strategies occur in Polonsky's screenplays for *Body and Soul* (1947)

and *Force of Evil* (1949) and the screenplays for Robert Aldrich's *Kiss Me Deadly* (1955) and *Autumn Leaves* (1957). See Tony Williams, *Body and Soul: The Cinematic Vision of Robert Aldrich* (Lanham, MD: Scarecrow Press, 2004), 56, 58, 73n37, 209. In many ways, the screenplays for both these Lewis westerns attempt to continue those choric resonances in the experiments of Abraham Polonsky, who attempted to equate image, actor, and word within the cinematic frame. As Polonsky mentions in his 1962 interview with William Pechter, "I varied the speed, intensity, congruence and conflict for design emotion and goal," liberating the language from "the burden of literary psychology and the role of crutch to the visual image." Quoted by Paul Buhle and Dave Wagner, *A Very Dangerous Citizen: Abraham Lincoln Polonsky and the Hollywood Left* (Berkeley: University of California Press, 2001), 123. Several of Lewis's long takes in *The Halliday Brand* and *Terror in a Texas Town* appear to be attempts to continue this artistic form of experimentation that the blacklist prevented from attaining full realization.

23. For one reading questioning the validity of Sanchez's confession in *Touch of Evil*, see James Naremore, *The Magic World of Orson Welles* (New York: Oxford University Press, 1989), 150.

24. Ibid., 148. See also Catherine L. Benamou, *It's All True: Orson Welles's Pan-American Odyssey* (Berkeley: University of California Press, 2007), 235–39.

25. Benamou, *It's All True*, 189.

26. Similar patterns of repetition occur in Polansky's screenplay for *Force of Evil* and A. I. Bezzerides's script for *Kiss Me Deadly*. It is more than coincidental that villains such as Bauer and Dr. Soberin usually engage in such rhetorical tropes. Bauer utters these lines to Doris before the second police raid on Leo Bauer's "business": "I wasn't feeling *so good* today, so I didn't *come in*, and then I decided to *come in*, but now I don't feel *so good* again." Dr. Soberin utters these departing lines to Lily Carver: "There is something *sad and melancholy* about trips. I always hate to go away. But one has to find a new place or it would be impossible to be *sad and melancholy* again" (my emphasis). It is impossible now to be certain as to whether this strategy of repetition was initiated by either Dalton Trumbo or Nedrick Young, but its use does suggest a conscious awareness of one of the screenwriting experiments of the pre-blacklist era that became nipped in the bud.

27. See Bordwell, *Poetics of Cinema*, 302–23, especially for relevant frames including this feature as well as staging in depth that also occur in *Terror in a Texas Town*.

28. See Glenn Erickson, DVD Savant review of *Terror in a Texas Town*, DVD Talk, http://www.dvdtalk.com/reviews/6479/terror-in-a-texas-town/?___rd=1. He also refers to the film as a "pretty shabby movie shot in undressed back-lot Western streets without townspeople, stagecoaches, extra horses, or anything else that might cost an extra nickel." However, the drabness of this film is not entirely the result of its low budget but another example of how style significantly contributes to meaning, a factor that Erickson appears unaware of. The

bleak interiors and exteriors of the town and its lack of population represent an ideal metaphor for the wasted landscape of a blacklist America. Also, the lack of people and witnesses ironically foreshadows the Northern Ireland landscape of an assassination culture that Alan Clarke documented in his exceptional British television play *Elephant* (1988). Erickson is also incorrect when he states that Young wears gloves to "avoid having to show the right hand mentioned in the dialogue." As noted above, we see this emphatically in the scene introducing Crale to the audience after the credits. Finally, George's movement to distract his opponent in the concluding scene parallels Dan Halliday's similar strategy against Chad Burris in *The Halliday Brand*.

29. See David Weddle, *"If They Move ... Kill 'Em!" The Life and Times of Sam Peckinpah* (New York: Grove Press, 1994), 233; Paul Seydor, *Peckinpah: The Western Films; a Reconsideration* (Urbana: University of Illinois Press, 1997), 83.

30. David Walsh, "An Interview: Filmmaker Jules Dassin, Witch-Hunting and Hollywood's Blacklists," *World Socialist Web Site*, April 7, 2008, http://www.wsws.org/articles/2008/apr2008/dass-a07.shtml.

3
Gun Crazy

12

CHRISTOPHER JUSTICE

Rejecting Everything

Gun Crazy *and the Radical Noir of Joseph H. Lewis*

In the heart of Joseph H. Lewis's cinematic art flows the aesthetic allure of contradiction. Although he never finished high school, Lewis became a respected Hollywood director. Unlike peers who worked in other visual arts or mass mediums, Lewis's art was restricted to film; nevertheless, he was a dynamic stylist. Often assigned to B pictures, he directed exquisite films boasting A picture qualities. Although Lewis forged strong relationships with some of Hollywood's leading moguls, he rarely initiated his own films, content to accept producers' assignments. He frequently worked in generic confines with limited budgets, but he used those boundaries to challenge and transcend his aesthetic impulses and each genre's conventions. Bogdanovich wrote, "Of all the directors I have met, Joe Lewis is the most idealistic and, strangely, the most innocent." Later, he added, "In a den of thieves, Lewis is the last honest man."[1] This blend of personal and professional idealism and honesty earned Lewis much respect, but valued for his candor, dignity, and humanity off set, Lewis on set was pure business and not afraid to criticize subordinates.

In 1991 the Public Theater in New York City coordinated a series of viewings celebrating auteurism. Lewis and his seminal 1950 lovers-on-the-run film, *Gun Crazy*, were featured. Critic Stanley Kauffmann wrote that the film is self-contradictory, suggesting that although the film aims for "ruthless realism," it fails due to its "wooden dialogue" and inferior acting. "It's flatly impossible to take *Gun Crazy* seriously as a whole, but it's not as a whole that it should be seen," Kauffmann wrote.[2] Since the film excels in its editing and cinematographic styles, Kauffmann argued, the acting and storytelling flaws should be overlooked and interpreted as complements that enhance Lewis's directorial signature, serving as frameworks for understanding it.

Kauffmann's implication—that Lewis intentionally chose weaker scripts to showcase his directorial style—assumes an ego not associated with Lewis and conflicts with Lewis's ethos that directors should not overshadow their films. Whether Lewis chose inferior scripts to distinguish his directorial style is an intentional fallacy better left for New Critics to debate. Lewis treated his films, regardless of budget, as professional assignments that deserved his best efforts. "I truly never knew the difference between an A picture, a B picture or a Q picture, except that one picture had more money to spend. The quality would not be different," he stated.[3] Hirsch countered Kauffmann's assessment of *Gun Crazy*, arguing that "when, for once in his career, with *Gun Crazy*, he was given a script that demanded little directorial-embroidery, he made a true genre classic in an unforced, masterly style."[4] However, Schrader disagreed, suggesting that *Gun Crazy* shines because of Lewis's directorial prowess: its "superlative qualities ... are precisely those which only the director can give: a combined sense of pacing, élan, and dynamic composition."[5] In Lewis's most important and celebrated film, contradictory interpretations abound.

Lewis's refusal to distinguish between A and B pictures and these contradictory interpretations are two reasons why critics debate his authorship. Consequently, as Nevins states, "Trying to see his body of work as a coherent whole is like trying to nail jelly to a wall." Some critics agree that Lewis's directorial style is unique, but others disagree about whether Lewis's films possess a consistent style or thematic pattern,[6] both hallmarks of American authorship. This tension resonates throughout scholarship surrounding the Lewis canon. Capp writes, "Lewis established himself as a director with a distinctive vision."[7] However, Thompson differs: "Lewis's scripts abound in outrageous elements or possibilities, but he rarely calls attention to them. . . . He prefers to remain comfortably within the bounds of his genres, to suggest and to underplay."[8] Keser offers another position, arguing that Lewis was beyond unique: "Lewis' wunderkind prodigality, his deliberate artistic approach, his baroque visual stylisation that transcends mere realism, his command of deep focus and long takes, his recurrent visual motifs and his players' intense performances: all these paint Lewis as a kind of Orson Welles of the B-movie. . . . Lewis constructed his own aesthetic, making every film, sometimes every shot, a personal statement."[9] In contrast, Thompson concludes that Lewis's genius existed in his self-effacing ability to blend into his films' backgrounds: "No consistent style of mise en scène is apparent, no Lewis look or Lewis POV or Lewis conceptual slant . . . can be spotted from film to film. . . . This separates him from the primary operation of authorship criticism on American directors: the analysis of consistent visual style to correlate it directly with consistent thematic vision. Lewis has areas of thematic interest or sensitivity, but he seems passive insofar as advancing a strong world-view of his own."[10] What is surprising is how starkly these opinions contradict one another and that Lewis's oeuvre and paradoxical style blossomed while working within classic Hollywood's machinelike, genre-driven system.

Lewis's contradictory, inconsistent style may be the most distinguishing characteristic of his directorial ethos, which reveals a radical departure from his contemporaries' predictable technical and thematic approaches to genre, particularly film noir. Although Lewis's most enduring contributions to that genre extend beyond *Gun Crazy* and *The Big Combo* (1955), his contributions are most prevalent in those two noir classics. What Lewis accomplished in those films reveals the consistent essence of his contradictory style: he blended conventional cinematic and editing techniques popular in film noir with unconventional techniques and used both to radically extend conventional noir themes into more sophisticated, complex expositions. By doing so, Lewis pushed noir's existential, nihilistic radicalism and the technical artistry that conveyed it further than any noir director.

Thompson suggests that notwithstanding the inconsistency in Lewis's overall style, his more distinguishing features were well suited for film noir, including "a taste for Bazinian depth of focus and for its temporal twin, the long take; for camera movement (relativity) rather than alternating static cuts (isolated specificity); for cinematographers with dramatic, concrete styles, often harshly black-and-white; for location shooting, or failing that, for modestly scaled back-lot work stressing character/environment interfaces rather than explicit spectacle."[11] Lewis's mastery of these established techniques allowed him to seamlessly assimilate into the noir universe. Depth of focus by the mid-1940s had already become a standard stroke on the film noir canvas; Orson Welles had exploited deep focus in film noir, most impressively in *Citizen Kane* (1941) and *The Lady from Shanghai* (1947). Similarly, the long take was featured in various noirs, most notably Robert Siodmak's *The Killers* (1946), and using distinctly talented cinematographers gave film noir its elegance. Collaborations between Anthony Mann and John Alton; Alfred Hitchcock and Robert Burks; Carol Reed and Robert Krasker; and Billy Wilder and John F. Seitz are examples. And using back lots to deemphasize location and "spectacle" and instead accentuate characters' interactions with settings was more an economic reality for noir directors than a stylistic choice. This assimilation allowed Lewis to plant seeds for his unconventional themes. However, to understand Lewis's creative vision, one must probe deeper. While Lewis's mastery of generic editing and cinematographic techniques earned him approvals within Hollywood, his unconventional techniques and radical treatment of popular themes in the genre—sexual duplicity, gender confusion, organized violence, and government's unprecedented expansion into citizens' lives—earned him recognition among Hollywood insiders.

Keser argues that in 1955's *The Big Combo* Lewis introduced "a visceral new brutality" into film noir,[12] and Dickos suggests that Lewis's display of violence and sex was unprecedented: "his noir sensibility" was "among the strongest in its appeal to violence and sex as the raison d'etre in noir filmmaking."[13] Capp adds that Lewis correlated man's violent and sexual obsessions in *The Big Combo*: "Lewis makes clear that *The Big Combo* is as much concerned with the dynamics of power, money and sexuality, as with the nexus between business, crime and the forces of law and order."[14] Considering how social science research about human sexuality such as the Kinsey reports, the first of which, *Sexual Behavior in the Human Male*, was published in January 1948 (two years prior to *Gun Crazy*'s January 1950 release), helped instigate America's sexual revolution, Lewis's sexual themes in *The Big Combo* played a pivotal role in fanning that revolution's flames. If sexuality and violence are profoundly connected, and if humans' sexual obsessions trigger their violence, then Lewis visually dramatized those realities in two of noir's most sadistic scenes.

Lewis's unique approach to sound editing amplified his radical portrayals of the relationships among sex, violence, and power. Mob boss Mr. Brown tortures his nemesis, Lieutenant Leonard Diamond, because of Diamond's obsession with Brown's girlfriend, Susan Lowell. Brown places one of his thug's hearing aids into Diamond's ear and forces Diamond to consume hair tonic. We visually experience Diamond's auditory agony, but we never hear it. Similarly, this same sound-editing technique is used later as Brown machineguns that same thug to death. Brown removes the thug's hearing aid, exclaiming, "You won't hear the bullets." Again, we visually experience the machine gun fire, awash in shadows and flame, but we never hear a single shot. However, in this dramatic finale, we are placed in the thug's subjective experience: like him without his hearing aid, we don't hear the shots. This disturbing absence of sound paradoxically makes our experience of violence louder, more sensual, and more subjective. We feel it as much as the characters do. That Lewis relies on this device twice only exacerbates the film's sadism.

Lewis's radicalism also resonates in his treatment of sexuality. That he addresses both homosexuality and heterosexuality so astutely in *The Big Combo* is impressive. Keser writes, "Lewis . . . ruptures mid-century American sensibilities with his pair of tender gay-coded henchmen."[15]

Lewis's depiction of these homosexual hit men, Fante and Mingo, is unique not because he cast gay characters into the film's hypermasculinized and testosterone-filled world of organized crime but because their relationship is the film's only "healthy" one. Although they're minor characters, Fante and Mingo's loyalty and respect for each other contradicts the dysfunctional heterosexual relationships between the film's protagonists: Mr. Brown, Diamond, and the beleaguered Lowell. Fante and Mingo offer a paradoxical parallel that laces Lewis's film with a radical political statement about homosexuality and gender politics in premodern Hollywood cinema: two gay men can experience a healthy relationship.

Mr. Brown's implied oral sex act, which Dickos believes—within the context of mid-1950s cinema—bordered on pornography,[16] is equally powerful. As Mr. Brown's face slowly descends down Lowell's back, the sexual implications are obvious (even to censors): his actions are a preview to cunnilingus. Lowell's tortured paradox—receiving pleasure from a man who dominates her—reminds us of the complexities inherent in heterosexuality and particularly in the relationships between power and gender. Although censors wanted the scene removed, Lewis cleverly avoided censorship by arguing that nothing specific could be seen; viewers must interpret what Mr. Brown's actions imply, and interpretation should not be regulated.[17] That Lewis fought to maintain the original scene's integrity reveals how important its thematic value was. Although *The Big Combo* beats loudly with Lewis's contradictory heart, the foundation for his radical treatment of sex and violence, which was "an abiding preoccupation" in his work, was established earlier in *Gun Crazy*.[18]

Lewis's direction of *Gun Crazy* along with his technical and thematic radicalism couldn't have arrived at a better time for the genre. As Schrader explains, film noir experienced three "broad phases": "the wartime period" from 1941 to 1946 of private eye and lone-wolf detective films; "the postwar realistic period" from 1945 to 1949 of police corruption and procedural films; and "the period of psychotic action and suicidal impulse" from 1949 to 1953 that featured psychologically deranged protagonists. Schrader suggests this final period naturally exuded a sense of self-awareness since it emerged during the genre's twilight,[19] and not coincidentally, *Gun Crazy* emerges at the third phase's start.

With *Gun Crazy*, Lewis refueled the genre during a time when its postwar conventions were running on empty. Police procedurals had traded places with detective mysteries; atomic and Communist angst had pushed aside femme fatale–induced dread; and the global, paranoiac intrigue of espionage thrillers had erased the urban thrill of gangster dramas. By the late 1940s, the genre had severed its ties to themes of postwar trauma and crawled into a darker, more sadistic period of thematic and stylistic self-analysis. While Welles may have eulogized the genre with 1958's self-deprecating *Touch of Evil*, Lewis christened its rebirth a decade earlier with *Gun Crazy*, leading the genre's charge into a more chaotic and intensely introspective period. Just as *The Big Combo* offered one final, sadistic breath of life into the police procedural and gangster noir subgenre, *Gun Crazy* introduced years earlier a radical, narcissistic temperament into 1950s noir that used contradiction and paradox to reject and celebrate conventions noir filmmakers had built. Lewis created a film that is visually and thematically identifiable as noir but radically extends, and even departs from, the genre's themes and conventions. While noir filmmakers and critics often attributed World War II for the chaos, insanity, ambiguity, and violence the genre revealed, by 1949 that excuse had lost its bite. The only element responsible for the madness noir exposed was ourselves. Lewis sharpened noir's blades and reloaded its guns while introducing new weapons into the genre's war on America's psyche. Consequently, the genre flourished not only into the 1950s but also into its contemporary iterations as neo-noir.

Boasting a screenplay penned by the blacklisted Dalton Trumbo and shot in approximately thirty days for about $400,000, *Gun Crazy*, Lewis's magnum opus, is the director's most contradictory film. *Gun Crazy* exaggerates many noir conventions, including the genre's focus on emasculated men and masculinized women. Although American audiences in the mid-1940s were "divided by gender,"[20] *Gun Crazy* doesn't fit the prototypical "tough wartime noir crime film" Biesen outlines: Bart was not "exposed to inordinate violence in combat"; Lewis never "encourages male camaraderie"; and the film offers no "male stars beating up female costars as hard-hitting realism."[21] While many noir films exploit gender confusion, *Gun Crazy* pushes this confusion to its extremes. Not only does Laurie assume masculine roles throughout the film, but her roles involve hypermasculinized men with militaristic, patriarchal traits. Laurie is an Oedipal figure for the fatherless, directionless Bart: "Bart's attraction to Laurie seems motivated by his desire to find someone who can embody the paternal position of power and authority." Later, when Bart threatens Packy, who is "the older man who lays claim to Laurie and who knows of her transgressive history," the scene becomes a "compressed scenario of Oedipal revolt."[22]

When the couple meet under a carnival tent, their sharpshooting duel represents a male ritual that challenges and affirms Bart's masculinity. Although Laurie arouses Bart, one must wonder if her physical body or the opportunity to publicly demonstrate his masculinity arouses him. Bart's military experience offered him opportunities to prove his masculinity, but his insecurities in that all-male environment, which originated from his fatherless youth, stunted those experiences, locking him into a prolonged adolescence. However, when Laurie offers him the opportunity to assert his masculinity, Bart is stimulated since her invitation is framed androgynously, an attractive offer since Bart was not only fatherless but motherless too. Her androgyny is also displayed during the couple's final heist when her female boss chastises her for wearing slacks and not a skirt. Within the context of business etiquette, her masculine attire is unacceptable; however, within the context of her criminal lifestyle, her masculine disguise is an asset. As an adult child, Bart needs every psychosocial benefit Laurie offers. Although she's dressed in a man's cowboy outfit during this shootout, Lewis frames her laterally to emphasize her buttocks, her belt is fitted loosely to emphasize her hips, and her black pants neatly outline her figure against the bright backdrop. Her erotic movements, particularly when she bends over to shoot between her legs (the gun representing an obvious phallus given its location), transform her into something more than a femme fatale: she hideously occupies both genders and multiple roles. Psychosocially, she is Bart's Oedipal mother and first love, but she is also the father figure he must compete with for approval.

Laurie's performance during the duel is identical to his, until the final round. In Bart's eyes, Laurie and he are essentially the same: initially, he believes, they see each other in themselves, and they see themselves in each other, so romantically they are ideal complements. He believes she fulfills his physical and psychological needs, serving as both his mother and father; but as their relationship continues, he slowly discovers how inaccurate and grotesque this belief is. Nevertheless, since he believes so fiercely in the compatibility of their personas, he cannot leave her. From their relationship's start, Bart needs Laurie to express his manhood, and consequently, she fills the vacuum of authority, love, and pleasure his parents never provided.

Gun Crazy also reveals how malleable identities become when individuals are forced to change, and Laurie's mercurial personality exemplifies this. She is a chameleon that switches gender roles quickly, cleverly, and conveniently: she "manipulates her femininity by playing upon Bart's emotions," and Bart eventually realizes that her "hermaphroditism" is "monstrous" and destructive.[23] Bart embraces her feminine/maternal and masculine/paternal qualities because he is physically attracted to the former and psychologically attracted to the latter. Since Bart is essentially an adolescent in adult's clothing, he needs parental guidance, especially since his sister, Ruby, served as his mother and father. According to Ruby's court testimony, Bart needed "a man around the house." Laurie represents for

Bart an "über-parent," but although this role is psychologically affirming, it's also destructive.

According to Gilmore, children perceive parental figures as monstrous due to their enormous size, power, and control over their lives, and, as he explains, "we have come to know the monster of the imagination as not simply a political metaphor, but also a project of some repressed part of the self. . . . The monster of the mind is always the familiar self disguised as the alien Other."[24] Laurie's hermaphroditism or shape-shifting is another quality found in monsters. While falling for Laurie, Bart gains a father, mother, and lover, but he also witnesses his grotesque incompleteness. This is why although Laurie looks good in uniforms, Bart feels uncomfortable in them. Nevertheless, Lewis does not settle with portraying Laurie as an extreme parent; he portrays her as a militaristic authority figure.

Laurie represents for Bart a hypermasculinized soldier, a portrayal that reveals additional layers of Bart's psychological composition. Laurie's masculinity earns Bart's respect because while she has proven her manhood, Bart's remains in limbo. Since Bart is fatherless, psychologically, his impulses as a child were left unchecked; his incarceration as a child is one example, and the police officer apprehending him becomes, symbolically, a father enforcing the law. After that scene, the state provides for him while he is in reform school and later in the military. However, neither institution effectively provided Bart the discipline he needed. This lack of a paternal, superego-like force in his life suggests that his emotional and physical attraction to Laurie may reflect narcissistic feelings about himself, making his infatuation with her self-fulfilling and masturbatory. When he shoots Packy, Bart sees his own image in the mirror and coincidentally shoots it, demonstrating that he will now immerse himself in Laurie's world (the scene also occurs in Laurie's room), a world that for him exists to satisfy his needs because in Bart's eyes Laurie represents an opportunity to resolve his psychological deficiencies. As he struggles to separate his ego/self from the world, his life is a constant hunt for pleasure signified by the one object that has pleased him throughout life: guns. And now Laurie represents the second object, and in Bart's eyes the two are indistinguishable. When he gazes at Laurie, Bart sees an elusive, unfulfilled image of himself and an opportunity to embrace the deranged pleasure embedded in narcissism.

The obvious militaristic quality they share is a passion and obsession for guns, a fatal attraction that incites their downward spiral, but the other similarities are striking. Bart falls for her in a "tent" with his buddies almost immediately after she displays her prowess as a "sharpshooter." Her surname is Starr, representing the stars military generals receive for exceptional leadership and a further reinforcement that she is an extreme, patriarchal figure, one whose approval Bart desires. Laurie is from London, which may evoke for Bart memories of the war's European theater. Since America was once a British colony, the geopolitical relationship between their homelands echoes the paternalistic relationship so common between empires and their colonies. If Laurie is an empire, Bart is the colony that depends on her for support. She dresses in men's uniforms throughout the film and, during the film's conclusion, crawls around a swamp with Bart, an action reminiscent of the reconnaissance missions soldiers undertake. If Bart's military service provided him direction or affirmation, thus putting his obsessive, pleasure-seeking mania for guns on hold, and if he perceives Laurie as a militaristic Oedipal figure, his crazy obsession for her is not as irrational as Schrader, who wrote, "There were no excuses given for the psychopathy in *Gun Crazy*—it was just 'crazy,'"[25] and others have stated. Psychologically, an underlying logic to their craziness lurks. Few lovers' relationships in the film noir canon have been composed with such psychological complexity as Bart and Laurie's.

The film's infatuation with guns combines two crucial themes: guns are the fetish that triggers the couple's lust, and guns are the instrument that facilitates their obsessions, haunts their journey, and pulls them apart. The film's soul is a gun, and while guns are an iconic image inherent in American culture, their symbolism is fundamentally paradoxical: "Guns here create mayhem and are very much a part of the American mythology of individual power in defense of law and order as well as of lawlessness."[26] No narrative in the noir canon addresses the symbolic meaning of guns as representing America's morality and immorality as powerfully as *Gun Crazy*. The film reminds us that guns are tools, instruments, and by-products of American democracy: they can build and destroy democratic states. Subsequently, they're one of the state's most potent instruments. While the US federal government constitutionally permits citizens to own guns through the Second Amendment, that same government uses guns to incarcerate its citizens. Cops and criminals, soldiers and enemies alike use guns, and America was created through the barrel of a gun. American democracy cannot survive without guns and the violence and peace that shadow them.

Considering how liberal American gun laws are in comparison to other Western countries', Lewis's narrative tapped into something fundamentally American. Dickos explains that *Gun Crazy* reveals "the amorality spawning senseless acts of violence akin to those we see on the nightly news. And Lewis understood this in 1949."[27] But who is to blame for this violence if the state legally allows gun use? Who is to blame if the state trains its citizens, within the context of national defense, to murder others with guns? Bart's obsession for guns represents these paradoxes: he is obsessed with guns but is paralyzed by their murderous capabilities. As his sister states before Judge Willoughby, there's "something else about guns that gets him." Since Bart can't kill anyone or anything (he refuses to aim at people or animals), he thrives on the self-affirming power guns offer, not their murderous consequences, and it's the state that provides this power. For Bart, the government possessed a unique power to regulate his gun usage. Consequently, Bart's journey specifically and *Gun Crazy* in general are for Lewis metaphorical retaliations against the government's mounting power and the state-sponsored aggression, both physical or psychological, that power promotes.

Bart's childhood relationship with guns was a positive experience until the state interfered. In school, when Bart revealed a revolver to his classmates, he gained much-needed recognition. Bart articulates the following statements while in court: "Shooting is what I'm good at. It's what I want to do when I grow up"; "I just gotta have a gun"; and "[I feel] awful good when I'm shooting them ... like I'm somebody." Guns give him an identity, but the court erases that identity. Judge Willoughby calls his obsession a "dangerous mania" and reminds Bart that "we all want things," but some objects such as guns must be regulated by law. Although his four years of reform school were not meant to punish Bart, they denied him access to guns, and by default, happiness. He was never reformed but rather deprived of a potentially valuable resource that could have, if properly integrated into his life, helped him positively develop. Since Bart's obsession with guns violently progresses throughout his life—first a sling shot, then a BB gun, then teaching soldiers how to shoot, and then planning to work for Remington—it's no surprise that someone with such an obsession who found the army dull should adopt a criminal lifestyle when coupled with Laurie Starr. Although Bart and Laurie's love affair serves psychological needs, thematically their affair is Lewis's most potent political statement: *Gun Crazy* is fundamentally a visual and narrative rejection of the state, and Bart's "fatherless state" is a metaphor for America's profound ineptness.

While Laurie and her relationship with Bart inspired the blueprint for their metaphorical rebellion against the state, Bart's institutionalization in a state-sponsored reform school and later in the US military laid its foundation. Since representatives of the state—a police officer, Judge Willoughby, military officials, and so on—have played key roles in Bart's development, typically retarding it, the state's omnipotence contributed to his mania, and, therefore, his criminal activity should be perceived as a radical rejection of state-sponsored institutions such as law enforcement agencies, federal banks, the FBI, the US military, a national park, and a state department of agriculture. Like a caged animal cornered by the oppressive tentacles of federal and state governments, Bart's rebellion is a symbolic "tearing" of those tentacles. Everywhere Bart turns, as a child and adult, the state is there to remind him of its presence or enforce its power.

The state's most powerful act of institutionalization is when Judge Willoughby sends Bart to reform school. "There is an explicit tension" between the "social problem case study" and the court's handling of Bart.[28] Judge Willoughby struggles to explain Bart's mania, but he cannot; instead, a pseudopsychological explanation is given that helps Willoughby render a verdict. However, the judge oversteps his expertise, and since he acts on behalf of the state, his—and the state's—failed judgment exacerbates Bart's mania, causing Bart long-term distress. The matter-of-fact testimony provided by Bart's teacher, who states, "It was as if the gun was something the boy just had to have," suggests that the war-shaken state is guilty for normalizing (and glorifying) guns, war, and violence. Equally important is that from *Gun Crazy*'s start we recognize that we're headed for a genre-defying experience. This opening court scene neuters the traditional "ordering" process of social-problem pictures.[29] In fact, no order unfolds; chaos reigns. The state cannot fix all of its problems, especially those it created. This is why Laurie states, "When are you going to begin to live? Four years in reform school, then the Army. I should think they'd owe you something for a change." Her "Us versus Them" mentality is effective because she taps into a sense of entitlement that haunts Bart, not because he feels the government owes him anything, but because the government has taken so much away.

When Bart returns from the army, his two childhood friends, Clyde and Dave, work as a sheriff and news reporter. Both occupations are extensions of the state, especially if the news media is considered the "fourth estate," an unofficial branch of the US federal government that, while fulfilling its watchdog duties, helps the federal government run effectively. While the state has helped them, it has failed Bart. When Bart and Laurie launch into their criminal escapade, obstacles representing extensions of federal or state governments serve as signposts throughout their journey. They rob banks, which in the late 1940s were heavily supported and newly insured by the US Department of Treasury. The FBI is heavily involved in chasing them, as are numerous county and state police officers. At one point during their journey, they consider settling in Mexico to shed their national identity—and US law enforcement's tentacles—and inherit a new national identity. When they arrive at the California state line, a state Department of Agriculture officer is conducting a traffic stop. And the film's final scene occurs in a national park, another triumph of the US federal government.

However, upon closer inspection, Lewis's depiction of these federal institutions reveals how inept the US federal government had become after its post-Depression and postwar successes.

The traffic stop conducted by the Department of Agriculture officer is bogus and a stark reminder of another failed federal institution. Additionally, American national parks have long been perceived as pristine natural utopias that the federal government has graciously protected; however, according to Lewis's portrayal of them, national parks are misleading. For many Americans, particularly those in the American West, government acquisition of public land is a major threat to personal freedom. In *Gun Crazy*, the national park is a vibrant reminder of death and tragedy. The film's final scene offers us "a beautiful series of images that display the abstractness of fear," and no institution in the 1950s conjured more "abstract fear" among Americans than its own "federal government." Through its involvement in creating the atomic bomb, wrongfully blacklisting alleged Communist sympathizers (the film's screenplay was written by a blacklisted screenwriter), expanding the military-industrial complex and the federal government's overall reach and size, or spying on its own citizens, the ambiguous face of the US federal government epitomized this "abstractness." That this final scene occurs "where Bart practiced target shooting as a boy"[30] returns us to Bart's original problem—his obsession with guns, an obsession the federal government has enabled. The cycle has been completed, and because the cycle is recursive, its self-destructive qualities are evident. Interestingly, a local cop, his childhood friend, shoots and murders Bart; no federal officer—FBI agent, national park officer, or state trooper—completes the job. Although the state terminates Bart, Lewis offers us this double-edged irony: the federal government's incompetence prevented it from apprehending its suspect, so the federal system's power ultimately rests in local governments. Nevertheless, even small local governments can destroy and oppress.

Bart's army service reflects the state's other act of institutionalization. Since one can reasonably assume that, like many US soldiers who entered the military during World War II, Bart may have been drafted, his time in the army may have been involuntary. Bart's army service did nothing to remedy his struggles: he returns home directionless and unfulfilled, and he feels no national pride or renewed purpose. If his military service wasn't a failure, it certainly wasn't a success. If Bart's first encounter with Laurie is meant to re-create a scenario common for many soldiers—socializing with buddies under a tent—then Lewis subverts that scenario by having Bart reject his buddies. Most important, Lewis offers no insights into Bart's army service, suggesting it was uneventful. In the context of film noir, which featured many World War II veterans struggling to integrate into civilian life, Lewis posits Bart's military experience in our unconscious, underneath the surface, constantly there but never visible, influencing everything. Laurie understands this when she succinctly states, "Four years in reform school, then the Army," effectively reducing Bart's existence into two neatly carved periods. Each period bookends a time when the state metaphorically held Bart hostage and retarded his growth. Laurie defines Bart's identity as a vengeful, rebellious veteran who cannot assimilate into domestic life. She ignores his life before reform school because the state had not yet interfered: she is only interested in defining him as a state-corrupted soul harboring a latent vengeance against the state. And she realizes she can use his rebelliousness against the state to her advantage. Unlike noir films such as *The Blue Dahlia* (1946) or *Act of Violence* (1948), where the protagonists' military experiences overtly impacted their postwar domestic lives, Lewis places Bart's military experience in a more implicit, understated, but nevertheless important, context.

Lewis's depiction of the military is problematic because minimal information is given about Bart's army service. Nevertheless, the open road and "on-the-run" aspects of *Gun Crazy*—both facilitated by automobiles—reveal another important motif. Dickos writes, "The car in the film noir is a complex symbol expressing the various kinds of escape its protagonists attempt." He argues that because automobiles are the "apex of industrial achievement," they have pushed America to its "ambiguous state of spiritual anxiety." Automobiles represent a fundamental contradiction: they symbolize American industrial and commercial success, but they also represent "that dangerous flight into the unknown."[31] Automobiles are also, however, a potent reminder of how the federal government and the war accelerated the automobile industry's growth. This marriage between the US federal government and automobile industry is another example of the federal government's complex relationship with private industry, and this relationship is a beneficiary of the federal government's mounting power and influence. Hollywood felt the brunt of this influence.

During the war, Hollywood's resources were severely limited, according to Biesen, and limitations on supplies, film stock, and electricity, among other commodities, "significantly influenced filmmaking practices." Furthermore, Biesen explains, the federal government heavily impacted Hollywood through antitrust legislation, consumption restrictions, and television research development, which helped facilitate the "dis-integration of the Hollywood studio system after the war," and the Office of War Information "infused political propaganda into Hollywood films."[32] The federal government's power contributed to the military-industrial complex that President Dwight D. Eisenhower warned Americans about in his 1961 exit speech. The ramifications of this complex—the automobile, a massive federal bureaucracy, a potent military, the atomic bomb—thrust America into a dangerous unknown, and Lewis was reminding us of its dangers in *Gun Crazy*.

Beyond these references to institutionalization, Bart and Laurie's rampage also represents a rejection of marriage, family, and traditional love stories. If marriage is a state-sponsored "institution," such an interpretation is consistent with Lewis's other state rejections. Keser writes, "*Gun Crazy*'s structure pivots on the lovers' rejection of the community."[33] Krutnik notes that this anarchistic approach to romantic relationships contradicts the accepted societal order: "The love is impossible because society is unjust and the couple seeks to establish a 'family-in-exile.' . . . Love is itself beyond the law, and cannot be contextualized within the terms of familial ordering."[34] Just as Bart's love of guns is beyond the law because the court cannot regulate his mania, Bart and Laurie's love is beyond traditional definitions of family and marriage. If marriage represents the hope of domestic and emo-

No ordinary bank heist: Lewis used this scene in *Gun Crazy* (1950) to radically reject two of America's most powerful institutions: the federal government and Hollywood.

tional stability, Laurie and Bart's relationship is the antithesis of marriage: domestic and emotional instability.

Gun Crazy doesn't fit conveniently into a social-problem film, as Krutnik notes, but it doesn't fit easily into film noir, either. This incongruence reflects Lewis's keen understanding of genre and his ability to manipulate generic boundaries to promote his aesthetic radicalism. Two overt subversions of film noir convention are Lewis's frequent thematic and visual reliance on rural "frontierism" and his portrayal of rural settings in broad daylight. Unlike the darkly lit, shadow-filled "asphalt jungles" that define so many noir landscapes, the city is nonexistent in *Gun Crazy*. Instead, Lewis frequently offers brightly lit landscape shots of mountains, national parks, open roads, and suburbs. Hirsch notes that *Gun Crazy* is a "true countrified noir thriller," but that it is unusual, explaining, "The city as a cradle of crime and a cauldron of negative energy is the inevitable setting for film noir. Country settings appear infrequently, and usually as a counterpoint to the festering city . . . (*Gun Crazy* has) a different narrative development. . . . Episodic, taking place in a greater number of locations than the usually claustrophobic noir thriller (it has) a picaresque flavor. . . . (The film has) a more open feeling."[35] Biesen explains that as Americans prepared for war, many citizens moved from the country to the city to obtain adequate employment. Also, since twenty-four-hour shifts and blackouts were common, Americans had become familiar with dark urban settings.[36] Lewis reveals that something was profoundly disturbing with the city itself and particularly with the wartime and postwar American city: America's militarization was corrupting its soul. By omitting urban locales, Lewis's omission is a profound act of commission: escaping state-induced militarization offers us the opportunity to re-create our identities, as Laurie and Bart have done, although their transformation is illegal, immoral, and tragic. Nevertheless, escape—narrative, social, and aesthetic—allows our personas to be redefined. As Dickos writes, "When Laurie and Bart marry, their union preserves a vaguely appropriate frontier patina—as if Annie Oakley were joining forces with Buffalo Bill."[37] Their union and its Wild West connotations place the couple symbolically outside society, the law, and genre, and for Lewis, this exodus is crucial because it's the inevitable by-product of institutional oppression. Specifically, in addition to the federal government, Lewis takes aim at the contradictory Hollywood industry that celebrated the optimism of democracy and other American values but ostracized and blacklisted alleged Communist sympathizers, ruining their careers due to unsubstantiated claims. According to Dickos, "The darker vision of such life ensconced in noir cinema could now be insinuated into an ideological purge for the national good, and, in the process, would lay just cause to the very impetus that gives the film noir its subversive authority."[38] *Gun Crazy* is not only an aesthetic rejection of film noir's popular motifs but also a rejection of the industry that supported them.

Like the road Laurie and Bart travel on, the legacy of *Gun Crazy* is long and winding. That's partly because it encompasses many noir subgenres: it's a lovers-on-the-run film, and it's also part heist film, part road picture, and part quasi-social-problem film. By representing much of what's exciting about noir, *Gun Crazy* extended the genre's boundaries into new terrain, particularly neo-noir. While the film's impact on Arthur Penn's *Bonnie and Clyde* (1967) has been well documented, what warrants further analysis is its impact on more contemporary noir installments. Dickos has argued that although violence in film noir emerged within a specific cultural context, *Gun Crazy* shattered that pattern because it's a "singularly fascinating exception . . . it appeals to the possibility of the irrational overtaking us, of violence providing an excitement that no substitute can."[39] The film's celebration of random violence is therefore a precursor to neo-noir's "aesthetics of violence." After *Gun Crazy*, violence became fun, sexy, and exhilarating, qualities abundant in neo-noir's canon, specifically in films such as David Lynch's *Wild at Heart* (1990) or Oliver Stone's *Natural Born Killers* (1994). Noting the work of B. Ruby Rich and Nicholas Christopher, Dickos attributes this irrationality to the popularity of "demonic narratives" with prominent Satan figures in neo-noir, including *The Usual Suspects* (1995; with Kaiser Soze as the devil) and *Angel Heart* (1987; with Louis Cyphre as Lucifer).[40] *Gun Crazy* bleeds with nihilism in both its narrative and aesthetic designs. Laurie and Bart's radical selfishness and fetishes for guns and violence profoundly rearrange the sordid values of even the most corrupt noir villains. The couple—often acting as one symbiotic unit—don't want power, nor do they necessarily want money; they want pleasure, and their lethal union—"We go together like guns and ammunition"—is a "sex-death fusion that predated fashionable nihilism."[41] If neo-noir helped make nihilism fashionable, *Gun Crazy* helped make neo-noir.

Gun Crazy's legacy is also embedded in Lewis's unique ability to deliver both a modernist and postmodernist masterpiece.[42] As modernist cinema, the film's self-conscious, amoral, genre-bending, and antiauthoritarian themes are obvious. As Keser writes, Lewis refuses to "sentimentalize his characters or moralize about their actions . . . (he) appeals to neither economic nor social nor psychological explanations."[43] No easy, explicit rationales are provided to explain Bart and Laurie's motivations. However, its postmodernist attributes—from its bricolage of cultural references (the Wild West costumes, carnival setting, military culture, and British character) to its celebration of absurdity and irrationality and blatant use of irony and contradiction—are evident. Few directors in the noir camp could deftly maneuver through so many cultural labyrinths as effectively as Lewis does throughout *Gun Crazy*.

Conventional and unconventional, generic and idiosyncratic, *Gun Crazy* defies easy analysis, interpretation, and categorization, and no scene exemplifies these traits better than its famous bank robbery scene. Lewis resuscitated a popular noir motif, the heist, by directing what many consider an exceptional sequence, one of Hollywood's best: a long single take full of unscripted dialogue that economically utilized resources. Nevins writes, "Lewis rented a stretch limousine with everything behind the front seats removed to make room for the crew. The cinematographer sat on a jockey's saddle thrown across a greased plank on legs and was pushed back and forth along the plank to simulate a dolly shot." Several microphones were hidden to record the lovers' frantic utterances and the locale's ambient sounds.[44] How such innovation could surface from limited resources amazed many in Hollywood. Billy Wilder and Joan Crawford, among others, expressed awe at Lewis's virtuosity. More important, the scene captures all that is contradictory about *Gun Crazy*: unlike noir's carefully planned heists, Bart and Laura's robbery is, like their chatter, unscripted and chaotic. However, they escape unlike other noir thieves who, notwithstanding their planning, often succumb to fate. If Borde and Chaumeton are correct, and "the moral ambivalence, the criminality, the complex contradictions in motives and events all conspire to make the (noir) viewer co-experience the anguish and insecurity which are the true emotions of contemporary film noir,"[45] then watching *Gun Crazy* is a delightfully anxious, unsettling experience that can teach us many lessons about how to use form, convention, and genre to transcend the present and create disorder and formlessness and ultimately avant-garde art. No film noir director made so much noise more quietly than Joseph H. Lewis.

Notes

1. Peter Bogdanovich, *Who the Devil Made It: Conversations with Legendary Film Directors* (New York: Ballantine Books, 1997), 640–41.

2. Stanley Kauffmann, "Not So Crazy," *New Republic*, June 24, 1991.

3. Francis M. Nevins, *Joseph H. Lewis: Overview, Interview, and Filmography* (Lanham, MD: Scarecrow Press, 1998), 25.

4. Foster Hirsch, *The Dark Side of the Screen: Film Noir* (New York: Da Capo Press, 1981), 135.

5. Paul Schrader, *Cinema,* 5(1), 44 (as quoted in Keser).

6. Nevins, *Joseph H. Lewis*, xii.

7. Rose Capp, "First Is First and Second Is Nobody: Hoodlums and Heroines in Joseph H. Lewis' *The Big Combo*," *Senses of Cinema*, no. 25 (February 2003), http://archive.sensesofcinema.com/contents/cteq/03/25/big_combo.html.

8. Rick Thompson, "Joseph H. Lewis," *Senses of Cinema*, no. 10 (October 2000), http://archive.sensesofcinema.com/contents/00/10/lewis.html.

9. Robert Keser, "Joseph H. Lewis," *Senses of Cinema*, no. 41 (September 2006), http://archive.sensesofcinema.com/contents/directors/06/lewis_joseph.html.

10. Thompson, "Joseph H. Lewis."

11. Ibid.

12. Keser, "Joseph H. Lewis."

13. Andrew Dickos, *Street with No Name: A History of the Classic American Film Noir* (Lexington: University Press of Kentucky, 2002), 151.

14. Capp, "First Is First."

15. Keser, "Joseph H. Lewis."

16. Dickos, *Street with No Name*, 151.

17. Bogdanovich, *Who the Devil*, 686.

18. Capp, "First Is First."

19. Paul Schrader, "Notes on Film Noir," in *Film Noir Reader*, ed. by Alain Silver and James Ursini (New York: Limelight Editions, 1999), 58–61.

20. Sheri Chinen Biesen, *Blackout: World War II and the Origins of Film Noir* (Baltimore: Johns Hopkins University Press, 2005), 150.

21. Ibid., 156.

22. Frank Krutnik, *In a Lonely Street: Film Noir, Genre, and Masculinity* (New York: Routledge, 1991), 221–22.

23. Ibid., 224.

24. David Gilmore, *Monsters: Evil Beings, Mythical Beasts, and All Manner of Imaginary Terrors* (Philadelphia: University of Pennsylvania Press, 2003), 16–18.

25. Schrader, "Notes," 59.

26. Dickos, *Street with No Name*, 153.

27. Ibid.

28. Krutnik, *Lonely Street*, 220–21.

29. Ibid.

30. Dickos, *Street with No Name*, 155.

31. Ibid., 176.

32. Biesen, *Blackout*, 68.

33. Keser, "Joseph H. Lewis."

34. Krutnik, *Lonely Street*, 226.

35. Hirsch, *Dark Side*, 83.

36. Biesen, *Blackout*, 62.

37. Dickos, *Street with No Name*, 153.

38. Ibid., 196.

39. Ibid., 240.

40. Ibid., 236.

41. Bryant Frazer, "*Gun Crazy*," Deep Focus, http://www.deep-focus.com/flicker/guncrazy.html.

42. Keser, "Joseph H. Lewis."

43. Ibid.

44. Nevins, *Joseph H. Lewis*, 39.

45. Raymond Borde and Etienne Chaumeton, "Towards a Definition of Film Noir," in Silver and Ursini, *Film Noir Reader*, 25.

MICHAEL LEE

Music, Masculinity, and Masochism in *Gun Crazy*

Gun Crazy, as its admirers and detractors invariably note, was a B movie. Pauline Kael provided one of the most celebrated assessments of the film when she said it was born of a "fascinating crumminess."[1] How then did a cheap film financed by notoriously thrifty producers Frank and Maurice King get a musical score from Victor Young, an A-list composer, whose career was anything but crummy? Young worked primarily on Paramount A product. By 1949, the year he went slumming with Joseph H. Lewis and the King brothers, Young had been nominated for Academy Awards for Best Score and Best Song numerous times, including earning four nominations twice in a single year on his way toward twenty-two total nominations and two Oscar wins. His success with the academy is only one trapping of a massively successful career in Hollywood. This chapter will not be able to answer the question of how the King brothers secured Young's services. Money, one supposes. It will strive, however, to situate Young's score in a larger context and theoretical frame that will hopefully add luster to its reputation among *Gun Crazy*'s many academic admirers who tend to emphasize director Joseph H. Lewis's visual sensibilities or the film's distinctive narrative patterns over the film's music. Young's score, and perhaps more particularly its use in the film, manages to problematize the gender role occupied by the film's antihero, Bart Tare, in ways that amplify much of the psychoanalytic analysis the film has enjoyed.

Situating Young's score in a larger context of music composed for film noirs reveals that Young's approach merits special attention. It resembles no other earlier effort more closely than David Raksin's score for *Laura* (1944) by offering a largely monothematic score that obsessively restates and varies a popular-sounding tune. Royal S. Brown's influential discussion of film music, *Overtones and Undertones: Reading Film Music* offers this opening to its substantial discussion of Raksin's *Laura* score:

> Perhaps the classic example of the fetishizing a woman via music (among other things) can be found in Otto Preminger's 1944 *Laura*. First and foremost, the monothematic nature of *Laura's* musical score by David Raksin strongly contributes to the obsessive atmosphere built up around the film's heroine, Laura Hunt (Gene Tierney). Almost every piece of music, diegetic and nondiegetic, heard in the film either is David Raksin's mysteriously chromatic fox-trot tune or else grows out of it particularly in the nondiegetic backing.[2]

Brown continues by pointing out the many diegetic appearances of the tune: the phonograph in Laura's apartment, the jazz combo playing in the café scene, ambient music at Waldo's party welcoming Laura back from the dead, and so forth. The nondiegetic track also finds Raksin consistently riffing on his own tune with subtle variations capturing the shifting mood of each particular scene but always, always obsessing on the person the tune references, Laura Hunt.

Like *Laura*, *Gun Crazy* features a sound track that obsesses on a popular tune written for the film. Whether the choice to emphasize a popular tune belonged to Young or Lewis or perhaps the King brothers lies outside the scope of what this chapter can claim. We cannot rule out the King brothers as a possibility, however strongly we might prefer to see the composer or director as the agent of such a choice. Hiring Victor Young and lyricist Ned Washington to team up to compose a song for the film may have stemmed from a desire to exploit the commercial potential of Young and Washington's successful collaboration on the hit song "Stella by Starlight" concocted by the team for the unlikely film vehicle *The Uninvited* (1944). Like "Stella by Starlight," "Mad about You" provides a surprisingly ambivalent and difficult to predict musical unfolding as its melody seemingly begins in one key and ends in a distantly related one. The King brothers certainly sought to profit from the ubiquitous presence of a Young/Washington song in their film. The press book for *Gun Crazy* encourages exhibitors to trumpet the presence of "'Mad About You,' recorded by Frank Sinatra, Kitty Kallen," and others in their ballyhoo for the film.[3] Because the song had to be performed during the Danceland Music Hall scene near the end of the film, Young had time to arrange getting it recorded before the film's release for having composed it in advance of production. By the time the film hit theaters, "Mad about You" had been recorded four times, most prominently by Frank Sinatra, who had previously recorded "Stella by Starlight" prior to the release of *The Uninvited*.[4]

Much like "Laura," "Mad about You" figures prominently in both the diegetic and nondiegetic music for the film. After an initial appearance for orchestra and wordless choir during the main title cue, "Mad about You" falls silent as Lewis treats the audience to Bart's backstory.[5] The tune emerges in the nondiegetic track only after the advent of Annie Laurie Starr in Bart's life. This first nondiegetic appearance unfolds rapturously as Bart, victorious in the shooting contest, returns Laurie's ring to her. Once it emerges on the sound track, Young seldom lets his song rest as the score provides restatements, variations, and fragmented versions all in the service of illustrating and intensifying Bart's obsession with Laurie and his willing submission to her will. "Mad about You" becomes the only important leitmotif in the film, always referencing Bart's subjective thoughts about Laurie.

Within the film's diegesis, we hear "Mad about You" on the radio in the shabby diner where Laurie and Bart wolf down hamburgers, hold the onions. A radio can be heard playing an instrumental version in the cheap motel room where Laurie makes her play to launch their crime spree by recourse to sexual blackmail. The couple slow dances to it in the Danceland scene as their crime spree approaches a fatal detour.

While Raksin's score for *Laura* provided the model for a crime drama score with one leitmotif derived wholly from a tune composed for the film, there are important nuances to Young's work on *Gun Crazy* that distance it from its apparent model. First, the song "Laura" didn't become a popular song until after the film's release. Johnny Mercer added the lyrics to David Raksin's tune in 1945 after the film became a hit. The tune is not sung in the film, nor is it ever heard from beginning to end. "Mad about You" is actually sung in the film *Gun Crazy*, rendering "Mad about You" a song, not a theme. Its lyrics indicate what it means with greater specificity than a leitmotif indicating the obsessive fetishizing of a woman.

Ned Washington's lyrics adopt a pleading tone, not unknown in the ballad literature, but rendered poignant by the singer's imploring words taking on a sad desperation. Important to the analysis to follow is the end of the first verse in which Washington's couplet captures the juxtaposition of reluctance and headlong pleasure the singer experiences. "Though I said to my heart, don't fall / How I love the enchantment of it all."[6]

The song closes with desperate lines that paraphrase Bart when he frequently adopts a pleading tone with Laurie. Bart rather explicitly paraphrases the song's concluding lines when he asks Laurie to join him in

Mexico, "Settle down, you gadabout, you, / Please don't make me sad about you, / Can't you see I'm mad about you, dear?"[7]

The song's music suits the lyrics for providing a weak and vacillating commitment to conventional harmonic goals. For their part, the lyrics speak on behalf of one character and one character only, Bart. He's the character who demonstrates reluctance within the couple, much as when the singer who says to her heart, "don't fall." Moreover, in a telling scene transitioning between bank robberies, it is Bart who compares his entire situation to the unreal while Laurie insists on his seeing only the reality of her lying next to him at night. Only Bart, the fantasist of the couple, could say he loves "the enchantment of it all." This situation effectively situates the music of the film in the service of illustrating the interiority, intensifying the emotions, and speaking the hopes of its male lead.

Even before the advent of "Mad about You" in the film, the nondiegetic orchestral score draws the viewer into Bart's interiority. We hear this in the film's opening sequence when Young's meticulous and obsessive small repeated passages draw the viewer into rapport with Bart's thinking during his failed attempt to feed his obsession by stealing guns.

This situation of linking the male character to the film's music inverts the more common approach to film music, which tends to align itself with the feminine, the irrational, and the subjective. Male leads don't ordinarily connect with music in crime dramas. While the obsession over Laura takes place in the male lead's head, the music remains steadfastly feminine for representing her, not him.

This situation of alienation between the masculine and music is almost as old as music itself. In her landmark case for a feminist musicology, Susan McClary almost passes over mention of music's historical femininity in the West, as she justifiably assumes her readers know this vast discourse already. However, she does not omit it but merely passes by it, quickly writing,

> Throughout its history in the West, music has been an activity fought over bitterly in terms of gender identity. The charge that musicians and devotees of music are "effeminate" goes back as far as recorded documentation about music, and music's association with the body (in dance or for sensuous pleasure) and with subjectivity has led to its being relegated in many historical periods to what was understood a "feminine" realm.[8]

One of these historical periods might well be studio-era Hollywood. Claudia Gorbman provides numerous instances of nondiegetic music connecting to the emotive and fantastic realm in her influential treatise on film music. During her discussion of the music for a scene in *Now, Voyager* (1942), Gorbman provides a cogent example.

> Music enters to satisfy a need to compensate for, fill in, the emotional depth not verbally representable. Bernard Herrmann: "The real reason for music is that a piece of film, by its nature, lacks a certain ability to convey emotional overtones. Many times in many films, dialogue may not give a clue to the feelings of a character." All music, say Eisler and Adorno, "belongs primarily to the sphere of subjective inwardness." It thus supplies that dimension to the film-perceptual fantasy which is felt lacking, and whose lack could pose a problem at particularly pregnant moments in the story's unfolding. To the "objectivity" of image and dialogue answers the subjectivity, interiority, depth of nondiegetic music.[9]

This link of sound and especially music to the subjective renders all it touches a measure of the irrational, emotional, and the feminine. The image track provides an empirical objectivity for having a physical presence, while material on the sound track does not. This lack in nondiegetic music has been successfully theorized as linking it to the subjective, emotional, and intuitive.[10] Peter Franklin has noted this situation in what some regard as the first important orchestral score for a nonmusical narrative film of the sound era, Cooper's *King Kong* (1933).[11] Franklin's argument provides a close reading of the film's score and notes how consistently composer Max Steiner aligns his orchestral music with the feminine, fantastical, and irrational to the notable exclusion of his male characters and their interiority.[12] Extending Franklin's observations, we can look at producer Val Lewton's protonoir sensibility as first manifested in Tourneur's *Cat People* (1942). The score for that film by Roy Webb features not one note of nondiegetic music to support any character other than Irena, the film's irrational female lead. All the leitmotifs within Webb's score reference Irena's beliefs, hopes, fears, and actions. From the earliest phase of Hollywood sound film with an orchestral track to an important wellspring of the noir style, music and the feminine align with each other.

In *Gun Crazy*, this tendency in Hollywood music to extend the link of music to the feminine manifests itself in the insistent use of "Mad about You" as crucial diegetic music and a nearly ubiquitous presence in the nondiegetic sound track after Laurie joins the story. That the song speaks for Bart aligns the film's male lead with the feminine enterprise of music and all music's attendant emotionalism.

The song speaks for Bart in the film, its lyrics paraphrasing his dialogue. More interesting still is the fact that the song eventually enjoys embodiment in *Gun Crazy* in the form of the young female singer seen at the dance hall and played by Francis Irvin, erroneously credited in the film as Francis Irwin, who favors Laurie and Bart with a rendition of "their" song.[13] Jim Kitses notes a special quality in Irvin: "Victim of a typographical error, Irvin is a small symbol of the 'going-nowhereness' of our fugitive couple, the film itself, and too many of its players, big and small."[14] For the purposes of this chapter, her meagerness as a figure as she sings the song that has been linked through most of the film with Bart further weakens the film's male lead. That the song speaks for Bart, yet falls on the lips of a young woman, places Bart's masculinity in greater crisis.

Critics have widely noted the effeminate or at minimum ineffectual role allocated to Bart in *Gun Crazy*. Rather than cite those, we might profitably consider how Bart might be understood at least provisionally or mildly as suffering from what Freud called "feminine masochism," a condition Freud almost exclusively connected with male subjects who embrace subservience to a woman.[15] The qualities associated with this perversion include power role reversals outside the scope of what society might tolerate, masquerades and role playing, a willing but much protested embrace of total subservience, antisocial conduct, and culmination in simulations of negations.[16] Ascribing such a perversion to the film's male lead may be too extreme for its failure to account for the robust mutual attraction the couple evinces or the important detail of Bart's final act of shooting Laurie. That Laurie and Bart are having sex seems obvious even though conventions of film narrative refused Lewis any opportunity to clarify this fact through overt depiction. Assuming that their specifically sexual conduct was in any sense normative seems a stretch insofar as the on-screen metaphors for sexuality in the film at minimum reach toward the near fringes of degeneracy where sex and violence link, and their public behavior draws comparison to that of wild animals. In their summary of *Gun Crazy*'s importance as a film, Alain Silver and Carl Macek argued, "Lewis' staging of a violent crime as if it were a sexual act is not unique in film noir; but his consistent stylization of *Gun Crazy* in those terms imbues the sexuality of Annie Laurie and Bart with a desperation and fatality that defines the noir vision."[17] That Laurie bullies Bart through sexual blackmail into joining in her crime spree indicates Bart's weaker position within the couple, a necessary and important position for the masochist. Laurie wields guns with reckless confidence and great skill, lending her symbolic access to phallic power. Meanwhile Bart is conflicted and seems incapable of making proper use of his gun by balking in every crisis save the last. Laurie's introduction into the film with guns wildly blazing finds her aiming squarely at Bart and pulling the trigger then later positioning her gun between her legs and firing at a female assistant. The sheer audacity and wide scope of Lewis's metaphor inspires awe. The power imbalance between the two receives a heavy handling.

Musically, Victor Young deploys a telling passage in his orchestral cue coinciding with the climax of the shooting contest. Typical of the music early in the film, this passage makes no reference to "Mad about You." It constitutes almost the last moment in the score to fail in this regard save some chattering ostinato patterns coinciding with the FBI's distribution of information in tracking down the fugitives. Having seen Laurie miss the last match on Bart's crown, Bart now grins broadly, looks significantly at Packett, and takes his sweet time igniting Laurie's last remaining match. The score features a growling descent in the bass instruments of the orchestra, culminating on a low, foreboding timpani roll. Why this dire-sounding music just as our hero is about to beat the carnival performer at her own game? For whom is Victor Young's orchestra churning out this doom-laden

In *Gun Crazy* (1950), Laurie Starr (Peggy Cummins) explodes into Bart's life while wearing a cowgirl costume.

music? Surely not the audience at the show, they've sided verbally with Bart. Surely it doesn't speak for Packett, whose interiority merits no such musical illustration. The orchestra seems to be anticipating a catastrophe for Bart. His victory will earn him the attentions of Laurie, attentions that will rapidly precipitate his fall. Young's orchestra speaks exclusively for Bart's situation.

Immediately after the timpani roll and Bart's triumph, "Mad about You" takes the reins of the score and never lets go. Even with the couple lying dead in the mountain marsh, a heavenly choir sings a wordless, soaring rendition of the song with sumptuous orchestral support. The earlier warning music gives way to the ecstasies of Bart's transgressive obsession with submission to Laurie. Those ecstasies get the last word musically, as the heavenly choir seems intent not only on illustrating Bart's interiority but also on sanctioning his choices, no matter how thoroughly they marginalize his masculinity. Young's final, triumphant chords are as subversive as anything in the film. Bart's interiority has been represented in music from the film's opening shot through the last in which we hear Young's music sanction Bart's choices with a heavenly chorus.

Between that low timpani roll and that soaring wordless choir at the film's close, Young charts Bart's inner state through his variations, fragmentations, and restatements of "Mad about You." Along the way, Young treats the audience to the shifting moods and feelings of the film's male lead, his ecstasies, his anxieties, his hesitations, so brilliantly married to John Dall's halting line deliveries and prolonged vacillations. Bart's interiority and subjectivity receive lavish illustration in Young's score, all conspiring to distance him from the normative treatment of cinematic masculinity by Hollywood composers.

Laurie eventually takes up the cause of dressing Bart. Her crime spree requires playacting. At first Bart makes no complaint, but over time he comes to hate her costuming choices. The success of their travesty of the boring couple as they flee from Hampton hinges on Laurie's supreme talent for manipulative make believe. In this regard Laurie resembles the pale and imperious Venus and Bart the ur-masochist of Leopold von Sacher-Masoch's novella *Venus in Furs* (1870) in which Wanda humiliates Severin by forcing him to dress in an outlandish costume of a Cracovian servant, one of several costume changes she imposes on her submissive lover.[18] At first he relishes his role, but before long he complains fruitlessly of the shame it causes him. Are Severin's or Bart's complaints genuine? More likely their role of the "feminine masochist" requires them to protest their degradations at the hands of the woman each serves.

The reversal of power in the film between Laurie and Bart is surely consensual. Bart's protests constitute flickering pangs of longing for the normalcy he once knew yet abandoned so readily. He does not really want to leave Laurie any more than Severin wants to abandon his servitude to Wanda. He has his chances to quit her, never more so than in the pas de deux they dance in their separate getaway cars after the Armour robbery. Bart participates in playacting of the sort common to masochistic relationships, enjoying his willing/forced alienation from wider society.

Summarizing the male masochist's inner state, Kaja Silverman wrote,

> What is it precisely that the male masochist displays, and what are the consequences of this self-exposure? To begin with, he acts out in an insistent and exaggerated way the basic conditions of cultural subjectivity, conditions that are normally disavowed; he loudly proclaims that his meaning comes to him from the Other, prostrates himself before the gaze even as he solicits it, exhibits his castration for all to see, and revels in the sacrificial basis of the social contract. The male masochist magnifies the losses of divisions upon which cultural identity is based, refusing to be sutured or recompensed. In short, he radiates a negativity inimical to the social order.[19]

While not all of Silverman's precision fits Bart exactly, there are ways that his situation reflects her formulation quite well. Most central to this formulation is the role played by Young's score. By insisting on inviting the audience into Bart's interiority, we find him through the various iterations of "Mad about You" running hyperbolically on the sound track, deriving his meaning from the other (Laurie) while spectacularly exhibiting his exaggerated subjectivity. The music provides this exaggerated subjectivity in a way that the image track or dialogue probably should not without risking total alienation between audience and antihero. Bart's emotional states represented by Young's score and gesturing constantly toward Washington's lyrics reveal him to be a supplicant to Laurie's power. His costumes and performances invite the gaze gesturing toward Washington's lyric, "Can't you see that I've got it bad about you?" His recurrent submissions to Laurie's will magnify the loss of division between masculine and feminine. His protests are urgent to the game's success.

Bart's inexplicable return to Cashville when the couple discovers that the money from the Armour meat-packing heist is hot offers his solicitation of the gaze of all those who mattered to him prior to his meeting Laurie. His sister asks why they came to her. He answers unsatisfactorily that they had nowhere else to go. He wants to be seen in all the glory of his powerlessness. By sharing in Laurie's project to meet an inevitable, violent end, he refuses to suture his alienation from social norms. Like Laurie, his conduct renders him inimical to the social order embodied in his sister, her absent husband, Ira, her "cute" kids, and his drab childhood friends now grown into versions of their drab fathers. The dire cue at the carnival warned that Bart's fall was inevitable on his winning that contest. "Mad about You" underscores what a sweet fall Bart is having.

One more popular song quoted in the film helps clarify how the music in *Gun Crazy* situates Bart in a masochistic role. As the musical interlude in "Mad about You" arrives at the Danceland Music Hall where Bart and Laurie spend their final peaceful moments together, we see a violinist approach from medium shot to close-up. His suave solo segues to a new song, also sung on-screen by Francis Irvin, "Laughing on the Outside" with music by Ben Raleigh and lyrics by Bernie Wayne. Composed in 1946, the song enjoyed three successful recordings that same year by Dinah Shore, Andy Russell, and Sammy Kaye. All three recordings reached the top ten on the *Billboard* charts.[20] Wayne's lyrics, which resonate with the vocabulary of "feminine masochism" when placed in the context of *Gun Crazy*, open with this verse:

> The crowd sees me out dancing
> Carefree and romancing
> Happy with my someone new
> I'm laughing on the outside
> Crying on the inside
> 'Cause I'm still in love with you.[21]

If the girl singer played by Francis Irvin has been lending her face and voice to concretize and ultimately feminize Bart's interiority as I've argued up to this point, her next selection seems uncannily apt to Bart's situation. The lyrics' dichotomy of laughing outwardly and crying inwardly captures the conflicted nature of masochism, which must protest wantonly the thing it craves in order to perform the degradation implicit in the compact that lends all power to the other. Of course all this only makes sense if Laurie is two people in the song. The film has so successfully isolated Bart and Laurie that little stretch is needed to allow Laurie multiple roles in Bart's mind. She must be both the "someone new" with whom Bart dances, for we see them dancing on the image track, while simultaneously serving as the object of desire that causes the song's singer so much suffering. In a sense, the Laurie that Bart dreams about does not exist. They are separated. Yet, much to his pain, he still loves that fantasy version of Laurie, and his pain transforms into pleasure as he consistently declines all opportunities for separation from the Laurie who torments him. The song's literal meaning must give way to Bart's subjectivity to allow this exaggeration of Laurie's importance as both object of immediate connection in the couple's dance and source of pain referenced repeatedly in the rueful refrain "Crying on the inside / 'Cause I'm still in love with you" to realize its full power. As an anthem of fractured identity, languishing subjectivity, and *amour fou* of a masochistic variety Lewis (or Young) couldn't have chosen more wisely.

Other critics have conducted psychoanalytic readings of Bart Tare and concluded similarly that he epitomizes the alienated, vacillating, doomed, masochistic antiheroes who populate so many film noirs. I believe that Victor Young's score for Joseph Lewis's *Gun Crazy* elevates Bart as an exemplar of his type by connecting him so thoroughly to the feminizing enterprise of music. Young's score constantly conjures Bart's subjectivity. John Dall's superbly "weak" performance is crucial to understanding the film, but Young's music elevates that performance by making all his hesitations, confusions, and vacillations sing. While Raksin's score for *Laura* provided Young with the necessary model, Young's music offers more than a classic leitmotif associated with a fetishized woman ever could.

With his film *The Big Combo* (1955), Lewis would eventually enjoy the services of David Raksin, architect of the monothematic popular song informing the entire nondiegetic track and key moments of the film's diegesis. Raksin provided Lewis with a monothematic score that deploys its brash and jazzy opening to represent the corrupt world in which the film unfolds. This later connection suggested why *Laura* was important to understanding how Young configured his score. As the story of *The Big Combo* unravels, Raksin spreads out the opening theme into a network of increasingly discordant variations suggestive of the unraveling of its villain's formerly secure world. The variation heard in the final scene at the airplane hangar finds the motives of the film's opening transformed into polyphonic modernist convolutions as the theme folds in on itself. Raksin, an enthusiast of musical modernism,[22] seems to be channeling Dmitri Shostakovich at his most strident. *The Big Combo* features a great score thanks to Raksin.

For all the terrific convolutions of *The Big Combo* score, Lewis got at least a comparably fine original score from Victor Young for *Gun Crazy*. Lewis was no passive figure in this story about the film he directed. Without John Dall's performance, Lewis's deft direction, and the screenplay's wanton sexual metaphors, nothing in Victor Young's score would make much sense. Whether we can quite say that the opposite is true constitutes a stretch, but we might admit that the score contributes mightily toward reading the film's intentions as regards its problematic male lead and his crisis of masculine identity.

Notes

1. Pauline Kael, *5001 Nights at the Movies* (New York: Holt, Rinehart, and Winston, 1982), 235.

2. Royal S. Brown, *Overtones and Undertones: Reading Film Music* (Berkeley: University of California Press, 1994), 86.

3. Jim Kitses, *Gun Crazy* (London: BFI, 1996), 81.

4. Frank Sinatra, "Mad about You" / "On the Island of Stromboli," Columbia Records 38613; and Kitty Kallen, *Kitty Kallen Favorites*, Mercury Records EP 1 3294A 1F 1. Both records were recorded in 1949 along with singles of "Mad about You" recorded by the Russ Case Orchestra with Stuart Foster, vocalist, and Charlie Spivak and His Orchestra, which appeared on London-648. This last record, while recorded in 1949, wasn't released until May 1950, making its mention in the *Gun Crazy* press book premature insofar as the film opened in January 1950.

5. My favorite detail in Young's score from this phase of the film concerns the moment when Bart kills the baby chick with his BB gun. Here Young channels Modest Musorgsky's *Pictures at an Exhibition* (1874) and specifically the movement "Ballet of the Unhatched Chicks." The chirping grace-note figures in the flute sound similar to the same figure, orchestrated by Maurice Ravel, in the ballet movement. Later we hear the same music when Bart fails to shoot the mountain lion. Young allows his score to conjure a memory within a flashback. It's one of many very nice moments early in the score.

6. Victor Young and Ned Washington, "Mad about You" (New York: Catherine Hinen/Patti Washington Music, 1949).

7. Ibid.

8. Susan McClary, *Feminine Endings: Music, Gender, and Sexuality* (Minneapolis: University of Minnesota Press, 1991), 17.

9. Claudia Gorbman, *Unheard Melodies: Narrative Film Music* (Bloomington: University of Indiana Press, 1987), 67.

10. Mary Ann Doane, "Ideology and the Practice of Sound Editing and Mixing," in *The Cinematic Apparatus*, ed. Teresa De Lauretis and Stephen Heath (London: Macmillan, 1980, 47–50.

11. Personally, I think this claim truly belongs to Max Steiner's score for *The Most Dangerous Game* (Pichel and Schoedsack, 1932), but that film and its wonderful score are generally overlooked in favor of *King Kong*.

12. Peter Franklin, "*King Kong* and Film on Music: Out of the Fog," in *Film Music: Critical Approaches*, ed. K. J. Donnelly (Edinburgh: University of Edinburgh Press, 2001), 88–102.

13. Kitses, *Gun Crazy*, 82.

14. Ibid.

15. Sigmund Freud, *The Ego and the Id* (1923), in *The Complete Works of Sigmund Freud, Standard Edition*, vol. 19, ed. by James Strachey (London: Hogart Press, 1953–74), 56.

16. A thorough discussion of "feminine masochism" appears in Kaja Silverman, *Male Subjectivity at the Margins* (New York: Routledge, 1992), 201–10.

17. Alain Silver and Carl Macek, "*Gun Crazy*," in *Film Noir: An Encyclopedic Reference to the American Style*, ed. Alain Silver and Elizabeth Ward (Woodstock, NY: Overlook Press, 1979), 118.

18. Leopold von Sacher-Masoch, *Venus in Furs*, trans. Uwe Moeller and Laura Lindgren (New York: Blast Books, 1989), 134.

19. Silverman, *Male Subjectivity*, 206.

20. Dinah Shore recorded "Laughing on the Outside" for Columbia Records (36964) and reached number three on the charts. Andy Russell recorded the song for Capitol Records (252) and peaked at number four. Sammy Kaye's version was recorded for RCA Victor Records (20-1856) and peaked at number seven. "Music Popularity Chart," *Billboard*, April 18 and 25; May 2, 9, 16, 23, and 30; and June 7 and 14, 1946.

21. Bernie Wayne, "Laughing on the Outside" (London: Campbell, Connelly, 1956).

22. Brown, *Overtones*, 282.

14

Phillip Sipiora

Ethos and Ethics

Reconsidering Gun Crazy

> Moral or ethical virtue is the product of habit (*ethos*).
> Aristotle, *The Nichomachean Ethics*

The culture of noir, fictive and cinematic, cuts a wide swath of expression. Joseph H. Lewis's *Gun Crazy* does and does not fit common stereotypes of crime drama. This electrifying film has all of the usual staple elements of noir—crime, sex, surrender to baser instincts, familiar camera angles, lighting and shadows, and of course a riveting femme fatale, the sine qua non of noir. Yet *Gun Crazy* is also a confrontational original treatment of characters, motifs, and techniques.[1] The resurrection of noir in the academy and in popular culture over the past generation has lifted the reputation of many forgotten crime dramas, including particularly aggressive, experimental films such as Lewis's midcentury masterpiece.[2] *Gun Crazy*, originally titled *Deadly Is the Female* and released in 1949, was not well received at the box office and reviews were mixed. The *New York Times* was negative, referring to it as "humdrum pulp fiction." The *Los Angeles Times* and *Variety* found some positive qualities in the low-budget film. Lewis had high hopes for the film and rereleased it six months later as *Gun Crazy*. Today there is no question that it has achieved cult status, but why?

Titles are usually synoptic metaphors representing themes and topics. The explicit ambiguity of the title *Gun Crazy* raises some grammatical and conceptual questions. Does the title refer to an obsession with guns? To a sense of "craziness" intertwined with guns? Is the title a compound noun or an implicit, unhyphenated compound adjective? If neither combination is a compound unit, which term is the noun and which term is the adjective? If the title is the combination of a noun and an adjective, which word is the modifier and which word is the substantive? Further, does the title refer to the psychological profile of the two leading characters? Annie Laurie Starr and Bart Tare are clearly "crazy" about guns, yet the title could reasonably refer to American audiences as "crazy" about gun movies and living vicariously through characters like Bart and Laurie. As James Naremore observes, "Because *Gun Crazy*'s lack of cinematic polish was homologous with the outlaw couple's disregard of bourgeois morality, viewers were given an opportunity to feel irresponsible and discriminating at the same time."[3] These interpretive possibilities suggest a range of thematic emphases, including those carrying ethical implications.

Ethos and Ethics

Ethics derives from *ethos*, a Greek word that means habit, custom, or usage, yet it also refers to a dwelling place, a physical locus as well as a metaphorical one. *Ethos* is a polysemous term of great significance in ancient thought. It denotes personal ethics as the sum total of a persona, the composite dwelling space or residence of personal existence, including cumulated experience—fore-structure (*vorhaben*) in the lexicon of Heidegger. As Michael J. Hyde argues in discussing the rhetorical implication of ethos, "Discourse is used to transform space and time into 'dwelling places' . . . where people can deliberate about and 'know together' (*con-scientia*) some matter of interest. Such dwelling places define the grounds, the abodes or habitats, where a person's ethics and moral character take form and develop."[4] Ethos calls attention to the importance of circumstance, context, and the exigencies of occasion or special time.

In one of his most densely packed dialogues, the *Phaedrus*, Plato explores complex connections between ethos and ethics and the relationship between the individual self and the possibilities of language. Plato advocated that language serve truth and eternal values, of course, but he also recognized the critical importance of the *medium* for the transmission/ acquisition of philosophic wisdom. For an "exchange" of truth to take place, whether through dialectic or rhetoric (a main theme in *Phaedrus*), the exposition must factor in the realization of the individual, including qualities of ethos as character.

A worthy moral compass is much more than the generative context or a product of the place of birth. Ethics as ethos suggests a dynamic ethic or tenor of character. An individual moral system is not a static register of beliefs and actions but rather a personal, evolving code of character that reveals a way of seeing the world and making value judgments according to the special circumstances of the moment. In his *Nichomachean Ethics*, Aristotle emphasizes the importance of "ethical stature as habit" precisely because ethical decisions are necessarily contingent on always-changing circumstances.[5] Laurie and Bart are involved in a series of critical moments that call for ethical judgments. When you have a gun in your hand pointed at someone, judgments and actions take on an uncommon urgency. Ethical stances, judgments, and behavior always involve issues of responsibility, which call attention to the importance of self-understanding. Ancient Greek systems of knowledge placed critical importance on knowing yourself (*gnothi seauton*) as an element of ethos. Laurie gives every indication that, indeed, she is acutely aware of her immoral nature and impulses. It is Bart who appears to have difficulty grasping his inner character, particularly in terms of his ever-changing ethical code.

The principle of "attending to oneself" (*epimeleia heautou*) is a critical dimension of *ethos* and is also seminal to Greek ethical philosophy, particularly in the schools of Isocrates, Plato, and Aristotle. The concept of attending to oneself is necessarily conjoined with knowing oneself. These paired principles are integrally intertwined in *Gun Crazy*. Socrates's warning to his judges in Plato's *Apology* is apt advice for Laurie and Bart: one's concern in life should be virtue rather than wealth. "Ethics," for Laurie and Bart, is much more than an abstract set of moral principles—it is a way of living, a lifestyle, a code of identification.[6] Indeed, it is a series of encounters complicated by value-laden opportunities available to them. The terrifying tandem are unfettered free spirits (one of the reasons they are so infectiously interesting to viewers) and as long as they are free to act according to their desires, they have the opportunity to make a full range of decisions—always with serious ethical implications. Laurie is clearly devoted to the principle of attending to herself—in the manner of acting selfishly—as her words and actions reveal her to be uninterested in the welfare of others, except, occasionally, for Bart. Laurie, unlike Bart, gives only slight indications that she (sometimes) realizes that the importance of attending to herself involves an internal struggle, deep within herself, in which her (dark) impulses are called into question, held in check. In the words of Foucault, "The practice of the self is conceived as a permanent battle. . . . The Individual must be given the weapons and the courage that will enable him [or her] to fight all his life."[7] Laurie engages in a number of battles, with fiery enthusiasm, but rarely with herself in moments of introspection.

The brilliance of Lewis lies in his ethical representations in *Gun Crazy*, particularly as he inverts a common contemporary understanding of "taking care of oneself" as self-centered behavior. *Gun Crazy* reinvokes the ancient principle by raising a question: Is "attending to oneself" where an individual's actions should be perceived within the context of a self-conscious responsibility toward a code of ethics that is collective rather than self-servingly individual? That is, *Gun Crazy* raises questions about why characters behave as ethically carelessly as they do, with little or no regard given to the effects and implications of their actions.

Thus Laurie's ethos is one of self-absorption, accompanied by a sense of grandeur and panache. Bart is apparently quite different, a somewhat selfless individual who is blindfolded by his obsession with Laurie, who in turn is blindfolded by her obsession with herself. There is no question that the gunslingers have an inexplicable dynamism between them. As Bart remarks to Laurie, "We go together like guns and ammunition!" Bart cogently anticipates how their criminal life will inevitably end and he is the brains of the crime team, yet he is incapable of derailing the inevitable results of their actions. However, he does have something of logic in him and he well understands the ways of the world, except when (often) his sexual compulsion overpowers his ability to make sound judgments.

Carnival Nights

Laurie grasps little of the precarious situation that she has put them in because of her insatiable lust for material goods and pleasures. She never understands that what she has allowed herself to become has jeopardized her relationship with Bart as well as both their lives. In the days of Athens, it was assumed that an individual could not attend to himself or herself morally (and in other ways) without guidance from others beyond what is learned as part of school training. Laurie's first known "mentor" is Packy, the sleazy carnival barker and her partner in the murder in St. Louis. (His audiences instinctively distrust the con-man, as illustrated by their demand for him to "show the money" for the marksmanship wager between Bart and Laurie.) Bart's carnival confidant is Bluey-Bluey, the traveling clown (an analogue of King Lear's court jester?) who attempts to teach Bart a little about self-understanding, but Bluey-Bluey concludes that "some guys are dumb" and Bart is one of them. The itinerant fool's words are insightful and even Bart acknowledges their accuracy, yet he appears to have little awareness into the tenuous, inevitable relationship between his personal behavior and social norms and mores. Bart's lack of self-perception goes back to his childhood when he has no answer for the judge as to his fascination for guns. Indeed, Bart's ethical consciousness may be more intriguing than Laurie's. Her impulses are not uncommon cravings for material possessions and a comfortable life, as she tells Bart. Her thirst for the existential excitement of bullets entering flesh is, however, frighteningly rare and inexplicable. Bart, on the other hand, has demonstrated a strong resistance to hurting any living thing. Unlike Laurie, however, Bart allows Laurie's sexual power over him to overpower his natural instincts to "take care of himself." If Bart were not involved with Laurie, there is no reason to believe that he would pursue a life of crime. Laurie, on the contrary, has proved (prior to meeting Bart) that crime and murder are in her blood. If Laurie behaves as she does because of a hidden, misanthropic madness deep within her, it diminishes her ability to take care of herself in making ethical decisions. Bart's record of antisocial behavior may suggest an inability to take care of himself that is more accountable because it is clearly not part of his nature. Is it more than a weakness of the flesh? Lewis dares to pose and probe such questions.

Gun Crazy is much more than a generic, woefully stereotypical crime film, as early critics claimed. All good (or great) noir cinema begins with interesting characters. *Gun Crazy*'s leading characters are seductively compelling precisely because they are fascinating outlaws who resist reductive, simplistic explanation. Laurie is a fascinating representation of evil in the vein of Norman Bates (*Psycho*, 1960) or Phyllis Dietrichson (*Double Indemnity*, 1944), captivating mad/evil characters who defy medical or legal classification beyond "sociopathic killer." Laurie, too, is ultimately inexplicable. As Stanley Kauffmann observes, "It's flatly impossible to take *Gun Crazy* seriously as a whole, but it's not as a whole that it should be seen."[8] Further, Andrew Dickos argues that "*Gun Crazy* is told in relatively unfettered moral terms."[9] The surface narrative is simple: public crimes are committed (not unlike those of another infamous tandem, Bonnie and Clyde) and the audience expects justice. However, the moral configurations of the two main characters are worth exploring because they are part of a continuous series of confrontations that engage the viewer. These encounters are intrapersonal, interpersonal, and include drawing the audience into the narrative in a search for meaning. What motivates Laurie and Bart to do what they do? They would seem to be driven by mysterious forces that include, but go beyond, physical passion.

Points of Departure

There are at least two critical points of departure in *Gun Crazy* that introduce the ethical profiles of the lead players.[10] The first incident is Bart's theft of the gun during the summer following his completion of the eighth grade. The opening scene magnifies the effect(s) of Bart's face on a rainy night as we see the lustful eyes of an early teenage boy staring obsessively at something of great beauty and attraction—a revolver in the window case of a hardware store. The late-night street appears to be deserted. Young Bart breaks the window, grabs the gun, and flees so swiftly with his object of lust that he slips on the wet street. The theft appears to have been premeditated as Bart approaches the hardware store with rock or brick already in hand, fully armed to steal the object of his obsession, his fetish. We see a piercing close-up of a face in fear as the fleeing juvenile slips and finds himself staring into the eyes of a lawman hovering above. The steely, squinty eyes of the law disapprovingly examine the boy's countenance. Not a word has yet been spoken, but the two faces tell a short story that needs no words. A young criminal is compelled to possess the object of his desires and the arm of the law intervenes, in a gesture of noir deus ex machina. Why does Bart steal the gun? It is an impulsive act, which he apparently cannot control (just as he apparently cannot control his subsequent obsession with Laurie). Right and wrong are issues of little concern. Satisfaction and deprivation are the controlling emotions of the moment. The stage has been set by and through two faces and without dialogue. We are introduced to a strategic motif: the critical significance of a character's ethical behavior coupled with a search for some kind of explanation.

The second (and equally important) point of departure in *Gun Crazy* involves the initial encounter between Bart and Laurie. They meet at a carnival and the atmosphere is carnivalesque—far beyond a country fair atmosphere of festivity and excitement—which serves for the setting of their first meeting in the shooting tent. The concept of the carnivalesque, as superimposed thematic architecture, implies atmosphere and mood that is surreal, intensely performative, heavily stylized, and "unnatural" in its emphasis on a mockery of traditions that involve masking, satire, and irony. Bart is mesmerized with Laurie and her sexually charged face and body, emphasized by exceptionally tight-fitting gunslinger's slacks. Once Laurie flashes her bedroom eyes, the race is on. Her twin six shooters add to her sexual allure, especially to a man who has a fetish for guns. From this encounter on, Laurie proves able to persuade Bart to do whatever she desires when she puts on her seductive face, even those actions he knows to be contrary to his nature.

Sex and guns, guns and sex—hardly a new motif, yet a signature movement in Lewis's chronicle of obsession. Bart's eyes nearly pop out of his head as he draws near the twin objects of his lust. There is an overriding sexual chemistry between Bart and Laurie that is continuously fueled by the film's overt phallic gun imagery, perhaps to the point of near absurdity, as commentators have noted. Yet there is little question that Laurie's control over Bart is directly related to her sexual power. Laurie is far more complicated than her sexual appeal, of course, and part of her appeal surely lies in her carnivalesque spirit. Laurie is an authentic "carney girl": experienced in carnival swindles, she quickly capitalizes on Bart's carnal cravings for her. Laurie, too, is reciprocally obsessed with Bart and his "gun" as well as his ability to handle guns. Their eyes say more to each other (and to the viewer) than words can convey. Laurie epitomizes carnivalesque in her embodiment of the surreal, the exciting, the taboo, the dangerous. Bart demonstrates reckless behavior in donning the crown of candles for their shooting contest in which a slight miss could mean his death. Laurie, too, displays an equally daredevil predisposition, trusting her life to someone whose ability to handle a gun has never been demonstrated to her (clearly a foreshadowing moment). Laurie later trusts Bart with her life a second time at film's end.

We soon learn that Laurie is no stranger to crime and her shady background includes more than carnival hustles. She has killed a man in a stickup in St. Louis with Packy, her lover and the manager of the carnival troupe. This revelation calls attention to Laurie's persona of guise and disguise. On the surface, she appears at first introduction to be a homespun "Annie Oakley," clad in snug western wear, which masks (and foreshadows) her identity as a cold-blooded killer. Is Laurie's guise also an internal disguise? Is she masking herself from herself? This observation is not to suggest schizophrenia (a difficult and redoubtable analysis), but how much explicit pretence is at work in her declamations? What does she believe and how might the viewer determine the "authenticity" of her beliefs? Which is the guise and which is the disguise? What we do know is that that neither Laurie nor Bart have an ethical system in place (at least a paradigm of positive ethics) that is built on a systematic set of principles. In antiquity, moral training was often compared to athletic development. One practiced specific physical moves in order to be successful when an opportunity presented itself. So, too, in ethical practice the individual was encouraged to be prepared to make "correct" ethical decisions in response to the exigencies of specific circumstances. There is no indication that Laurie or Bart has ever developed any kind of ethical regimen, and it is the wanton violence of the film that raises ethical questions about Bart and Laurie that extend beyond classifying them as simply amoral or immoral without qualification.

Field(s) of Experience

The relationship between Laurie and Bart is one that evolves over time as a result of the encounters between them. Foucault's theory of the "field of experience" is pertinent to the configuration of the conditions involving

Laurie and Bart and their matrix of experiences. As Foucault argues, "It [a field of experience] is basically a matter of different examples in which the three fundamental elements of any experience are implicated: a game of truth, relations of power, and forms of relations to oneself and to others."[11] "Truth" is clearly a game between Laurie and Bart and, arguably, a game within themselves. It is clear from the beginning of their relationship that Laurie is gaming Bart, repeatedly telling him what he wants to hear, especially her pledges to give up their life of crime as soon as they are financially independent. She immunizes him, through sexual and romantic chemistry, against his resistant inner ethical voice that crime is wrong. Truth, for Laurie, lies deep within that impenetrable, undecipherable topography of her subconscious mind, yet we are given hints that Laurie's self-understanding occasionally bubbles to the surface. I would suggest that these moments of self-recognition are implied by Laurie's look of silence after Bart penetrates her steely shell with challenging questions and statements.[12] As Bart tells her, "I was an honest guy." The implication is clear: until he met Laurie he possessed a "standard" code of ethics. The collective field of experience between Laurie and Bart is catalyzed by her assertion of control, always energized by Bart's obsession with her. There is a power vacuum in their relationship that she does not hesitate to fill. Bart remains frozen in a continual pattern of deferral to her will and whims. Thus their alliance is dependent on a critical primary cause: Laurie's deference to her unchecked desires for material gain.

The identities of the outlaws are in ongoing transformation, and, along with their ethical stances, their identities are the cumulative result of encounters with each other and within themselves. As Foucault observes in defining ethics, "If by ethics you mean the relationship you have to yourself when you act, then I would say that it intends to be an ethics."[13] Laurie and Bart are engaged, respectively, in an incessant, futile search to create some kind of meaning in their lives and their quests, which are clearly not the same, and they are affected by the satisfaction or frustration of their particular objectives and desires. Their mutual sexual lust is complemented and catalyzed by their obsession with guns. Laurie's material motivation is powerful and it consistently overpowers Bart's conscience. However, Bart was, arguably, a reasonable and ethical person when he first meets Laurie.

Laurie is instinctively and irredeemably evil, as revealed in her assertion to Bart following their posthaste wedding (a ceremony probably included because of the Hays Code): "You're not getting any bargain. I've got a funny feeling that I want to be good. I don't know. Maybe I can't." Her self-portrait as constitutionally bad is an ironic, almost laughable response to Bart's naive confession to her that he had stolen a gun as a youth (this to a woman who has committed murder). This marked difference in their respective "coming clean" exchanges reveals a dramatic difference between the characters. Bart is simple and naive, as revealed in his recognition of his sense of himself: "I don't want to look in the mirror and see nothing but a stickup man starring back at me." Although Bart seems to "knows himself," he never fully grasps Laurie's sociopathic nature. In confronting her, he wildly blurts out a rhetorical question (which is near comic): "Why do you murder people? Why can't you let them live?"[14] Bart might as well ask why the sun rises. This exchange reveals Laurie to be cunningly depraved, yet not without insight into herself. It also raises the nagging question about her essential orientation toward human interaction. If it is her "nature" to be evil (in comparison to choosing evil), how does this knowledge affect our reception of her? (The same question might be asked regarding *Detour*'s Vera and *Double Indemnity*'s Phyllis Dietrichson). Bart has a significantly different self-perception, as revealed by his categorical assessment of what he is not: "Laurie, I'm not a killer. I don't want to be a killer." Bart's words foreshadow, again, the one and only time that he becomes a killer. Bart's language also reminds us that words always carry judgments. As V. N. Volosinov points out, "No utterance can be put together without value judgment. Every utterance is above all an evaluative orientation. Therefore, each element in living utterance not only has a meaning but also has a value."[15] Values, of course, always carry ethical qualities, and the language of Laurie and Bart says as much about their ethics as their actions and perhaps more because their words provide possible clues to their motives.

These intriguing portraits reveal a series of figural displacements from the very beginning when Annie Laurie Starr is introduced as "straight from England"—something she is not.[16] One of the major reasons why these characters are so infectiously captivating is their seductive portraits of ethical representations.[17] *Gun Crazy*, like all noir cinema, is steeped in moral issues that underlie interpersonal and criminal behavior. Lewis challenges tradition—and not only that of crime drama but of cinematic narrative in general. *Gun Crazy* calls into question not only the importance (and disregard) of virtue but, more important, the film questions the very possibility of virtue in the central characters. I would suggest that the film is a litany of moral questions, an inquiry and exploration into ethics rather than a demonstration of failed ethics, which is how the film has often been received for over half a century.

There is a double gesture at work in the early scenes: characters express themselves through disguise, or misrepresentation of what "appears to be." The gun-toting duo continually don disguises to facilitate their safe conduct through police checkpoints: Bart wears a navy uniform, they both dress like suburban middle-class travelers, Bart becomes a meat handler, and Laurie becomes an office worker in their attempt to pull off a meat-packing heist of great magnitude. Hence a structural mode of tension is introduced—the difference between one face, mask, or guise and one or more alternative representations of a character, a calculus of "misrepresentations." These differences, I would suggest, do not signify a reductive interpretation of character as "appearance" and "reality." Rather, they suggest a multiplicity of appearances that deny the possibility of piercing the outer veil to expose the inner, "real" character and his or her ethical center. Consider Bart's juvenile gun theft and the subsequent courtroom scene: a scene of order and social restoration. Bart is admonished by the judge for the youthful offender's obsession with guns and sent to reform school, where he remains until he is old enough to join the army, which makes him a firearms instructor. Bart has committed a serious crime, of course, but it is apparent that he suffers from an inexplicable psychological "condition." How important to our ethical judgment of a character is something that a character cannot control?

Ethical Responsibility

Young Bart's experience opens a series of ethical questions: To whom does one bear an ethical responsibility? To oneself? To others? To a lover? A series of ethical obligations are intertwined in the tapestry of possibilities in *Gun Crazy*, which perhaps explains its half-century appeal. Yet there is a surface, explicit ethical structure to the film: Laurie and Bart commit crimes. There are ethical codes at work in the work of criminals. There is an "ethics of encounter," an ethics of interrelationship between Bart and Laurie from the very beginning of the film. Emmanuel Levinas, phenomenologist and ethical theorist, examines personal, interactive relationships between and among individuals as the foundation for the determination of ethical positioning. His perspective focuses on encounters in which there is often a precondition of established relationship. (Laurie and Bart fit into this paradigm.) There is a moral umbilical cord attached between those configured in encounters, and interactions between individuals determines ethical positioning. Scenes of encounter, according to Levinas, reveal identity, particularly as they denote ethical values. Collaborators in these scenes necessarily reveal their ethical status precisely because of the encounter, which provides the condition(s) for ethical exposition. In the words of Levinas, "For me, the term ethics always signifies the fact of the encounter, of the relation of myself with the Other: a scission of Being in the encounter—without coincidence!"[18] Ethics, then, is necessarily determined by our interactions with others. Bart most likely would not have become an adult criminal without his encounter with Laurie. Laurie probably would not have elected to pursue a series of violent road crimes without the gun expertise and emotional support of Bart. Their initial encounter was the birthing cauldron for their brief life of crime.

The verbal and physical interchanges between Bart and Laurie reveal overt moral meaning. Indeed, many of their conversations deal directly with the moral nature of their acts as well as their ethical implications; for example, their elaborate planning and rehearsal of the meat-packing robbery. As Kenneth Burke points out, it is a failure of semantic reality to fail to acknowledge this imperative: "It fosters, sometimes explicitly, sometimes by implication, the notion that one may comprehensively discuss human and social events in a nonmoral vocabulary, and that perception itself is a nonmoral act. It is the moral impulse that motivates perception, giving it both intensity and direction, suggesting what to look for and what to look out for."[19] Bart cannot anticipate with certainty that Laurie will kill two people without cause in the robbery, but Laurie gives every indication that she will do whatever is necessary and that includes murder. Her murderous acts are ethical violations that Bart should have anticipated were he not mesmerized by Laurie.

The calculus of ethics goes further than antisocial behavior, and their interpersonal relationship is part of the woof and warp of Laurie and Bart. At a deeper level there is an internal ethical scope in play in Laurie and Bart, and their ranges are clearly distinct. Further, the words and actions of both characters raise compelling questions about their respective psychological instabilities, which in turn raises another series of questions about the dimensions of ethical responsibility in individuals who are criminally driven. Undoubtedly, Laurie exhibits sociopathic behavior that invokes questions about her fitness of mind. She displays a zeitgeist of evil in full provocation. As Aaron Lazenby argues, "Not content to let her past drive her into her shell, Annie lashes out at the world and demands that she be paid back, with interest, for the injuries she's endured."[20] And if her mental state is dysfunction, as I think it is, what conclusions might be drawn about her ethical status? Laurie, especially, is a psychological sticky wicket not given, I believe, to reductive classification. She is an exemplary femme fatale, about as evil a character one finds in the murky, lurid world of noir.

Character Is Destiny

Heraclitus said that character is destiny and apparently Lewis agreed with him because the destinies of Laurie and Bart are the direct result of their

Deadly is the female: Joseph H. Lewis's *Gun Crazy* (1950).

actions within explicit moral contexts. If Aristotle is correct that moral virtue is a habit, then an absence of morality is also a habit and this possibility is in play from the opening of *Gun Crazy*. Heraclitus also believed that all phenomena exist in a state of tension with their opposites, which is sometimes referred to as a "state of flux." At some point the tension between forces in opposition is often reconciled. *Gun Crazy* is a portrait of characters in tension, but it is a complex interrelated configuration of opposites that is ultimately never reconciled. At one level, Bart and Laurie reveal internal tensions within themselves. At other times, there is discernable tension between the two of them. And there is the usual noir pattern of tension between the criminal duo and society at large, including the audience. The daring meat-packing robbery dramatically reveals Laurie's character as she shoots Augustine Sifert, an "old biddy" in Laurie's words, and then shoots a guard as they exit the plant. Laurie is now seen to be the killer that we anticipated, By the time of their last robbery, Laurie has killed at least three people, including the St. Louis murder. Bart has shot nothing since he killed a baby chick in his youth.

Laurie loves the thrill of crime and the smell of blood. She also loves the financial rewards of crime. Bart has no interest in material things, and he has no natural interest in crime. At one point he muses about his life before Lady Oakley: "I *was* a fairly honest guy." He hopelessly and selflessly craves the love of his woman. Even his fascination with guns seems to fade over the course of the film. He surrenders everything for her, even his life, and Bart loses his perspective on life, the price of his unexamined ethos. When he reads about the deaths in their big heist, Bart is "shocked," in spite of the fact that he witnessed Laurie firing her gun on both occasions.

What are we to make of the bizarre final scenes of *Gun Crazy*? Bart and Laurie manage to stowaway on a train to the home of Ruby, sister of Bart. The outlaws literally take over the house, and Laurie refuses to take her eyes off of Ruby out of fear that she will call the police. The ethical codes of both Laurie and Bart have evolved to the point where the disruption of Bart's family is a natural segment in the developing chain of events. Indeed, the disruption of family life is now a necessary part of their modus operandi. As Sylvia Harvey points out, "In *Gun Crazy* the isolation of the couple as well as their nonconformity to certain social norms is emphasized by the way in which they are presented as outsiders to the family and family life. Taking refuge with Bart's family at the end of the film, they so clearly do not belong; they constitute a violent eruption into the ordered patterns of family life."[21] The "violent eruption" of the home invasion is yet another thread in the duo's tapestry of immorality.

All narratives reveal change over time and cause and effect. The final scene is perhaps *Gun Crazy*'s utmost encounter—the murder of a lover by a lover. This final act of violence defies expectations. The relationship between Bart and Laurie begins and ends with the trauma of guns and shooting. Either character could easily have been killed in their initial encounter. Laurie mentioned that once before she had "shot low," presumably shooting someone wearing the crown of candles. What was Laurie thinking about as she paused, extensively, before firing her sixth candle shot above Bart's head? Was she fearful of killing Bart? Perhaps. If so, perhaps she does have a small remnant of a conscience. Yet she had killed before and continues to attempt to kill before she is killed.

Ethical questions are raised by the bizarre killing of Laurie of the film, which in turn (presumably) causes the killing of Bart by Sheriff Clyde. On one level, Bart shooting Laurie is a fitting, although ironic, adjudication of her life and crimes. Laurie, thoroughly and inexplicably evil, has shown little conscience, in spite of her occasional protests to the contrary. The resolution of the film calls for her to be dispatched, but death by Bart, a lover and gunman who does not have it in him to shoot an animal? The dreamlike quality of the end of the film serves both as macroimage and synecdoche for the film's representation of a hazy world of ethical values. A Hollywood resolution gives the audience what it wants, but it is an ironic conclusion. Bart is not a killer—yet he kills the one person he loves. By film's end there remains a suffusion of unanswered ethical questions. However, Bart and Laurie have earned their fates, as character is destiny.

Notes

1. I refer to originality that goes beyond Lewis's backseat single-take bank robbery scene that is usually identified as his signature mark as a seminal auteur.

2. A significant segment of the American film audience has long been obsessed with the concept of "crazy," which means much more than mental illness. In ancient times, "madness" (especially Platonic madness) also meant inspiration, obsession, and complicated irrationality. In Plato's *Phaedrus*, for example, it is necessary for madness to combine with reason in order to express philosophical truth through the art of rhetoric. In *Gun Crazy* there is an element of the "cunningly crazy" in the behavior of the characters, especially Laurie. There is also craziness in the wanton rebellion against society's ethical norms.

3. James Naremore, *More than Night: Film Noir in Its Contexts*, updated and expanded ed. (Berkeley: University of California Press, 2008), 151.

4. Michael J. Hyde, "Introduction: Rhetorically, We Dwell," in *The Ethos of Rhetoric* (Columbia: University of South Carolina Press, 2004), xiii–xxviii.

5. This kind of special, circumstantial time is *kairos*, another dominant concept from ancient Greece that has particular relevance to ethics. All ethical judgments and acts are made in response to the qualities of specific circumstances. For a discussion of the historical dimensions of *kairos* in ancient Greece, see Phillip Sipiora, "The Ancient Concept of *Kairos*," in *Kairos and Rhetoric: Essays in History, Theory, and Praxis*, ed. Phillip Sipiora and James S. Baumlin (Albany: SUNY Press, 2002), 1–22.

6. An important premise of my analysis is recognition of Lewis as a director whose films are shaped by his philosophical perspectives, his cultural sensibilities. Although he is a highly stylized representative of auteur theory in practice, I would extend his involvement to include much more than control of character, cameras, angles, locations, shots, and so forth. It is his understanding of human experience with which I am most concerned. The elements of filmmaking for which he is recognized are only part of his work as an artist—some of which lies in the realm of the subconscious of his characters. What is accessible to analysis, of course, is the "surface" cinematic product (the *interpretant* in Heidegger's lexicon).

7. Michel Foucault, *Ethics: Subjectivity and Truth*, ed. Paul Rabinow (New York: New Press, 1997), 97.

8. Stanley Kauffmann, "Not So Crazy," *New Republic*, June 24, 1991, 26.

9. Andrew Dickos, *Street with No Name: A History of the Classic American Film Noir* (Lexington: University Press of Kentucky, 2002), 153.

10. A point of departure (*point de départ*) is a critical element in literary interpretation in the theoretical work of Belgian critic Georges Poulet, who argues that an author chooses a particular point (or points) of entry to introduce (and thereby emphasize) strategic elements of character identification through the phenomenological interactions of characters, which carry strategic implications. These phenomenological gestures, I would argue, are also integral to the establishment of cinematic characters' respective ethical identities. An interpretation of *Gun Crazy* is significantly shaped by Bart's introduction to the viewer as an obsessed thief. Laurie's introduction as a (seemingly) unstable sharpshooter shaped by her obsession with Bart says a great deal about her character. For Poulet's theoretical work, see Georges Poulet, *Le point de départ* (Paris: Plon, 1964).

11. Foucault, *Ethics*, 117.

12. A striking example is the moment before Bart kills Laurie when he warns her not to shoot Clyde and Dave. Laurie says nothing, but the look in her eyes suggests that she knows exactly how close death is, perhaps denying to herself that it will come at the hand of Bart. The many implied silences in *Gun Crazy* are a reservoir of speculation, particularly in regard to Foucault's attention to the significance of silence(s). Foucault, *Ethics*, 122ff.

13. Ibid., 131.

14. There is a double gesture to Bart's question. If the question is rhetorical, it declaims his contempt and frustration for her murderous ways. If the question is grammatical, it signifies a search for meaning behind Laurie's behavior, some kind of explanation for her instinctive, pervasive immorality.

15. V. N. Volosinov, *Marxism and the Philosophy of Language*, trans. Ladislav Matejka and I. R. Titunik (New York: Seminar Press, 1973), 105.

16. Peggy Cummins, who played Annie Laure Starr, was born in Wales and appeared on the London stage as early as 1938 at the age of thirteen. We are told by Laurie that she hails from California.

17. The study of ethics has always been concerned with the relationship between principles or rule of morality and the relationship of individual behavior to general codes. In antiquity there was a much stronger emphasis on standardizing or "normalizing" individual behavior to generic norms in comparison to today's more eclectic approaches to the relationship between the individual and society.

18. Quoted in Simon Critchley, *The Ethics of Deconstruction* (Oxford: Blackwell, 1992), 17.

19. Kenneth Burke, *The Philosophy of Literary Form: Studies in Symbolic Action* (Berkeley: University of California Press 1969), 164.

20. Aaron Lazenby, "Gun Crazy," Filmcritic.com, March 17, 2004, http://www.filmcritic.com/reviews/1949/gun-crazy/.

21. Sylvia Harvey, "Woman's Place: The Absent Family of Film Noir," *Women in Film Noir*, new ed., ed. Ann Kaplan (London: BFI, 1998), 43.

Contributors

Lance Duerfahrd is assistant professor of film and photography studies in the English Department at Purdue University. He is the author of essays on Frederick Wiseman, Billy Wilder, Ed Wood, and Klaus Kinski (in the *Blackwell Companion to Werner Herzog*, forthcoming). He is completing a manuscript on Samuel Beckett and the work of poverty.

Michael E. Grost is a mystery writer, abstract painter, and film historian who lives near Detroit, Michigan. His film website (http://mikegrost.com/film.htm) contains his detailed critical studies of over one hundred directors, including book-length works on Fritz Lang, Vincente Minnelli, Raoul Walsh, and Joseph H. Lewis. His website also includes his mystery short stories, a large-scale history of detective fiction, and an equally massive critical study of golden age and silver age American comic books.

David J. Hogan is a division publisher with Chicago-based Publications International Ltd. He has conceived and cowritten many books of illustrated history on topics as diverse as the Holocaust, the American civil rights movement, World War II, the American West, and the 1950s. He has been a published film historian since 1973, with articles and reviews in *Cinefantastique, Photon, Filmfax, Moviegoer*, and others. His books include *Who's Who of the Horrors and Other Fantasy Films; Dark Romance: Sexuality in the Horror Film* (US and British editions); and a multiauthor essay collection, *Science Fiction America*. A BMW fancier, Hogan writes on vintage cars for *Collectible Automobile* magazine and has contributed to books of auto and aviation history. He lives with his wife, Kim, their three children, and a menagerie of animals in suburban Chicago, in a house that bulges ominously with books, music, and movies.

Brian Hoyle is a lecturer in film studies and English at the University of Dundee. He completed his PhD on British art cinema at the University of Hull in 2006. He has written articles on Derek Jarman, Sally Potter, Orson Welles, and the relationship between gangster films and comics. He has also recently contributed a chapter to the new study *Ken Russell: Re-Viewing Britain's Last Mannerist* (Scarecrow, 2009) and has an article on Chris Petit's *Radio On* in a forthcoming edition of the *British Journal of Cinema and Television*. He is currently writing a monograph on the films of John Boorman.

Christopher Justice is a lecturer at the University of Baltimore and its director of expository writing. He teaches writing, literature, film, and journalism courses. An alumnus of the University of Massachusetts Amherst, Loyola College, the University of New Mexico, and Rutgers University, he writes widely about various topics including auteurism, genre studies, and film history. Recent essays have explored the sexploitation films of Edgar G. Ulmer, the role of travel in Michael Haneke's films, and the political rhetoric of Robert Zemeckis; he's also working on a chapter about depictions of the Arctic in eco-trauma films. His monthly column, "The Tackle Box," appears in *PopMatters* and explores the confluence of fishing and popular culture. Born and raised in New Jersey, he currently resides in Owings Mills, Maryland, with his wife and children.

Michael Lee holds the Sam K. Viersen Jr. Professorship in Musicology at the University of Oklahoma. He researches and publishes on the Ballets Russes, American experimental music, and film music. His current large-scale project concerns Roy Webb's music for the films of Val Lewton. He is managing editor for the journal *Horror Studies*.

Hugh S. Manon is director of screen studies at Clark University where he specializes in Lacanian theory and film noir. He has published in *Cinema Journal, Film Criticism, Framework*, and the *International Journal of Žižek Studies*, as well as in numerous anthologies, including articles on Tod Browning, Edgar G. Ulmer, George Romero, Billy Wilder's *Double Indemnity*, Michael Haneke's *Caché*, and Stanley Kubrick's film noirs. He is interested in lo-fi and punk representation in relation to the psychodynamics of failure and is currently developing a book project titled "Lack and Lossless-ness: Toward a Lacanian Aesthetics."

Francis M. Nevins is a professor at St. Louis University School of Law, where he has taught since 1971. In addition to his writings on legal subjects he is the author of six mystery novels. He has also written about forty short stories, which have appeared in *Ellery Queen, Alfred Hitchcock*, and other national magazines and many of which have been reprinted in leading mystery anthologies. He has edited more than fifteen mystery anthologies and collections and has written several nonfiction books on the genre. He has also published many articles dealing with movies and four books on the same subject: *The Films of Hopalong Cassidy* (1988), *The Films of the Cisco Kid* (1998), *Joseph H. Lewis: Overview, Interview, and Filmography* (1998), and *Paul Landres: A Director's Stories* (2000).

Gary D. Rhodes is lecturer and codirector of film studies at The Queen's University of Belfast, Northern Ireland. He is the author of such books as *Lugosi* (McFarland, 1997), *White Zombie: Anatomy of a Horror Film* (McFarland, 2002), and *The Perils of Moviegoing in America, 1896–1950* (Continuum, 2011), as well as the editor of such anthologies as *Horror at the Drive-In* (McFarland, 2001) and *Edgar G. Ulmer: Detour on Poverty Row* (Lexington, 2008). Rhodes is also the writer-director of such documentary films as *Fiddlin' Man: The Life and Times of Bob Wills* (1994), *Chair* (2000), and *Banned in Oklahoma* (2004).

Marlisa Santos is an associate professor and director of the division of humanities in the Farquhar College of Arts and Sciences at Nova Southeastern University in Fort Lauderdale, Florida. She has published and presented various papers on film in edited anthologies and at national conferences. Her most recent publications are essays on Edgar Ulmer and Martin Scorsese for film and popular culture anthologies. Her latest project is *The Dark Mirror: Psychiatry and Film Noir* (Lexington, 2010).

Robert Singer is a professor of English at Kingsborough, CUNY and adjunct professor of liberal studies and film studies (pending) at the Graduate Center, CUNY. He received a PhD from New York University in comparative literature. His areas of expertise include literary and film interrelations, interdisciplinary research in film history and aesthetics, and comparative studies. He coedited *Zola and Film* (2005), *The Brooklyn Film* (2003), and he also coauthored the text *The History of Brooklyn's Three Major Performing Arts Institutions* (2003). He is the vice president of AIZEN, and he has written and directed several independent short films.

Phillip Sipiora is professor of English and film studies at the University of South Florida. He is the author or editor of three books and has published approximately three dozen scholarly essays, including articles on the work of Edgar G. Ulmer, Billy Wilder, and Stanley Kubrick. He has lectured nationally and internationally on twentieth-century literature and film and is the founding editor of the *Mailer Review*.

Brian Taves (PhD, University of Southern California) has been a film archivist with the Library of Congress since 1990. He is the author of such books as *Robert Florey, the French Expressionist* (Scarecrow, 1986), *The Romance of Adventure: The Genre of Historical Adventure Movies* (University Press of Mississippi, 1993), *Talbot Mundy, Philosopher of Adventure* (McFarland, 2005), and *P. G. Wodehouse: Screenwriting, Satire, and Adaptation* (McFarland, 2006). He has edited several other books, has written well over a hundred articles and chapters in other volumes, and is currently completing books on Thomas H. Ince and on the three hundred film and television adaptations of Jules Verne produced worldwide.

Yannis Tzioumakis is a lecturer in communication and media at the University of Liverpool. His research specializes in American cinema and the business of media entertainment. His books include *American Independent Cinema: An Introduction* (2006) *The Spanish Prisoner* (2009), *Hollywood's Indies: Classics Divisions, Specialty Labels and the American Film Market* (2012), all for Edinburgh University Press, and, as a coeditor, *Greek Cinema: Texts, Forms, Identities* (2011) for Intellect. He is currently coediting *The Time of Our Lives: Dirty Dancing and Popular Culture* (Wayne State University Press) and *American Independent Cinema: Indie, Indiewood and Beyond* (Routledge). He is also coediting the American Indies series for Edinburgh University Press, which has published five volumes since 2009.

Tony Williams is professor and head of film studies in the Department of English at Southern Illinois University at Carbondale. He is author of *The Cinema of George A. Romero: Knight of the Living Dead* (Wallflower Press, 2003), *Body and Soul: The Cinematic Vision of Robert Aldrich* (Scarecrow Press, 2004), and *John Woo's Bullet in the Head* (Hong Kong University Press, 2009), and coeditor (with Steven Jay Schneider) of *Horror International* (Wayne State University Press, 2005).

Index

Page numbers in italics refer to illustrations.

Across to Singapore (1928), 118
Act of Violence (1948), 235
"Actress, The" (1961), 64, 65, 72
Adams, Ernie, 48, 86, 88
Al Capone (1959), 197
Alcoa Theatre (1959), 77
Aldrich, Robert, 103, 113, 178, 180, 202
Allen, Lewis, 197
Alton, John, 180, 182, 196, 225
Andrew, Geoff, 152
Angel Heart (1987), 147, 238
Angels Wash Their Faces, The (1938), 22
Angels with Dirty Faces (1938), 21, 22
Anger, Kenneth, 197
Ape Man The (1943), 84, 97
Arizona Cyclone (1941), 74
Armetta, Henry, 92
Armstrong, R. G., 214
Arnaz, Desi, 188
Arnold, Martin, 60
Arsenic and Old Lace (1944), 86
Ashby, Hal, 194
Asphalt Jungle, The (1950), 163, 164
Asther, Nils, 117
Attack! (1956), 202
Atwill, Lionel, 100
Autumn Leaves (1957), 202

Bad and the Beautiful, The (1952), 197
Baker, Bob, 68
Ball, Lucille, 188
"Baranca" (1960), 65, 70, 71

Barnett, Vince, 97
Barricade (1939), 116
Barrios, Richard, 188
Bauer, Christian, xi
Bazin, André, 46, 114, 225
Beaudine, William, 97
Berger, Harris, 22
Beyond the Forest (1949), 218
Biesen, Sheri Chinen, 235, 237
Bigamist, The (1953), 200
Big Combo, The (1955), 3, 6, 11, 13, 50, 67, 72, 95, 99, 108, 134, 140, 146, 151, 157, 169, 177, 178–197, 203, 225, 226, 227, 228, 252
Big Heat, The (1953), 158, 166, 167, 183, 186
Big Knife, The (1955), 202
Big Valley, The (1965–69), 11, 63, 65, 73, 75, 76, 124
Birth of a Nation, The (1915), 81
Bitter Tea of General Yen, The (1932), 117
Bitter Victory (1957), 202
Black Cat, The (1934), 85, 92, 94
Black Dragons (1942), 84
Blade Runner (1982), 113
Blair, Betsy, 201, 216
Blazing Six Shooters (1940), 64, 66
Block, Lawrence, ix
Blue Dahlia, The (1946), 235
Boehm, Sydney, 166
Boetticher, Budd, 201

275

Bogdanovich, Peter, 38, 41, 86, 110, 191, 200, 208, 223
Bombs over Burma (1942), 5, 35, 68, 72, 116–133
Bonanza (1959–73), 63, 65, 78
Bond, Ward, 201, *203*
Bonnie and Clyde (1967), 238
"Boomerang" (1959), 78
"Boots with My Father's Name" (1965), 124
Borde, Raymond, 178, 179, 192, 239
Border Wolves (1938), 68
Bordwell, David, 147, 150, 199, 201, 216, 217
Boss of Hangtown Mesa (1942), 64, 72, 74, 82
Bottom of the Bottle (1956), 218
Bowery at Midnight (1942), 84, 97
Boy of the Streets (1937), 16
Boys of the City (1940), 12, 25–30, 34
Branded (1965–66), 68, 69, 200
Breck, Peter, 75
Bresson, Robert, 154, 156
Bride of Frankenstein (1935), 93
Bride of the Monster (1955), 84
Broken Lance (1954), 202
Brontë, Emily, 202
Brooks, Richard, 196
Brown, Royal S., 243
Browning, Tod, 83
Brute Force (1947), 187
Buck, Pearl S., 131
"Bullet, The" (1963), 65, 66, 71
Burks, Robert, 225

Cabot, Sebastian, 209
Call Northside 777 (1948), 164
Capp, Rose, 224, 226
Carr, Trem, 15
Caruso, Anthony, 173
Casablanca (1943), 180
Cat and the Canary, The (1927), 93, 94
Cat People (1942), 246
Catered Affair, The (1956), 196
Caught (1949), 156, 157
Chaplin, Charles, 196

Chaumeton, Étienne, 178, 179, 192, 239
Cheirel, Michele, 146
Chester, Hal E., 22
Christopher, Nicholas, 135, 139, 144
Citizen Kane (1941), 81, 83, 96, 202, 216, 218, 225
City of Bad Men (1953), 200
Clarens, Carlos, 180
Clarke, Alan, 220
Cline, Robert E., 23
Clockwork Orange, A (1971), 93
"Closer Than a Brother" (1961), 71
Club Havana (1945), 110
Codee, Ann, 3
Cohen, Larry, 200
Columbia Pictures, 12, 13, 20, 146, 153
Coming Home (1978), 194
Compson, Betty, 48
Connections (1981–92), 65
Connors, Chuck, 62, 72, 77
Consolidated Film Industries, 16
Conte, Richard, 50, 181, 191, 193
Conti, Albert, 92
Continental Talking Pictures, 15
Cooper, Jackie, 16, 19,
Cooper, James Fenimore, 20
Coppola, Francis Ford, 185–186
Corey, Wendell, 201
Corpse Vanishes, The (1942), 84, 97
Cotten, Joseph, 3, 200, 201, 202, *203*, 206, 218
Courage of the West (1937), 64, 68, 72, 111
Cowie, Elizabeth, 140
Craven, Wes, 86
Crawford, Joan, 239
Crawford, Johnny, 77
Criminals Within (1943), 122
Crimson City, The (1928), 120
Crimson Kimono, The (1959), 201
Cronyn, Hume, 187
Cry of the Hunted (1953), 6, 12
Cummins, Peggy, 3, 49, 51, 183, *236*, 248, 266, 269
Currie, Louise, 97
Curtiz, Michael, 83, 180

Dall, John, 3, 49, 51
Daniel Boone (1964–70), 11, 64, 68, 70
Dark, Christopher, 202
Dark Waters (1944), 139
Darro, Frankie, 22
Dassin, Jules, 164, 165, 187
Daughter of the Dragon (1931), 130
Daughter of Shanghai (1937), 119, 129
Davis, Bette, 41, 59
"Day of the Hunter" (1960), 76
Dead End (1937), 21
Deadly Is the Female (1950). See *Gun Crazy* (1950)
"Deadly Wait, The," 63, 64, 75, 78
Deanimated (2002), 60
Dead End Kids, The, 22
"Death Never Rides Alone" (1962), 70
Defiant Ones, The (1958), 208
Dell, Lucy, 123
Denison, Leslie, 123, *126*, 127
"Deserter, The," (1960), 63, 68, 70, 71
Detectives Starring Robert Taylor, The (1959–62), 63, 68
Detour (1945), 56, 160, 187, 263
Devil Bat, The (1940), 84
Dickos, Andrew, 134, 144, 226, 227, 231, 237, 259
Dick Powell Show, The (1962), 77
Dieterle, William, 83
Dmytryk, Edward, 202
Doane, Mary Ann, 142
Dodd, Claire, 100
Donlevy, Brian, 184
Donner, Richard, 72
Double Indemnity (1944), 259, 263
Douglas, Kirk, 208
Dr. Jekyll and Mr. Hyde (1932), 92
Dr. Strangelove (1964), 209
Dracula (1931), 83, 92, 95
Dragon Seed (1944), 131
Drifting (1923), 120
Duel in the Sun (1946), 206, 207, 218
"Duel of Honor" (1958), 63, 69–72
Duerfahrd, Lance, 5, 271
Duff, Howard, 177
Dumb Waiter, The (1957), 190

Dwan, Allan, 201

Eagle-Lion Films, 120
East Side Kids (1940), 13, 22, 25, 28,
East Side Kids, The, 5, 11, 12, 15, 19, 21, 23, 26, 27, 30, 32, 34
Easy Rider (1969), 51
"Eddie's Daughter" (1959), 72
Edwards, Vince, 184
Eichberg, Richard, 119
Eisenhower, President Dwight D., 236
Eisenstein, Sergei, 112
Elephant (1988), 220
Ellery Queen's Penthouse Mystery (1941), 119
Elliott, William, 71
Empire Films, 15
Essex, 196
Everson, William K., 35
Exterminating Angel, The (1962), 110

"Face of Yesterday" (1961), 65, 69
Falcon in San Francisco, The (1945), 12, 124
Fallen Angel (1945), 150
Fat Man, The (ca. 1958), 67–68
Feeney, Edward F., 21
Fix, Paul, 77
Fleming, Victor, 83
Flippen, Jay C., 206
Florey, Robert, 83
Flying Wild (1941), 13, 34
Flynn, Charles, 14,
Foch, Nina, 3, 39, 45, 134, 170, *174*
Force of Evil (1948), 212, 219
Ford, Glenn, 75, 167, *174, 175,* 176, 183, 192
Ford, John, 150, 201
Foucault, Michel, 269
Four Star Productions, 63, 208
"Fourflusher, The" (1960), 64
Frankenstein (1931), 83
Franklin, Peter, 246
Frazer, Robert, 89
Freeman, Helen, 42
Friedan, Betty, 187

Index 277

Fuller, Sam, 114, 150, 201
Furies, The (1951), 201, 203, 217

Gagnon, John, 189
Gallery of Mme. Liu-Tsong, The (1951), 118
General Died at Dawn, The (1936), 116
George, George W., 200
Geray, Steven, 42, 47, 141, 146, *148*
Gerrard, Charles, 92
Ghosts on the Loose (1943), 84, 97
Gleason, James, 17
Glen or Glenda (1953), 84
Godfather, The (1972), 186
Godfather, Part II, The (1974), 186
Godfather, Part III, The (1990), 186
Gorcey, Leo, 21, 22, *23*, 31
Godard, Jean-Luc, 93
Good Earth, The (1937) 116, 117, 130, 131
Gordon, C. Henry, 117
Gould, Harvey, 97
Gorbman, Claudia, 245–246
Grahame, Gloria, 192
Grand National Films, 12, 16
Griffith, D. W., 102
Grost, Michael E., 5, 217, 271
Gun Crazy (1950), ix, xi, *4*, *7*, 12, 13, 44, 45, 46, 49, *50*, 51–52, 54, 55, 56, 58, 64, 68, 70, 82, 95, 99, 110, 127, 134, 146, 157, 167, 169, 177, 178, 216, 223–241, 242–254, 255–269
Gunsmoke (1955–75), 11, 65

Halliday Brand, The (1957), 3, 6, 64, 73, 108, 124, 199, 200, 201–208, 209, 210, 211, 212, 215, 216, 217, 218, 219, 220
Halperin, Victor, 94
"Hangman, The" (1960), 64
Hard, Fast, and Beautiful (1951), 200
Harington, Joy, 38
Harvey, Sylvia, 139, 267
Hathaway, Henry, 164
Hawks, Howard, 77, 150
Hayden, Sterling, 58, 209, 210, 211, *213*, 215, 218

He Walked by Night (1948), 165, 196
Hell on Frisco Bay (1955), 166
"Heller" (1960), 65
"Hero" (1960), 70, 78
Herrmann, Bernard, 246
Hervey, Harry, 120
Hickox, Douglas, 86
"Hiding Place, The" (1959), 68
High Wall (1947), 166
Hill, Robert F., 13, 28
Hirsch, Foster, 135, 237
Hitchcock, Alfred, 76, 112, 138, 147, 152, 225
Hitchhiker, The (1953), 200
Hitler—Beast of Berlin (1939), 120
Hogan, David J., 6, 271
Höller, Carsten, 65
Hollywood on Parade (1933), 86
Hollywood Revue of 1929, The (1929), 86
"Honest Abe" (1961), 64, 69, 70, 71, 75
Hopper, Dennis, 51
Hopper, Edward, 181
Hopper, Hedda, 130
House on 92nd Street, The (1945), 164
House Un-American Activities Committee (HUAC), 204, 209, 210
Hoyle, Brian, 5, 272
Hoyt, John, 3
Hurst, Richard Maurice, 14
Huston, John, 89

I, the Jury (1953), 196
I Love Lucy (1951–57), 188
"Incident at Dry Creek" (1965), 71
"I Take This Woman" (1962), 72
Ingraham, Lloyd, 88
International Settlement (1938), 117
Intimate Interviews (1932), 86
Investigators, The (1961), 77
Invincible Pictures, 15
Invisible Ghost (1941), 3, 5, 34, 42, 47, *48*, 49, 56, 64, 65, 69, 81–97, 105, 107, 113, 125, 151, 157, 160
Irey, Elmer L., 168
Irving, Washington, 18, 19
Island of Lost Men (1939), 119, 129

Johnny Guitar (1954), 201, 202, 205, 211
Johnston, W. Ray, 15, 18, 20
Jolson Story, The (1946), 72
Jones, Marcia May, 19, 20, 21
Jordan, Bobby, 21, 22, 23, 25
Joseph H. Lewis:, Overview, Interview, and Filmography (1998), 3, 11
"Journey Back, The" (1961), 69
Journey into Fear (1942), 218
Judell, Ben, 120
Justice, Christopher, 7, 272

Kael, Pauline, 58
Kallen, Kitty, 243
Kaprow, Allan, 65
Karloff, Boris, 18, 83, 86, 116
Katzman, Sam, 21, 22, 23, 34
Kauffmann, Stanley, 223–224, 259
Kaye, Sammy, 251, 254
Kelley, Barry, 171, *175*
Kelly, Carol, 210
Kelsey, Fred, 92
Kerr, Paul, 23, 24, 157
Keser, Robert, 202, 217, 224, 226, 236, 238
Killer Is Loose, The (1956), 201
Killer's Kiss (1955), 178
The Killers (1946), 225
Killing, The (1956), 184
King, Frank and Maurice, 242, 243
King of Chinatown (1939), 119, 129
King Klunk (1933), 86
King Kong (1933), 86, 246
Kinsey, Dr. Alfred, 226
Kirshner, Lewis, 40, 55
Kiss Me Deadly (1955), 103, 113, 178, 180, 219
Kitses, Jim, 3, 46, 51, 54, 147
Kovács, László, 51
Kracauer, Siegfried, 98, 99
Krasker, Robert, 225
Kruger, Otto, 43, 152, 153
Krutnik, Frank, 237
Kubrick, Stanley, 90, 93, 178, 184, 209
Kuntzel, Thierry, 209
Kurosawa, Akira, 177

Kyrou, Ado, 110

Lacan, Jacques, 38, 40, 44, 52, 53, 55, 56
Lackey, William T., 21
Lackteen, Frank, 123
Lady from Chungking (1942), 120, 121, 125, 129, 131
Lady from Shanghai, The (1947), 81, 211, 225
Lady in the Lake, The (1947), 216
Lady without Passport, A (1950), 12, 44, 45, 69, 99, 108, 124
Lancelot du lac (1973), 154
Landers, Lew, 94
Landon, Michael, 65
Lang, Fritz, 158, 183, 185, 192, 210
Last Stand, The (1938), 66
Laughing at Danger (1940) 22
Laura (1944), 197, 242, 243, 252
Laurel-Hardy Murder Case, The (1930), 92
Lawless Street, A (1955), 3, 69, 73, 74, 76, 115, 124, 200
Lawrence, Marc, 201, 216
Lazenby, Aaron, 265
Lazer, Joan, 173, *174*
Lee, Michael, 7, 272
Leni, Paul, 93
Le Picard, Marcel, 97
Lesser, Sol, 85
L'étoile de mer (1928), 48
Letter, The (1940), 41, 46, 47, 59
Letter from an Unknown Woman (1948), 156
Lewis, Buena, xi
Lewton, Val, 94, 246
Liberty Pictures, 16
Limehouse Blues (1934), 130
Lindfors, Viveca, 202
Little Foxes, The (1941), 41, 59
Lola Montés (1955), 76
London, Jack, 18, 19
"Long Gun from Tucson" (1961), 75
Long Hot Summer, The (1958), 211
Loo, Richard, 122
Luciano, Michael, 202

Lugosi, Bela, 1, 3, 42, 47, *48*, 81, 82, 83–86, *87*, 89, 90, 91, 92, 96, 160
Luke, Keye, 117, 118
Lupino, Ida, 200
Lynch, David, 238

Macbeth (1948), 201
MacDonald, J. Farrell, 97
Macek, Carl, 202, 247
MacReady, George, 44, 135
Mad Doctor of Market Street, The (1942), 5, 82, 98–115
Madison, Noel, *128*
Magnificent Ambersons, The (1942), 216, 218
Majestic Pictures, 16
Major Dundee (1965), 214
Maltese Falcon, The (1941), 89
Malvern, Paul, 21
Mamoulian, Rouben, 92
Man Called Shenandoah, A (1965–66), 71
Man from Laramie, The (1955), 217
"Man from Nowhere, The" (1966), 76, 125
Man from Tumbleweeds, The (1940), 64, 71, 74
Man in the Shadow (1957), 200, 211
Mankiewicz, Joseph, 141
Mann, Anthony, 24, 164, 165, 176, 196, 201, 217, 218, 225
Manon, Hugh, 5, 38, 272
Marshall, Herbert, 41
Martin, Al and Helen, 85
Mascot Pictures, 14, 18, 209
Mayo, Archie L., 90
McCarthy, Kevin, 73
McCarthy, Todd, 14
McGuire, John, 42, 87, 88
McIntire, John, 163
McKay, Wanda, 97
McVey, Tyler, 212
Meisel, Myron, 82, 96, 110, 136, 218
Mercer, Johnny, 244
Merkel, Una, 100, *109*
Metropolis (1926), 210

Metz, Christian, 105
MGM Studios, 13, 117
Michael, Gertrude, 129
Middleton, Robert, 183
Milian, Victor, 210
Minciotti, Esther, 172, *174*
Minnelli, Vincente (1956), 69, 76, 150, 197
Minstrel Man (1944), 65, 107
Modern Times (1936), 196
Monogram Pictures Corporation, 12, 13, 15–17, 18, 19, 20, 25, 31, 33, 35, 47, 82, 83, 84, 85, 120
Monsoon (1945), 14
Moran, Jackie, 19, 21
Morley, Karen, 218
Morris, Errol, 163
Most Dangerous Game, The (1932), 253
Moya, Billy, 129
Mulvey, Laura, 156, 178
Mundy, Robert, 54, 58
Murnau, F. W., 43, 63, 83, 107
Muse, Clarence, 88, 92
Mussorgsky, Modest, 253
My Name Is Julia Ross (1945), 3, 5, 11, 35, 38–39, 44, *45*, 46, 82, 95, 99, 108, 125, 134–145, 148
Mystery Street (1950), 166, 167

Naked City, The (1948), 164, 165–166, 177
Naremore, James, 178, 196, 211
Natural Born Killers (1994), 238
Nesmith, Ottola, 48
Neufeld, Sam, 120
Nevins, Francis M., ix, x, xii, 3, 11, 12, 41, 62, 152, 200, 202, 217, 224, 239, 272–273
Niagara (1952), 218
"Night of the Wolf" (1965), 65, 73, 75, 76, 78
Nochimson, Martha P., 194
North of Shanghai (1939), 117
Nosferatu (1922), 107
Now, Voyager (1942), 246

Oakman, Wheeler, 97
O'Brien, Dave, 84, 97
O'Connor, Una, 93
Oland, Warner, 116, 120
Old Dark House, The (1932), 93, 94
"Old Tony" (1963), 65
Oliver, Edna May, 17
On Dangerous Ground (1951), 201
On Dress Parade (1939), 22
"One Killer on Ice" (1965), 65
Ophüls, Max, 43, 76, 156, 157
Osterloh, Robert, 170, 171
Othello (1952), 211
Outrage (1951), 200

Painted Veil, The (1934), 116
Palmer, R. Barton, 180
"Panic" (1959), 70
Panorama de film noir Américan (1941–53), 179
Paramount Pictures, 13, 17, 24
Parker, Alan, 147
Parks, Larry, 211
Peckinpah, Sam, 214
Pembroke, George, 90, 97
Pendelton, Nat, *109*
Penn, Arthur, 238
Penn, Leo, 174
Pennington, Jody W., 179
Perry, Ben L., 208
"Pet, The" (1959), 65, 66
Phantom Empire, The (1935), 14
Pierson, Carl, 23, 97
Pinter, Harold, 190
Plan 9 from Outer Space (1959), 84
Poetics of Cinema (2007), 199
Polonsky, Abraham, 209, 212
"Pompey" (1964), 63, 68, 70
Porfirio, Robert, 202
Poulet, Georges, 269
Preminger, Otto, 160, 196, 243
Pride of the Bowery (1941), 12, 13, 32–34, 67, 72
"Prisoner, The" (1961), 69
Prisoner of Japan (1942), 129
Private Hell 36 (1954), 177, 200

Producers Releasing Corporation (PRC), 12, 13, 24, 35, 84, 120, 125, 129
Psycho (1960), 147, 259
Pushover (1954), 177

"Quality of Mercy, The" (1963), 65
Queen of the Yukon (1940), 21

Raimi, Sam, 93
Rains, Claude, 39
Raison, Milton, 121
Raksin, David, 180, 242, 243, 244, 252
Raleigh, Ben, 251
Randall, Jack, 18, 20
Ravel, Maurice, 253
Raven, The (1935), 94
Ray, Man, 48
Ray, Nicholas, 201, 217
Rayns, Tony, 146, 153
Rebel without a Cause (1955), 202
Reckless Moment, The (1949), 157
Reed, Carol, 225
Reingold, Gail, xi
Rendezvous in Black (1948), x
Republic Pictures, 13, 14, 16, 24, 120
Retreat, Hell! (1952), 65, 68, 70
Return of the Ape Man, The (1944), 84, 97
Return of Chandu, The (1934), 85
Return of October, The (1948), 64, 68, 75
Return of Wild Bill, The (1940), 65
Rhodes, Gary D., 273
Richards, Addison, 60
Ride Back, The (1957), 202
Rifleman, The (1958–63), 11, 62, 63, 64, 65, 66, 68, 69, 70, 71, 72, 73, 75, 76
Ritter, Tex, 20, 21
RKO Pictures, 13, 16, 17, 18
Roar of the Dragon (1932), 117
Robe, The (1953), 217
Rogue Cop (1954), 166
Romeo and Juliet (1936), 99
Rooney, Mickey, 17
Rope (1948), 152, 216
Rosen, Phil, 97
Rossitto, Angelo, 97

Index 281

Rowland, Roy, 139
Russell, Andy, 251, 254

"Safe Guard, The" (1958), 78
Salt, Barry, 150–151
Sanders, George, 117
Sangster, Georgia, xi
Santos, Marlisa, 5, 273
Sarris, Andrew, 58, 81, 82, 96, 111, 115
Savage, Ann, 56
Schallert, Edwin, 124
Schatz, Thomas, 13
Schnitzer, Gerald, 97
Schrader, Paul, 46, 51, 54, 55, 157, 224, 227, 231
Scott, Randolph, 3, 69, 200
Scott, Ridley, 113
Scourby, Alexander, 183
Scream (1996), 86
Searchers, The (1956), 200, 203
Secrets of a Co-Ed (1943), 35, 43, 44, 60, 151, 160
Seitz, John F., 225
7th Cavalry (1956), 3, 69, 200
Seventh Victim, The (1943), 94
Sexual Behavior in the Human Male (1948), 226
Seymour, Dan, 123
Shanghai Express (1932), 116, 120, 121, 130
"Shattered Idol, The" (1961), 65, 70, 75
Shaw, Anabel, 50
"Sheer Terror" (1961), 72, 73, 76
Shining, The (1980), 90
"Shivaree" (1959), 70, 76
Shock Corridor (1963), 114
Shore, Dinah, 251, 254
Side Street (1950), 166, 177
"Sidewinder" (1963), 70
Siegel, Don, 200
Silver, Alain, 247
Silver Bullet, The (1942), 72, 74
Silverman, Kaja, 250
Sinatra, Frank, 243, 244
Singer, Robert, 6, 273
Siodmak, Robert, 225

Sipiora, Philip, 7, 273–274
Slavin, George F., 200
Snow, Michael, 73
So Dark the Night (1946), 3, 12, 42, 47, 64, 99, 115, 134, 141, 146–162
Somewhere in the Night (1946), 141
Son of Frankenstein (1939), 83
Sopranos, The (1999–2007), 194
Spartacus (1960), 208
Spivak, Charlie
Spooks Run Wild (1941), 84, 97
Spy Ring, The (1938), 64, 65, 74
Stahl, John, 150
"Stand-In, The" (1961), 75
Stanhope, Ted, 3
Starrett, Charles, 67
Steiner, Max, 253
Stone, Oliver, 238
"Strange Town" (1960), 70, 71
Stray Dog (1949), 177
Streets of Shanghai (1927), 120
Suddenly (1954), 197
Supreme Pictures, 15
"Surveyors" (1959), 67, 72–74
"Suspicion" (1963), 73
Svengali (1931), 91
Swordsman, The (1948), 47
Syndicate Film Exchange, 15

Tacha, Athena, 65
Tamiroff, Akim, 116
Targets (1968), 86
Taves, Brian, 5, 25, 274
Tax Dodgers, The (1948), 168
Tea and Symphony (1958), 69
Terror in a Texas Town (1958), 3, 6, 11, 42, 58, 70, 74, 95, 127, 151, 199, 200, 202, 208–215, 217, 219
Tesson, Charles, 109
Test Site (2006), 65
Texas Stagecoach (1940), 65, 72, 75
That Gang of Mine (1940), 12, 25, 30–32, 34
Thayer, Tina, 43, 152
Theatre of Blood (1973), 86
Thief of Bagdad, The (1924), 118

They Made Me a Criminal (1938), 22
Third Man, The (1949), 206, 218
Thirer, Irene, 33
Thompson, Rick, 110
Tierney, Gene, 243
Tight Spot (1955), 177
T-Men (1947), 164–165, 168, 196
Toll of the Sea, The (1922), 118, 120
Touch of Evil (1958), 81, 200, 211, 228
Tourneur, Jacques, 24, 78, 246
Tracey, Grant, 182, 186, 193
Tracy, Spencer, 202
"The Trade" (1959), 73
Trent, John 19, 21
Trumbo, Dalton, 208, 210, 228
20th Century Fox, 13, 16, 17, 18, 117
Tzioumakis, Yannis, 5, 274

Ulmer, Edgar G., 14, 35, 56, 83, 85, 110, 146, 150, 160, 187
Under Capricorn (1948), 218
Undercover Man, The (1949), 2, 6, 12, 47, 50, 66, 67, 108, 163–177
"Undercover Man: He Trapped Capone" (1947), 168
Undersea Kingdom (1936), 14
Union Station (1950), 166
United Artists, 13, 17
Universal Studios, 12, 13, 16, 35, 83, 117
Up in the Air (1940), 22
Urecal, Minerva, 97
Usual Suspects, The (1995), 238

"Vacqueros, The" (1961), 72
Varno, Roland, 135
Venus in Furs (1870), 249
Vertigo (1958), 138
Victory Pictures, 15, 21
"Vindicators, The" (1965), 68, 69
Violent Saturday (1955), 166, 167
Visconti, Luchino, 77
"Visitor, The" (1960), 72
Voodoo Man (1944), 97

Waggner, George, 92
Wagner, Robert, 202

Walker, Helen, 187
Walker, Terry, 88, 97
Walsh, Raoul, 83, 177, 201
Warner Bros., 13, 16, 17, 22
Washington, Ned, 243, 250
Wavelength (1966), 73
Wayne, Bernie, 251
Wayne, John, 216
Webb, Jack, 177
Webb, Roy, 246
Welles, Orson, 81, 112, 150, 201, 211, 224, 228
Werker, Alfred L., 165, 196
West, Dorothy, 86
West, William, 13, 34
West of Shanghai (1937), 117
Wexley, John, 218
Whale, James, 93
When Were You Born (1939), 119, 129
White, Patricia, 174
White Heat (1949), 177
Whiteread, Rachel, 65
White Zombie (1932), 84, 89, 90, 91, 94
Whitfield, Stephen J., 183
Whitley, Tom, 123
Whitmore, James, 170, *174*
Whitty, Dame May, 44, 135, *137*
Wild at Heart (1990), 238
Wild Boys of the Road (1933), 22
Wilde, Cornel, 192, 194
Wilder, Billy, 225, 239
Williams, Bill, *203*
Williams, Tony, 6, 274
Wilson, Frank J., 168
Wilson, Richard, 197
Windsor, Marie, 184
Witness to Murder (1954), 139
Wolf Man, The (1941), 92
Woman on Pier 13 (1949), 200
Wong, Anna May, 5, 116, 118–120, 121, 125, *126*, *128*, 129, 130, 131, 133
Wong, James Lee, 17, 18, 19
Wood, Edward D. Jr., 84
Woolrich, Cornell, x, xi, xii
Wurtzel, Sol, 17, 18
Wyler, William, 41, 46, 47, 150, 202

"Wyoming Story, The" (1961), 64, 72, 78

Yard (1961), 65
Yordan, Philip, 180
You'll Find Out (1940), 86
Young, Collier, 200
Young, Nedrick, 3, 42, 58, 123, *126*, 200, 201, 208, 209, 210, 215
Young, Polly Ann, 42
Young, Victor, 242, 243, 248, 249, 252, 253
"Young Man's Fancy, A" (1962), 64, 65

www.ingramcontent.com/pod-product-compliance
Lightning Source LLC
Chambersburg PA
CBHW051537230426

43669CB00015B/2625